ADVENTISTICA

# Studies in Adventist History and Theology – New Series

Series Editors:
Johannes Hartlapp, Daniel Heinz,
Stefan Höschele, Rolf J. Pöhler

PUBLISHED BY
THE INSTITUTE OF ADVENTIST STUDIES
OF FRIEDENSAU ADVENTIST UNIVERSITY

Volume 1

# PERCEPTIONS OF THE PROTESTANT REFORMATION IN SEVENTH-DAY ADVENTISM

Rolf J. Pöhler
Editor

ADVENTISTICA
Studies in Adventist History and Theology – New Series
Editors: Johannes Hartlapp, Daniel Heinz, Stefan Höschele, Rolf J. Pöhler

Volume 1
Perceptions of the Protestant Reformation in Seventh-day Adventism

Editor: Rolf J. Pöhler
Editorial Assistant: Filip Kapusta
Copy Editors: Jamie G. Boucher, Daniel Edwards

Cover: © rasani.design Leipzig

© 2018 Institute of Adventist Studies
Friedensau Adventist University
(Theologische Hochschule Friedensau)
39291 Möckern-Friedensau, Germany
Internet: www.thh-friedensau.de
E-Mail: ias@thh-friedensau.de

Printed by: BoD - Books on Demand, Norderstedt
Germany

This title is also available as e-book.

All parts of this publication are protected by copyright. Any utilization outside the strict limits of the copyright law, without the permission of the publisher, is forbidden and liable to prosecution. This applies in particular to reproductions, translations, microfilming, and storage and processing in electronic retrieval systems.

ISBN Print: 978-3-935480-51-2

# Contents

Introduction 7

*Stefan Höschele*
Reform, Reformation – Protest, Protestant:
Adventist Terminology and Rhetoric 13

*Nicholas Miller*
The Reformation and the Remnant:
The Reformers, the Great Controversy and the Sabbath 31

## I. Martin Luther in Seventh-day Adventist Perspective

*Denis Kaiser*
"God Is Our Refuge and Strength" –
Martin Luther in the Perception of Ellen G. White 49

*Daniel Heinz*
"Komm, lieber jüngster Tag!"
An Appraisal of Luther's Eschatological Worldview 67

*Jón Hjörleifur Stefánsson*
Luther's Antichrist and His Reception by Seventh-day Adventists 79

*Christian Lutsch*
Martin Luther's View of the Scripture Principle 99

*Sully Sanon*
*Sola Scriptura* as *Devotio:* An Appeal to Theological Dialogue 117

## II. Perspectives on the Magisterial and Radical Reformation

*Michael Campbell*
Martin Luther, Seventh-day Adventism and the Lord's Supper 139

*Thomas Domanyi*
John Calvin's Legacy in Seventh-day Adventist Belief 155

Reinder Bruinsma
The Sixteenth-Century Reformation and Adventist Ecclesiology   165

Timothy Arena
The Soteriology of Philip Melanchthon
and the Importance of Its Legacy for Seventh-day Adventists   179

Martin Rothkegel
The Anabaptist Reformation Experience   205

Trevor O'Reggio
The Radical Reformers (Anabaptists) and Seventh-day Adventism   219

Charles Scriven
The Radical Reformation and the Transformation of Adventism:
The Legacy of James William McClendon, Jr.   239

## III. The Impact of the Reformation on Seventh-day Adventism

Woodrow W. Whidden
The Ground-Breaking General Conference of 1888:
What Kind of Reformation Experience Was It About?   253

Johannes Hartlapp
Ludwig Richard Conradi's Understanding of Luther's Reformation   263

Gilbert M. Valentine
The Reformation and the Shaping of Conflict over the Meaning of
"Righteousness by Faith" in Seventh-day Adventism 1960–1978   287

Rolf J. Pöhler
Are Seventh-day Adventists "Heirs of the Reformation"?
Between Aspiration and Reality   311

Contributors   319

*Rolf J. Pöhler*

# Introduction

Few incidents in Western Christian civilization have had more repercussions on the church and on society than Martin Luther's nailing of the 95 theses on the door of the All Saints' Church in the university town of Wittenberg on October 31, 1517. While some historians question the historicity of the event, there can be no doubt about the manifold and lasting echo of the 95 theses. It was on the same day that the young Bible professor was writing a letter to archbishop Albrecht of Magdeburg and Mainz petitioning him to stop the practice of indulgences – albeit to no avail.

The long-term impact of Luther's letter of protest was becoming visible in the years and centuries to come. Beginning in 1617, the commemoration of the "Reformation Day" became a much-honored tradition in the churches owing their existence to the sixteenth-century Reformation. Mediated by the Methodist and Baptist traditions, the Seventh-day Adventist Church, too, sees itself as an heir of the Protestant Reformation. In the 1880s, Adventists began to wrestle with the theological insights and beliefs of the Reformers, which were increasingly regarded as integral parts of the Adventist message and mission.

It is no surprise, then, that the quincentenary of the Reformation received widespread attention, not only in the Protestant (and even Catholic) world, but also by Adventists around the world. Conferences and symposia were organized, pastors' meetings conducted, public lectures given, evangelistic sermons held. Noteworthy publications dealing with various aspects of the Protestant Reformation in relation to Seventh-day Adventism are Nicholas P. Miller's *The Reformation and the Remnant* (2016) and *Here We Stand: Luther, the Reformation, and Seventh-day Adventism*, edited by Michael W. Campbell and Nikolaus Satelmajer (2017, both Pacific Press).

In May, 2016, the Institute of Adventist Studies at Friedensau University held its Second International Symposium, dealing with "Perceptions of the Protestant Reformation in Seventh-day Adventism." Eighteen scholarly papers were read at the conference. Part of the program was an excursion to Lutherstadt Wittenberg, located just 50 miles from Friedensau. The Adventist University in Germany feels honored to be in the vicinity of the birthplace of the Reformation and is committed to uphold the principles of the Reformation in the framework of the Adventist faith.

The stand-up display of the symposium (see back cover) related the historic 1888 General Conference and Ellen White's seminal book *The Great Controversy* to the great Reformer, thereby indicating the leading questions of the symposium and of this book: how have Seventh-day Adventists perceived the Protestant Reformation in the past and how do they see their relation to it today? This question is no less timely and relevant now as it was during the quincentenary in 2017.

The eighteen chapters of the book are divided in three main sections. Following the two introductory chapters, five authors look at Martin Luther from an Adventist perspective (Part I). After that, seven chapters deal with various aspects of both the Magisterial and the Radical Reformation (Part II). The concluding four chapters analyze the impact of the Reformation on Seventh-day Adventism (Part III).

In the opening essay, *Stefan Höschele* presents a fascinating analysis of the changing meaning of the terms reform/ation and protest/ant as used by Adventists over the years. He traces the development from a mainly negative view of Protestants and a fully positive use of "reform" to a differentiated and rather positive notion of both "Protestantism" and the Reformation. He identifies five different views that are still found in various Adventist discourses today. Towards the end, Höschele lists major Adventist studies on the Protestant Reformation and on Adventism's self-perceived relationship with it as well as to the Reformation churches.

The opening presentation at the symposium was given by *Nicholas Miller*; it was based on his book *The Reformation and the Remnant*, which had just come off the press. He traced the free will and moral government of God view through four centuries, arguing that Jacob Arminius (1560–1609), Hugo Grotius (1583–1645), John Wesley (1703–1791) – all of them echoing the free will position of the Radical (Anabaptist) Reformers – as well as Albert Barnes (1798–1870) – the Bible commentator whose works were highly appreciated by Ellen White – exerted the strongest influence on the unique and distinctive Adventist beliefs, particularly the great controversy motif and the sanctuary doctrine. Unsurprisingly, the free will and moral government of God position leads to a concern for the social justice issues of the day.

Occasioned as it was by the quincentenary of the posting of the 95 thesis, several symposium papers focused on Martin Luther from an Adventist perspective (Part I).

*Denis Kaiser* analyzes in detail how Ellen White perceived and valued the person, life and work of the great sixteenth-century reformer in three publications from the 1880s (and 1911). She lauded his stand on the Bible and justification by faith, and regarded his separation from the Catholic church as a consequential step. White placed her story of Luther in the context of the great controversy metanarrative.

Focusing on Luther's eschatology, *Daniel Heinz* describes his end-time orientation that made him a staunch "Adventist." His comprehensive apocalyptic worldview was reflected in his keen interest in Bible prophecy and end-time signs and in his joyful longing for, and heightened expectation of, the "dear last day." Justification in Christ now and final redemption at his *parousia* – the present and the future kingdom of God – are the two cornerstones of salvation according to the Reformer.

Arising from biblical apocalypticism is the notion of an end-time antichrist, which Luther saw fulfilled in the papacy. *Jón Hjörleifur Stefánsson* closely investigates the similarities and differences between the Reformer's and the Adventist view. While Luther was personally confronted by a foe with blatantly antichristian pretensions and performance, Adventists expect severe persecution from the papacy in the projected future, focused on the Sabbath-Sunday issue. According to Luther and White, there is a direct affinity between self-righteousness and the spirit of Antichrist – a sobering thought for Adventists who self-identify as Laodiceans – apathetic to Christ and the gospel. For a fair appraisal, they also need to update their knowledge of Catholicism.

The following two chapters deal with the formal principle of the Reformation as set forth by Luther and adopted by others. They were written by two young scholars while they were still graduate students at Friedensau University. *Christian Lutsch* traces the background, development, and meaning of Luther's Sola Scriptura view. His Scripture Principle was not drafted as a dogmatic formula but grew out of an existential encounter with Christ, the living Word and true subject matter of Scripture, and the Gospel, the proclaimed word, in the Bible. The Holy Spirit impresses the saving truth upon the heart, thus joining Christ and the believer/hearer. This is indispensable for a correct understanding of Scripture as the *viva vox evangelii*.

*Sully Sanon* builds upon this crucial insight in his stimulating treatise on sola scriptura as *devotio*, which entails both a commitment to the primacy and sufficiency of Scripture and an appeal to an open-minded theological dialogue about and with Scripture. In contrast to both a polemical use of the slogan in the service of religious-political power struggles and its individualistic appropriation leading to hermeneutical chaos, a commitment to interpretive humility and the willingness to submit to scripture and to learn from one another in the community of believers is needed. In this way, Scripture interprets our lives and reigns in the *(semper reformanda)* church.

Part II broadens the scope from Luther to other sixteenth-century Reformers – both Magisterial and Radical – whose legacy likewise can be found in the Seventh-day Adventist Church – John Calvin, Philip Melanchthon, and the Anabaptists. In seven chapters a broad spectrum of topics is discussed from an Adventist perspective.

To begin with, *Michael Campbell* once again turns to Martin Luther, this time focusing on his interpretation of the Lord's Supper in comparison to the Catholic and other contemporary Protestant views and also to the Adventist understanding and practice (including footwashing), placed in the American religious setting and set forth in its development (e.g., from closed to open communion). Early Adventists, coming from other Protestant traditions – chiefly Baptist and Methodist – simply carried over with them their (little thought out) understanding and practice of the Lord's Supper.

*Thomas Domanyi* sees a conspicuous ideational relationship between the writings of John Calvin and Adventist beliefs. He gives an overview of some fundamental beliefs where his influence can be felt: the doctrine of the church, the anti-creedal, Biblicist attitude, the esteem for the Old Testament, and the working of the Holy Spirit.

*Reinder Bruinsma* shows that the Adventist model of church governance is indebted to the various traditions from which the early Adventist leaders came (in particular Methodism and the Christian Connexion), which, in turn, were deeply influenced by the Calvinist roots they shared with American Protestantism. They also show some influence of Lutheranism and, especially, of the "free church" tradition that was much indebted to the Radical Reformation.

According to *Timothy J. Arena*, Philip Melanchthon's soteriological legacy is of special significance for Adventists through its echoes in Arminius, Wesley, and Ellen White. The author – who was not able to present at the symposium – adds important insights to this book by examining Melanchthon's influential thought on hamartiology/anthropology (free will), justification (forensic imputation), and sanctification (law/good works). White's writings can be seen as a continuation and affirmation of Melanchthon's significant and continually pertinent soteriological legacy.

The following three chapters examine the Anabaptist Reformation experience and its continued relevancy for Seventh-day Adventists. *Martin Rothkegel*, a Baptist church historian (and the only non-Adventist contributor to this volume), provides a detailed overview of the various Anabaptist movements and groups (including Sabbatarians), the forerunners of the free church *(Freikirchen)* tradition. Recent historiography has shown the polygenetic origin and peculiar features of sixteenth-century Anabaptism. Their "sectarian" views included believers' baptism; several groups also propagated religious liberty, pacifism, and the separation of church and state.

*Trevor O'Reggio* explores the extent and nature of the Anabaptist influence on Adventism, and the (indirect) historical links of Adventism to the Radical Reformers, mediated mainly through the Christian Connexion, the Baptists, and the Methodists. A survey of Adventist doctrines and practices reveals striking resemblances with those taught by the Anabaptists. Adventism emerged from groups constituting the radical tradition of Protestantism that were strongly influenced by the Anabaptists. Therefore, it owes a debt of gratitude to the Radical Reformers for the rich tradition that has been handed down to them.

To complete the portrayal of Anabaptism, *Charles Scriven* reflects on the contribution of James McClendon, Neo-Anabaptism's most important systematic theologian. According to the author, McClendon provides four leverage points for renewal in Adventism: his definition of theology as community-transforming, his practical understanding of doctrine as being about discipleship, his Christocentrism, and his view on eschatology as including earthly concerns, not withdrawal or escapism.

The third and final part of the book concerns the impact of the sixteenth-century Reformation on Seventh-day Adventism. Four authors examine significant phases in the history of the church spanning 130 years – from 1888 until today. These case studies yield some ambiguous, if not sobering, results for a people claiming to be (the) heirs of the Reformation. The conclusions drawn by these authors are not beyond dispute. For this, they give all the more reason for further critical reflections.

*Woodrow W. Whidden* looks at the ground-breaking 1888 General Conference and asks the question: What kind of "reformation" was this divisive event about? He draws a sharp line between James and Ellen White, the "Protestant" champions of early Adventism, on the one hand, and E. J. Waggoner and A. T. Jones, the other key players of 1888 fame, who gradually drifted away from the Reformation emphasis, on the other hand. Assuming the perspective of "faithful" Ellen White, other, more interlinking interpretations of the 1888 experience are left out of consideration.

Another very influential leader of the young denomination, Ludwig R. Conradi, draws the interest of *Johannes Hartlapp*, who analyzes the European pioneer's understanding of the Protestant Reformation. Conradi viewed Luther and other Reformers mainly from the perspective of a historicist interpretation of Bible prophecy (Daniel and Revelation; Antichrist, Second Coming) and the Sabbath (law), neglecting in turn Luther's essential soteriological concerns (*sola gratia, sola fide, solus Christus*). This tragically betrays a one-sided understanding and misinterpretation of the Reformation.

*Gilbert M. Valentine* recounts the story of the 1960s and 1970s when Adventism got involved in intense debates about the exact meaning of "righteousness by faith," especially in the South Pacific and North America. Perfectionistic views clashed with a strictly forensic definition of justification. Among the contentious points was the question of the Reformation view of justification; black-and-white positioning and opposing attitudes shaped the contours of this controversy. The two perspectives still stand in tension with each other and continue to polarize the denomination.

The last essay raises a question that was hovering over the entire symposium; it also looms large behind the contributions in this volume: Are Seventh-day Adventists true heirs of the sixteenth-century Protestant Reformation? What do Adventists mean by this claim and how did they live up to it? According to *Rolf J. Pöhler*, the question requires a nuanced answer. Taking his clues from the other papers in this book and measuring the Adventist claim by its correspondence to both Protestant and Adventist history and theology, he concludes that this assertion is valid as long as Adventism remains a genuine movement – as the sixteenth-century Reformation had been – that embodies the spirit of the Reformers and continues to move forward. The church will always experience a tension between aspiration and reality.

No publication of this size and purview is the work of a single mind and hand. Special thanks are due to Filip Kapusta, my reliable and competent student assistant, who had a large share in preparing the manuscripts for publication. I will miss his watchful eye and thoughtful support. Four papers were translated into English by Frieder Schmid and Jamie G. Boucher; the latter did an excellent job in handling exacting footnotes. Copy editing was done by him and mostly by Daniel Edwards. Our gratitude extends to the eighteen contributors to this volume who have spent much time and effort both in preparing excellent presentations for the symposium and in reworking them for this publication. We are proud to see the names of two recent Friedensau graduates among the roster of international authors.

We are publishing this book in the hope that it will provide helpful information and stimulating ideas for church historians, theologians, theology students, church members and others who take an active interest in the Seventh-day Adventist Church and its theological discourse. May it also contribute to the needed reflection on what it means to be a church in a continuous process of reformation – ecclesia semper reformanda. Sepp Herberger, German football coach of 1954 World Cup fame coined the phrase: "After the game is before the game." With regard to Christianity in general and Adventism in particular, it may also be said: "After the reformation is before the reformation."

Friedensau,
July 2018

*Stefan Höschele*

# Reform, Reformation – Protest, Protestant: Adventist Terminology and Rhetoric

Abstract

The Adventist use of the terms "reform," "reformation" and "protest," "Protestant" illustrates the changing theological moods of the denomination and its precursor movements. Starting from a partly neutral and partly negative view of Protestantism among the Millerites and the first Sabbatarian Adventists, this discourse was supplemented with a positive "reform" rhetoric in the 1850s, which also implied an affirmative view of "reformation" as a moral cause and of the sixteenth-century Reformation. Only in the early twentieth century did "Protestant" assume a pronounced positive meaning. It is on this basis that a more dialogical relationship with other Protestants developed in the second part of the century, implying a differentiated look at the Reformation and at Protestantism at large.

From their beginnings, Seventh-day Adventists have developed not only a peculiar theology and culture, but also a language of their own. Some elements in the terminology and rhetoric of the Adventist community were, of course, inherited from antecedent movements – the Puritans, the restorationist Christian Connexion, and revivalists of various backgrounds.[1] Others were borrowed from the Holiness movement, which advanced in parallel steps with the young Seventh-day Adventist denomination, and, later, from North American Fundamentalists. But a significant part of the phraseology in the burgeoning Seventh-day Adventist community was home-made; its roots were mostly biblical apocalyptic passages, and phrases often became dear to the Advent people as their leaders used them over and over again.[2] Unsurprisingly, the Adventist supply of magazines produced a similar phenomenon, with recurring vocabulary such as the many "Heralds," "Messengers" and "Signs."

1   Cf. Bryan W. Ball, *The English Connection: The Puritan Roots of Seventh-Day Adventist Belief* (Cambridge: Clarke, 1981); Jonathan Butler, "Seventh-Day Adventism's Legacy of Modern Revivalism," *Spectrum* 5.1 (1973): 89–99; and (on the Adventist-Christian Connexion linkage and the Adventist move away from it) Stefan Höschele, "Constructions of Catholicity and Denominational Particularity: Key Stations in the Seventh-day Adventist Doctrinal Journey," in *Christliche Traditionen zwischen Katholizität und Partikularität / Christian Traditions between Catholicity and Particularity*, ed. Leo J. Koffeman (Frankfurt a. M.: Lembeck, 2009), 131–147.
2   Examples abound, so a few terms will suffice: "present truth," "Loud Cry," "Spirit of Prophecy," "remnant church," "investigative judgement," "third angel's message." A longer list is found in Taiko Takaya, "A Bilingual (English-Japanese) List of Seventh-day Adventist Terminology with Suggestions for Use" (MA thesis, Loma Linda University, 1968).

An exception to these common patterns in Adventist publishing was a paper that appeared only for seven years: *The Protestant Magazine*. Published from 1909 to 1915 by the General Conference Religious Liberty Department,[3] the title page announced its main orientation: "The Protestant Magazine. Advocating Primitive Christianity. Protesting against Apostasy. Human Authority vs. Divine Revelation." This magazine and its name remained a short-lived[4] and rather unique experiment,[5] but its existence *and* discontinuance imply important insights on the denomination's self-understanding, its view of Protestantism, and its relationship to the Protestant world at large. More observations on this episode will be presented later; at this point it should suffice to note that *The Protestant Magazine* illustrates (1) the Adventists' will to present their movement as the most consistent form of Protestantism, (2) the fact that this tendency became stronger towards the end of the denominational pioneers' period, and (3) a certain degree of uneasiness that remained in identifying with Protestantism at large.

In this paper, I intend to give an overview of the way in which Adventists talked about the terms "Reformation" and "reform," about "Protestantism" and "protest" – in short, about the manner in which their perception of their reformation origin and of others in the large Protestant family revealed itself in their discourse. Different from the denomination's inbred vocabulary, these words reached Adventists with meanings and ascriptions that had their roots centuries earlier, and that had already developed a life of their own. This inheritance, then, led to constructions enriched with strands of typically Adventist thinking. I should add immediately that it is impossible to present a truly comprehensive account of this subject; a thorough evaluation would certainly need serious and systematic discourse analysis with a scope of no less than a Master's thesis or even two. Another preliminary observation that needs to be kept in mind is that all of these terms – reform/ation, protest/ant – are non-biblical. Like the term "revival," the canon offers but a weak foundation with regard to this terminology, which may be one reason why Adventists took time to appropriate some of it with positive theological connotations and some degree of differentiation.

[3] It appeared quarterly from 1909 to October 1912 and monthly from November 1912 to 1915 and was published under the leadership of W. W. Prescott.

[4] The fact that the magazine was not continued beyond 1915 may be attributed to several factors, the most important being that in 1915 Prescott moved to another responsibility and the circulation Manager, A. J. S. Bourdeau, died in the same year; moreover, the subscription situation was apparently not very good. Whether the war had any impact cannot be ascertained, but evidently after seven years of publication, the major themes were exhausted – some had been repeated several times – especially when a magazine was to be published monthly.

[5] With one exception: In Germany, there was also a magazine entitled *Der Protestant* from 1910 to 1914, with an emphasis on religious liberty issues, Roman Catholicism, and articles on what Protestantism entails. The title page said, "The Protestant. Quarterly for the Liberty of Faith and Conscience as well as Fostering True Protestantism." Possibly this paper was inspired by the American Adventist *Protestant Magazine*.

## Protestantism as Babylon: The Earliest Adventists

The Millerite revival had largely been an intra-Protestant movement, but the Millerites' attitudes to their denominations of origin was complex. With their generally anti-sectarian perspective, their future-orientation and particularly after the increasingly conflictual developments in 1843, the roots in Reformation history that they shared with other Evangelicals seemed largely irrelevant. Miller remained a Baptist, but his skepticism of denominationalism translated into interpreting the existence of so many Protestant "sects" as "conclusive sign by which we may know we live on the eve of finishing the prophecies."[6] In general, Miller used "Protestant" in a neutral manner when explaining fulfilled prophecy, but with a negative connotation when utilized as a synonym to the "worldly," "popular churches."[7]

The earliest Sabbatarian Adventists' view and use of "Protestantism" was shaped by the fact that they all originated in the radical Bridegroom (or Shut-Door) Adventist group. This means they initially considered not only Roman Catholics and Protestants, but even the moderate Adventists beyond hope of salvation. It is, therefore, not surprising that the earliest references to Protestantism among them – in Bates' 1847 pamphlet *Second Advent Way Marks and High Heaps* – are consistently negative.[8] The paradox of this treatise is, however, that it represents the first quasi-salvation-historical approach to theological thinking by a future Seventh-day Adventist, and thus indirectly opened the way for later theological constructions in which the Reformation played a positive role.

But for the time being, a dark picture of Protestantism prevailed. With her few fellow believers, Ellen White expected an imminent persecution of Sabbath keepers while "the churches [i.e., Protestants and Catholics] and nominal Adventists" were "enraged" because of the Sabbatarian proclamation.[9] In the same period, an expectancy of "false reformations" designed "to deceive God's people" developed in

---

6   William Miller, *Evidence from Scripture and History of the Second Coming of Christ, about the Year 1843* (Boston, MA: Himes, 1842), 112. Miller interpreted the division of Protestantism as the fulfilment of the predicted "scattering of the holy people" (Dan 12:7); see ibid., 113.
7   See, e.g., William Miller, *William Miller's Works*, vol. 3 (Boston, MA: Himes, 1842), 77, where he says: "Yea, they that work wickedness are SET UP *[sic]*. This is certainly the effect, more or less, of all our Protestant sects at this time." Cf. also William Miller, *Remarks on Revelations Thirteenth, Seventeenth and Eighteenth* (Boston, MA: Himes, 1844), 38, 40.
8   Joseph Bates, *Second Advent Way Marks and High Heaps, or, A Connected View of the Fulfillment of Prophecy, by God's Peculiar People from the Year 1840 to 1847* (New Bedford, MA: Benjamin Lindsey, 1847), has seven references to Protestants (pp. 22, 24, 25, 27, 28). The two 1846 publications by Bates do not contain the term "Protestant" or "Reformation"/"reform," nor does the important booklet by James White, Joseph Bates, and Ellen G. White, *A Word to the "Little Flock"* (Brunswick, ME [By the Authors], 1847).
9   Ellen G. White, *A Sketch of the Christian Experience and Views of Ellen G. White* (Saratoga Springs, NY: James White, 1851), 17 (reference to 1847: p. 15).

White's writings, thus marking the first uses of the term "reformation" as negative.[10] Among Sabbatarian Adventists of the period, Protestantism was universally viewed as part of apocalyptic Babylon; the only difference among the movement's leaders was the question of whether Protestants were *equal* to "Babylon" or merely formed *part* of it.[11] James White held the former view, which implied that prophecies were fulfilled in the very present and, therefore, increased the urgency of proclaiming the need for separation from them. With regard to perspectives on Protestantism in general, these two varieties made little difference: all the churches had "fallen" (Rev 14:8).

The logical consequence was that developments, activities and even revivals in Protestant denominations had to be considered spurious.[12] In 1857–1858, when an evangelical revival spread from New York to other cities,[13] Sabbatarian Adventists quickly rejected it as deceptive.[14] Such awakenings or "reformations," as they were also labeled,[15] had to be non-genuine. After all, Protestants were in an apostate condition;[16] thus argued Uriah Smith, the editor of the Sabbatarian Adventist paper Review and Herald, in 1859,

> we know of course that they cannot recover from that condition [of being fallen], until they first repent of the steps that led them to it – until they grieve for their past neglect,

10  Ellen G. White, "Dear Brethren and Sisters," *Present Truth* [vol. 1, no. 3], August 1849, 22; similar wording is found in her booklet *A Sketch of the Christian Experience*, 27. The same idea appears in her letter "My Dear Brethren and Sisters," *Present Truth* [vol. 1, no. 8], March, 1850, 64, where she adds the shut-door explanation that "[t]he excitements and false reformations of this day do not move us, for we know that the Master of the house rose up in 1844, and shut the door of the first apartment of the heavenly tabernacle."

11  For details, see Samuel Kibungei Chemurtoi, "James White and J. N. Andrews' Debate on the Identity of Babylon, 1850–1868" (MA thesis, Adventist International Institute of Advanced Studies, 2005).

12  Already in 1847, Joseph Bates, *Second Advent Way Marks*, 53, argued, "How can you have faith in Babylonish revivals, after Babylon has fallen?" In 1854, a *Review* reader applied Ellen White's statement on "false reformations" to a local revival; see E. R. Seaman, "Can Ye not Discern the Signs of the Times?" *Review and Herald [RH]*, February 21, 1854, 37.

13  Cf. Kathryn T. Long, *The Revival of 1857-58: Interpreting an American Religious Awakening* (New York, NY: Oxford University Press, 1998).

14  See, e.g., "Extracts from Letters," *RH*, February 4, 1858, 103; Jesse Dorcas, "Exhort One Another," *RH*, June 17, 1858, 37. For further source references, see P. Gerard Damsteegt, *Foundations of the Seventh-day Adventist Message and Mission* (Grand Rapids, MI: Eerdmans, 1977), 184–185.

15  A. S. H., "Reformations in the Nominal Churches," *RH*, March 11, 1858, 136.

16  Cf. a Millerite pamphlet republished in 1854 by Sabbath-keeping Adventists, Robert Atkins, *A True Picture or Description of the State of the Churches* (Rochester, NY: Advent Review Office, [1854]): "Apostasy, apostasy, apostasy is engraven on the very front of every church" (ibid., 6). The significance of Atkins's pamphlet and the views it propagated is seen in the fact that Ellen White quotes material from it in her 1888 and 1911 editions of *The Great Controversy Between Christ and Satan* (Oakland, CA: Pacific Press, 1888), 387–388; 1911 edition: 388.

and walk up to the abundant light that now shines forth from the word of God. Nothing of this kind have they done; and yet they claim that a wonderful revival has taken place among them.[17]

In its earliest period, therefore, Sabbath-keeping Adventists quite consistently used the term "Protestant" and reports connected with it in a negative manner. There were scant exceptions – such as a case when James White claimed that originally "the Bible alone is the religion of Protestants" and called this "the Protestant principle."[18] But even in this instance the argument was that the churches originating in the Reformation had actually turned away from the Sabbath. Thus references to them generally implied the reproach of having dishonored God's law, the verdict of having fallen from God's favor, and the expectation of a soon-coming crisis, in which they would stand opposed to God's faithful. This view of "Protestantism" was more or less unconsciously built on earlier traditions of anti-sectarianism, which were particularly powerful in the Restorationist movements such as the Christian Connexion, but received its strength through the appeal to apocalyptic passages of the Bible and Sabbatarianism.

## Moral Reform Everywhere: Ellen G. White and the Incipient Denomination

It is only with the background of this general picture that another line of development can be appreciated. It started in the mid-1850s. For a few years, the fledgling Sabbatarian Adventist movement had experienced years of enormous numerical growth and developed first local organizational arrangements. When the first dissidents threatened to split the body of Sabbath keepers in 1853–1854,[19] the need for solid leadership structures became more evident, and slowly a self-understanding as "church" evolved. This was visible both in increasing calls for "gospel order" and in the first publications that utilized the term "church" in a positive way. Heretofore "the churches" had been synonymous to "Babylon" and "Protestantism"; now the singular began to denote Sabbatarian Adventism.[20]

This subtle change of self-understanding can be noticed in Ellen White's writings as well. She started her *Testimonies for the Church* series in late 1855,

17 [Uriah Smith,] "The Recent Revivals," *RH*, April 21, 1859, 172. For a similar view of similar phenomena in Ireland, see [Uriah Smith,] "The Revival in Ireland," *RH*, November 24, 1859, 4.
18 James White, "Twenty Reasons for Keeping Holy in Each Week the Seventh Day instead of the First Day," *Present Truth* [vol. 1, no. 3], August 1849, 23.
19 On the "Messenger Party" as well as the Stephenson and Hall split in Wisconsin, see Richard W. Schwarz and Floyd Greenleaf, *Light Bearers: A History of the Seventh-day Adventist Church* (Nampa, ID: Pacific Press, 2000), 89.
20 One notable example – apparently the first to use "church" in a positive way in a publication title of the movement – is a 64-page booklet by Merritt E. Cornell, *The Last Work of the True Church* (Rochester, NY: Advent Review Office, 1855).

addressing what she viewed as the dearth of spirituality and dedication to the cause in "the Church" – i.e., Adventist Sabbath keepers.[21] The parallels to the Adventist criticisms of "Protestantism" are striking! Further "Testimonies" were full of reproof and exhortation for fellow Sabbatarians as well, focusing on moral behavior, family issues, general commitment, church life, health and dress.[22] One expression that steadily gains significance in these admonitions is "reform." Appearing in individual instances in the 1850s and denoting a change of individual attitude or lifestyle, the term acquires crucial importance in the 1860s and connects particularly frequently with "dress" and "health." Ellen White used it about 100 times in what was to become the first *Testimonies* volume.

In fact, at this juncture "reform" was soon found almost everywhere. While the official church papers continued focusing on theological issues, on exegetical questions, the Sabbath and eschatology, it appears that Ellen White re-formed the general Adventist discourse almost single-handedly and moved it into the direction of Christian ethics. What is of fundamental importance in her use of terms is that "reform" and "reformation" are actually synonymous;[23] to her, both terms imply seriousness, the willingness to pursue a totally ethical lifestyle, and courage in a world that opposes faithful Christian conduct.

It is against this backdrop of the equality of "reform" and "reformation" that Ellen White's first comments on the Reformation of the sixteenth century can be best understood. Both in her 1863 *Testimonies* and in the first version of her *Great Controversy*, the volume *Spiritual Gifts* published in 1858, the Reformation is largely depicted as the clash of those who represented faithfulness to God and those who indulged in or supported a worldly, sinful church. In other words, the Reformation was about ethics – it was an event in which morality triumphed. In the short chapter devoted to the sixteenth century in *Spiritual Gifts* (covering only five rather small pages), White mentions the conflict, protest, or disgust regarding the

---

21 Ellen G. White's *Testimony for the Church* (Battle Creek: Advent Review Office, 1855) contains strong words of rebuke, which resemble the evaluation of other Protestant bodies: "I saw that the Spirit of the Lord has been dying away from the Church [i.e., Sabbath keepers]" (1); "I asked the angel why simplicity had been shut out from the Church" (2); "I saw that the spirit of sacrifice was almost gone from the Church" (3); "The Church have nearly lost their spirituality and faith" (8).

22 In vol. 1 of Ellen G. White, *Testimonies for the Church*, 9 vols. (Mountain View, CA: Pacific Press, 1948), containing her *Testimonies* from 1855 to 1868, these were the issues addressed in five or more sections.

23 Some examples from vol. 1 of her *Testimonies*: 1857: "reformation in the life" (154); "Beg of God to work in you a thorough reformation" (158); 1863: "when the truth is believed by them from the heart, it will work an entire change in their lives. They will immediately commence the work of reformation" (415); "unpleasant necessity of individual reformation and exertion" (441); 1865: "A reformation is needed among the people, but it should first begin its purifying work with the ministers" (469); "Many professed Sabbathkeepers will be no special benefit to the cause of God or the church without a thorough reformation on their part" (533).

sins of church leaders no less than seven times in addition to two other major recurring themes: the courage and zeal of Luther and an ecclesiology of purity, that is, a church which consisted only of the faithful. These stood in opposition to the "priests ... [who] did not wish to be reformed. They chose to be left in ease, in wanton pleasure, in wickedness. They wished the church kept in darkness."[24] To Ellen White, the Great Controversy was, even in Reformation times, essentially a moral controversy.

Such mid-nineteenth-century interpretations of sixteenth-century events were certainly colored by American reform attitudes and figures of thinking. It is consistent, therefore, that a few years later Ellen White asserted about Adventists at large, "We are reformers."[25] The main aim of her messages was evidently to encourage Sabbath-keeping Adventists to uphold this reform spirit: to remain faithful and active, to attract others to their convictions by standing firm. In this thinking, Luther was a reformer rather than a theologian, and not so much a herald of justification but a lover of the Bible, and more of a bold protester than a university professor.

It is not surprising, therefore, that Ellen White's second major reference to the Reformation (in her *Testimonies* in 1863, a message directed to Adventist preachers) echoes the same orientation. "Ministers who are preaching present truth," the prophet insisted, were not nearly as zealous as Luther and his contemporaries. Like the reformers, they were to display the character and boldness needed for God's cause. Even here, "Reformation" essentially meant a protest against the fallen church, the insistence on God's truth, a life of true Christian values, and the moral courage to stand for what is right.[26]

Interestingly, Ellen White included one reference to the actual content of Luther's gospel understanding in her 1858 book. According to her, he "was not satisfied until a gleam of light from heaven drove the darkness from his mind, and led him to trust, not in works, but in the merits of the blood of Christ; and to come to God for himself, not through popes nor confessors, but through Jesus Christ alone."[27] This experiential description (combined, again, with some protest language) remains the only place where something like a *sola gratia* notion occurs in this earliest section on the Reformation – yet even here redemption, with its language of merit that implies a satisfaction model of atonement, appears as having a strong moral slant.

---

24 Ellen G. White, *Spiritual Gifts*, vol. 1: *The Great Controversy between Christ and His Angels, and Satan and His Angels* (Battle Creek, MI: James White, 1858), 121–122.
25 Ellen G. White, *Testimonies for the Church*, vol. 3 (Mountain View, CA: Pacific Press, 1948), 159. Here the context is educational reform; the original text is from the year 1872.
26 Ellen G. White, *Testimonies for the Church*, vol. 1 (Mountain View, CA: Pacific Press, 1948), 372–376. A thematic analysis of this text yields these four major emphases, with each being addressed four times (except protest against the fallen church, which is mentioned three times).
27 White, *Spiritual Gifts*, vol. 1, 120.

## Protestantism-Reformation Dialectic: The Second Generation

The organizational changes that Sabbatarian Adventism experienced in the 1860s not only went hand in hand with theological development – particularly in the field of ecclesiology – but also influenced the use of terminology in various realms. As Seventh-day Adventists organized themselves into a denomination, their intense apocalypticism was balanced by an increasing ecclesial consciousness, which both provided and demanded a theology with a certain measure of stability. It is salvation-historical thinking – building on Miller's interpretations, having been present in Joseph Bates' earliest Adventist theologizing, and appearing in Ellen White's first version of the *Great Controversy* – which evolved into a framework that could serve this demand of stability. This development would soon also be felt in the Adventist discourse on "Protestantism."

On the one hand, "Protestantism" continued to represent the "fallen churches," those who had become "Babylon" in 1843 or at least belonged to apostate Christianity because of their "moral fall" or general state. It is logical, therefore, that the persecution scenario that Adventist Sabbath keepers had referred to already in the late 1840s continued to be referred to and even became a crucial part of Ellen White's 1884 version of the *Great Controversy*. Her now famous words implied a continuing mistrust of "the churches" among Adventists in spite of the fact that they had become a denomination themselves.

> Protestantism will yet stretch her hand across the gulf to grasp the hand of Spiritualism; she will reach over the abyss to clasp hands with the Roman power; and under the influence of this threefold union, our country will follow in the steps of Rome in trampling on the rights of conscience.[28]

> The Protestant churches ... are now adopting a course which will lead to the persecution of those who conscientiously refuse to do what the rest of the Christian world are doing, and acknowledge the claims of the papal Sabbath.[29]

On the other hand, the same book by Ellen White contained four chapters on Luther and the German Reformation; in addition, one deals with "Early Reformers" (John Wycliffe and Jan Hus) and one with "Later Reformers" (Tyndale, Knox, the Wesleys, and the English Seventh Day Baptists). If the logic inherent in this chiastic scheme is extended, the Waldenses, who "planted the seeds of the Reformation," with a separate chapter before the "Early Reformers," correspond to William

---

28 Ellen G. White, *The Spirit of Prophecy*, vol. 4: *The Great Controversy between Christ and Satan from the Destruction of Jerusalem to the End of the Controversy* (Oakland, CA: Pacific Press, 1884), 405.
29 Ibid., 409–410.

Miller, who is also called one of the "reformers."[30] With this significant attention given to key figures of Protestantism and other reform personalities, a perception that strikingly differed from the end-time expectancy of turmoil was present in the writings of the foremost leader in Adventism after James White died.

The double perspective of extolling the Reformation and condemning Protestant churches was a tension that could not easily be upheld in the following period. Both "apostate Protestantism" and "courageous reformers" were figures of thought that had existed alongside each other, but as time went by, the inherent dialectic in this interpretation[31] was difficult to uphold. One area in which this is visible was the issue of mission. Starting with an anti-mission shut-door ideology, Adventist Sabbath keepers were initially utterly skeptical regarding the missionary activities of other Protestant bodies. To them mission, like attempts of Evangelical revivalism, was a futile endeavor at best[32] and anti-biblical at worst – for it was frequently linked with what was then called "the world's conversion," the postmillennialist vision of an entirely Christianized globe.[33]

After some time, however, this opposition to Protestant mission activities mellowed, and when Adventists had begun serious international missionary activities of their own in the 1870s, they commended the mission efforts of other Protestant denominations.[34] In a few instances, Protestant mission projects were even depicted

---

30 Ibid., 202. Ellen White actually puts him in line with "many other reformers." Cf. also the table of contents, where a part of this chapter is thus summarized: "The World Opposes Reformers" (ix).
31 Ellen White's assessment of what happened in the generations following the Reformation was the following: "Thus the spirit inspired by the Reformation gradually died out, until there was almost as great need of reform in the Protestant churches as in the Roman Church in the time of Luther. There was the same spiritual stupor, the same respect for the opinions of men, the same spirit of worldliness, the same substitution of human theories for the teachings of God's word. Pride and extravagance were fostered under the guise of religion. The churches became corrupted by allying themselves with the world. Thus were degraded the great principles for which Luther and his fellow-laborers had done and suffered so much" (ibid., 194).
32 Uriah Smith argued that evangelism would not have any significant results anyway: "He who foresaw the end from the beginning, has told us that goodness and virtue should gradually cease to find an abode in the hearts of men; that wickedness and vice in most hideous forms, should increase and flourish." Only as a result of the Adventist proclamation "a few may be saved." See [Uriah Smith,] "Evangelizing the World," *RH*, November 6, 1856, 8. Cf. also J[oseph] B. Frisbie, "The World's Conversion," *RH*, August 19, 1858, 105, who argued that conversions were "of a doubtful character" anyway, and, later, "Converting the Heathen," *RH*, June 9, 1868, 396; "Missionaries in Asia: Anglican Exclusiveness in India," *RH*, July 21, 1868, 70–71; and "Missionary Work in Africa," *RH*, July 19, 1881, 61.
33 Cf. the six-part article series in 1865 by R. F. Cottrell, "The World's Conversion," *RH*, June 27, 29; July 11, 45–46; July 18, 53; July 25, 61; August, 1, 69; and August 15, 84; see also "Evangelizing the World," *RH*, December 20, 1870, 5.
34 Cf. the fourteen-part series on mission in the *Review and Herald*, starting January 4, 1881, 12, and ending April 26, 1881, 268. In the January 11, 1881, issue, for instance, the author

as examples for Adventists.³⁵ The climax of these new bouts of sympathy came with the non-denominational Student Volunteer Movement for Foreign Missions (SVM) in the 1890s.³⁶ An Adventist report on an SVM World Convention insisted,

> [T]he Student Volunteer Movement is one which merits the full sympathy and co-operation of Seventh-day Adventists. Unselfish, unsectarian (so far as concerns Protestant sects), animated by pure zeal and devotion to the cause of Christ, and seeking only to bring the sound of his gospel to the millions whose ears it has never reached, it is a part of the great gospel work which God is doing for the world in this last generation of its history, and in which it has pleased him to assign us so wonderful a part.³⁷

With regard to mission, Protestants appeared to revive the reformers' ethos, and the SVM with its non-denominational course and identity as a "movement" appealed to the anti-sectarian feelings that underlay the original Millerite Adventist reasoning. Thus Seventh-day Adventists could, for the first time, view contemporary Protestantism in an utterly positive manner – at least with regard to its dedication to worldwide gospel proclamation.

It appears that Ellen White's role was crucial in steering a course that would lead to a differentiated Adventist view of Protestantism. Her learning experiences in Europe in the 1880s, her contributions to the Christocentric turn in 1888 (albeit with little reference to the Reformation and its core)³⁸ and her calls for caution in

---

noted, "true piety and Christian simplicity have characterized the early history of all Christian denominations" (28).

35 See, e.g., M. L. R., "A Mission Established by the Baptists," *RH*, January 24, 1882, 55; "Beginnings of Protestant Missions," *RH*, February 4, 1890, 70; "The Pioneer of Chinese Missions," *RH*, March 25, 1890, 182.

36 Cf. Michael Parker, *The Kingdom of Character: The Student Volunteer Movement for Foreign Missions, 1886–1926* (Lanham, MD: University Press of America, 1998).

37 L. A. S[mith], "The World's Convention of Student Volunteers for Foreign Mission," *RH*, March 17, 1891, 168–169, here 169. Cf. also "International Convention of the Student Volunteer Movement," *RH*, February 17, 1891, 102, where the authors states, "We know of no enterprise for the advancement of foreign mission work, that we indorse more heartily than the Student Volunteer Movement. It is undenominational in character, but has sympathy and encouragement from all Christian bodies."

38 In Ellen G. White, *The Ellen G. White 1888 Materials*, 4 vols. (Washington, DC: Ellen G. White Estate, 1987), among the dozens of references to "reform" or "reformation" (which almost all refer to change in conduct or attitude), only one alludes to the issue of justification, viz. grace, and even here the theme is couched in 19th-century holiness language: "Christ's followers must walk in the light of his glorious example, and at whatever cost or labor or suffering, must maintain the purity of the soul and spirit through the grace of Christ, yielding complete allegiance to the reformatory doctrines of the gospel of Christ, without mingling self with the work. Keep self subdued, and keep Jesus ever lifted up, and push the triumphs of the cross of Christ. Let it be your work while life shall last to extend the borders of his kingdom, and wage a daily war against all sin and ungodliness, whatever others may think of you" (969; from an 1891 letter to S. N. Haskell).

relating to other Christians[39] combined into a direction that upheld the unique Adventist mission while acknowledging praiseworthy elements among other Protestants. In fact, in her thinking of the period, Adventists were to be the truest Protestants *and* Reformers; her confidently anachronistic 1886 reflection on *Christ* as "Reformer" and "Protestant" even implies that to Adventists this terminology effectively indicated eternal principles, not references to specific periods of history.

> Christ was a protestant. He protested against the formal worship of the Jewish nation, who rejected the counsel of God against themselves ... The Reformers date back to Christ and the apostles. They came out and separated themselves from a religion of forms and ceremonies. Luther and his followers did not invent the reformed religion. They simply accepted it as presented by Christ and the apostles.[40]

## Reform Movement or Protestant Church? The Early Twentieth Century

Ellen White's merger of "Reformer" and "protest/Protestant" language indicates a shift that would manifest itself in an even more pronounced manner in the early twentieth century. Adventists increasingly began to present themselves as Protestants or even the *true* Protestants. *The Protestant Magazine*, mentioned in the introduction of this paper, was only one visible indication of this trend. Theologically, Adventists moved significantly closer to the Evangelical mainstream in the 1890s and the 1900s in terms of soteriology and Christology as well as the gradual adoption of trinitarianism.[41] It is as if the somewhat isolated Seventh-day Adventist denomination now sought allies rhetorically in its immediate religious neighborhood. After all, it also began to form some kind of coalitions where this seemed opportune, as in the student mission movement, the temperance cause,[42] and anti-Catholic activism, the latter being a major thrust of *The Protestant Magazine*.

And there were even more pronounced versions of Adventist self-identification with "Protestantism." Alonzo Jones, for instance, who had left Adventism in the context of the Kellogg crisis but remained doctrinally attached to his former faith,

---

39 For a collection of these statements, see Stefan Höschele, *Interchurch and Interfaith Relations: Seventh-day Adventist Statements and Documents*, Adventistica 10 (Frankfurt a.M.: Lang, 2010), 21–30.
40 Ellen G. White, "Visit to the Vaudois Valleys," *RH*, June 1, 1886, 2 [338].
41 Rolf Pöhler's thorough study of Adventist theological development evaluates these changes as indicating a movement from "heterodox to orthodox," from "distinctive to fundamental" and from "legalism to evangelicalism"; see his "Change in Seventh-day Adventist Theology: A Study of the Problem of Doctrinal Development" (ThD diss., Andrews University, 1995), 285–288 (section headings).
42 Cf. Yvonne D. Anderson, "The Bible, the Bottle and the Ballot: Seventh-day Adventist Political Activism, 1850–1900," *Adventist Heritage* 7.2 (1982): 38–52, and Richard Rice, "Tempered Enthusiasm: Adventists and the Temperance Movement," *Spes Christiana* 25–26 (2014–2015): forthcoming.

wrote a large monograph to explain what the Reformation "meant then" and "what it means now."[43] To Jones, it implied the most far-reaching religious freedom possible and, consequently, minimal ecclesial authority. The Protestant principle, to him, was to proclaim and defend "the full and complete liberty of every individual, himself alone ... the sole and complete responsibility of the individual soul to God only, in all things pertaining to religion or faith."[44] The Bible was, of course, to be the basis, "all-sufficient in all things pertaining to religion and faith,"[45] but denominations were not to introduce any restrictions "on the full preaching of the word of God, even on 'controverted points,' to every creature everywhere and always."[46] This reformation view and its concomitant advocacy of extreme individualism, which was reminiscent of the somewhat chaotic Millerite post-disappointment phase, did evidently not match the generally uniform Seventh-day Adventist approach to faith in the period. It arose, however, from a typically Adventist impulse – an apocalyptic and individualist transformation of radical strands of Protestantism.

A line of thought and action that took the Adventist "reform" philosophy one step further into another direction was born in the crisis of World War I. The heightening of apocalyptic expectations, debates on ethical questions such as military service – especially on the Sabbath day –, the Adventist tradition of strictness in the context of diversified responses to burning issues, and the absence of a prophetic voice after the death of Ellen White all contributed to a novel movement that aimed at taking up the cause of reform. The Reform Movement (or Reformation Movement, as its adherents preferred to call themselves) aimed at carrying the traditional Adventist logic of a pure, "reform" church to the end – and thus paradoxically reversed some of the steps towards Protestantism that Seventh-day Adventists had travelled.

In the 1910s the Adventist denomination had, in fact, transformed from a protest movement to a Protestant church. Its protest ethos was still alive, at least rhetorically; but the necessities of establishing and safeguarding the denominational organization and building its missionary machinery shaped it in such a way that analogies with other Protestant churches were ubiquitous. It is, therefore, natural that close contacts in the so-called mission field finally led to an Adventist recognition of other Protestant mission agencies as part of God's involvement in the history of the world. In the context of mission rivalry and cooperation in China, Seventh-day Adventist leaders of the Eastern Asia Division issued a declaration entitled "Our Relationship to Other Societies" in 1919,[47] which included the following statements:

43 Alonzo T. Jones, *The Reformation, 14th–16th Century: What It Meant Then; What It Means Now* (N. p.: By the author, 1913).
44 Ibid., 44.
45 Ibid.
46 Ibid., 43.
47 W. A. Spicer – [J. L.] Shaw, March 21, 1919, Archives, General Conference of Seventh-day Adventists (GCA), 21/1919/Spicer; first publication: *RH*, August 19, 1920, 5–6 (1061–

1. We recognize every agency that lifts up Christ before men as a part of the divine plan for the evangelization of the world, and we hold in high esteem the Christian men and women in other communions who are engaged in winning souls to Christ.
2. Wherever the prosecution of the gospel work brings us into touch with other societies and their work, the spirit of Christian courtesy, frankness, and fairness should at all times guide in dealing with mission problems ...
3. As to the matter of territorial divisions and the restriction of operations to designated areas, our attitude must be shaped by these considerations:
a. As in generations past, in the providence of God and the historical development of his work for men, denominational bodies and religious movements have arisen to give special emphasis to different phases of gospel truth, so we find in the origin and rise of the Seventh-day Adventist people, the burden laid upon us to emphasize the gospel of Christ's second coming as an event 'even at the door,' calling for the proclamation of the special message of preparation of the way of the Lord as revealed in Holy Scripture.

This declaration, which would soon become part of the denomination's *General Conference Working Policy*[48] was a long way from the earlier insistence on Protestantism being wholly apostate. While it did not actually amount to the "comity statement" of mutual non-interference that the other mission societies desired, and did not mention Protestant missions (as opposed to Catholics), it is evident that the text almost exclusively aimed at fellow Protestants: the China Continuation Committee (CCC) of the Edinburgh World Missionary Conference, to whom it was sent, consisted solely of such organizations. Whatever the wording, the significance of the text is that Seventh-day Adventists publicly expressed, for the first time, how much they appreciated the ministry of other denominations, especially those that were fellow heirs of the Reformation.

## Observations on the Discourse in the Post-Pioneer Period

The Adventist use of "reform" and "protest" rhetoric and of the terms "Reformation" and "Protestant" in the post-pioneer period constitutes a large field of research of its own; here only a few observations can be presented, which indicate how the inherited discourses continued and were reinforced or modified.

(1) Involvement with other Protestants in the missionary realm continued and expanded. The Seventh-day Adventist Church joined the (Protestant) Foreign Mission Conference of North America (FMCNA) in the 1930s, an organization

---

1062). For a more detailed account on the background of this declaration, see Stefan Höschele, "From Mission Comity to Interdenominational Relations: The Development of the Adventist Statement on Relationships with Other Christian Churches," *Exploring the Frontiers of Faith: Festschrift in Honour of Dr. Jan Paulsen*, ed. Børge Schantz and Reinder Bruinsma (Lüneburg: Advent-Verlag, 2010), 389–404.

48   The text had been intended for use solely in Eastern Asia, but the first edition of the *General Conference Working Policy*, published in 1926, included it and thus raised its importance to a global level. In a slightly modified form, it is still part of the same *Working Policy* today.

that encompassed a very broad spectrum of churches: Fundamentalist-type denominations, Presbyterians, Methodists and Baptists, African American mission organizations, Pentecostals and (initially) even Universalists.[49] Soon, Adventists served on a significant number of committees, thus indicating that at least in the support of mission, they no longer distanced themselves from Protestantism at large organizationally.[50]

(2) In the context of the Fundamentalist/Modernist controversy, Adventists clearly positioned themselves on the Fundamentalist side. In spite of uneasy relations with the Fundamentalist mainstream, which generally regarded Adventism as cultic, heretic, or at best odd, the Seventh-day Adventist self-identification as the most genuine Fundamentalists[51] squarely categorized them as Protestants – or, indeed, the *truest* Protestants of all.[52]

(3) The Evangelical-Adventist conversations in the 1950s, which led to the publication of *Questions on Doctrine* (QOD), reinforced this general perception. Adventists presented themselves as conservative Protestants and emphasized what they held in common with other Christians and, particularly, Protestants.[53] While these conversations and QOD caused quite a stir both within the Adventist community and the North American Evangelical world, the episode was indicative of a direction in thought that could not be reversed. "Protestantism" was now viewed, by a majority of Adventist thought leaders, as an ally rather than an enemy. While QOD mainly addressed a context shaped by Calvinism (and, therefore, only one type of Reformation heirs) and, therefore, the Reformation as such was not a major theme, it emphasized both the continuity with Protestantism and the Adventist will to "complete" the Reformation.[54]

49  Cecil M. Robeck, "The Assemblies of God and Ecumenical Cooperation, 1920–1965," *Pentecostalism in Context: Essays in Honor of William W. Menzies*, ed. Wonsuk Ma and Robert Menzies (Sheffield: Sheffield Academic Press, 1997), 110–112.
50  For a more extensive account, see Stefan Höschele, "Interchurch Relations in Seventh-day Adventist History: A Study in Ecumenics" (Habilitation thesis, University of Prague, 2016), 230–238.
51  Cf. F. M. Wilcox, "Forsaking the Foundations of Faith," *RH*, November 28, 1929, 13–14 (here Adventists are called "the chief of Fundamentalists today"); William H. Branson, "Loyalty in an Age of Doubt," *Ministry*, October 1933, 3 ("fundamentalists of Fundamentalists"). Cf. also Francis D. Nichol, "Modernism's Inadequacy Is Our Opportunity," *Ministry*, February 1936, 13–14, 22.
52  Some Adventist leaders also attended Fundamentalist "Prophetic Conferences" in 1918 and 1919 and mostly reported favorably; see Michael W. Campbell, "The 1919 Bible Conference and Its Significance for Seventh-day Adventist History and Theology" (PhD diss., Andrews University, 2008), 41–56.
53  *Seventh-day Adventists Answer Questions on Doctrine: An Explanation of Certain Major Aspects of Seventh-day Adventist Belief* (Washington, DC: Review and Herald, 1957), 21–25.
54  Two quotations may suffice to illustrate this: "We definitely feel that we must emphasize certain neglected truths, must restore others that most Protestant bodies no longer stress, and must continue the work of the Reformation" (ibid., 189). "We, as Adventists, profoundly

(4) Although Adventism did not produce many Reformation scholars, a few Adventist theologians did develop interest in Reformation studies from the 1960s onward. This added a new dimension to the Adventist discourse on both Protestantism and the Reformation; scholarship helped to differentiate earlier perspectives and interpret historical and dogmatic developments in a more contextual manner. An outstanding researcher in this field was Kenneth Strand,[55] who edited several works on the Reformation, published a good number of articles on the subject (especially in Andrews University Seminary Studies)[56] and specialized in Reformation Bibles[57] – a fitting research niche for someone from a tradition that has a strong biblical emphasis.

(5) Another line of – mainly academic – discussion opened in the 1970s and came to flourish in the 1980: the historical and dogmatic relationship between Reformation churches and Seventh-day Adventism. New studies documented the significant connection between Puritanism and Adventism[58] and the link of Sabbath theologies in some strands of the Reformation with Seventh-day Adventist thought[59] and thus reinforced the affirmation that Adventists were inheritors of Reformation elements. (Yet the peculiar Adventist view of the Reformation seems not to have been made a topic of research of any major study then and until the present, whence the symposium and this publication.)

(6) The idea that Adventists were the true "heirs of the Reformation" is rooted in the movement's nineteenth-century self-reflection, but this particular formulation came up later. LeRoy E. Froom used it in 1931, presumably for the first time in Adventist print;[60] his massive collections *The Prophetic Faith of Our Fathers*

---

believe that in these last days God is calling for the completion of the arrested Protestant Reformation and for the full and final restoration of gospel truth" (615).
55 Another scholar is Johann Heinz, who wrote his dissertation on "Justification and Merit: The Interpretation and Evaluation of the Concept of Merit in Modern Catholic Theology in Relation to Luther's Doctrine of Justification" (ThD diss., Andrews University, 1982).
56 Strand contributed fifteen articles to *AUSS* on Reformation topics and, as an editor of the journal, initiated a special issue on Luther (1984).
57 This all connected with his dissertation: Kenneth A. Strand, "A Low-German Edition of the Gospels and Book of Acts Based on Hieronymus Emser's Version and Published by the Brethren of the Common Life at Rostock about 1530" (PhD diss., University of Michigan, 1958). Some of his significant publications are Kenneth A. Strand, *Reformation Bibles in the Crossfire* (Ann Arbor, MI: Ann Arbor Publishers, 1961); idem, *German Bibles Before Luther* (Grand Rapids, MI: Eerdmans, 1966); idem, *Introduction to the Religious Thought of Luther, Zwingli, and Calvin* (Ann Arbor, MI: Braun-Brumfield, 1974); idem, *Paul's Epistle to the Romans from the December Bible and Wittenberg Editions of 1530, 1534, and 1545* (Ann Arbor, MI: Ann Arbor Publishers, 1972), and idem, ed., *Essays on Luther* (Ann Arbor, MI: Ann Arbor Publishers, 1969).
58 Cf. Ball, *The English Connection* (1981).
59 See Richard Müller, *Adventisten – Sabbat – Reformation*, Studia Theologica Lundensia 38 (Lund: Gleerup, 1979).
60 LeRoy E. Froom, "Build upon the Foundations," *Ministry*, November 1931, 7.

and *The Conditionalist Faith of Our Fathers*[61] actually mirrored this self-understanding. In later decades, "Heirs of the Reformation" became a more frequent metaphor in Adventist publications.[62]

(7) In several interchurch dialogues taking place from the 1990s onward, Seventh-day Adventists continued to invoke significant continuity with the Protestant Reformation. Naturally, this emphasis appeared most strongly in the Lutheran-Adventist dialogue during the 1990s ("shared heritage from the Reformation"; "deep appreciation for the work and teachings of Martin Luther"; "heirs of the Protestant Reformation"; "children of Luther").[63] The report summarized,

> Adventists have a high appreciation for the Reformation. They see themselves as heirs of Luther and other Reformers, especially in their adherence to the great principles of *sola scriptura, sola gratia, sola fide, solo Christo.* Teachings which others may view as distinctive of Adventists are seen by them as the continuation of the Reformation's recovery of Biblical truth.[64]

While the Adventist-Mennonite conversations of 2011–2012 and the Adventist-Evangelical dialogue of 2006–2007 do not highlight aspects of the Reformation in their final reports,[65] Seventh-day Adventist "indebtedness ... to the Reformation

---

61 LeRoy E. Froom, *The Prophetic Faith of Our Fathers: The Historical Development of Prophetic Interpretation*, 4 vols. (Washington, DC: Review and Herald, 1950); idem, *The Conditionalist Faith of Our Fathers*, 2 vols. (Washington, DC: Review and Herald, 1966).
62 It even made its way into Geoffrey J. Paxton, *The Shaking of Adventism* (Grand Rapids, MI: Baker, 1978), and entitles his first chapter: "Adventists: Heirs of the Reformation." The popular book by Walter L. Emmerson, *The Reformation and the Advent Movement* (Washington, DC: Review and Herald, 1983), is a book-length attempt at demonstrating the continuity between the (Radical) Reformation and Adventism. In a short history of Adventism in Europe of 1997, the "heirs" phrase actually serves as the book title: Hugh I. Dunton, Daniel Heinz, Dennis Porter and Ronald Strasdowsky, *Heirs of the Reformation: The Story of Seventh-day Adventists in Europe* (Grantham: Stanborough, 1997).
63 *Lutherans and Adventists in Conversation: Report and Papers Presented 1994–1998* (Silver Spring, MD: General Conference of Seventh-day Adventists; Geneva: The Lutheran World Federation, 2000), 7–8.
64 Ibid., 16–17.
65 It is somewhat odd that the Seventh-day Adventist–Mennonite dialogue report mentions the Reformation but does not draw any conclusion for the common heritage and relationship of Adventists and Mennonites. See "Living the Christian Life in Today's World: Adventists and Mennonites in Conversation, 2011–2012," in *Living the Christian Life in Today's World: A Conversation between Mennonite World Conference and the Seventh-day Adventist Church*, ed. Carol E. Rasmussen (Silver Spring, MD: Public Affairs and Religious Liberty Department, General Conference of Seventh-day Adventists; n.p.: Mennonite World Conference, 2014), 263–270. In the report on the dialogue between the World Evangelical Alliance and the Seventh-day Adventist Church, there is no reference to the Reformation, only the remark that "Adventists can subscribe to the WEA Statement of Faith," thus placing the Seventh-day Adventist Church in the Evangelical Protestant community. See "Joint Statement of the World Evangelical Alliance and the Seventh-day Adventist Church." 2007

heritage" is emphasized in the Reformed-Adventist dialogue of 2001 as well.[66] The continuity with the Reformation, therefore, is what remains the most prominent legacy of earlier Adventist discourses in the twenty-first century.

## Conclusion

Our walk through a section of the Adventist language landscape is ending here. Five major emphases have been discerned: (1) a *consistently negative* image of *Protestantism* during the earliest Adventist period, in which Protestants were equated to apostate Christianity (and pictured as future persecutors of the true believers); (2) a *consistently positive* view of *reform* in the period when the Seventh-day Adventist denomination emerged and was organized; in it, the *moral reform rhetoric* of nineteenth-century America combined with the theological emphases of the young movement and strongly colored its interpretation of the Reformation as well; (3) the period from the 1880s onward, in which *Reformers* were seen as *precursors of Adventism*, moral examples to be followed, and in which even their other Protestant offspring appeared more acceptable than previously, at least with regard to their mission orientation; (4) a self-identification as the *true Protestants*, particularly in the early twentieth century; and (5) a more *dialogical relationship with other Protestants*, implying a differentiated (and more academic) look at the Reformation and at Protestantism at large.

All of these five options have continued in Adventist discourses until the present. As contradictory as some may seem, and although some reflected ahistorical or unhistorical points of view, together these perspectives and their implied attitudes form a variegated tradition from which any approach can be retrieved by some subgroup of contemporary Adventism, especially because earlier skeptical views have persisted in the writings of Ellen White and other Adventist pioneers. Yet all in all, a clear development can be recognized: from a mainly negative view of Protestants and a fully positive use of "reform" to a differentiated and rather positive notion of both "Protestantism" and the Reformation.

---

(https://goo.gl/ti8xNc, November 28, 2017; published also in Höschele, *Interchurch and Interfaith Relations*, 157–160). A report on a lengthy series of conversations (from 2004 to 2008) with the Salvation Army does not refer to the Reformation, presumably because the two traditions are linked in Methodism rather than 16th-century developments; see "Joint Salvation Army/Seventh-day Adventist Statement Arising from 2004–2008 Bilateral Theological Dialogues," Council on Interchurch/Interreligion Affairs, January 17, 2008, Religious Liberty Department, General Conference of Seventh-day Adventists.

66 "Report of the International Theological Dialogue between the Seventh-day Adventist Church and the World Alliance of Reformed Churches," Jongny sur Vevey, Switzerland, 1–7 April 2001 (https://goo.gl/prG8Sz, November 28, 2017). The report also says (about both traditions): "We acknowledge our debt to the Reformation with its biblical emphasis upon salvation by grace alone (sola gratia) through faith alone (sola fide) in Christ alone (solus Christus)."

*Nicholas Miller*

# The Reformation and the Remnant: The Reformers, the Great Controversy and the Sabbath

## Abstract

While all the main sixteenth-century Protestant reformers made important contributions to Adventist theological understanding and identity, those contributing most directly to the unique beliefs of Adventism were the radical reformers, as mediated and informed by the work of Jacob Arminius and Hugo Grotius. These two articulated most fully the free-will Protestant tradition inside a moral government of God framework, which served as the foundations for Adventist views on the great controversy and the sanctuary. That God oversaw a moral government implied both that God had opened up His actions and character for examination by the universe, and that human governments should also behave in a responsible and moral manner. Thus, Adventist pioneers were concerned with the justice and character of God, as well social issues of their day, such as slavery and alcohol prohibition. We are only truly heirs of the reformation as we bring the great "solas" of the reformers to bear in protest on current-day abuse and misuse of religious and social power.[1]

The question of which one of the sixteenth-century reformers was the most important or influential in relation to the Adventist church is impossible to answer. There are at least three or four reformers that are truly indispensable, and without which Adventism would not be Adventism as we know it. Martin Luther's contributions of the authority and primacy of Scripture, the truth of justification by faith, and the priesthood of all believers are absolutely essential to early and modern Adventism. But equally indispensable, most would believe, was Calvin's balancing of justification with sanctification, in his understanding of the third use of the law, with its continuing role in the Christian life, and basic church order and organization, without which there would be no worldwide Adventist church. And then of course there are the radical reformers, such as Anabaptist leaders Michael Sattler and Balthasar Hubmaier in Austria and Germany, and Menno Simons in Holland. With these, we share such views as believers' baptism, voluntary church membership, separation of church and state, holy living, and nonviolence.

Asking which is most important to Adventism is a little like asking which tire on a car is the most important, or what is the most important wing on a plane. They are all essential. But if we ask a slightly different question, that is, "Which reformer was most critical to the *unique* identity of Adventism?" we can attempt an answer.

1   This essay contains revised material that was originally published in Nicholas Miller, *The Reformation and the Remnant* (Nampa, ID: Pacific Press, 2016).

Many of the beliefs listed above we share with other Christian churches, whether it be scriptural authority, or justification, or even the perpetuity of the Ten Commandments. But where do we find those things that make Adventism uniquely Adventist?

Some might tag the radical reformers with this role, and I believe there is some truth to this. The trouble with making this the full answer is that tracing a path of actual influence from the radicals to Adventism is very difficult. They had no great names or central writings whose influence one can trace in an unbroken line from the sixteenth-century radicals to the nineteenth-century Adventists. Apart from a brief mention of Menno Simons, Ellen White omits the radical reformers from her discussion of the Reformation in the *Great Controversy*. In the nineteenth century, Anabaptist historiography was more associated with the excesses of the radical Zwickau prophets, the rabble rousing Thomas Müntzer, and the fanatical, violent, and short-lived theocracy of the City of Münster.

It is very doubtful that the Adventist pioneers read the radicals directly, or even indirectly. Their influence was dim and distant, and in most instances more of a parallel movement rather than a direct influence. There are some exceptions to this, especially in the area of church and state, the believers' baptism, and possibly even the Sabbath, where the influence of the Baptists, heirs of the Anabaptists, can be seen on the early Adventists. More on this later.

The sixteenth-century reformer I choose as the most significant for the uniqueness of Adventism is one that interacted with the radicals, but during his life was generally considered an opponent of them. He also comes at the end of the sixteenth century, not at the beginning like most of the iconic reformer names. I am speaking of James or Jacob Arminius, theologian of the Dutch Reformed Church, and foremost expositor of the Arminian, free-will tradition of Protestant theology. Arminius actually died as a member and professor in good standing of the Dutch Reformed Church. Only after his death were his followers and their views anathematized at the Synod of Dort in 1618.

To understand Arminius' significance for Adventism, one must understand that human free will was only part of a larger theological framework held by Arminius, and articulated by one of his leading supporters by the name of Hugo Grotius, called the moral government of God. I believe this theme helped provide the foundation for the Adventist theme of the great controversy as well as the sanctuary message.

I am going fast forward now about four centuries, to show a connection between Adventism, Ellen White, and the moral government of God heritage in Protestant thought. It is found in her biography, written by her grandson, Arthur White. He records that while in Australia in 1900 "she wrote to Edson calling for her library to be sent to Australia: 'I have sent for four or five large volumes of Barnes' notes on the Bible. I think they are in Battle Creek in my house now sold, somewhere with my books ... I may never visit America again, and my *best books* should come to me when it is convenient' (emphasis added)."[2]

How is it that an Adventist prophet would view the biblical commentaries of a non-Adventist scholar, Albert Barnes, as among her "best books," ones that were indispensable to her in her Australian work?

That any leader of the Adventist church would find high value in the commentaries of Barnes, a Calvinist/Reformed scholar of the Presbyterian Church – who was once tried for heresy – is somewhat paradoxical. Raised a Methodist, Ellen White lived and taught on the opposite end of the theological spectrum from Barnes, embracing a free-will, Arminian perspective of human choice and salvation, as Adventists generally do today. But these two Bible students, White and Barnes, were connected by a commitment to the powerful idea that God runs a moral government and that He is willing for His created beings to evaluate the fairness of that government.

It was within this moral government framework that Ellen White developed and refined her ideas of the sanctuary and its great controversy theme between Christ and Satan. It is a theme that many Adventist scholars view as the central and organizing motif of her writings. It is also a key to understanding the heart of Adventist theodicy (defending God's dealings with humanity) and is a crucial point of connection for many Adventist doctrines. But it is somewhat more complex and profound than a mere battle between good and evil, which most Christians, and even Hollywood, understands as being at the heart of the human story.

The moral government of God was a view that God Himself operates in a just and moral manner toward the beings He has created. Further, He can be seen to be moral and just by people as well as by an onlooking universe, who themselves are moral beings, able to understand and choose between good and evil. This framework, at least in its modern form, originated with the Arminian, free-will strand of Protestantism. But such was the force of its appeal that it also manifested itself in certain Calvinistic, Reformed circles, especially in America in the late eighteenth and early nineteenth centuries. That is why it can be found in the writings and commentaries of a progressive Presbyterian like Albert Barnes, which explains why Ellen White referred to his writings as being among her "best books."

An understanding of the Reformation roots of the concept of God's moral government provides insights into the heritage and richness of the great controversy motif, its role in the sanctuary, and its importance for Adventist doctrine today. But to understand this story, we need to go back to at least its early modern beginnings in the struggle over predestination and human free will, which laid the foundations for the moral government of God theme.

---

2   Letter 189, 1900. As quoted in Arthur L. White, *Ellen G. White: Volume 4, The Australian Years* (Washington, DC, and Hagerstown, MD: Review and Herald, 1983), 448.

## Arminius and the Roots of Free-Will Theology

Most Adventists have at least heard of Jacob Arminius, the great Dutch theologian of the late sixteenth and early seventeenth century. Arminius (1560-1609) launched a modification of Calvinist theology to allow for the human will to play some role in the acceptance of salvation. Arminian theology has become synonymous with a rejection of rigid human predestination, an atonement limited only to an elect few, and the arbitrary sovereignty of God in choosing who will be saved.

The strong identification of Arminius with free-will theology is somewhat unfortunate. It tends to obscure the fact that, prior to Arminius, other groups and individuals within the Protestant reformation also held two versions of human freedom in salvation. These included Lutheran theologian Philip Melanchthon and the entire evangelical Anabaptist movement. Emphasizing Arminius as the originator of free will within Protestantism makes it seem as though this emphasis was a later, third- or fourth-generation addition to genuine Protestant thought. This perception is used to imply, or even declare, that ideas about human free will are a corruption of an earlier, purer form of Protestantism. This continues to be the view of many Reformed thinkers, even up to the present day.

But this view of free will as a late-comer to the Reformation is just not accurate. It is true that both Luther and Calvin emphasized mankind's helplessness and bondage in reaction against a tendency in medieval scholasticism to underplay the severity of humanity's fall into sin. This scholasticism also overplayed human ability to both know and do the good and the right. In his debate with Erasmus over the freedom of the will, Luther wanted to emphasize man's absolute helplessness absent the grace of God. In doing so, he slid into the other ditch of making man almost a puppet in the hands of God. Both Luther and Calvin believed in God's essentially arbitrary predestination of certain people to be saved.

But not all first-generation Reformers held to this position of universal human helplessness and lack of free will. The Anabaptist theologian Balthasar Hubmaier wrote, in the 1520s, two treatises on the freedom of the will. In these works, he carefully avoided Pelagianism (the doctrine that man can save himself through good choice) and embraced a fully fallen, corrupted human nature. Yet he still asserted that "whoever denies the freedom of the human will, denies and rejects more than half of the Holy Scriptures."[3] For Hubmaier, God's atonement was for all humanity, and not just the elect, as Calvin held. These views on free will and the general availability of the atonement for all humanity came to characterize the views of the evangelical Anabaptists. These Anabaptists were found in both Austria and the Netherlands, where Anabaptist leader Menno Simons expressed similar views.[4]

---

3   Henry Clay Vedder, *Balthasar Hubmaier: The Leader of the Anabaptists* (New York, NY: G. Putnam's Sons, the Knickerbocker Press, 1905), 197.
4   Cornelius J. Dyck, *An Introduction to Mennonite History*, 3rd ed. (Scottdale, PA: Herald Press, 1993), 142.

Arminius began pastoring in Amsterdam in the 1580s. We know that he had contact with Mennonite Anabaptists as well as proponents of Melanchthon's views.[5] Was Arminius influenced by the Anabaptists, by Melanchthon, and/or by others in shaping his own views on grace and free will? The extent of such influence is historically contested. What we do know is that he developed a careful expression of Calvinism that allowed him to affirm almost all the existing reformed creeds on sin and salvation, yet to do so in a way that allowed for genuine human free choice in accepting salvation. But, importantly for our purposes in examining the roots of theodicy and the great controversy theme, his reason for elevating human freedom was not primarily because of a concern for human dignity, or human importance, or human liberty. Rather, his primary concern was that of the early Anabaptists – the sovereign glory and reputation of God. As church historian Roger Olson puts it,

> Arminius' strongest objection was that [unconditional predestination is] injurious to the glory of God [because] from these premises we deduce, as a further conclusion, that God really sins ... that God is the only sinner ... that sin is not sin. Arminius never tired of arguing that the strong Calvinist doctrine of predestination cannot help making God the author of sin, and if God is the author of sin, then sin is not truly sin because whatever God authors is good.[6]

Luther and Calvin, while unshackled from much error of the medieval church, still clung, perhaps unconsciously, to classical conceptions of a God who was timeless and untouched by our temporal experiences and concerns. Such a God was ultimately unknowable by humanity who could not enter the timeless realm that God inhabited. Thus, they viewed God as essentially unknowable in His essential being. This was the "hidden God," the "Deus absconditus," that Luther believed lay behind the face of God we have in the Bible. It was this hidden God who arbitrarily elected some to salvation and left the others to burn in hell. Between God's essential being, which we cannot know, and humanity's, there was no connection.[7]

5   Carl Bangs, *Arminius: A Study in the Dutch Reformation* (Eugene, OR: Wipf and Stock Publishers, 1985), 169–171, 193–194.
6   Roger E. Olson, *The Story of Christian Theology: Twenty Centuries of Tradition & Reform* (Downers Grove, IL: InterVarsity, 1999), 467.
7   Fernando Canale has explored in some detail these philosophical questions of divine and human ontology in classical thought and its impact on Protestant thought. Fernando Canale, "Philosophical Foundations and the Biblical Sanctuary," *Andrews University Seminary Studies* 36:2 (1998): 183–206. Canale has provided powerful insights into the philosophical underpinnings of much of Protestant thought, and how its conceptions of God and salvation have been molded, both consciously and unconsciously by classical conceptions of God's timelessness and immutability. Cf. idem, "The Eclipse of Scripture and the Protestantization of the Adventist Mind: Part 1," *Journal of the Adventist Theological Society* 21:1–2 (2010): 133–165; idem, "The Eclipse of Scripture and the Protestantization of the Adventist Mind: Part 2," *Journal of the Adventist Theological Society* 22:1 (2011): 102–133. My work supplements Canale's philosophical story by showing, in part, how it unfolded historically. I make no claim that Arminius or Grotius or Wesley explicitly repudiated the classical onto-

Arminius began to take steps that began, perhaps even unconsciously, to move away from this Greek, classical conception of a timeless, impassive, immovable God. He recognized that the gap between the divine Being and the created being is huge, even approaching "infinite." Mere beings, he believed, could never be raised to "divine equality with God." But despite this gap and distance, and that "the human mind is finite in nature," Arminius believed that we could understand something of God, though not in His entirety. As he put it, the human mind is "a partaker of infinity – because it apprehends Infinite Being and the Chief Truth, although it is incapable of comprehending them."[8] In other words, Arminius believed that humans were capable of knowing God as He truly is, at least in part – apprehending but not comprehending.

According to this view, when Christ revealed God, He showed us true things about the actual, real, eternal nature of God, and that there are not further, hidden natures that are contrary to this revealed nature. Of the qualities of God's nature, Arminius was very clear. "Concerning his nature; that it is worthy to receive adoration, on account of its justice; that it is qualified to form a right judgment of that worship, on account of its wisdom."[9] This "worthy" nature of God Arminius sought to defend from accusations of His being the creator of evil. God was not, Arminius insisted, the arbitrary divider of humanity into the vast camp of the eternally damned, who had no choice but to sin, and a small group of the saved elect.

It was in this context of defending God against being the arbitrary author of evil that he re-emphasized the biblical teaching of the role human choice played in accepting salvation. This choice played a role in determining which destiny a human would receive, that of the first Adam or that of the second Adam. Even for Arminius, this was not an unaided human choice, but a choice that the human will

logy of God's timelessness. But I believe that these men's theological movement towards a God that is fundamentally knowable, rational, relational, and responsive to human action was in profound conflict with this classical ontology. They paved the way for future Protestants, especially Adventists, to leave this classical ontology for one with greater consistency with the Bible. Canale, as a philosopher, wants to emphasize the discontinuity between classical ontology and the Adventist, biblical view, and hence emphasizes the differences between Adventists and other Protestants. My concern as a historian is to show the continuity of how this shift in views of God, both theologically and philosophically, actually unfolded on the ground. I think that my story shows that Adventism built on a growing body of truth about the nature of God and man, and did not erect a new structure wholesale. I believe that for most people, including pastors and theologians, shifts in philosophical outlook are driven by a combination of theology and practical experience, and not vice versa. Thus, Arminius, Grotius, Wesley, and the other theologians of our story began to shift their views of God's ontology, even if they did not think explicitly in terms of temporality, timelessness or ontology.

8  Jacob Arminius, *Works of Jacob Arminius, Vol. 1* (Montoursville, PA: Lamppost Books, 2009), 13.
9  Ibid., 15.

could make only under the influence of God's prevenient grace. This grace was given to all, in this sense it was inescapable, but for Arminius it was not irresistible. This prevenient, universal grace of God could be resisted and refused.[10]

## The Remonstrants, Hugo Grotius, and the Moral Government of God

It was in pursuit of the vindication of God's worthy nature that the story of the Dutch Remonstrants, supporters of Jacob Arminius, unfolded in Holland. The keepers of Calvinist orthodoxy were anxious to squash these "progressive" ideas about God. Shortly after Arminius died in 1609, his followers drafted a "remonstrance" against the official orthodoxy of the state church. The five points of the remonstrance did not deal directly with larger questions of theodicy or the defense of God's character. Rather, they focused on the immediate issues in dispute in relation to predestination, grace, and choice: conditional election, unlimited atonement, total depravity, prevenient grace, and continued choice (opposition to once saved, always saved).

These points, while not framed in terms of a theodicy, carry obvious implications for these questions. The ideas of conditional election and unlimited atonement convey the view that God has made a way for all to be saved, and the choice is in their hands as to whether to respond to the grace He has given. These ideas paint a very different picture of God than the high Calvinist view that Christ's atonement was made only for an arbitrarily chosen elect.

One of the Remonstrants, a lawyer by the name of Hugo Grotius (1583-1645), saw the importance of these points to understanding God as a gracious and fair ruler. These insights caused him to weave the ideas of the general atonement, prevenient grace, and human freedom into a larger conception of God and his government that came to be known as the moral government of God. Grotius is a well-known name in legal circles, being considered the father of international law, the law of war and peace, and Protestant conceptions of natural law. But in his day, he was equally famous for his theological writings.

One of his seminal theological works was *Concerning the Satisfaction of Christ*, in which he explored theories of the atonement in light of his new conceptions regarding God's moral relationship to human choice. He brought his legal background to bear, constructing what came to be known as the theory of the moral government of God. As one nineteenth-century Grotius scholar has put it,

> Grotius believed that there must be a reason back of every act of God, and accordingly could not accept the idea of a mechanical, self-acting, and insatiate justice blindly calling for the exact satisfaction of its claims. The justice of God was justice with a reason, and because He was a governor it became rectoral justice. God's government

10 Jacob Arminius, *Works of Jacob Arminius, Vol. 1* (Montoursville, PA: Lamppost Books, 2009), 188-191.

flowed from His character. That character was love, and the government of God was accordingly one of the many displays of his eternal love. This is the idea of the Grotian system.[11]

This moral government of God can only function in a universe of moral beings who have the freedom to make responsible, moral choices, and to evaluate the moral choices of others. Of course, fallen humans have lost the ability to make good moral choices, but through God's prevenient grace can make the one choice that matters, to choose God's help. At this point, true free will is restored, and they can once again make other moral choices. It is thus easy to see the close connection between a belief in human free will and God's moral government.

A second doctrine that is deeply connected to the moral government theory is the moral government theory of the atonement of Christ; it is best understood in relation to earlier views. Grotius' model did not so much displace these older views, but rather clarified, refined, and enriched them. Several centuries before Grotius, Anselm had famously argued that Christ must die in our place to satisfy the impaired *honor* of God. John Calvin had modified Anselm's view somewhat to describe the death of Christ as providing satisfaction to the offended *holiness*, law, or justice of God, as our guilt, sin, and punishment are mysteriously transferred to Christ.

Grotius did not deny God's honor, holiness, justice, or law. He accepted that these had indeed been breached and offended by sin. But he went further and addressed the question as to why God could not forgive this breach by merely accepting the genuine sorrow and repentance of the sinner. If humans can extend forgiveness without requiring sacrifice or suffering, why cannot God do the same? He answered that God could not merely freely forgive the sinner because it was not His role merely as an *individual offended Deity* that was involved. Rather, or in addition, it was His role as *Ruler of the universe*, a universe that can function only in peace and safety according to certain moral guidelines.[12]

This shift of God from offended Supreme Being to offended Supreme Ruler means that in enforcing His law – in requiring the payment of a penalty – He is not doing it out of some personal sense of pique, pride, or impaired glory. Rather, He is acting on behalf of the benefit of all the beings of the universe, beings who depend on the stability, fairness, and morality of His government. In defending His honor and character, He defends, as Ruler of the universe, the very thing that allows the universe itself to have the order, stability, and security that make it a safe and hospitable place for all its inhabitants.

Sometimes this view of Grotius is confused with the *moral influence* theory of the atonement, but the two are quite different. While both theories are concerned

11  Frank Hugh Foster, "Translator's Notes," in Hugo Grotius, *A Defense of the Catholic Faith Concerning the Satisfaction of Christ against Faustus Socinus* (Andover, MA: Warren F. Draper, 1889), 280.
12  Ibid., "Historical Introduction," xi–xv.

with "moral" aspects of God, the governmental theory holds that Christ saved us from a "necessary" punishment that was required to uphold the stability of God's universal government, and that Christ was thus truly a substitute for human beings. The moral influence theory tends to deny the necessity of both the punishment as well as the substitution.

Hugo Grotius exerted meaningful influence in the theological arena, especially in England, and then eventually America, for quite some time. Some of the names connected with Grotius in the English-speaking world need no introduction. John Milton, when on a tour of Europe as a young gentleman in 1638, stayed with Grotius in Paris for a period. Milton had a strong Calvinist, Puritan background, and yet emerged as a believer in freedom of the will, unlimited atonement, and very definitely the moral government of God. His *Paradise Lost*, of course, was written with the specific purpose to "assert Eternal Providence, and justify the ways of God to men."[13]

Milton's defense and explanation of God's ways and judgments is not a Calvinist ideal, which would have emphasized God's sovereignty. It is, though, a very Arminian, Grotian, moral government of God way of looking at the world. It also laid the foundation for viewing the activity of God as being part of an ongoing trial in the universe, of an investigative judgment, carried out in God's sanctuary, where the ways of God are being assessed in the manner in which He engages with humanity, and humanity with Him.

John Locke was known to possess all the main works of Hugo Grotius and often referred to him as an authority on both legal and religious matters. His conceptions of limited government and a state bound by principles of natural law and morality to the individual reflect very much the framework articulated by Grotius, whom he frequently acknowledges in his writings on government and natural law.

A contemporary of John Locke, a Seventh Day Baptist by the name of Thomas Tillam, wrote not just on God's government as being the center of a great controversy, but also tied that controversy to the seventh-day Sabbath and the conflict between Sabbath and Sunday observance. Tillam was influenced by a strand of Sabbath-keeping thought that had its roots in continental Anabaptism. Indeed, the dean of radical church history, George Williams of Harvard identified Anabaptist Oswald Glait as the first professor of "seventh-day Adventism" of the Reformation era, as he espoused both the Second Advent and the Sabbath in 1529.[14]

Adventist scholar W. L. Emmerson, in his book *The Reformation and the Advent Movement*, details these Anabaptists roots of modern Sabbath-keeping.[15] He discusses Glait, and the tract he published, *Concerning the Keeping of the Sabbath*, possibly the first written defense in the early modern era of the seventh-

---

13  John Milton, *Paradise Lost, Book 1*, in *The Student's Milton*, ed. Frank Allen Patterson (New York, NY: Appleton-Century-Crofts, Inc., 1957), 160.
14  G. H. Williams, *The Radical Reformation* (London: Weidenfeld and Nicolson, 1962), 257.
15  W. L. Emmerson, *The Reformation and the Advent Movement* (Hagerstown, MD: Review and Herald, 1983).

day Sabbath.[16] He traces the development and spread of Anabaptist Sabbatarians from Silesia, to Bohemia, Moravia, France, and even into Scandinavia by the middle of the sixteenth century.[17]

It would seem to be no coincidence that the branch of the Reformation that believed in human free will and the importance of the moral aspects of God's nature and government should be the branch to contain the first modern Sabbath keepers. This connection ties Sabbath-keeping not to a kind of arbitrary rediscovery of the fourth commandment, but to a coherent understanding of the moral nature of God and man, and the moral nature of God's law.

To return to the seventeenth-century Baptist, Thomas Tillam, we can see these connections between morality, the Sabbath, and the great controversy between God and Satan made explicit. Tillam was a Puritan who converted to become a Seventh Day Baptist in the 1640s in New England. Ironically, there was even greater persecution in New England at the time than in old England, and so Tillam moved back to Britain. There he wrote a tract in 1657 in support of the seventh-day Sabbath. The long title of the tract reveals its main argument:

> The Seventh-Day Sabbath Sought out and Celebrated, or, The Saints last Design upon the man of sin, with their advance of God's first institution to its primitive perfection, being a clear discovery of that black character in the head of the little Horn, Dan. 7:25. – The Change of TIMES AND LAWS – With the Christians glorious Conquest over that mark of the Beast, and the recovery of the long-slighted Seventh day, to its ancient glory ...[18]

Not only does Tillam, in his title, indicate that the conflict over Sabbath and Sunday is of great importance, but that it involves the efforts of the little horn and is connected with the mark of the beast. It only gets more interesting as one delves into the book. He titles chapter one, "The Seventh-day Sabbath, Sought Out and Celebrated, by Saints Obtaining the Victory Over the Mark of the Beast." He begins that chapter with these words: "The first Royal Law that ever Jehovah instituted, and for our Example celebrated, (namely His blessed Seventh-day Sabbath,) is in these very last days become the last great controversy between the Saints and the Man of Sin, The Changer of Times and Laws."[19]

Notice how Tillam identifies God's law in general, "the Royal Law," and the Sabbath commandment in particular, as being at the heart of a final conflict which he terms the "last great controversy." It is remarkable language that prefigures and even parallels in part Adventist eschatology more than two hundred years before it was written.

---

16   Ibid., 74–75.
17   Ibid., 76–79.
18   Thomas Tillam, *The Seventh-Day Sabbath Sought out and Celebrated, etc.*, Livewell Chapman, London, 1657.
19   Ibid., 1.

Tillam also makes a moralist argument about God's law that distinguishes himself from the "hidden God" of Luther and Calvin, and aligns him with the moral God of the Anabaptists, Arminius, and Grotius. He says that God's moral law is "not merely good because commanded, but it is therefore commanded because it is good and such is the nature of the seventh-day"[20] The recovery of the Sabbath was thus part of the re-building of a larger image of the picture of God and His moral government.[21]

Before discussing how Grotius' ideas came to America, and eventually Adventism, it must be noted how the moral government of God theory made a very practical, social difference in the lives of those who held it. It seems to be no coincidence that those that advocated freedom of human choice and the fact of God's moral government also began to seek civil freedoms and to expect higher standards of morality from human governments.

Methodists, who embraced Grotius' ideas of moral government, were against slavery from near their beginnings. William Wilberforce, the great British parliamentarian who ended the British slave trade, was raised a Methodist. After his conversion as an adult, he associated with non-conformist ministers – including Methodists – who opposed slavery. In the middle of his fight against the slave trade, Wilberforce received what may have been the last letter that John Wesley ever wrote supporting him in his war against "that execrable villainy which is the scandal of religion, of England, and of human nature." Wesley exhorted him, "O be not weary of well doing! Go on, in the name of God and in the power of his might, till even American slavery (the vilest that ever saw the sun) shall vanish away before it."[22]

20 Ibid., 10–11.
21 The writings of Tillam also inform a current debate among some Adventists over the role of Sunday laws in prophecy. In some academic circles it is popular to criticize the Adventist view of end-time Sunday laws as an artifact of late 19th-century Adventist experience. The argument is that our view of the prophecy regarding the mark of the beast and the seal of God arose in the 1880s, when Sunday laws were a big issue in the United States. But now, some argue that the great threat to our Sabbath is not coercive Sunday legislation, but secularization. Because of this, it is proposed, that the final conflict will be over issues other than sacred time and the Sabbath.
But we now have an understanding that the connection of the Sabbath with the seal of God was actually understood and believed more than 200 years before that. This interpretation is not dependent on the culture and events of the 1880s, but is much older than Ellen White, Uriah Smith, or Joseph Bates. Thomas Tillam, two centuries earlier and on another continent, is some evidence that White, Smith and Bates were not merely captive to their own cultural view. Now, just because a Baptist, more than three hundred years ago, believed in this view of the Sabbath and the final conflict over the seal of God and the mark of the beast does not make that interpretation correct. And yet it does respond to the argument that the interpretation was purely a product of late 19th-century American Protestantism.
22 John Wesley to William Wilberforce, February 24, 1791, quoted in Eric Metaxas, *Amazing Grace: William Wilberforce and the Heroic Campaign to End Slavery* (Toronto, ON: HarperCollins Publishers, 2007), 144.

Importantly, this anti-slavery stance came to be shared by the other branch, or prong, of moral government of God influence that came into America. This branch developed within reformed churches, ironically, and became a renewal movement within American Congregationalism and Presbyterianism. It is this strand that brings us to an understanding of the revivalist Charles Finney, the Biblical commentator Albert Barnes, and Ellen White herself, all of whom wrote significant works against the evils of slavery and in favor of its abolition. To the American fruition of the principles of the moral government of God we next turn.

## God's Moral Government Comes to America

Grotius' Arminian teachings about God's moral government were brought directly to America in two distinct ways. The first, touched on above, was through Methodism. One of the best-known inheritors of Grotius' teachings was John Wesley (1703-1791), the founder of Methodism. We know that Wesley's parents, Samuel and Susanna, were supporters of those in the Church of England that supported an Arminian, free-will outlook. Samuel's favorite biblical commentator was Hugo Grotius, and he recommended him to John. The writings of Grotius came to be a great theological resource for Wesley and his friends at Oxford.[23]

Through the influence of Wesley, Methodism, in both England and America, came to formally embrace the moral government of God view of the atonement, along with the teachings of unlimited atonement and freedom of the will. As we know, Ellen White was raised a Methodist and she no doubt encountered these views during her time as a young person in the Methodist Church. However, as a mature adult she seems to have been influenced even more by a second stream of Grotian thought.

This second stream came through the American Puritans and their Presbyterian, Calvinistic heirs. We know that Grotius was read in New England as early as the 1650s, and a copy of his *Satisfaction of Christ* was in the Harvard College Library as early as 1723. Grotius was also widely quoted in writings of the Puritan Richard Baxter, who was widely read in New England.[24] It would take a book on its own to trace the manner in which the New England divines largely rejected Arminianism in terms of will and predestination, but were influenced by and eventually embraced notions of God's moral government.[25]

---

23 Richard P. Heitzenrater, ed., *Diary of an Oxford Methodist: Benjamin Ingham, 1733–34* (Durham, NC: Duke Univ. Press, 1985).
24 Hugo Grotius, "Historical Introduction," in *A Defense of the Catholic Faith Concerning the Satisfaction of Christ against Faustus Socinius*, trans. Frank H. Foster (Andover, MA: Warren F. Draper, 1889), xliv.
25 Ibid., xliii–lvi.

## New Haven Theology and the Soil of Adventism

This new synthesis of Reformed thought emerged in the decades prior to the rise of Adventism. It became known as the New Haven Theology among the Congregational Calvinists and as New School Presbyterianism among the Presbyterians. This developing theological system was part of the backdrop out of which Adventism grew. This was especially true of Adventist views on the moral government of God as seen in Ellen White's writings on the sanctuary and the great controversy.

The theologian at the center of this new movement was Nathaniel Taylor, professor of theology at Yale University from 1822 to 1858. Taylor was a biblically conservative and devout Congregationalist teaching from within the Reformed tradition. He followed the moral government of God theory to its logical conclusion, that is, that a truly moral God would provide opportunity for all to be saved.

His listeners attested to both his piety and his passion for the moral government of God. A former student said, "While lecturing, his voice often trembled, and at times the tears would start, especially when speaking of the moral government of God."[26] For Taylor, it was an understanding of the absolute morality and fairness of God's government that stood against the claims of high Calvinism that only an elect had an opportunity for salvation. He came to embrace the general view of the atonement that Christ died for all.

For Taylor, this was the good news of God's moral government, that *all* were invited to partake of God's wonderful offer of grace and mercy. As he put it:

> Let ... the impression be made full, strong, unqualified on every guilty mind, that God in his law, and God in the invitations of his mercy, means exactly what he says. Let the full-orbed sincerity of a redeeming God, like the sun in mid-heaven, be made to pour its melting beams on the dark and guilty mind of the sinner against God ... If there is any one thing more than another, which would give new power to New England preaching, I cannot but think, it is to make a fuller impression of the true-hearted sincerity of God in his calls of mercy.[27]

Taylor regularly taught a class, the notes of which were collected and placed into a volume entitled *Lectures on the Moral Government of God*. Most of us have heard of neither him nor his lectures. Yet we have heard of those whom his ideas impacted. These would be men like Charles Finney, the great evangelist of the Second Great Awakening, and of course, Albert Barnes, the great commentator, whose works Ellen White was so anxious to have with her in Australia.

Finney and Barnes were New School Presbyterians, a reformed group that embraced a general atonement and the free choice of man in salvation. This new movement also contained some of the most ardent anti-slavery activists in the evangelical

---

26 Douglas A. Sweeney, *Nathaniel Taylor, New Haven Theology, and the Legacy of Jonathan Edwards* (New York, NY: Oxford University Press, 2003), 91.
27 Nathaniel Taylor, "The Peculiar Power of the Gospel on the Human Mind," 23–24, quoted in Sweeney, *Nathaniel Taylor*, 91.

world. Their "old school" opponents were typically men who wrote in defense of slavery.

Albert Barnes himself, put on trial for heresy because of his embrace of unlimited atonement and freedom of the will, wrote two major works against slavery in the period leading up to the American Civil War. Finney was the evangelist of the moral government movement in the Second Great Awakening. His revival meetings in New England and New York in the early 1830s defined the religious experiences and spiritual environment of the childhood of many of the pioneers of the Adventist Church.[28]

But it was the writer Albert Barnes, whose commentaries forcefully encapsulated the moral government theory, who had the broad, long-lasting, and popular impact on the subject. It is estimated that Barnes' *Notes on the New Testament*, which was on my father's shelves when I was a boy, sold more than a million copies by 1870. In his commentary on Romans 3:26 – "that he might be just and the justifier of the one who has faith in Jesus" –, Barnes clearly set out the moral government view of the atonement. "This verse contains the substance of the gospel," he wrote.

> It refers to the fact that God had retained the integrity of his character as moral governor; that he had shown a due regard to his law, and to the penalty of the law, by his plan of salvation. Should he forgive sinners without an atonement, justice would be sacrificed and abandoned ... He is, in all this great transaction, a just moral governor, as just to his law, to himself, to his Son, to the universe, when he pardons, as when he sends the incorrigible sinner down to hell.[29]

## Ellen White, God's Moral Government, and the Sanctuary

So we come now, full circle, to the request by Ellen White that Barnes' commentaries be sent to her in Australia, as they were among her "best books." There can be little doubt that Ellen White was heir to a moral government of God outlook, both through her Methodist roots and through her acquaintance with Barnes' commentaries. Of course, this is not to deny the fruits of her own Bible study and visions, which reinforced and expanded on the moral government of God theme. She especially brought into clearer focus the central role that love plays in both the character of God and the workings of His government. Indeed, under the gaze and pen of Ellen White's vision, the moral government of God blossoms fully into God's moral government of *love*.

Once one's eyes are opened to the conception and framework of the moral government of God, it can be seen throughout the writings of Ellen White. The

---

28   See the descriptions of the meeting of Finney and Miller in David L. Rowe, *God's Strange Work: William Miller and the End of the World* (Grand Rapids, MI: Eerdmans, 2008), 138–139; Charles E. Hambrick-Stowe, *Charles G. Finney and the Spirit of American Evangelicalism* (Grand Rapids, MI: Eerdmans, 1996), 206–207.

29   Albert Barnes, *Barnes' Notes on the New Testament*, ed. Ingram Cobbin (Grand Rapids, MI: Kregel Publications, 1976), 573–574.

doctrine of the heavenly sanctuary provided the place from which God's moral government is administered. It took a notion that was somewhat abstract and nebulous, and gave it a sense of concrete reality. Adventist theologian Fernando Canale has impressively argued that the teaching about the physical reality of the heavenly sanctuary, where God's presence is especially found, ensures that the actuality of God's being is part of our own time and space, as well as moral world.[30]

In this view, the teaching of a literal, heavenly sanctuary provides a firewall against classical conceptions of God's timelessness, immutability, and utter transcendence. He really participates in our realm, can know us, love us, have relationship with us, through His Word, both Christ and Scripture. And in knowing this Word, we do actually know Him. There is no *Deus Absconditus* whose character, motives, morality, and will are a complete and utter mystery.

While all this sounds a bit theoretical, its impact was immediate and practical. Those that embraced the larger sanctuary message of God's moral government were active in anti-slavery and temperance reform. Adventists that gained a particular insight into the heavenly cleansing of the sanctuary saw these social reform movements as of particular importance. They believed that the cleansing of the heavenly sanctuary was meant to involve a parallel cleansing of God's people on earth, both individually and the church as a whole.

As Ellen White put it, "we do not follow Him into the sanctuary as we should. Christ and angels work in the hearts of the children of men. The church above united with the church below is warring the good warfare upon the earth. There must be a purifying of the soul here upon the earth, in harmony with Christ's cleansing of the sanctuary in heaven."[31]

She viewed the institution of slavery as one of the evils from which the church and its members were to be cleansed. "There are a few in the ranks of Sabbath-keepers who sympathize with the slaveholder. When they embraced the truth, they did not leave behind them all the errors they should have left. They need a more thorough draft from the cleansing fountain of truth."[32]

As a people, the Adventist Church should be mindful that its prophetic heritage and sanctuary message is closely tied in with movements to bring greater justice and equality to those that are marginalized and oppressed.

Beyond being a stimulus to good social deeds, the sanctuary-based moral government of God concept provided the frame in which Ellen White expressed her ideas about the great controversy between Christ and Satan, as well as a number of apparently disparate doctrines, such as creation, hellfire, and even the Sabbath. It is the theological hermeneutical principle that helped our pioneers see that in the Bible,

---

30 Fernando Canale, "Philosophical Foundations and the Biblical Sanctuary," *Andrews University Seminary Studies* 36:2 (1998), 183–206.
31 Ellen G. White, *Maranatha: The Lord Is Coming* (Washington, DC: Review and Herald Pub. Assn., 1976), 249.
32 Ellen G. White, *Testimonies for the Church*, vol. 1 (Mountain View, CA: Pacific Press Pub. Assn., 1948), 358.

terms like "forever" did not mean an "eternity" of hellfire, that "slavery" did not justify the racial, brutal, kidnapping, chattel slavery of the South, that "wine" did not always mean strong drink that caused men to abuse women and children, and that a God of love did not make a "good" creation through the pain and suffering of theistic evolution.

If we continue to understand and embrace our Arminian/Grotian heritage of God's moral government, we will continue to see these good things, and add many others to them, such as: how to relate justly and kindly to our immigrant neighbors in need; how to critique the war on terror based on the shared human dignity we have with foreigners; how to relate to our Muslim neighbors; and how to relate to systems of thought, whether religious, political, or ideological, that would scapegoat and demonize the minorities and outsiders in our midst, including those that continue to value traditional and biblical concepts of the family and sexual morality.

It is this moral government framework that provides the impetus for the continuing "protest" of the Reformation heritage. Luther's ideas of Scripture and grace were not viewed as important and dangerous until he applied them to an institution of religious and social wrong and injustice of his day – the system of indulgences. We may tenaciously hold onto the *solae* of the Reformation, but if we are not applying them to the religious and social wrongs and injustices of our day, we are not truly heirs of the "Protest" of the Reformers.

# PART I

# MARTIN LUTHER IN SEVENTH-DAY ADVENTIST PERSPECTIVE

*Denis Kaiser*

## "God Is Our Refuge and Strength"[1] – Martin Luther in the Perception of Ellen G. White

**Abstract**

Ellen White was deeply interested in the life and experience of Martin Luther. In her three primary publications he emerges as *the* Protestant Reformer par excellence. The material of her narrative was essentially complete by 1883, and it was streamlined by her in 1884, only to be slightly expanded four years later to give a more direct voice to Luther himself. She emphasized the authority of Scripture and salvation by faith in Christ against the backdrop of the great controversy between light and darkness, and God's providential working to set an example for those preparing for coming events.

Although separated by an ocean, different cultures, educational backgrounds, and three hundred and forty years, they had much in common. Both Martin Luther (1483–1546) and Ellen G. White (1827–1915) were at the forefront of religious reform and revival movements in their own nations and beyond. The churches of their childhood and youth expelled them for the circulation of their religious convictions. Both highlighted the ultimate significance of Scripture as the basis for faith and practice, Scripture's role as its own interpreter, the close relationship between the Old and New Testament, and the central role of Christ. While they strongly believed in the merits of Christ's atoning sacrifice as the provision for the justification of the sinner by faith, for both Luther and White, salvation was accompanied by a conspicuous eschatological outlook. Their theological framework has influenced their fellow believers and is still held in high regard by their respective denominational traditions, to the point that it still impacts broader surrounding culture.

---

1 These words are from the first verse of Ps 46 (KJV). The entire psalm has been set to music and appears in numerous hymnals. Martin Luther echoes it in his famous song "A Mighty Fortress is Our God." Applying the significance of that psalm in Luther's experience to her readership, Ellen White wrote, "When Martin Luther received discouraging news, he would often say, 'Come, let us sing the forty-sixth psalm.' This psalm commences with the words, 'God is our refuge and strength, a very present help in trouble. Therefore will we not fear, though the earth be removed, and though the mountains be carried into the midst of the sea.' Instead of mourning, weeping, and despairing, when troubles gather about us like a flood and threaten to overwhelm us, if we would not only pray for help from God, but would praise him for so many blessings left, – praise him that he is able to help us, – our course would be more pleasing to him, and we would see more of his salvation." See Ellen G. White, "Cheerfulness in Affliction," *Review and Herald*, November 1, 1881, 273; Ellen G. White, *Life Sketches of Ellen G. White* (Mountain View, CA: Pacific Press, 1915), 258.

Others have referred to them as prophets of God, a designation both felt did not describe them accurately. Despite these commonalities, there are many differences that could be invoked as one gives a level look to the particulars of their theological and philosophical views. A case in point is their soteriology, a central and significant part of their respective belief systems. While Luther held what I would call somewhat anachronistically a Lutheran soteriology, White's understanding of salvation was throughout her life essentially Wesleyan-Arminian.[2]

One may be surprised nevertheless to find her talking far less about John Wesley, John Calvin, Huldrych Zwingli, John Knox or Philip Melanchthon than about Luther. A brief search in *The Published Ellen G. White Writings* CD-ROM shows that Luther appears 964 times in her publications (modern compilations and duplications included) whereas the other five reformers are mentioned only a combined 222 times.[3] The sheer number of occurrences of his name in her writings, both published and unpublished, is overwhelming. In her view, Martin Luther was obviously *the* Protestant Reformer par excellence.

Surprisingly, only few Adventist scholars have discovered the study of White's perception of Luther so far. First, in 1981, Ron Graybill compared the literary relationship between her handwritten and published accounts of Luther's experience from Worms to the Wartburg Castle and the sources used to fill in historical details.[4] Second, in 2013, the *Ellen G. White Encyclopedia* made available a fine summary by Hans Heinz of White's sketch of the German reformer's life, activities, and teachings as found in the 1911 edition of the *Great Controversy*.[5]

The present chapter discusses differences and similarities between White's primary publications on the famous German reformer, her chronological treatment of his life, and the particular emphases found in her Luther narrative.

2   George R. Knight, *A Search for Identity: The Development of Seventh-day Adventist Beliefs*, Adventist Heritage Series (Hagerstown, MD: Review and Herald, 2000), 32–33; Woodrow W. Whidden, *The Judgment and Assurance: The Dynamics of Personal Salvation*, Library of Adventist Theology, vol. 4 (Hagerstown, MD: Review and Herald, 2012), 13–16, 42–43; Denis Fortin, "The Theology of Ellen G. White," in *The Ellen G. White Encyclopedia*, ed. Denis Fortin and Jerry Moon (Hagerstown, MD: Review and Herald, 2013), 248–255.
3   Melanchthon occurs 23 times, Zwingli 36 times, Calvin 44 times, Knox 43 times, and Wesley 76 times. Thus about one third of the combined references fall on Wesley who was actually not a $16^{th}$-century Protestant Reformer. Occurrences of Luther and the other Reformers in White's unpublished writings (available online since July 2015) have been disregarded in this calculation. In 1877, Luther's name appears for the first time in the extent unpublished letters and manuscripts. The highest concentration of Luther's name in the unpublished letters and manuscripts is in the 1880s. Compared with occurrences in the published writings, appearances in the letters and manuscripts are nevertheless far less frequent (1x in the 1870s, 12x in the 1880s, 5x in 1890s, and 2x in 1900s).
4   Ronald D. Graybill, *Analysis of E. G. White's Luther Manuscript*, White Estate Shelf Document, no. 226-B (Washington, DC: Ellen G. White Estate, 1981).
5   Johann Heinz, "Luther, Martin (1483–1546)," in *The Ellen G. White Encyclopedia*, ed. Denis Fortin and Jerry Moon (Hagerstown, MD: Review and Herald, 2013), 954–956.

## Major Publications about Martin Luther

The experience of the famous German Reformer captivated Ellen White's attention for more than fifty years. The book *Spiritual Gifts*, vol. 1 (1858), contains her first treatment of Martin Luther. Seated in her discussion of the Protestant Reformation, she treated the story of Luther and Philip Melanchthon in less than 800 words.[6] Five years later she discussed Luther's experience and his courage at the diets at Augsburg and Worms on about four pages in *Testimony for the Church*, no. 9. Seated in an appeal to Adventist ministers, she presented Luther's courage as an example for them to emulate in their preaching of present truth.[7] The third, and largest, discussion of Luther appeared in a series of twenty articles in the *Signs of the Times* from May 31 to November 1, 1883.[8] As *Spirit of Prophecy*, vol. 4 (1884), was sold to the American public, her Luther narrative was made available to a wider audience. The insertion of numerous illustrations made the book even more attractive.[9] The last discussion of Luther's life is found in the *Great Controversy* (1888, 1911).[10] As the latter three publications do not just contain incidental mentions of his name but distinctive chronological treatments of his experience, the following two sections compare only these three sets of publications.

6  Ellen G. White, *Spiritual Gifts: Great Controversy Between Christ and His Angels, and Satan and His Angels*, vol. 1 (Battle Creek, MI: James White, 1858), 120–22. Although Luther is mentioned twice on p. 123, these occurrences are excluded from the count as they focus on other individuals and Luther only serves as a subject of comparison.
7  Ellen G. White, *Testimony for the Church*, no. 9 (Battle Creek, MI: Steam Press of the Seventh-day Adventist Pub. Assn., 1863), 16–20.
8  The articles appeared consecutively in the periodical, except for the September 13, 27, and October 4, 1883 issues which did not carry articles on Luther or the Reformation. There is a handwritten rough draft manuscript of fifty-one pages that precedes the *Signs of the Times* series and seems to exhibit, at least partially, a close literary relationship to that series of articles. Ron Graybill has compared the first six pages of the manuscript with D'Aubigné, Charles Adams, these *Signs* articles, *Spirit of Prophecy*, vol. 4, and the two editions of the *Great Controversy*. Graybill notes that "materials in the manuscript which are fully unique to Ellen White and not found in the historical sources she evidently consulted are carried forward into the *Signs of the Times* articles." See Graybill, *Analysis of E. G. White's Luther Manuscript*, 1.
9  Ellen G. White, *Spirit of Prophecy: Great Controversy Between Christ and Satan from the Destruction of Jerusalem to the End of the Controversy*, vol. 4 (Battle Creek, MI: Steam Press of the Seventh-day Adventist Pub. Assn., 1884), 94–169; "Bound Books," *Review and Herald*, August 26, 1884, 559.
10 Ellen G. White, *The Great Controversy: Between Christ and Satan During the Christian Dispensation*, rev. and enl. ed. (Oakland, CA: Pacific Press, 1888), 120–170, 185–210; Ellen G. White, *The Great Controversy Between Christ and Satan: The Conflict of the Ages in the Christian Dispensation* (Washington, DC: Review and Herald, 1911), 120–170, 185–210.

## Continuation and Consolidation: From the Signs of the Times Articles to Spirit of Prophecy, Vol. 4

A comparison of the Luther narratives in White's twenty *Signs* articles and *Spirit of Prophecy*, vol. 4, reveals considerable similarities. Much of the textual material has been carried over into the new work, yet it differs from the earlier treatment in that a more economic use of the language cut the amount of words almost in half. The differences may generally be divided into three classes – minor, moderate-size, and major changes.

There are multiple minor changes such as altering the tense of verbs from present to perfect, modifying the punctuation, capitalizing lower-case words, replacing words with synonyms, inserting references for Bible quotations, modifying the spelling of names, improving the sentence structure, and omitting words to remove redundancy. Some changes seem more significant. When White quoted Staupitz's explanation on the importance of Jesus' death, she omitted, for example, the word "expiatory" from the original technical term "expiatory sacrifice," and later in *Spirit of Prophecy*, vol. 4, she replaced it with the word "atonement," suggesting that Christ's death does, in fact, atone.[11]

Other changes could be described as moderate-size alterations. Thus in some places entire sentences or paragraphs were omitted, eliminating frequently the application of general principles (education, Christian life) to the modern reader. As White combined several articles from her *Signs* series in one chapter, she may have wanted to relinquish parenetic paragraphs at the end of the articles, explanatory (historical details) and hortatory statements frequently interspersing the articles, and remarks comparing Luther's experience with that of the reader.

Some of the alterations manifest major material changes. Thus in her earlier account she stated that one day "Luther was ascending the stairway to St. Peter" whereas one year later she relocated that event to "Pilate's staircase,"[12] leading to a corridor of the old Lateran Palace. Another major difference is the addition of an entire chapter. Whereas her articles in the *Signs* covered Luther's life only until 1522, her new chapter, entitled "The Protest of the Princes," deals with events and developments from 1526 to 1530, particularly the second Diet of Spires (1529) and the Diet of Augsburg (1530).[13] The material was all new except for one paragraph that explained God's protective influence on those engaged in the work

---

11 Ellen G. White, "Martin Luther--His Character and Early Life," *Signs of the Times*, May 31, 1883, 242; White, *Spirit of Prophecy*, 4:98. Cf. Jean Henri Merle d'Aubigné, *History of the Great Reformation of the Sixteenth Century in Germany, Switzerland, etc.* (Philadelphia, PA: Porter & Coates, 1870), 48.
12 Ellen G. White, "Luther at Wittenberg," *Signs of the Times*, June 7, 1883, 253–254; White, *Spirit of Prophecy*, 4:100.
13 White, *Spirit of Prophecy*, 4:156–169.

of reform.[14] It seems that her previous discussion of Luther's interaction with Henry VIII, king of England, had to give way to the subjects in the new chapter.[15]

While the majority of the text of the *Signs* articles reappeared in only slightly modified form in *Spirit of Prophecy*, vol. 4, expanded by a few additions of material, the body of the text was streamlined and shortened to present a clear line of argument.

## *Retention and Expansion: From* Spirit of Prophecy, *vol. 4, to the* Great Controversy

The four chapters narrating the story of Martin Luther carry the same titles in the two volumes.[16] Ellen White inserted a new chapter on the Swiss Reformer Huldrych Zwingli between the second and third chapter on Luther in the *Great Controversy*.[17] Like the previous section, the present one discusses three types of differences between the two works.

Most changes were of minor stylistic nature such as the replacing of words with synonyms, the capitalization of lower-case words, the un-capitalizing of capitalized terms, the modification of the spelling of names, and the improvement of the sentence structure.

Moderate-size changes were, for example, the insertion of explanatory remarks that added clarity and smoothness to the text. In one instance a quotation from Luther was substituted with a more complete and better translation of the statement.[18]

A number of additions constitute the biggest difference between the two books. For instance, adding a whole new paragraph, White introduced Melanchthon earlier

14 Cf. Ellen G. White, "Triumph of the Reformation," *Signs of the Times*, November 1, 1883, 481–482; White, *Spirit of Prophecy*, 4:168.
15 White, "Triumph of the Reformation," 481.
16 The chapter titles in both books: "Luther's Separation from Rome," "Luther Before the Diet," "Progress of the Reformation," and "Protest of the Princes."
17 Interestingly, as D'Aubigné quit talking about Luther having been brought to the Wartburg in May 1521, he turned his focus to Huldrych Zwingli and the Reformation in Switzerland. See Jean Henri Merle d'Aubigné, *History of the Reformation of the Sixteenth Century*, 5 vols. (New York, NY: Robert Carter & Brothers, 1864), 276–279. On the other hand, Ellen White continued her discussion of Luther until the winter of 1521/1522 before turning her attention to the Reformation in Switzerland. See White, *The Great Controversy Between Christ and Satan*, 168–171. While this is certainly a difference between the two accounts, it needs to be acknowledged that, similar to D'Aubigné, she, rather than continuing her Luther narrative at this point, turned her attention to the early life of the Swiss reformer and the beginnings of the Reformation in Switzerland.
18 Cf. White, *Spirit of Prophecy*, 4:133–134; White, *The Great Controversy*, [1888], 160. See *The History of the Reformation in Europe: With a Chronology of the Reformation* (London: Religious Tract Society, 1853), 89–90; D'Aubigné, *History of the Great Reformation of the Sixteenth Century in Germany, Switzerland, etc.*, 203.

in the narrative (1518 instead of 1521) by describing his personality and significance to Luther.[19] Another type of additional material came in the form of quotations. While the majority of these quotations were direct statements of Luther and his contemporaries,[20] there were a few other statements coming from historians.[21] A quick glance at the source references of the quotations suggests that she quoted primarily from J. H. Merle d'Aubigné's *History of the Reformation of the Sixteenth Century*. A few scattered quotes stem from J. A. Wylie's *History of Protestantism*. In a few cases she added quotations from the Bible.[22] In her intro-

19  Cf. White, *Spirit of Prophecy*, 4:111; White, *The Great Controversy*, [1888], 134.
20  White, *The Great Controversy*, [1888], 123 ("I was indeed ... even to death."), 136 ("In so doing ... his imperious language."), 138 ("Since Doctor Martin ... from our States."), 140 ("We have all ... ago, and burned."), 142, 143 ("My enemies have ... by his might." "Who knows if ... not with them." "I feel more ... against these doubts."), 147 ("It was a ... she was condemned."), 150 ("What a loss ... carry it through."), 151 ("If I do ... will matter little."), 152 ("Peace be unto ... saith the Lord." "Since God has ... a mere pretense."), 154 ("had all been freed by my gospel."), 155 ("This appearance was ... caused this humiliation."), 157 ("O God, ... and my stronghold."), 158 ("Most serene emperor, ... glory of God."), 161 ("This man will never make a heretic of me." "The monk speaks with intrepid heart and unshaken courage." "I have no ... have already given."), 163 ("A single monk, ... like faithful Christians." "The Rhine ... a century ago." ), 164 ("I would not like to blush like Sigismund."), 165 ("The doctor's little ... who presented themselves."), 166 ("In what concerns ... be for him."), 167 ("God is my ... to the Creator." "I have never ... nor will I."), 188, 189 ("Be it known ... most availing defense." "Behold me ready ... punish our nation."), 189, 190 ("The mass is ... of the land."), 191 ("He who hath ... Holy Scriptures."), 194 ("Whatever Luther and ... these enterprising colporteurs."), 195, 196 ("Opposed to the ... to deserved contempt."), 199–201 ("What is to ... liberties of Christendom."), 203 ("We therefore reject ... and legitimate duty."), 206 ("Was it not ... not abandon us." "A strong tower is our God."), 209 ("the doctrine of the gospel ... and sinful mistrust." "Satan is raging ... let them pray."), 209, 210 ("We cannot in our conscience ... risk and peril.").
21  Ibid., [1888], 147.
22  Ibid., [1888], 144 (John 15:19–20; Luke 6:26). Graybill points out that although it has been known for a long time that Ellen White drew from D'Aubigné, there is "a more immediate source of the mundane historical facts found in the manuscript. On page 3 of the handwritten manuscript, Mrs. White breaks into her narrative with the following note: 'See *Words That Shook the World*, 240 pages [a book authored by Charles Adams].'" Graybill further notes that Adam's book was "basically a condensation of D'Aubigné," yet he did not slavishly copy D'Aubigné as is evident from the fact that he omitted elements from D'Aubigné material and added his own comments and thoughts. Interestingly, where Ellen White dealt with objective historical facts her account is identical to Adams' and D'Aubigné's accounts. Graybill further states that the quotations from D'Aubigné found in Adams and White stem from the same edition (A. A. Turnstall's translation in the 1847 edition). Nevertheless, in 1911 C. C. Crisler suggested to Ellen White to use another translation, one that D'Aubigné himself had approved, and she accepted his suggestion in the 1911 edition of the *Great Controversy*. Graybill notes, "She has no historical facts not found in Adams, and her paraphrases are obviously based on Adams, not D'Aubigné." She

duction to the book she stated that quotations of historians were "not given for the purpose of citing that writer as authority, but because his statement affords a ready and forcible presentation of the subject."[23]

While she re-wrote some of the material, the basic set of information and the purpose of the presentation remained unchanged. White merely expanded her previous narrative by inserting numerous primary source quotations, therefore giving Luther an opportunity to speak for himself.

## The Chronological Treatment of Luther's Life

When discussing Ellen White's Luther narrative, at least four principles should be kept in mind. First, in outlining the history of the church, she did not intend to provide an authoritative account of dates and events, but she wanted to ascribe a new significance to developments, "well known and universally acknowledged by the Protestant world," in order to highlight the principles operating in the conflict between the powers of good and evil so as to prepare people for "coming events."[24] Hence she may have laid different foci, leaving some events unmentioned that modern scholars deem important. Second, as the visions generally did not provide her with the historical setting of the "flash-light pictures," she used the works of Uriah Smith and secular historians to locate them in time and space. Third, she utilized these books further to help her "describe many of the events and ... movements" seen "in vision."[25] She respected those historians who traced the divine work of reform in human history and discerned a correspondence with biblical prophecy. Nevertheless, she "never thought that readers would take it [The Great Controversy] as an authority on historical data and use it to settle controversies."[26] Fourth, she initially gave a "partial description" of the scenes,[27] and, later, when she rewrote and expanded her description of particular scenes, they were frequently shown her again in "visions of the night so that they were fresh and vivid" in her

---

nevertheless contributed her own thoughts to the narrative. See Graybill, *Analysis of E. G. White's Luther Manuscript*, 1.
23 White, *The Great Controversy*, [1888], h.
24 Ibid.
25 W. C. White, "Great Controversy--New Edition: A Statement Made by W. C. White Before the General Conference Council," October 30, 1911, Ellen G. White Estate, Silver Spring, MD.
26 In fact, Ellen White "never wished our brethren to treat them [her writings] as authority on history." See W. C. White to S. N. Haskell, October 31, 1912, W. C. White Correspondence File, Ellen G. White Estate, Silver Spring, MD. That she agreed with the statements of her son is evident from the fact that she added the following words to that letter, "I approve of the remarks made in this letter, Ellen G. White."
27 Ibid.

mind.[28] As White's narratives of the German Reformer do not really exhibit material differences, a look at her outline in the most recent and readily available 1911 edition of the *Great Controversy* will suffice.

The first chapter covers the years from Luther's childhood to the beginnings of the Protestant Reformation (1483–1520). Ellen White discussed the lack of love and rigidity that Luther experienced in his parental home. While she perceived these circumstances as less than ideal, she observed that his early education nevertheless also produced good fruits in his character and personality.[29] At this point, her *Signs* articles added some advice on parenting and character development.[30]

Her sketch of Luther's life generally follows a chronological sequence, yet some events seem to be in the wrong order. For example, she mentioned his lectures on the Psalms, the Gospels, and the Epistles as well as his sermons before both his visit to Rome (winter 1510/1511) and the conferral of his doctoral degree (October 1512).[31] As all these events are mentioned in the same *Signs* article and repeated in the exact same way in later publications, it may well be that the arrangement was intended to be topical rather than chronological.[32] The fact that the information on his lectures appears briefly in connection with his work at the university seems to lend credence to that conclusion.

Hans Heinz suggests that her account of Luther's salvational insight ("The just shall live by faith"), when ascending the Lateran staircase in Rome (1510/1511), as based on D'Aubigné's *History of the Reformation of the Sixteenth Century*, or more specifically on Paul Luther's account, "reflects the Luther research of her era" but is regarded as a "mistake of memory" by modern historians.[33] Heinz seems to overlook, however, a couple of facts. D'Aubigné argued that while Luther read the passage already in 1509, the words continued to ring in his ears at different occasions.[34] Unlike Ellen White, he placed the insight during Luther's period of

---

28   Ellen G. White to F. M. Wilcox, July 25, 1911, Lt 56, 1911, quoted in Ellen G. White, *Selected Messages*, vol. 3 (Washington, DC: Review and Herald, 1980), 123.
29   White, *The Great Controversy Between Christ and Satan*, 120–121.
30   White, "Martin Luther--His Character and Early Life," 241–242.
31   White, *The Great Controversy Between Christ and Satan*, 124. Luther lectured on the Psalms (1513–1515), Romans (1515–1516), Galatians (1516–1517), and Hebrews (1517–1518). See Georg Buchwald and Gustav Kawerau, *Luther-Kalendarium und Verzeichnis von Luthers Schriften*, Schriften des Vereins für Reformationsgeschichte, 47/2 (Leipzig: M. Heinsius Nachfolger Eger & Sievers, 1929), 2–4; Stephen Strehle, *The Catholic Roots of the Protestant Gospel: Encounter Between the Middle Ages and the Reformation*, Studies in the History of Christian Thought, vol. 60 (Leiden: Brill, 1995), 16–17. It is unclear to what Gospel lectures Ellen White was referring to.
32   White, "Luther at Wittenberg," 253; White, *Spirit of Prophecy*, 4:98–100; White, *The Great Controversy Between Christ and Satan*, 124–125.
33   Heinz, "Luther, Martin (1483–1546)," 954–955. Cf. White, *The Great Controversy Between Christ and Satan*, 125.
34   D'Aubigné, *History of the Reformation of the Sixteenth Century*, 1:196.

sickness in Bologna in December 1510.[35] Further, Heinz notes that White neglected to mention "Luther's reformational breakthrough, the so-called *Turmerlebnis* (tower experience), between 1512 and 1518" as it was not until 1904 that it gained prominence in Reformation studies.[36] However, Luther's vast corpus of writings mentions that event only once, in 1545.[37] Many historians place the incident about 1514, three years prior to the ninety-five theses, and some suppose it did not occur until after the nailing of the theses (about 1518). Still others assert that his reformational discovery was a process over a longer period rather than a single event.[38] Historians in the twentieth century may have perhaps been a little too optimistic about the significance of the *Turmerlebnis*. Be that as it may, White's view of a longer process of growth is quite possible.

Considering that Ellen White devoted almost an entire chapter to the main events during and surrounding the Diet of Worms in the spring of 1521, the council seemed to constitute a significant event for her – one third of her sketch on Luther centering on about two months.[39] The diet brought the conflict between Rome and Luther, between darkness and light, face to face. The character and foundation of each side were manifested more directly than ever before. She depicted the scene of Luther standing before Charles V, the papal party, and the German nobility as a showdown between the two parties. In fact, she considered the circumstance of Luther appearing before the diet as a sign of the success for the Reformation – a condemned heretic being granted safe conduct and allowed to present his teachings before the assembly. "To institute inquiry into a case in which the pope had already pronounced sentence of condemnation would be to cast contempt upon the authority of the sovereign pontiff."[40]

Although in the next two chapters she continued her account of the Reformation in Germany from 1522 to 1530, remarks on Luther himself become less frequent. The third chapter focuses particularly on his return to Wittenberg and his efforts to check the activities and ideas of spiritualizing fanatics who emphasized emotion and direct spiritual communications over the written word of God. White refers particularly to his preaching and the translation of the Bible into German.[41] The last chapter deals with events from 1526 to 1530, specifically the diets of

35 Cf. D'Aubigné, *History of the Reformation of the Sixteenth Century*, 1:200; White, *The Great Controversy Between Christ and Satan*, 125.
36 Heinz, "Luther, Martin (1483–1546)," 955.
37 Martin H. Jung, *Reformation und konfessionelles Zeitalter (1517–1648)*, Basiswissen Theologie und Religionswissenschaft, vol. 3628 (Göttingen: Vandenhoeck & Ruprecht, 2012), 27.
38 Ibid., 28. See also Christian Danz, *Einführung in die Theologie Martin Luthers*, Einführung Theologie (Darmstadt: Wissenschaftliche Buchgesellschaft, 2013), 24–29. Danz observes that the debate about the early or late dating of the reformational insight fails to do justice to "the complex development of the Reformer between 1510 and 1520." See ibid., 24.
39 White, *The Great Controversy Between Christ and Satan*, 145–170.
40 Ibid., 146.
41 Ibid., 185–196.

Spires (1526, 1529) and the one at Augsburg (1530). Luther was dealt with merely in the background; "God had raised up" some of Luther's "colaborers and the princes ... to defend His cause in this emergency."[42]

Ellen White's absolute silence on Luther's development in his last twenty-some years may be interpreted variously. First, she may have described only such scenes as she had been shown through special revelation, and as she refrained from writing about Luther's later life, she probably had not been shown anything regarding it. Second, as Luther got entangled with the political authorities to secure the continued existence of Protestantism against both Roman Catholics and ideological extremists after 1522, she may have preferred to focus on the early Luther's somewhat naïve advocacy of his new discoveries to avoid marring his positive example. Third, as she utilized the works of historians in illustrating the scenes presented to her, she may have gone only as far as these works described Luther's life. D'Aubigné's five volumes of the *History of Reformation of the Sixteenth Century* practically end the detailed account of Luther with his return from the Wartburg and his encounter with the Zwickau prophets, with the exception of brief accounts of Luther's interaction with Henry VIII, the progress of the Reformation, and his marriage.[43] Likewise, White did not extend her discussion of Luther's life beyond his skirmish with the king of England and the progress of the Reformation.[44] She could have chosen to complete her Luther narrative from other supplementary material, yet she deliberately chose to conclude her account at that point, thus using that part of Luther's life best suited to provide an exemplary illustration for her readers.

## Emphases of the Martin Luther Narrative

The central emphases that characterized her writings in general also appeared as recurrent themes in her Luther narrative. The authority of Scripture, justification by faith in Christ, the great controversy between light and darkness as seen in Luther's increasing separation from Roman Catholicism and God's providential guidance were interwoven in the chronological account of his life.

White placed special emphasis on the value and importance of Scripture. Writing about Luther's finding of a Latin Bible in the university library, she stated that he was filled with awe and his heart was stirred as he read "the words of life" for the first time for himself. As Luther sighed, "O that God would give me such a book for myself," angels enlightened his understanding and led him to a deep

---

42  Ibid., 197–210, esp. 198.
43  See Jean Henri Merle d'Aubigné, *The Life and Times of Martin Luther* (Chicago, IL: Moody Press, 1950), for a selection of the Martin Luther passages in his *History of the Reformation of the Sixteenth Century*.
44  White, *The Great Controversy Between Christ and Satan*, 185–210. Luther's interaction with Henry VIII is only reported in her *Signs* articles series but was later omitted. See White, "Triumph of the Reformation," 481.

conviction of his own sinfulness.[45] And as he greatly delighted to study the Bible, "chained to the convent wall," he was convicted even more and, as a result, he tried to earn the forgiveness of his sins by his own works.[46] Ellen White stated that Staupitz eventually explained the Bible to Luther and asked him to look away from self to Jesus.[47] At Wittenberg he was able to study Scripture in its original languages and soon he lectured on the biblical books. She stressed that he needed Staupitz's encouragement to preach the Word of God because he himself felt unworthy.[48] When, in 1512, he earned the doctoral degree and became a professor at the university, "he was [now] at liberty to devote himself, as never before, to the Scriptures that he loved." She saw that it was at this point that he made several important decisions. He wanted to study the Bible carefully and to teach others faithfully in it. He chose to receive only such doctrines that rested on the authority of Scripture, pointing already to "the vital principle of the Reformation."[49] He believed that, beyond intellect and study, one needed to pray with an open heart for God, the author of Scripture, to give a better understanding of it.[50] She stressed that Luther considered Scripture as the only rule of faith and practice,[51] requesting even his detractors "to show him his errors from the Scriptures."[52] She further stated that he was "filling his lamp from the storehouse of truth" during his stay at the Wartburg Castle.[53] Luther did not only turn against Roman Catholicism and Rationalism; he also opposed the spiritualizing fanaticism of the Zwickau prophets and Thomas Müntzer who stressed the importance of spiritual communications to the neglect of Scripture.[54] Interestingly, White sided with Luther in his rejection of the violent abolishment of the mass because she believed that the power of the word of God was more effective in turning people away from both apostate worship and fanatical excitement than the employment of force.[55] Hence his translation of the Bible into the language of his native people was one of his primary contributions to point people to Scripture and the gospel.[56]

---

45 White, *The Great Controversy Between Christ and Satan*, 122.
46 Ibid., 123.
47 Ibid.
48 Ibid., 124.
49 Ibid., 126, see also 186–187.
50 Ibid., 132.
51 Ibid., 132–133.
52 Ibid., 138, see also 151, 152, 156, 157, 159, 160, 166–68. Because of his use of Scripture she seemed to view him as the prime advocate of "true Christianity." See ibid., 193.
53 Ibid., 168.
54 Ibid., 186–188, 191, 193.
55 Ibid., 189–190.
56 Ibid., 193–194.

Denis Fortin notes that White ascribed to Luther "the greatest role in restoring the second distinctive doctrine of Protestantism: salvation through faith in Christ."[57] She stated that Luther rediscovered "the great truth of justification by faith, ... a mighty beacon to guide repentant sinners into the way of life."[58] He was seeking peace and forgiveness of his sins through discipline and spiritual exercises when Staupitz finally asked him to "look away from himself" and the "infinite punishment for the violation of God's law, and look to Jesus, his sin-pardoning Saviour."[59] That advice was helpful, yet it evidently failed to fully transform his understanding of salvation. In the winter of 1510/1511, Luther, like others, "devoutly" climbed the Scala Sancta in Rome when "suddenly a voice like thunder seemed to say to him: 'The just shall live by faith' (Rom 1:17)." Leaving the scene in horror, "that text never lost its power upon his soul." He realized "more clearly than ever before the fallacy of trusting to human works for salvation, and the necessity of constant faith in the merits of Christ."[60] While she did not mention the *Turmerlebnis*, she commented on the content and effect of his teachings from 1512 to 1517 as follows: "The glad tidings of a Saviour's love, the assurance of pardon and peace through His atoning blood, rejoiced their hearts and inspired within them an immortal hope."[61] Replying to those who expected absolution from their sins without repentance and a desire for reform because they had purchased Johann Tetzel's indulgences, she wrote,

> Nothing but repentance toward God and faith in Christ can save the sinner. The grace of Christ cannot be purchased; it is a free gift. He [Luther] counseled the people not to buy indulgences, but to look in faith to a crucified Redeemer. He related his own painful experience in vainly seeking by humiliation and penance to secure salvation, and assured his hearers that it was by looking away from himself and believing in Christ that he found peace and joy.[62]

Many secular and religious dignitaries refused to accept Luther's teachings once they realized that accepting the idea of "looking to Christ alone for salvation would overthrow the pontiff's throne and eventually destroy their own authority."[63] While Luther thought that the gospel was and had to be a cause of trouble, offense, and

---

57 Fortin, "The Theology of Ellen G. White," 246. Hans Heinz states that by discovering that teaching, Luther established the material principle of the Reformation. See Heinz, "Luther, Martin (1483–1546)," 954.
58 Ellen G. White, *Acts of the Apostles* (Mountain View, CA: Pacific Press, 1911), 373.
59 White, *The Great Controversy Between Christ and Satan*, 123–124.
60 Ibid., 125.
61 Ibid., 126.
62 Ibid., 129. Talking about the effect of his 95 theses, White stated, "It was also clearly shown that the gospel of Christ is the most valuable treasure of the church, and that the grace of God, therein revealed, is freely bestowed upon all who seek it by repentance and faith." See ibid., 130.
63 Ibid., 131.

dissension (Matt 10:34),[64] he viewed it as something that was freeing people, regardless of their societal status.[65] In a sermon at Erfurt, on his way to Worms, Luther encapsulated the doctrine of salvation quite well. "We are saved by his [Christ's] work, not by our own," and "since God has saved us" through him, we are to live as saved ones, extending self-sacrificing love to those in need. White felt that Luther's sermon was "the bread of life ... broken to those starving souls." Seeking to present Jesus only "as the sinner's Redeemer," "he hid behind the Man of Calvary," "lost sight of self," and the peril of his own situation.[66]

Ellen White believed that God took an active interest in Luther's life, pointing to numerous experiences as Heaven's providential working. Talking about his despondency in the cloister, she stressed that "God raised up a friend and helper [Staupitz] for him."[67] She considered Luther's visit to Rome providential because it was during that trip that he was confronted with the dichotomy between ecclesiastical realities and biblical sentiments.[68] Many recognized "the voice of God" in his ninety-five theses feeling "that the Lord had graciously set His hand to arrest the rapidly swelling tide of corruption."[69] She believed that Luther had indeed been moved by the Holy Spirit to begin his work,[70] and that angels of heaven were frequently sent to protect him.[71] She further believed that it had been "God's providence [that] sent Melanchthon to Wittenberg" because they would complement each other and strengthen the Reformation.[72]

White considered even some actions of pronounced enemies of the Reformation as results of divine providence. Thus Luther saw the Emperor's call to present his views at Worms as the call of God himself.[73] In her view, the appearance of Jerome Aleander (1480–1542), "the ablest of [Rome's] orators," was also ordered by divine providence to bring both positions to a direct encounter.[74] She further asserted that God worked on the heart of Duke George of Saxony, "a determined enemy of the Reformation," to denounce the papal tyranny, offering a better critique than Luther himself could have given. She perceived the presence of the angels of heaven and the power of God in the assembly, "opening minds and hearts

64  Ibid., 159, 165.
65  Ibid., 154.
66  Ibid., 152.
67  White, "Martin Luther--His Character and Early Life," 242; White, *Spirit of Prophecy*, 4:98; White, *The Great Controversy*, 123.
68  White, "Luther at Wittenberg," 253; White, *Spirit of Prophecy*, 4:99.
69  White, *The Great Controversy Between Christ and Satan*, 130, cf. 128.
70  Ibid., 131, see also 142 on Luther's own remarks on his divine calling, and 188 on the Holy Spirit's operation on Luther to urge him forward in the work of reform.
71  Ibid., 133, 140, 208. Resounding the theme of Ps 46:1 and other psalms, she referred to Luther's belief in God as his defense. See ibid., 153.
72  Ibid., 134. She believed that God had placed Melanchthon in his position at Wittenberg. See ibid., 135.
73  Ibid., 146.
74  Ibid., 147.

to the reception of truth."⁷⁵ When Luther prepared his final answer for the council, the despondency coming over him was, according to Ellen White, permitted by "an all-wise Providence" for "Luther to realize his peril, that he might not trust to his own strength and rush presumptuously into danger." Like Jacob, he was wrestling with God and "in his utter helplessness his faith fastened upon Christ, the mighty Deliverer."⁷⁶ Then, after Luther had related his speech in German, he was asked to repeat it in Latin. She saw it again as a circumstance directed by "God's providence" for some to understand the force of Luther's argument because they had not felt it the first time.⁷⁷

As one might expect, White saw Luther's abduction on his way home as God's "way of escape" in the hour of peril by giving "wisdom to Frederick of Saxony to devise a plan for the Reformer's preservation."⁷⁸ She thought that there were some even more significant results to be gained from his abduction. Shut out from the public and human praise, he would be "saved from pride and self-confidence" that often result from success. As humans often extol and praise the leaders of revivals, attention is drawn to God's instrument rather than God himself. Rather than allowing the efforts of the Reformation to be thwarted, God wanted to prepare Luther "again to walk safely upon the dizzy heights to which he had been so suddenly exalted."⁷⁹ White firmly believed that through Luther "God accomplished a great work for the reformation of the church and the enlightenment of the world."⁸⁰

Interestingly, when commenting on the opposition that all those have to face who "God employs to present truths especially applicable to their time," White remarked that as "there was a present truth in the days of Luther, a truth at that time of special importance, there is [similarly] a present truth for the church today."⁸¹ Although "present truth" was a concept that was highly significant for early Seventh-day Adventists and Ellen White,⁸² it appears only two times in the *Great Controversy*, both times in that one sentence. Thus, in her view, Luther's

---

75   Ibid., 149–150. Others were convinced too that "that a divine influence attended" Luther, encouraging him unexpectedly on his way to the council. See ibid., 154–155.
76   Ibid., 156–157.
77   Ibid., 159. As Luther was fully depended on God – "May God be my helper, for I can retract nothing." – White felt that it was Christ himself who had spoken and manifested himself through Luther working on those attending the council. See ibid., 161–162, see also 160, 164, 166. In fact, as people in the audience listened to the "divine power [that] had spoken through Luther," many of them experienced the pleading of the Holy Spirit "for the last time," alluding to a subjective or personal close of probation as seen in the life of Pilate, Felix, and Agrippa. See ibid., 164.
78   Ibid., 168.
79   Ibid., 169–170.
80   White, "Martin Luther--His Character and Early Life," 241; White, *Spirit of Prophecy*, 4:94; White, *The Great Controversy*, 120.
81   White, *The Great Controversy*, 143.
82   The term appears 1,921 times in her published writings on the Ellen G. White CD-ROM.

courage in preaching "present truth" in the face of opposition seemed to be an example for those called by God to promote the "present truth" in the end-time.

Whereas one might think that Ellen White merely intended to outline Luther's early years (1483–1521) in her first chapter on him in the *Great Controversy*, a closer look reveals a particular focus on his inner dissociation from the Roman Catholic system. Thus after describing Luther's joy of studying the Bible and the relief coming as a result from Staupitz's advice, she stressed that for years, he was "still a true son of the papal church" who "had no thought that he would ever be anything else."[83] In her sketch of Luther's visit to Rome, she noted that he became aware more than ever before of the futility of trusting in human works for salvation and the need to believe in Christ's merits.[84] She stated, "His eyes had been opened, and were never again to be closed, to the delusions of the papacy. When he turned his face from Rome he had turned away also in heart, and from that time the separation grew wider, until he severed all connection with the papal church."[85]

After completing his doctoral degree, Luther "declared that Christians should receive no other doctrines than those which rest on the authority of the Sacred Scriptures," a principle that "struck at the very foundation of papal supremacy."[86] However, when pointing out the horror Luther experienced as he learned about Tetzel's "blasphemous assumptions" in 1517, White viewed him "still [as] a papist of the straightest sort."[87] In fact, even after his return from the Diet of Augsburg in late 1518, she considered him "still a supporter of the Roman Church," having "no thought that he could ever separate from her communion."[88] While in her view the separation process lasted thus over some years,[89] she eventually suggested that the final inner and outward separation occurred when Luther, after a terrible inner struggle, burned the papal bull in December 1520.[90] Ellen White encapsulated this theme of an extended separation process, which runs through the entire chapter, aptly in the title of that chapter – "Luther's Separation from Rome." The remaining three chapters trace how the gap widens even more after his final separation.

## Summary and Conclusion

The present chapter analyzed the relationship between Ellen White's primary publications on Martin Luther, her chronological treatment of the German Reformer, and the emphases of that narrative.

---

83 Ibid., 124.
84 Ibid., 125.
85 Ibid.
86 Ibid., 126.
87 Ibid., 128.
88 Ibid., 139.
89 This description of a longer development is also noted in Heinz, "Luther, Martin (1483–1546)," 955.
90 White, *The Great Controversy*, 142–143.

The comparison of the three substantial versions of the Luther narrative has shown that the text of the *Signs* articles (1883) was evidently shortened in preparation for the four chapters on Luther in *Spirit of Prophecy*, vol. 4 (1884), only to be expanded again with quotations and explanatory remarks in preparation for the *Great Controversy* (1888). Such literary and editorial changes were in line with her more dynamic understanding of inspiration, which excluded the ideas of mechanical inspiration or a general verbal inspiration.[91]

While the two latter publications were unequivocally placed within the context of the universal conflict between the powers of good and evil, Christ and Satan, a closer look at the *Signs* articles reveals that the presentation of the famous German Reformer's experience was already highlighting the metanarrative of the great controversy. The foundational role of Scripture and the significance of salvation by faith in Christ are recurrent themes in these publications. Luther's holding fast to these two basic points put him in close relationship to God and set him on a path away from the papal system. Although she emphasized God's guidance in Luther's life and the important role he played in restoring the knowledge of fundamental truths, she did not necessarily agree with every point of his theology and everything he did.[92] Interestingly, some of the themes appearing in her Luther narrative were also prominent in her sermons and other writings about the same time.[93]

Although she created a stark contrast between Romanism and Protestantism, she described developments of Luther and other individuals that illustrate a paradox in their lives. Luther was moving away from Rome and was placing his faith on a different foundation – Scripture and salvation by Christ – yet he was still a strict supporter of the papal system. Thus Ellen White illustrated the tension between the two great principles in one's daily experience. She wanted her readers to

---

91   Denis Kaiser, "Ellen White's View of Divine Inspiration," Perspective Digest 19, no. 2 (2014), https://goo.gl/T5Ri9i (November 29, 2017).
92   George R. Knight, *Reading Ellen White: How to Understand and Apply Her Writings* (Hagerstown, MD: Review and Herald, 1997), 121.
93   At the General Conference session in late 1883 Ellen White tried to impress Adventist ministers and delegates with the thought to look away from self and focus on cross – "Look and live." While she employed the phrase already earlier, it is worth noting that the phrase seems to resound the core of Staupitz's admonition. She used the phrase as early as 1870 against the backdrop of Num 21:8. See Ellen G. White, *Spirit of Prophecy: The Great Controversy between Christ and His Angels and Satan and His Angels*, vol. 1 (Battle Creek, MI: Steam Press of the Seventh-day Adventist Pub. Assn., 1870), 317; Ellen G. White, "The Fiery Serpents," *Signs of the Times*, October 28, 1880, 469–470. Staupitz's statement appeared in White, "Martin Luther--His Character and Early Life," 241–242. Thus right at the time her *Signs* articles appeared, she frequently emphasized the need to refrain from focusing on one's own lack of perfection and to look firmly to Christ for one's personal salvation. See Ellen G. White, "The Christian's Refuge," *Review and Herald*, April 15, 1884, 241; Ellen G. White, "Effectual Prayer," *Review and Herald*, April 22, 1884, 257–258; Ellen G. White, "Christ's Followers the Light of the World," *Review and Herald*, May 13, 1884, 306; Ellen G. White, "Our Mighty Helper," *Review and Herald*, July 1, 1884, 417.

understand the nature of the two principles that are contending for supremacy, …
[and] see how this controversy enters into every phase of human experience; how in
every act of life he himself reveals the one or the other of the two antagonistic motives;
and how, whether he will or not, he is even now deciding upon which side of the
controversy he will be found.[94]

Whereas we tend to judge individuals based on "occasional good deeds and occasional misdeeds," she stressed the significance of "the tendency of the habitual words and acts."[95] Her Luther narrative was to be an illustration of the tension between the two contending principles in human lives and an example for those seeking to prepare themselves for the coming events. Whatever the denominational affiliation of her readers, White intended to impress upon them the need to cling fast to Jesus and Scripture, to make God their "refuge and strength" (Ps 46:1).

---

94  Ellen G. White, *Education* (Oakland, CA: Pacific Press, 1903), 190. The two contending principles in the great controversy may be defined as follows: divine, self-sacrificing, other-oriented love vs. selfish, self-oriented love. These principles content for supremacy in each person's life. Projecting his own character on God, Satan claims that God's principle of government is selfish, and that his own principle is for the good of humanity, society, and the universe. Individuals and systems are in the midst of that conflict, sometimes exerting the one principle, sometimes the other one. Thus a knowledge of the great controversy does not only intend to provide believers with an understanding of the great metanarrative but with a comprehension of the real struggle that they experience constantly in themselves (emotionally, physically, mentally, and spiritually). Actions, behaviors, and habits relating to their personal lifestyle feed the strength of these contenting principles in their life. The purpose of the plan of redemption is to restore God's image, his character in them. It is its goal to turn them away from self-oriented love to other-oriented love so that they do truly live within the boundaries of God's Decalogue, showing what love is not, and exert creatively and innovatively love to God and others. The more they get to the end of time the clearer will become the tendencies of each person's life until finally there are only two groups for the entire universe to witness the pure fruits of both principles. Eventually God's character and his government (of other-oriented love) will stand vindicated and Satan's principle will appear for what it really is (self-love). The *inclusio* of White's Conflict of the Ages Series stresses the core of God's character ("God is love") and its center manifests Christ as the ultimate revelation of that love (*The Desire of Ages*). See Ellen G. White, *Patiarchs and Prophets: or, The Great Conflict between Good and Evil as Illustrated in the Lives of Holy Men of Old* (Oakland, CA: Pacific Press, 1890), 33; White, *The Great Controversy Between Christ and Satan*, 678; Ellen G. White, *The Desire of Ages* (Oakland, CA: Pacific Press, 1898).

95  Ellen G. White, *Steps to Christ* (1892; reprint, Battle Creek, MI: Review and Herald, 1896), 58.

*Daniel Heinz*

# "Komm, lieber Jüngster Tag!"
# An Appraisal of Luther's Eschatological Worldview

Abstract

With his deep longing for the redemption of the entire creation through the return of Christ at the end of time, Martin Luther took up an authentic biblical stance. To view this as merely historically conditioned and bound to the spirit of his time does not do justice to the Reformer's genuine end-time orientation. The relevance of his eschatological views is especially evident when viewed in light of the historical impact and pertinence of the prophetic word of the Bible. In this sense, Luther was a staunch "Adventist." His joyful expectation of a new world gives hope and comfort to Christians to this day.

A look at Martin Luther's work and legacy reveals two distinct and equally continuous lines of thought that represent a faith pattern, from the time of his Reformation breakthrough until the end of his life: his doctrine of justification by faith in Jesus Christ alone, and his expectation of the imminent return of Christ. Even though Luther was not familiar with, and thus did not utilize the term "eschatology," his entire theological mindset or *Weltanschauung* was eschatologically grounded.

The clear eschatological/apocalyptic character of Luther's theology has long been overlooked. Luther expert Paul Althaus is especially to be credited with bringing about a turning point.[1] In the mid-twentieth century, Althaus proposed the solidly-supported thesis that Luther, with his positive view of the end, did not merely re-transmit the tradition of early Christians; rather, with his hopeful and joyful expectation of the Second Coming of Christ, Luther also proved to be a Reformer of the doctrine of "last things" (eschatology).[2] Luther scholars such as Ole Modalsli and Bernhard Lohse came to similar conclusions in the second half of the twentieth century.[3]

---

1  See Paul Althaus, "Luthers Gedanken über die letzten Dinge," *Luther-Jahrbuch* 23 (1941): 11.
2  Ibid.
3  Ole Modalsli, "Luther über die letzten Dinge," in *Leben und Werk Martin Luthers von 1526–1546,* ed. Helmar Junghans (Berlin: Ev. Verlagsanstalt, 1983), 1:331; Bernhard Lohse, *Luthers Theologie in ihrer historischen Entwicklung und in ihrem systematischen Zusammenhang* (Göttingen: Vandenhoeck & Ruprecht, 1995), 349.

Althaus criticized earlier Luther scholarship because there "Luther's thought concerning last things largely recedes into the background."[4] Scholars either gave Luther's eschatology absolutely no attention, as in the case of Theodosius Harnack, Reinhold Seeberg and Erich Seeberg, or else they abbreviated the treatment of the subject, as in the case of Julius Köstlin and Johannes von Walter.[5] However, the importance of the connection between present and eschatological salvation was exemplified by Karl Heim by an illustration in his work, *Jesus der Weltvollender* (1952). It compares the Christian concept of salvation to a bridge suspended between two towers. The one represents Golgotha, the other the *parousia* of Christ.[6] The former guarantees salvation in faith, the latter promises salvation in sight. If one of the towers is neglected or even brought crashing down, the entire bridge will ultimately be destroyed.

This tension between "justified by faith now" and "saved through the *parousia* thereafter" constitutes the foundation of the Christian expectancy. Luther found this concept above all in the writings of Paul. Therefore, Paul Althaus could correctly say of Luther that "His faith is eager to know about last things."[7] Modern Luther scholarship has attempted to rectify the deficiency of the past and views the tension between Luther's approach to the cross and the Second Coming as a *heilsökonomischer Dualismus* ("dualism in the economy of salvation") typical of Luther. The cross and the Second Coming become *Urdaten* ("raw data") of his eschatological expectation.[8]

The thesis "to have" and its antithesis "to not yet have," of "to be" and "to not yet be," leads to the eschatological synthesis in which present and future salvation unite. "Luther's theology [is] eschatological through and through in the strict sense of final expectation."[9] The connection between present justification – declaring the sinner to be righteous before the judgment seat of God on the basis of his faith through the salvific act of Christ on the cross – and the future final salvation on the Judgment Day is of "fundamental significance" for Luther's theology.[10] It affects his doctrine of salvation as well as his anthropology and interpretation of history. His entire theological thought was placed within the matrix of the end-times, so that one can speak of a comprehensive eschatological/apocalyptic worldview in Luther.

---

4   Althaus, "Luthers Gedanken," 9 („Luthers Gedanken über die letzten Dinge sehr zurücktreten").
5   Ibid.
6   Karl Heim, *Jesus der Weltvollender* (Hamburg: Furche, 1952), 150.
7   Althaus, "Luthers Gedanken," 10.
8   Ulrich Asendorf, *Eschatologie bei Luther* (Göttingen: Vandenhoeck & Ruprecht, 1967), 14.
9   "... Luthers Theologie durch und durch eschatologisch im strengen Sinn der Enderwartung." Paul Althaus, *Die Theologie Martin Luthers*, 4th ed. (Gütersloh: G. Mohn, 1975), 339.
10  Lohse, *Luthers Theologie*, 345f.

## Affirming the Joyful Advent Hope of the Early Christians

Just as the Reformer with his understanding of the doctrine of justification became a rediscoverer of the Pauline gospel,[11] which had been concealed for centuries by the church's view of righteousness by works – so also his eschatological/apocalyptic orientation represented a part of both, tradition and reformation. In his eschatology, Luther appealed to important eschatological forerunners such as Augustine, Bernard of Clairvaux, Joachim of Fiore, and Peter John Olivi. He did not simply adopt and retransmit this tradition; rather, as an exclusively biblically-oriented theologian, he rediscovered the joyful end-time expectation of the earliest Christians and kept it fresh: "[We should] be ready for [the Last Day], hope for it with joy ... as the Day which delivers us from sin, death, and hell."[12]

The first Christians were of course filled with this joy to the fullest. Because they absolutely trusted the word of their Lord, "I will come back" (John 14:3), the Apostle Paul was able to burst out with hope to the church in Philippi: "Rejoice in the Lord always ... the Lord is at hand" (Phil 4:4-5). Likewise, he was able to comfort the Thessalonians with the words, "sorrow not, even as others which have no hope ... For the Lord himself shall descend ... and the dead in Christ shall rise first" (1 Thess 4:13,16). And, at the end of the epistle, he assures them that Jesus Christ "died for us, that ... we should live together with him" (1 Thess 5:10).[13]

The same conviction is found in the epistles of Peter. Hoping for the end of suffering and death, the apostle encourages persecuted Christians of all times that "the end of all things is at hand" (1 Pet 4:7); "we, according to his promise, look for new heavens and a new earth, wherein dwelleth righteousness" (2 Pet 3:13).

However, as all New Testament writers were emphasizing, Christians do not know when these promises will be fulfilled. Yet they live in a state of permanent hope that the promises could be fulfilled at any time. Just as the prophecies of the first coming of Christ were fulfilled, so they hope that at the right point in time, which God alone has determined, the prophecies concerning the Second Coming will also be fulfilled. "Cast not away therefore your confidence, which hath great recompence of reward," the book of Hebrews reads, "For ye have need of patience, that, after ye have done the will of God, ye might receive the promise" (Heb

---

11  Hans Küng, "Katholische Besinnung auf Luthers Rechtfertigungslehre," in *Theologie im Wandel*, ed. Katholische Fakultät Tübingen (München: E. Wewel, 1967), 464.
12  LW 30:197 (Sermons on the Second Epistle of Peter). All citations are from *Luther's Works, American Edition*, 55 vols., edited by Jaroslav Pelikan and Helmut T. Lehman (Philadelphia: Muehlenberg Press and Fortress Press; and St. Louis: Concordia, 1955–1986). Original found in WA 14, 72. ("Wir sollen für den Jüngsten Tag bereit sein, mit Freuden auf ihn hoffen ... als auf den, der uns erlöst von Sünden, Tod und Hölle.") All citations are from *Weimarer Ausgabe: D. Martin Luthers Werke, Kritische Gesamtausgabe*, 127 vols. (Weimar: H. Böhlau, 1883–2009). It is grouped into Schriften/Werke [Writings] (WA), Tischreden [Table talks] (WA TR), Deutsche Bibel [German Bible] (WA DB) and Briefwechsel [Exchange of letters] (WA BR).
13  All Bible quotations in this chapter are taken from the King James Version (KJV).

10:35–36). Every Christian generation must walk this line. Because Christians know neither the time of Christ's appearing nor the time lapse until the *parousia* (Acts 1:7), they must exercise patience, accomplish their allotted task, and at the same time be prepared for the end that means completion and a new beginning.

This eschatological posture going back to the earliest Christians lent itself well to the Reformer. Now, as he was never tired of emphasizing, we are living in a "long winter" after which shall follow the "eternal summer" of the new world of God. The fact that the dawning of this new era does not reveal itself to those waiting for it must not unsettle them, for they already witness the signs of the waning world and already live in the anticipatory joy of the coming one.

It is precisely this joy that distinguishes Luther's hope in the *parousia* from the fearful doomsday expectation of the Middle Ages. The vision of the end was alive and ever-present during that era – one must only think of the doomsday fears concerning the year AD 1000, the expectation of Joachim of Fiore that the Age of the Spirit would dawn in AD 1260, and the calculations of the astronomer John of Toledo, according to whom this age of the world would come to an end in AD 1186. However, most of these medieval end-time scenarios were lacking the joy that had characterized the early Christian hope concerning the promise of another and better world.

The fearful and negative attitude in regard to the end of the world did not originate just in the Middle Ages. While the first Christians greeted each other with the phrase *Marana tha* (1 Cor 16:22 – literally "our Lord is coming"), already in the second to fourth centuries the thought began to take hold of the ancient church that the end of the world would be so horrible for everyone that one should not long for it, but rather should ask God to postpone it. This attitude also increased through the acceptance of pagan myths, such as that described in Plato's *Phaedo* (ch. 62). There the philosopher speculates on the condition of the dead and develops ideas about a place of punishment and purification that later crept into Catholic Christianity as the doctrines of hell and purgatory. Thus people were threatened not only with the final judgment, but even before that with a judgment immediately following death. Robbed of the biblical assurance of salvation, one lived in fear and trembling as to how well one would fare before the heavenly Judge.

The unbiblical doctrine of an already existing hell and the misrepresentation of the benevolent Christ as a merciless judge resulted in people being more likely to tremble than to rejoice. The "Day of the Lord," the day of Christ's Second Coming, was, above all, considered to be the *dies irae*, the "Day of Wrath" which even the believer must fear.

Viewing the *Inferno* of Dante and Michelangelo's *The Last Judgment*, one gets an impression of what stirred the people of the time. The invocation of Mary and the saints, the cult of relics and indulgences, pilgrimages and asceticism, were supposed to aid the fear-filled mind, and yet were unable to alleviate the agony of the soul. Martin Luther himself had experienced this condition. At the end of his life he confessed of his time spent as a monk before his reformation break-through,

"[I was] in dread of the last day, nevertheless from the depth of my heart wanted to be saved."[14]

The new content and tone of Luther's joyful end-time expectation – bursting forth from his rediscovery of the Gospel – was fittingly characterized by historian Walter Nigg:

> For the world, the last day will prove to be 'pure terror and trembling, death and poison and hellish ordeal,' but for the Christian, 'pure sweetness.' What a monumental turning point is apparent in this invitation to consider the last day a day of joy, in contrast to the crippling horror of that day with which the medieval person quaked. A more radical turn-around is not possible. These joyful words of Luther are the bright rays of sunshine that broke through the dark clouds of the late Middle Ages. In the view of this reassessment, Luther's religious triumph over the Middle Ages is palpable. With this new and simultaneously ancient understanding, the Reformer really found his way back to early Christianity.[15]

Through this approach, Luther, as a strictly biblical theologian, was also able to integrate the somber mood of crisis in his apocalyptic, for eschatology (consciousness of the end) and apocalyptic (end-time events) formed a unity in his thinking, just as they formed a unity in the message of Jesus. "In Jesus of Nazareth," one can summarize, "the apocalyptic dimension of the Kingdom of God became the center of the eschatological message of Luther."[16]

## The Existential Longing for the "Dear Last Day"

Since Martin Luther consistently thought in strictly biblical terms, the eschatological/apocalyptic character of his work remained constant, even when his focus on an individual salvation perspective condensed into a perspective of universal completion. The themes that constantly resounded were: the pitiful condition of the world, the significance of the signs of the times, the divine promise of the *parousia*, the *parousia* as the visible and audible return of Christ in power and majesty, and the

---

14  LW 34:328 (Preface to the Complete Edition of Luther's Latin Writings, 1545). Original in WA 54, 179 ("Ich hatte eine furchtbare Angst vor dem Jüngsten Tag und begehrte doch von Herzens Grunde, gerettet zu werden.")
15  "Für die Welt wird der Jüngste Tag 'eitel Schrecken und Zittern, Tod und Gift und höllische Marter zeigen,' aber für die Christen 'eitel Zucker.' Welch gewaltiger Umschwung zeigt sich doch in dieser Aufforderung, den Jüngsten Tag als Freudentag zu betrachten, gegenüber dem lähmenden Entsetzen, mit dem der mittelalterliche Mensch vor diesem Tag bebte. Eine radikalere Umdrehung ist nicht möglich; diese freudigen Worte Luthers sind der helle Sonnenstrahl, der durch das dunkle Gewölk des Spätmittelalters hindurchdrang. Angesichts dieser Umwertung ist Luthers religiöse Überwindung des Mittelalters mit Händen zu greifen. Mit dieser neuen und zugleich alten Auffassung hat der Reformator tatsächlich wieder zum Urchristentum zurückgefunden." Walter Nigg, *Das ewige Reich* (München: Siebenstern, 1967), 177f.
16  Hans Schwarz, *Jenseits von Utopie und Resignation* (Wuppertal: Brockhaus, 1990), 50.

imminent expectation and longing of the Christian for the last day. To appropriate and internalize these perspectives, unequivocal trust in God and humble clinging to the Scriptures are essential. God speaks through the biblical Word to human beings. Whoever hears and does not resist, will be cut to the heart. Thus, the hearers of the truth of the Word become confident, overcome the objections of doubt, and trust the future promise, even if the latter surpasses reason and experience in its otherness and extensiveness. "Whoever reads the Word of God, to him the Holy Spirit speaks ... [and] embosoms the letters. This completely transforms the person, and such a one is confident ... having no doubts."[17]

Luther's own eschatological/apocalyptic constant unfolded at the moment when he was swept into the major controversies of his time as a public figure. As a Bible-affirming Christian, he believed that the relevant answers to the questions concerning the trajectory and goal of the world were only to be found in the Scriptures. Thus the conflict between the pope, the emperor, and the sultan further nourished his end-time expectation. The corresponding biblical-realistic understanding of the condition of the world matured him into the "prophet of the end-time," which he remained to the end of his life.[18]

During his time of maturing into a Reformer, the personal aspect of salvation stood in the foreground as Luther wrestled as a monk with his own salvation. However, with the groundbreaking recognition of the justification of the sinner through faith in Christ alone, and the corresponding assurance of salvation, the eschatological/apocalyptic outlook brought forth a new perspective. Now, for Luther, the end meant not fear and horror, but joy and peace. The eschatological *topoi* remained the same for him, but his perspective in interpreting them had been transformed. His initial personal struggle with the Gospel-message opened his view to its final universal aspect. Christian faith not only encompasses the renewal of the individual, but aims toward the re-creation of the entire world. Both – becoming righteous before God (justification) as well as becoming righteous in life (sanctification), along with the renewal of the entire world – are evidently two sides of the same coin and may not be separated. Both – redemption in an unredeemed world at the first Advent and redemption of the entire world through the Second Advent – served as cornerstones of his new concept of salvation.

This salvation perspective was first evidenced with the young Reformer and became increasingly clear throughout his latter days. In April 1519, a few weeks before his pivotal Leipzig Disputation with John Eck, his theological archenemy, Luther published the work *Deutsche Auslegung des Vaterunsers für die einfältigen Laien* (An Exposition of the Lord's Prayer for Simple Laymen). At several instances

---

17 Original in WA 47, 184 ("Wer das Wort Gottes liest, mit dem redet der Heilige Geist ... [und] drückt die Buchstaben ins Herz. Dann werden die Menschen ganz anders und ein solcher ist gewiss ... dass er keinen Zweifel habe.")

18 Cf. Volker Leppin, "Apokalyptische Strömungen in der Reformationszeit," in *Apokalyptik und kein Ende?*, ed. by Bernd U. Schipper and Georg Plasger (Göttingen: Vandenhoeck & Ruprecht, 2007), 77, 80.

therein he addressed the theme of the condition of the world. The Christian lives "among cruel foes, robbed of the dearest Father's land [fatherland]." According to the prayer instructed by Christ, there are "two kingdoms." The first is the "kingdom of the devil" in which the world is enslaved, until "God's kingdom" comes. The latter is already present since Christ's first coming, but it is not yet complete. Thus the plea, "Thy kingdom come" is an expression of longing: "Dear Father, do not let us sojourn very long here ... that ... we may be delivered from the devil's kingdom."[19]

After it became ever clearer to Martin Luther that Rome was completely unwilling to engage in church reform, in August 1520, in a document dedicated to emperor Charles V, entitled *An den christlichen Adel deutscher Nation von des christlichen Standes Besserung* (To the Christian Nobility of the German Nation Concerning the Reform of the Christian Estate), he made an appeal to the nobility to undertake the needed work of reform. Although this profound document ("gewaltige Schrift")[20] is primarily concerned with the issues of Reformation at that time – Luther spoke of "three walls"[21] erected by Rome that needed tearing down: that the power of the church takes precedence over the power of the state; that only the Roman *magisterium* has the right to validly interpret Scripture; and that councils can only be called by the pope – ultimately everything culminated in Luther's hope and desire not only for present change, but for a final and permanent consummation. "O Christ, my Lord, look down: let the day of your judgment break [through] ... I hope that the day of judgment is at hand. Things could not possibly be worse than the state of affairs the Romanist See is promoting. If he is not the Antichrist, then somebody tell me who is!"[22]

In the Wartburg castle, where Luther had been in hiding since 1521, he occupied himself with the end-time sermon of Jesus, especially with the passage from Luke 21:29–36, which formed the core of his persistent Advent hope. Over the years, at numerous points in his career, he preached on this passage almost without alteration.[23] The recurring allusions to this passage clearly show that the imminent expectation of the Second Coming of Christ was a thoroughgoing constant in his

---

19 LW 42:37, 40 (An Exposition of the Lord's Prayer for Simple Laymen, 1519). Original in WA 2, 97 ("unter grausamen Feinden, beraubt des allerliebsten Vaterlandes" and "Lieber Vater, lass uns hier nicht lange bleiben ... damit wir gänzlich erlöst werden von des Teufels Reich.")
20 Ernst Staehelin, *Die Verkündigung des Reiches Gottes in der Kirche Jesu Christi*, vol. 4 (Basel: Reinhardt, 1957), 35.
21 WA 6, 381ff.
22 LW 44:194–195 (To the Christian Nobility of the German Nation Concerning the Reform of the Christian Estate, 1520). Original in WA 6, 453f. ("Ach, Christus, mein Herr, siehe herab, lass' hereinbrechen deinen Jüngsten Tag ... Ich hoffe, der Jüngste Tag sei vor der Tür. Es kann und darf ja nicht ärger werden, als es der römische Stuhl treibt. Gottes Gebot drückt er herunter, sein Gebot erhebt er darüber. Ist das nicht der Antichrist, so sage ein anderer, wer es sein möge!").
23 Cf. Modalsli, 332.

faith and life. "I neither wish to force nor to pressure anyone to believe me. However, no one can shake me from my belief that the Last Day is not far off."[24]

In contrast to the enthusiastic expectation of the *Schwärmer*, the Reformer's attitude was characterized by biblical sobriety. Luther expected a maturation and growth of the signs in the area of moral decay and spiritual deformation. Despite some extreme views, such as the conjecture that the catastrophes of his time could hardly be exceeded, and that world history would only endure 6,000 years,[25] his understanding was in fact influenced less by calculations than by the sober observation of the condition of the world, demonstrating "that Christ must come soon, because ... [people] are coaxing the Judgment Day along through their defiance so much that it has to come upon them sooner rather than later."[26]

## Apocalyptic Threat and Comfort

In face of this deep and strong eschatological/apocalyptic orientation, Luther's early criticism of the Revelation of John, the book about the Second Coming of Christ, seems completely out of place. In his *Vorrede auf die Offenbarung* (Preface to Revelation) of 1522, one finds surprisingly derogatory comments regarding the last book of the Bible with its comforting promises of the glorious future and its solemn ending: "He which testifieth these things saith, Surely I come quickly. Amen. Even so, come, Lord Jesus" (Rev 22:20).

The Bible interpreter from 1522 considered the book to be "neither apostolic nor prophetic,"[27] because it is not written with "clear and concise words" like the Gospels and Epistles, but rather consists of "images."[28] The reason why Luther could not hold the Revelation in high esteem is that "Christ is neither taught nor acknowledged in it."[29] This verdict seems all the more astounding because the Johannine apocalypse is a thoroughly Christocentric book, commencing with the Resurrected One (Rev 1:18), recalling the Sacrificed One (Rev 5:6, 9, 12), continuing on with the Exalted One (Rev 3:21; 5:12–14), and ending with the Coming One (Rev 22:12, 20); it has been called the "Crown of the New Testament."

In 1530, Luther moderated his earlier verdict. Now he left open the question of apostolic origin,[30] and credited the book with usefulness and profitability,

---

24 Original in WA 10 I, 2, 95 ("Ich will niemanden zwingen noch dringen, mir zu glauben. Ich will mir es aber auch wiederum von niemandem nehmen lassen, dass ich dafür halte, der Jüngste Tag sei nicht ferne.").
25 Cf. Staehelin, *Die Verkündigung des Reiches Gottes*, 65.
26 Ibid., 41 ("... dass Christus bald kommen müsse, denn ... [die Menschen] reizen mit ihrem Trotz den Jüngsten Tag zu sehr, er muss über sie fallen, ehe es lange währt.").
27 Heinrich Bornkamm, ed., *Luthers Vorreden zur Bibel* (Frankfurt am Main: Insel, 1983), 218.
28 Ibid., 219.
29 Ibid.
30 Ibid., 221.

first for comfort, that no violence or lie ... no affliction or sorrow will suppress Christianity, but that it will finally obtain victory ... And next, as a warning against the great, dangerous offense of ... calling the Christian Church what in reality is the worst enemy of the Christian Church, and in turn calling those who are the true Christian Church, heretics.[31]

Not only declaring the Evangelical Church heretical from within Christianity aggrieved and irritated Luther in those years, but also the serious threat from the outside against the faith. At the end of the 1520s, the Turkish crisis reached the borders of the *Reich* for the first time. These events caused all of Europe to hold its breath, they also made a deep impression on Luther. In the year when the Turks besieged Vienna, he published his famous writings *Vom Krieg wider die Türken* and *Eine Heerpredigt wider den Türken* ("On War Against the Turks" and "A Sermon Against the Turk"). Since war and turmoil posed a significant "sign of the times" (Matt 24:6, 7; Mark 13:7; Luke 21:9), Luther heard the warning call of God amidst the upheaval of this time. These threatening events deepened his end-time convictions to the utmost. The fact that the pope and the French king, the *res publica christiana* of Christian Europe, refused to help against the Turks, leaving the emperor alone, was for him clear evidence of an end-time moral collapse.

In the spring of 1529 – the Turkish military troops crept slowly but surely up to the border of the Empire – Luther's *Large Catechism* and *Small Catechism* appeared, handbooks for instruction and strengthening in the faith, written for pastors and heads of household. Both addressed the Lord's Prayer and especially its plea "Thy kingdom come." While in the *Small Catechism* the fulfillment of the plea was predominantly explained in present terms – the kingdom comes "when the Heavenly Father gives us His Spirit" – he added to the *German Catechism*, known since 1541 as the *Large Catechism*, an explanation regarding the double meaning of the term "kingdom": It currently breaks through in the "Word and faith, but thereafter in eternity, when it shall be truly manifest."[32] The latter is understood as the Second Coming of Christ and the recreation of God's new world. "May the devil's kingdom be vanquished, that he might have no more right nor might over us, so long until he is finally totally destroyed, and sin, death, and hell are annihilated, that we might have eternal life in full righteousness and bliss."[33]

---

31  Ibid., 229 ("Erstlich zur Tröstung, dass keine Gewalt noch Lüge ... keine Trübsal noch Leid werden die Christenheit unterdrücken, sondern sie soll endlich den Sieg behalten ... Zum andern, zur Warnung wider das große, gefährliche Ärgernis ... das christliche Kirche zu heißen, welches doch der christlichen Kirche ärgste Feinde sind, und wiederum das verdammte Ketzer zu heißen, die doch rechte christliche Kirche sind.").
32  Martin Luther, *Der Große Katechismus* (München: Siebenstern, 1964), 115.
33  Luther, *Der Große Katechismus,* 115f. ("Lass' des Teufels Reich überwunden werden, dass er kein Recht und keine Gewalt mehr über uns habe, solange bis es schließlich ganz zerstört und Sünde, Tod und Hölle vertilgt wird, dass wir dann ewig leben in voller Gerechtigkeit und Seligkeit.").

This tension between the "Now" and the "Thereafter" pervades Luther's thought from beginning to end, and is fundamental to his Bible-centered understanding of theology. In his *Deutsche Auslegung des Vaterunsers* (Exposition of the Lord's Prayer) in 1519, he had already carved out his twofold concept of the present and future kingdom. The kingdom is primarily "the kingdom within us," but then above all "the kingdom before us," because the "now" is the "being away from home" and with it, the waiting for "consummation."[34]

How deeply the Reformer was impressed by this eschatological hope is evident in the 1530 edition of the translation of the prophet Daniel, even before the translation of the New Testament was completed and the first edition of the Luther Bible could be released in 1543. The translation and preface – including an overview of the meaning of the most important symbols and prophecies of the book – were dedicated to the Saxon Prince Johann Friedrich, the son of Elector Johann, both of them faithful followers of Luther. The Reformer had long been convicted that the book of Daniel especially was for the "comfort" of all Christians, but was above all a handbook of the theology of history for sovereigns and regents, a royal and princely book.[35]

This special and early publication *(Der Prophet Daniel deutsch)* flowed out from the personal conviction of Luther that he was facing the end of the world.

> The world runs and rushes on so splendidly towards its end, that often strong impressions come to my mind, as if the Last Day were to dawn before we could possibly come to completely translate the Scriptures into German ... such thoughts and similar ones have prompted us to put out this prophet Daniel before the others that have not yet come out, so that it could come out before that day will come when everything is dissolved, and to allow it to fulfill its role in comforting miserable Christians, for whose sake it was written, and preserved and reserved for these last times.[36]

In 1541, Luther added to the final verses of the book (Dan 11:36–12:13) an additional explanation of the signs of the end.

> As for myself, however, I am satisfied that the Last Day must be at the door. For the signs that Christ and the Apostles Peter and Paul proclaimed are almost all come to pass. And the trees are budding, Scripture is greening and blooming. Whether we can know the exact day is irrelevant ... it is certainly all at an end. Therefore we also see here that in Daniel all the visions and dreams, no matter how dreadful they are, always end with joy, that is, with Christ's kingdom and future.[37]

For Luther, the "Last Day" had a universal eschatological significance, since amidst the ending of the world it manifests the new beginning, the resurrection of the dead and the establishment of the kingdom of God. Herein lies the basis for his deep

---

34  Martin Luther, *Auslegung des Vaterunsers* (München: Siebenstern, 1965), 33f., 38.
35  Cf. Bornkamm, *Luthers Vorreden zur Bibel*, 123.
36  Staehelin, *Die Verkündigung des Reiches Gottes*, 4:56f.
37  Bornkamm, *Luthers Vorreden zur Bibel*, 121–122, 125.

longing, "Come, dear Last Day!" From this perspective Luther gained the strength for his daily fight of faith.[38]

## The "Eschatological" Luther – Summary and Conclusion

The eschatological force of Luther's theology is evident. His urgent expectation of the "Last Day" makes him a true "Adventist" believer. Tragically, his strong endtime orientation has been lost by many modern Protestant churches after five hundred years since the Reformation event.

In summary, Luther rejected a golden age on earth and believed in the imminent return of Christ. Thus, he joyfully longed for the day when Christ would put an end to all corruption, wickedness, strife and death. He saw the fate of the world fulfilled in Christ's eternal kingdom. To him, Bible prophecy and the signs of the times served as an orientation and preparation for the dawning of the Last Day. In his eschatological conviction that the world had reached its final stage, Luther saw humanity in his time engaged in a great battle between divine and demonic forces. The wickedness of the world would become unbearable, were it not for the fact that God would "strike vigorously" and thus remain victorious over evil and sin. Therefore, the final verdict, terrifying as it would be for many, was for Luther a joyful prospect more than it was a fearsome one. His apocalyptic hope culminated in the Christ triumphant. God's Kingdom would come at last and the true followers of Christ would be fully rehabilitated.

It is surprising that Seventh-day Adventists have not given more attention to Luther's eschatology so far, even though they like to see themselves as heirs of the Reformation. Of course, the role of Luther as church Reformer is held in high esteem by Adventists, especially by Ellen G. White. It seems, however, that Adventists have focused more on the Reformer's historical battle against Rome and his theological interpretation of the pope as Antichrist, without giving enough attention to his eschatological worldview as a whole. Have we fully grasped what it meant when Luther reinterpreted his eschatological worldview, which had been determined by medieval fear and anger, in the light of his fundamental experience of justification by faith? It was the deep existential experience of being lost without God's forgiving grace that led Luther to the rediscovery of the assurance of salvation *hic et nunc* – here and now. This turning point in his theological development opened his eyes for a reevaluation of biblical eschatology in the sense of the future as a redemptive and liberating process of God acting in history. In Luther's own words: "*Zukunft ist Erlösung* – future is redemption."[39]

---

38   LW 50:220 (Letter 292 To Mrs. Martin Luther, July 16, 1540). Original in WA BR 9, 175. The exact wording of Luther is "Come, Day. Amen!" In order to clarify Luther's intention, "dear last" has been added by the editors. Cf. Hans-Martin Barth, *The Theology of Martin Luther* (Minneapolis: Fortress Press 2013), 397.
39   Cf. WA 10 I, 2, 110f.

Thus for Luther, "future" became increasingly a synonym for "salvation". The "Here and Now" – the present individual assurance of salvation – will ultimately experience full restoration at the end of time. Consequently, assurance of salvation reaches into eternity. Luther did not teach universal salvation, but he linked the forgiving presence of God with His eschatological consummation at the return of Christ. This transformation, based on the joyous experience of salvation assurance, and the urgent and hopeful awaiting of Christ's soon-coming kingdom, created a new understanding of the salvific work of God in history. Under Luther's apocalyptic lens, history turns into a redemptive, "liberated" history, a "long winter" of captivity into a joyful "summer" of divine deliverance, "a summer that will never end."[40]

---

40   WA 34 II, 481.

*Jón Hjörleifur Stefánsson*

# Luther's Antichrist and His Reception by Seventh-day Adventists

Abstract

The Antichrist looms large in the apocalypticism of both Luther and Seventh-day Adventists. Luther's belief that the church was apostate led him to conclude that the long-awaited Antichrist had already come centuries ago, being none other than the pope himself. Adventists inherited this Protestant view of the papacy but adapted it to their own time and theology. Whereas Luther clashed with the pope in the present over authority and salvation, Adventists believe the same issues will lead to their own clash with the pope in the future, but with the new focal point of the seventh-day Sabbath.

The prophetic tenet of the papal Antichrist was popularized by Martin Luther and for the ensuing centuries became part and parcel of Protestant apocalypticism. Three centuries later, the Seventh-day Adventists[1] were among those who continued this identification of the end-time nemesis. Yet apocalyptic prophecy was not the only source for this doctrine. Theology, history, and prophecy interacted and brought to view Antichrist's entire career as it was portrayed in the apocalyptic texts. When compared to Luther's description of him, it can be seen that Adventists' portrait of the enemy is not an unchanged photo from the inherited Reformation family album. To both Luther and the Adventists, the papal Antichrist is their ultimate and greatest opponent. But a comparison of how Luther and Adventists viewed this enemy in the light of theology, history, and prophecy, shows him to be similar where they agree, and a foe different where they do not.[2]

1   Hereafter (almost always) Adventists.
2   In this essay, I limit myself to *Luther's Works,* American Edition, 55 vols., edited by Jaroslav Pelikan and Helmut T. Lehman (Philadelphia: Muehlenberg Press and Fortress Press; and St. Louis: Concordia, 1955–1986), from now on LW. This leaves out a wealth of material, both in German and Latin, as well as Luther's exposition of Daniel 8 in his answer to Ambrosius Catharinus. The most recent English translation is *The Pope Confounded and His Kingdom Exposed, in a Divine Opening of Daniel VIII.23–25,* transl. Henry Cole (London: James Nisbet, 1836). Denis Kaiser has written a helpful paper on this work entitled "Offenbarung des Endchrists aus dem Propheten Daniel (1524). Martin Luther and Seventh-day Adventists on Daniel 8: Approach and Interpretation" (term paper, Andrews University, 2008), Center for Adventist Research, James White Library, Andrews University, Berrien Springs, MI.
    Adventists have produced much literature on apocalyptic prophecy; I can only convey a fraction of it. But if Zipf's Law holds true, it should not be too detrimental that I limit myself to few influential and representative works. The third delimitation is to Adventist reception rather than perception of Luther's Antichrist. For Adventist academic research on

## Luther's Antichrist

In the late medieval period, the idea of Antichrist was an accepted tenet of eschatology in Christianity, and his coming was expected. Antichrist would be the final enemy of the church, arising to power shortly before the return of Christ. His arrival would constitute a clear sign of the end times. The Antichrist would not only be the final foe of the church, he would be its greatest.[3] This wicked man would rise to power through deception on the one hand and scheming and war on the other. He would present himself as the Messiah, and false miracles would be wrought to lead Jews and Christians to worship him. All dissenters would face fierce persecution. Theology had traditionally seen temptation as coming from the Devil, the world, and oneself ("the flesh"). The reign of Antichrist – as befits the apocalyptic climax of evil – would be a snare woven out of all three strands. Being specially guided by Satan, the Antichrist would offer the kingdom of this world to the saints if they would only worship him. Validated by signs and wonders as the true worship of God, and finding resonance with the flesh, this crowning temptation of the Devil would be nearly irresistible. If it were possible, it would deceive the very elect.

The scriptural marrow for this belief was the apocalyptic writings of Scripture, such as Daniel, the Olivet Discourse, 2 Thessalonians, and Revelation. Taking cues from many other scriptures, the acts of the Antichrist were developed further by adding details about his life, such as his birth in Babylon and lineage of the tribe of Dan. Taken at face value, such a remarkable life quenched all attempts at identifying the Antichrist – no one in the medieval period fit these criteria and thus could not be the Antichrist. But another line of interpretation ignored most of these details. Instead, it suspected that the Antichrist would arise from within the church, and saw the way being paved for his arrival by the heretics and the ungodly. If he was to seek to deceive and lord it over Christendom, and since the pope was the head of the church, ascending the seat of Peter would be the perfect hiding in plain sight by the master deceiver. Thus the belief arose that the Antichrist would be an antipope, a usurper of the Holy See. Some even pointed to certain popes as being the Antichrist.[4]

---

Luther's Antichrist, see Leif Kr. Tobiassen, "An Investigation into the Evolution of Martin Luther's Views Concerning Antichrist" (MA thesis, Seventh-day Adventist Theological Seminary, 1948); William M. Landeen, "Martin Luther on the Antichrist," in *The Stature of Christ: Essays in Honor of Edward Heppenstall* (Loma Linda, CA: Privately published, 1970), 127–135; Winfried Vogel, "The Eschatological Theology of Martin Luther. Part I: Luther's Basic Concepts," *Andrews University Seminary Studies* 24, no. 3 (1986): 249–264; idem, "The Eschatological Theology of Martin Luther. Part I: Luther's Exposition of Daniel and Revelation," *Andrews University Seminary Studies* 25, no. 2 (1987): 183–199.

3  For the medieval interpretation of the Antichrist, see Richard Kenneth Emmerson, *Antichrist in the Middle Ages: A Study of Medieval Apocalypticism, Art, and Literature* (Seattle: University of Washington Press, 1981), 74–107.

4  This interpretation started before AD 1000 and included expositors such as Joachim of Fiore, the Spirituals and Fraticelli, and others until the 15$^{th}$ century, when Wycliffe began the new

## In Theology

Luther's earliest writings show little concern for the Antichrist.[5] What preoccupied the young monk were not future apocalyptic temptations, but his present *Anfechtungen*, the great distress caused by being immersed in the religious life while still being unable to grasp the hand of God. But then Luther found peace in Christ. And as his evangelical theology grew clearer, and the church's resistance to it stronger, this lack of concern changed.[6] Wherever Luther looked, he saw forms of things Christian but without the right shape or essence. It was as if a strangling fig of human traditions had overgrown the original tree and nearly choked it.[7] The Church was not only formal and corrupt, it had apostatized from the gospel.[8]

The late medieval understanding of Matthew 24:15 and 2 Thessalonians 2 warned Christians that Antichrist might rise from within the church and with this Luther agreed.[9] But whereas some thought the Antichrist might usurp the papal throne, Luther's theology pushed him further. A future pope, no matter how heretical, could scarcely add to the damage,[10] for the apostasy crystallized in the office and claims of the Papal See itself. The Antichrist was already tyrannizing and deceiving

---

trend of equating Antichrist not with a papal usurper, but any sitting pope, i.e., the papacy itself. See Bernard McGinn, *Antichrist: Two Thousand Years of the Human Fascination with Evil* (New York, NY: Columbia University Press, 2000), 142–181.

5  See for instance LW 10:114, 244, 282, 449; 11:476, 551 (1513–1514). During these years Luther applied some of the antichrist texts to heretics (or, sometimes, to bad Christians) and the Turks. LW 10:437–438; 11:100, 235, 279 (1513–1514). Luther emphasized that the reason why Antichrist could attack the church was that she was spiritually apathetic and Laodicean. LW 10:351–356. Luther's opinion of her spirituality was not high: "The church was hardly ever in worse condition." LW 10:358 (1513–1514).

6  For the connection between Luther's evangelical theology and his views on the papal Antichrist, see Scott H. Hendrix, *Luther and the Papacy: Stages in a Reformation Conflict* (Philadelphia, PA: Fortress Press, 1981).

7  While distorted and obscured, Luther believed that the Bible and its religion had survived in the midst of the apostasy. LW 40:231–234 (1528); 35:201 (1530); 22:102 (1537–1538). During the Reformation they were then restored to their original form and meaning. LW 24:368 (1537).

8  In one of the many instances where Luther described the apostasy from the original gospel, he wrote: "There are still more innovations, like purgatory, relics, consecration of churches, swarms of decrees and decretals, and many more countless books full of vain, new inventions, of which neither the ancient church nor the apostles knew anything … In this matter it is enough for the present to demonstrate how shamefully the papists lie … when they call us the new, apostate, heretical church … They have abandoned the ancient church and its ancient bridegroom and have not only become apostate and heretical … but Antichrist and 'antigod'." LW 41:205 (1541).

9  LW 31:393 (1520); 36:72 (1520); 28:373 (1528); 40:231–234 (1528); 46:180 (1529); 26:24, 257 (1535); 54:101 (1533); 3:122–123 (1535–1538); 22:470 (1538–1540); 41:209 (1541); 41:339 (1545).

10  LW 31:336–337 (1520); 31:393 (1520).

Christians under the guise of being their true head and shepherd. The Antichrist was not a single pope, he was *the Pope*. This meant that the apostle's warning did not apply to a single heretical tyrant, but marked out the centuries of the papacy.[11]

In his treatment of the papal Antichrist, Luther dwelt primarily on how he had exalted himself above God, both by demanding things that belonged to God alone and by opposing him (Dan 11:37; 2 Thess 2:4). This exaltation constituted Antichrist's tyranny and deception and had many facets: The papacy had exalted its laws above God's law, thus making it a greater sin to disobey the pope than Christ.[12] It taught that the requirement for salvation was good works (often defined as obeying canon law) instead of faith in Christ.[13] It was rightly called "Man of Sin" for it taught sin where there was no sin, and no sin where there was sin.[14] The papacy sat in judgment over the Bible, either contradicting it or misinterpreting it by its traditions and laws.[15] Thus the gospel of the Bible was not taught,[16] and instead of being liberated by the good news, the conscience was subjugated to the tyranny of the hierarchy.[17] Instead of leading people to worship God, the papacy had set up a worship of itself.[18] The very office of the papacy was a priesthood "of which Christ and the Scriptures know nothing" that eclipsed the Savior.[19] Instead of Christ's holy example, the lives of the Antichrist and his court were deeply corrupt.[20] And all opposition and dissidents, whether kings, heretics, or true worshipers of God,

---

11 Luther rejected both the contemporary understanding of the Antichrist as well as most of the contemporary textual support for the Antichrist. LW 20:127, 130, 320, 337 (1524–1527); 8:282–284 (1543–1545). Yet identifying the Holy See as the seat of Antichrist was not a novelty begun by Luther, but a further development of the antipope Antichrist interpretation that had started with Wycliffe. See Emmerson, *Antichrist*, 181. The claim that Luther first identified a single pope as the Antichrist is groundless and contradicts everything that Luther wrote about the papal Antichrist. For instance, when Luther wondered whether the pope was the Antichrist or not during his preparation for the Leipzig debate, this suspicion was born from reviewing papal decretals issued by many various popes. Thus, what he had in mind was the pope as the head of the church, not as a single ruling individual.
12 LW 36:72 (1520); 52:21 (1522); 20:264 (1524–1527); 30:288 (1528); 37:367 (1528); 40:330 (1530); 26:385–386, 408 (1535); 38:190 (1533); 3:121 (1535–1538); 22:67 (1537–1538); 24:355 (1537); 34:237 (1538).
13 LW 36:83 (1520); 20:264 (1524–1527); 30:314 (1528); 40:330 (1530); 26:180, 408 (1535); 47:53–54 (1531); 38:190 (1533); 22:67 (1537–1538); 24:308 (1537); 8:185 (1543–1545).
14 LW 31:392 (1520); 32:63 (1521); 30:107 (1523); 40:348–349 (1530); 27:110 (1535); 41:339 (1545).
15 LW 32:71 (1521); 52:21 (1522); 30:99 (1523); 39:307 (1523); 38:174–175, 190 (1533); 13:330 (1534–1535); 24:308 (1537); 34:237 (1538); 22:470 (1538–1540).
16 LW 52:21 (1522); 38:190 (1533); 22:67 (1537–1538).
17 LW 29:42 (1527); 26:385–386, 408 (1535); 27:110 (1535).
18 LW 9:67 (1523–1524); 20:264 (1524–1527); 30:288 (1528); 41:339 (1545).
19 LW 13:330 (1534–1535).
20 LW 47:40 (1531).

the papacy met with ruthless and unreasoning wrath and persecution.[21] The terrible net result was that massive numbers of souls were going to perdition for Antichrist had led them away from their Savior, while they still believed they were Christians.[22] All of this was included in the Antichrist's tyrannical and deceitful exaltation above God, and sitting in the temple as if he were God.

Other prophetic identifying markers of the Antichrist highlighted some of the papacy's theological atrocities. Antichrist's gathering of treasures (Dan 11:38, 43) referred to the papacy's opulence and unjust amassing of wealth.[23] The papacy's enforced celibacy for clergy (and unjust marriage rules for laity) were intended both when Daniel said the Antichrist would fail to "regard the love of women, that is, the estate of marriage" (Dan 11:37) and when the apostle warned that the latter-day apostasy would include "forbidding marriage" (1 Tim 4:3).[24] The ecclesiastical regulations for when the consumption of certain food items was allowed lay behind Paul's further warning that the false teaching would include abstinence from lawful foods.[25] And finally, the papal mass was depicted when Daniel said Antichrist would opulently worship Maozim, a god unknown to his Christian forefathers, and that those in charge of this worship would distribute the lands and their wealth (Dan 11:38–39).[26]

What marked the papacy as apostate to Luther was its opposition to true Christianity, which Luther believed the evangelical teaching had restored. The clearest way to identify the Antichrist was therefore by comparing his gospel to the gospel of Christ. Then people would be able to say:

> 'Thus Christ spoke and did. But the pope teaches and does the very opposite. Christ says yes. But the pope says no. Now because they are at loggerheads, one of them must surely be lying. Now Christ surely does not lie. Therefore I conclude that the pope is a liar, and, in addition, is the real Antichrist.' Thus you must be so well armed with Scripture that you not only can call the pope an antichrist but know how to give clear proof of this, that you can confidently stake your life on this and prevail against the devil when you die.[27]

The gospel did not only identify the Antichrist, it was also the only way to withstand him successfully. While the Antichrist was the pope, the unlawful head of

21  LW 31:393 (1520); 39:84 (1520); 52:6 (1522); 46:180 (1529); 23:212 (1530–1532); 27:110 (1535); 24:308 (1537).
22  LW 31:375 (1520); 36:72 (1520); 52:137 (1522); 13:282 (1534–1535); 22:61 (1537–1538); 41:339 (1545).
23  LW 39:60 (1520); 45:289 (1524); 35:306 (1530).
24  LW 31:391 (1520); 36:98, 102 (1520); 39:84 (1520); 39:210, 212 (1521); 51:80 (1522); 30:107 (1523); 28:339 (1528); 34:40–41 (1530); 45:144 (1530); 35:313 (1530); 38:232–233 (1534).
25  LW 39:84 (1520).
26  LW 38:232–233 (1534).
27  LW 30:138 (1523); see also LW 36:157–158 (1521); 52:247–248 (1522); 26:258–259 (1535); 38:210–211 (1533).

Christendom, his apostasy had its roots in the human nature common to all. This meant that to fight the Antichrist coincided with the fight against one's own self. Luther acknowledged this when he wrote: "That ambition to be God still inheres in us. We, too, want to be gods, as Paul says to the Thessalonians (2 Thess 2:4) concerning the Antichrist."[28] The war against this tendency had to be waged on the inner and the outer front – against pope and one's own sinful heart – and with the same gospel weapons.

## In History

Luther's study of councils, decretals and canon law – i.e., of the papal past – was a vital factor in his identification of the papal Antichrist.[29] When he denounced the pope as Antichrist, Luther was not merely denouncing the contemporary pope and curia – he was rejecting the system of centuries in its entirety. Once the Antichrist had been identified as ruling within Christendom – the abomination in the holy place and the son of perdition sitting in the temple – the question arose how the Antichrist had ascended the throne.

Luther often wrote on the history of the papacy, but the purpose was to refute its unscriptural and historically inaccurate claims,[30] and therefore he did not write any contiguous "history of the papacy." However, in his last treatise, which contains the most comprehensive treatment of the subject, Luther dated the apostasy back to the sixth century. He counted St. Gregory as the last Roman bishop, for he had been content with his local bishopric and had refused the title "universal bishop." After him came Sabinian, whom Luther regarded as pope for having wanted to burn Gregory's books, and then Boniface III, who persuaded the emperor to make him "pope, or chief of all the bishops in the whole world."[31]

The prophecies had situated the Antichrist roughly in time and space by placing his rule after the fall of the Roman Empire[32] and within Christianity[33]

---

28  LW 17:19 (1527). Other similar statements are also illuminating: "Paul and the other apostles did not dwell on and denounce any sin more vehemently than the contempt of grace and the denial of Christ. Yet we commit this sin so very easily. This is why especially Paul inveighs so severely against Antichrist, because he abolishes grace and denies the blessing of Christ" and "has established the doctrine of works and the kingdom of ceremonies." LW 26:179–180 (1535). "I am more afraid of my own heart than of the pope and all his cardinals. I have within me that great pope self." Quoted in *Signs of the Times*, January 1, 1931, 7.
29  While Luther was studying canon law in preparation for the Leipzig debate with Dr. Eck, he wrote in a letter to his friend Spalatin: "Confidentially, I do not know whether the pope is the Antichrist himself or whether he is his apostle, so miserably is Christ (that is, truth) corrupted and crucified by the pope in the decretals." LW 48:113 (1519).
30  Among those were the claims that Matt 16:13–19 and John 21:15–17 demonstrated Peter's primacy over the church.
31  LW 41:291–292 (1545).
32  LW 20:192 (1524–1527); 35:387 (1546 [1522]).

(according to Daniel's four kingdoms, Matt 24, and 2 Thess 2). But apart from identifying the Antichrist, Luther did not see many details of the papal past embedded in the prophecies. 1 John 2 and 4 showed that the future apostasy was already present in embryo in the heresies of the apostolic age,[34] that false wonders that would deceive Christendom had been fulfilled by the miracle-filled history of the saints (Matt 24:24; 2 Thess 2:9–10),[35] and the reign of the papacy was the great tribulation preceding the Last Day (Dan 12:1; 2 Thess 2:9–10).[36] These are historical elements which are only loosely connected. The closest to an overarching history would be the seven trumpets of Revelation (Rev 7–13),[37] but though Luther explained them as the history of succeeding heresies culminating in the papacy, these heresies were miscellaneous, and did not constitute a continuum. Nor was any such detailed prophetic historical overview necessary to Luther. The apostles had predicted that the apostasy had begun as "the spirit of the Antichrist" in their day and that it would grow until it would find its final expression in the Antichrist himself.[38] Having identified the papacy as the Antichrist, the records of its past were open for all to study how the son of perdition had taken his seat in the temple of God.

Luther understood history in general within the apocalyptic framework of the conflict between good and evil.[39] Church history could be read against the backdrop of Satan's war against the church. In the early centuries, he had sought to conquer her by persecution; when that did not work he resorted to compromise.[40] But where Christ had resisted the crowning temptation by refusing the kingdoms of this world, the church had failed. Having explained that the triple tiara signifies "the world's empire," Luther wrote: "This is the crown the devil offered our Lord, Matthew 4, when he led him up the high mountain and showed him all the kingdoms of the world and their splendor, and said, 'All these I will give you, if you

---

33  LW 21:63 (1530–1532); 38:210–211 (1533); 35:387 (1546 [1522]).
34  LW 30:149 (1523–1524); 30:251–254, 284–288 (1528); 22:67 (1537–1538); 35:393 (1546 [1522]).
35  LW 17:118 (1527); 21:271–272 (1530–1532); 24:75, 368–369 (1537–1538); 35:387 (1546 [1522]). Earlier Luther emphasized the working of the Wicked One through lies rather than miracles. See LW 39:134 (1520); 32:64 (1521); 41:339 (1545).
36  LW 41:210 (1541).
37  LW 35:402–407 (1546 [1530]). According to Luther, the angel in chapter 10 was the angel of the sixth trumpet, and chapter 13 depicted the woe of the seventh trumpet.
38  "John confirms this public statement of the church, namely, that the Antichrist will rule. Although he already sees his spirit, he predicts that the true Antichrist himself will come. Indeed, he had already come with the first fruits of his spirit. But the kingdom of the pope, which is nothing else than the kingdom of unrighteousness, grew gradually until the pope exalted himself above the kingdom of Christ." LW 30:288 (1528).
39  Hence the title of Heiko Oberman's biography: *Luther: Man between God and the Devil*, transl. Eileen Walliser-Schwarzbart (New York, NY: Image Books, 1992).
40  LW 40:49 (1524).

will fall down and worship me.' But the Lord said to him, 'Begone, Satan!' But what does the pope say? 'Come here, Satan!'"[41]

An important point to note here is that Luther did not believe that the apostasy had to have happened. Nor was it preordained to continue.[42] Luther simply believed that the apostasy was so pervasive that reformation would never happen.[43] And this, in turn, shaped Luther's outlook on the future of the Antichrist.

## In the Future

Since Antichrist would reign in the end time, and had now been identified as having ruled already for centuries, Luther believed that history was at sunset.[44] So what did he think of Antichrist's future? As has been noted, Luther had no hope of the papacy being reformed. His lifelong struggle against it continually strengthened this conviction. And while Luther had seen the gospel advance, not all who denounced the papacy accepted the Reformation.[45] Luther's apocalyptic was the future prolongation of his contemporary realities mingled with the hope God would intervene at last: The Antichrist would continue[46] to decay until Christ would utterly destroy him at the Last Day.

Luther stated that Jan Hus and later the Reformation had exposed the papal Antichrist for what he was and this had begun his decay.[47] This partial victory had not been gained by armed resistance but by prayer and preaching of the truth. This was in harmony with Scripture (Isa 11:4; Dan 8:25; 2 Thess 2:8a) that stated that the Lord would consume his foe "with the spirit of his mouth," that is, the gospel. Luther urged that this was the biblically sanctioned way to wage war against the

---

41  LW 41:334 (1545).
42  "If the example of St. Augustine," who was "the first and almost the only one who determined to be subject to the Holy Scriptures alone," "had been followed, the pope would not have become Antichrist, and that countless mass of books, which is like a crawling swarm of vermin, would not have found its way into the church, and the Bible would have remained on the pulpit." LW 34:285 (1539). See also LW 36:72 (1520).
43  LW 31:336–337 (1520).
44  LW 36:158, 219 (1521); 32:141, 147 (1521); 48:215 (1521); 40:49 (1524); 35:306 (1530); 24:367 (1537); 34:240 (1538); 41:205 (1541).
45  This was also prophetic. An old book about the Antichrist taught that "before the Last Day [people] will fall into such errors that they will deny the existence of God and ridicule everything that is preached about Christ and the Last Day. This is true, no matter what its source may be." LW 30:192–193 (1523–1524). And again: "Now is the time which was predicted to come after the fall of Antichrist, when people will be epicureans and atheists, so that the word of Christ might be fulfilled: 'As it was in the days of Noah and Lot, so will it be on the day of the arrival of the Son of man.'" LW 50:243–244 (1543).
46  Luther believed that the texts that foretold the rise of Antichrist within the church also meant that he would stay there until the Last Day. LW 40:231–234 (1528); 38:210–211 (1533).
47  LW 45:359 (1524); 13:417 (1526); 22:470 (1538–1540).

Antichrist, and stated that this process would continue until little of the papacy would remain.[48] Yet since Antichrist would remain within the temple of Christendom till the end, it was necessary that in opposing him one tear down only his accretions and not the temple itself.[49] Luther hoped that the Antichrist's decline could be hastened by gospel work and often expressed his wish that the Last Day would come soon.[50] The ultimate demise of the Antichrist, as his decline, was reserved to God. On the Last Day, he would be broken without any human agency (Dan 8:25) for Jesus would return and destroy him with the brightness of his appearance (2 Thess 2:8b).[51]

Luther's entire theological enterprise can be seen as apocalyptic when set in the framework of his defense of the true gospel against the papal Antichrist, the last-day foe of the church. Yet that struggle remained the Reformer's present – not future – focus all his life, and can thus also be seen as the delimitation of his apocalyptic. Luther's interest in the future eschatological aspects of the Antichrist did not find enough of his time and ink to advance beyond the broad strokes.

## Adventists' Antichrist

The Seventh-day Adventists established their church in the United States in 1863, and, as a Protestant denomination, they claimed Luther's Reformation against the papal Antichrist as their historical heritage and ongoing role.[52] Yet Adventists were

48 LW 36:219 (1521); 39:279 (1522); 45:59–61 (1522); 40:58 (1524); 26:86, 223, 383 (1535); 35:351 (1533); 34:240 (1538); 35:387 (1546 [1522]).
49 LW 40:231–234 (1528).
50 LW 39:202–203 (1521); 49:13 (1522); 46:181 (1529); 26:86, 383 (1535); 35:352 (1533); 13:188 (1534–1535); 22:61 (1537–1538). One of the strongest examples of the possibility of hastening the end is when Luther wrote: "Now when the papal villainy has been thus exposed and the breath of Christ's mouth prevails, so that men no longer esteem but despise the pope and his lies, then the Last Day will break in and, as Paul says [II Thess. 2:8], Christ will utterly destroy the pope by His coming." LW 45:60 (1522).
51 "These texts have convinced me that the papacy and the clerical estate will not be destroyed by the hand of men, or by insurrection." LW 45:61 (1522). See also LW 31:392 (1520); 36:219 (1521); 39:202–203 (1521); 39:278–279 (1522); 45:59–62 (1522); 49:13 (1522); 26:383 (1535); 13:258 (1534–1535); 24:367, 371 (1537); 35:387 (1546 [1522]); 41:273 (1545).
Despite this conviction, Luther sometimes wondered whether human agency would inflict some future damage on the Antichrist. Once he noted that according to an old prophecy, once the Antichrist had been exposed, people would turn liberty to licentiousness, and would (in harmony with Rev 17:16) turn on the papacy. LW 13:190 (1534–1535). Again, he wrote: God "will find someone to ruin both the Turk and the pope with his tyrants. Or else, reaching down from heaven, He will finish them Himself." LW 13:258 (1534–1535).
52 The *Great Controversy* by Ellen G. White, one of the founders of Adventism, is the classic Adventist understanding of church history. Its more Lutheresque title could have been the *Tale of the Two Churches*, with the false church being the papacy, and the true church faithful believers throughout the centuries, Luther being a key figure for his time, and the

separated from both Luther and the papacy in several ways, for between them lay three centuries and the Atlantic Ocean. As an American church, Adventists could for the most part only read English and not much of Luther had been translated. Until the twentieth century – when a large American edition of Luther's works started to be published[53] – their understanding of Luther and his opposition to the papacy was mostly informed secondhand by Protestant writings in English.[54] And as an American church, Adventists lived mostly in a Protestant country. Their direct contact with the papacy was non-existent, let alone a conflict between the two, whereas Luther had lived in Catholic Europe and had struggled directly with the then mighty papacy.

Protestant expositors of prophecy had also had to explain three centuries more of history than Luther and had worked untiringly on filling out the apocalyptic canvas of the Reformer in much greater detail.[55] For instance, many of them had tried to demarcate the Antichrist's career by situating papal supremacy within the apocalyptic epoch of the 1260 years. In the early nineteenth century, a common terminus of the 1260 years was 1798, the year when Napoleon's army had invaded Italy and dissolved the papacy.[56] Among those who accepted this year into their eschatology were the Millerites.[57] Since the Antichrist had declined until his formal reign had ended, his destruction must be imminent. In tandem with this fact, the Millerites believed that Jesus would return in 1844 (soon after 1798), the year when all the prophetic lines would meet and end. When that did not happen, some Millerites – those who eventually became the Seventh-day Adventists – realigned and extended their prophetic interpretation to cover the unsuspected blank time from 1844 to the eventual return of Jesus. And in this extension Antichrist made his re-appearance.

---

Adventists his end-time counterparts. On Luther's Reformation, White stated in this work: "The Reformation did not, as many suppose, end with Luther. It is to be continued to the close of this world's history." Ellen G. White, *The Great Controversy between Christ and Satan: The Conflict of the Ages in the Christian Dispensation*, rev. ed. (Mountain View, CA: Pacific Press, 1911), 148.

53  See above, note 2.

54  Reinder Bruinsma, *Seventh-day Adventist Attitudes toward Roman Catholicism 1844–1965* (Berrien Springs, MI: Andrews University Press, 1994), 159–160, 297.

55  Over the last few decades, interest in the history of apocalypticism (or prophetic interpretation in Adventist terminology) has been growing. There are many scholarly books that focus either on certain expositor(s) or time periods. For emphasis on those prophetic strands that continued from Luther to Adventism, see LeRoy Edwin Froom, *The Prophetic Faith of Our Fathers: The Historical Development of Prophetic Interpretation*, 4 vols. (Washington, DC: Review and Herald, 1946–1954), 2:241–4:1173.

56  Froom, *Prophetic Faith of Our Fathers*, 2:765–782; Bruinsma, *Adventist Attitudes toward Catholicism*, 13–14.

57  Damsteegt, P. Gerard. *Foundations of the Seventh-day Adventist Message and Mission* (Grand Rapids, MI: Eerdmans, 1977), 21–25. For the role of the papacy and the Catholic Church in Millerite prophetic interpretation, see Bruinsma, *Adventist Attitudes toward Catholicism*, 45–63.

## In Theology

The first two main differences one notices between Luther's prophetic interpretation of the papal Antichrist and that of Adventists are that the latter emphasized other apocalyptic texts and tenses of the Antichrist's career. Luther's most frequently used Antichrist scriptures were Daniel 8:25, Daniel 11, Matthew 24:15, and 2 Thessalonians 2. Adventists preferred Dan 7 and Rev 13 and did not apply some of Luther's key texts to the papacy.[58] This variance in textual preference reflects both a different understanding of the prophecies as well as new concerns about the Antichrist. Luther had discovered what the Antichrist *was* doing – Adventists discovered what he *would* do.

Adventists believed that Providence had allowed the mistaken expectation of Christ's return in 1844 as a test to awaken Protestants out of their backslidings so that they would finish the Reformation and be fully prepared to meet their Lord. By rejecting this wake-up call, Protestants showed that they had no desire for further reformation and hardened their worldliness into apostasy.[59] The faithful Protestant remnant who awaited the Last Day discovered that on this disappointing date Christ had begun the last phase of his intercession before his – still imminent – return. During this intercession, the believers were to renounce the last vestiges of papal errors, preach the fully restored gospel to the world, and thus complete the Reformation initiated by Luther.[60] Looking into the late night sky, Adventists configured all these new truths into an apocalyptic constellation, with the Sabbath one magnitude brighter than the other stars.

As Adventists accepted the seventh-day Sabbath as the biblical interpretation of the fourth commandment, they investigated how this truth had been abandoned by Christians. Their study of history led them to conclude that Sunday-keeping was a pagan tradition that the papal Antichrist had enshrined into Christian belief.

---

58  Adventists understood "the abomination of desolation" in Matthew 24 as referring to the Roman armies surrounding Jerusalem in the first century. See, for instance, White, *Great Controversy*, 25–26. On Dan 11:36–45, Adventists held conflicting views, and in the one popularized by Uriah Smith, the papacy did not feature at all. Jón Hjörleifur Stefánsson, "Approaching Armageddon: The Fall of the Ottoman Empire in Adventist Eschatology, 1833–1922" in Rolf J. Pöhler, ed., *The Impact of World War I on Seventh-day Adventism: Prophetic Disconfirmation and Conscientious Cooperation,* Adventistica: Studies in Adventist History and Theology, New Series, vol. 2 (Friedensau, Germany: Theologische Hochschule Friedensau, 2018) – forthcoming; Uriah Smith, *Daniel and the Revelation* (Battle Creek, MI: Review and Herald, 1897), 264–292.
59  Ellen G. White, *Great Controversy*, 297–298, 311, 379–390.
60  "Said my accompanying angel, They are again disappointed in their expectations. Jesus cannot yet come to earth. They must yet suffer for Jesus and endure greater trials. They must give up errors and traditions received from men, and turn wholly to God and his word." "…that they might divest themselves of errors which have been handed down from the heathen and papists." "When this work shall have been accomplished, the followers of Christ will be ready for his appearing." Ellen G. White, *Spiritual Gifts*, vol. 1 (Battle Creek, MI: James White, 1858), 146, 155; *Great Controversy*, 425.

Therefore it was not a biblical teaching as commonly believed by Protestants, but a Catholic dogma. This heretofore unrealized aspect of the apostasy was encoded in the prophecies. The little horn's attempt to change times and laws (Dan 7:25) was seen as the papacy's change of the fourth commandment by declaring Sunday the Sabbath instead of Saturday. The presumption of the Roman Church to change the divine law was also what the apostle had in mind when he stated that the Antichrist would exalt himself above God (2 Thess 2). This change was more than a dogma. It was the seal of Catholic authority, challenging God's rightful authority (Rev 13:16–17)[61] as prescribed in the Decalogue and sealed by the fourth commandment. These conflicting expressions of authority would be at the heart of the final, future conflict with the Antichrist. All in all, this meant that what was involved in which day to keep holy was the weighty matters of whether one would follow the Bible or tradition, obey divine or human law, and be free in faith in Christ or submit to the tyranny of the Antichrist. At stake were the very issues raised by the Reformation.

Ellen G. White, one of the founders of the Adventist Church, also agreed with Luther on the affinity of the enemy without and the enemy within. Commenting on the principles of the hierarchy in Christ's day, she wrote that they were "characteristic of humanity in all ages" for "the spirit of Phariseeism is the spirit of human nature."[62] In a similar vein she likened at times both the papacy and Adventists to the Pharisees: "The popery is the religion of human nature," resembling the Pharisees "in superstition and formality," and the Adventists were in danger of being "Laodiceans," manifesting "hollow formalism, and Pharisaic pride."[63] This meant that Adventists were in danger of harboring the essence of Antichrist in their heart while outwardly denouncing him.

Thus Adventists agreed with Luther's reasons for denouncing the papacy as the Antichrist, while they simultaneously disagreed with the Reformer, for he had not gone far enough. This might explain why Adventists investigated Catholic theology so selectively.[64] They chose to focus on those aspects of the Antichrist's teachings

---

61 On the Sabbath change coded in Dan 7 and Rev 13, see Smith, *Daniel and Revelation*, 550–559; White, *Great Controversy*, 51–54, 446–450. On Dan 7 and 2 Thess 2, White writes: "An intentional, deliberate change is brought to view: 'He shall *think* to change times and laws.' The change in the fourth commandment exactly fulfills the prophecy. For this change the only authority claimed is that of the church. Here the papal power openly sets itself above God." "Those who were tampering with the divine law were not ignorant of the character of their work. They were deliberately setting themselves above God." *Spirit of Prophecy*, vol. 4 (Oakland, CA: Pacific Press, 1884), 279–280; 395.

62 Ellen G. White, *Thoughts from the Mount of Blessing* (Mountain View, CA: Pacific Press, 1896), 79.

63 Ibid., "Romanism the Religion of Human Nature," *Signs of the Times*, February 19, 1894, 8; *Spiritual Gifts*, vol. 3 (Steam Press of the Seventh-day Adventist Pub. Assn., 1864), 44; "'Hold Fast, and Repent,'" *Advent Review and Sabbath Herald*, November 2, 1886, 1.

64 During the period 1863–1915, "there was hardly any systematic treatment of Catholic doctrine and theology in Adventist publications, and likewise there was no methodical way of commenting on issues in the Catholic Church in general and in the American Catholic

which Protestants still harbored – mostly Sunday-keeping – and saw little need in studying the Catholic teachings Protestants had already abandoned. To some the aspects of Catholicism that Protestants had abandoned did not matter much, if at all. This becomes clearer when we look at how Adventists saw the past of the Antichrist.

## In History

The first obvious difference between Luther and Adventists' study of the Antichrist's past is the time difference. When Adventists formed their church in the nineteenth century, the papal past had become three centuries longer, with Luther and the Reformation now being a part of it. The two used different sources as well. Luther had been a Catholic monk and theology professor and was therefore well acquainted with Catholic canon law. Adventists used some of the most infamous utterances of the popes, but did not study the primary sources directly as Luther did. Yet another difference was the weight of history. To Luther, the papacy had been a present foe, but while nineteenth-century Adventists (as other Protestants) feared Catholic takeover of America,[65] these fears were based on the growing influence of Catholicism, but not on the pope's actual and present power. Adventists could not turn to the Vatican to see the pope ruling as the tyrannical Antichrist. For that, they had to turn back to history, which they read, like Luther, through the lens of prophecy.[66]

Adventists saw the career of the Antichrist mapped out in much more prophetic detail than Luther had. They saw his history, both religious and political, covered in nearly all the visions of Daniel and Revelation.[67] Some examples must suffice. The apostles had warned of the coming apostasy and stated that it had already begun in their day (1 John 4:3; 2 Thess 2:7). The letters to the seven

---

Church in particular." Bruinsma, *Adventist Attitudes toward Catholicism*, 163. While the study of Catholicism diversified 1915–1965, it still remained largely selective. Ibid., 235, 292. Bruinsma mentions another important reason for Adventist indifference to the study of Catholicism: They believed that "Rome never changes," and that rendered further study pointless. Ibid., 197–199, 201–202, 280–281.

65 Bruinsma, *Adventist Attitudes toward Catholicism*, 166–168.
66 Ibid., 114, 158, 297.
67 Adventist interpretation of the papal Antichrist in the prophecies of Daniel and Revelation has remained strikingly consistent to this day. This can be seen quickly by comparing some of the commentaries published throughout the denomination's history, such as Uriah Smith, *Daniel and Revelation* (last edited by the author in 1897; rev. ed. 1944); Stephen N. Haskell, *The Story of Daniel the Prophet* (Battle Creek, MI: Review and Herald, 1901); idem, *The Story of the Seer of Patmos* (South Lancaster, MA: South Lancaster Printing Company, 1905); C. Mervyn Maxwell, *God Cares*, 2 vols. (Nampa, ID: Pacific Press, 1981/1985); Roy Allan Anderson, *Unfolding Daniel's Prophecies* (Pacific Press, 1975); idem, *Unfolding the Revelation* (Pacific Press, 1953; rev. ed. 1974); Zdravko Stefanovic, *Daniel: Wisdom to the Wise* (Pacific Press, 2007); and Ranko Stefanovic, *Revelation of Jesus Christ: Commentary on the Book of Revelation*, 2nd ed. (Berrien Springs, MI: Andrews University Press, 2009).

churches spelled out the church's faltering steps from its first love (Ephesus) and breasting early persecutions (Smyrna) to its compromise with paganism (Pergamos) and establishment of the false hierarchy (Thyatira). The church's illicit union with the state was foretold by the harlot's adultery with the kings of the earth (Rev 17:2; 18:3, 9). The 1260 years showed the span of papal supremacy. They began in 538, once the three horns of Vandals, Heruli, and Ostrogoths had been uprooted by the Byzantine general Belisarius (Dan 7:8, 24) and Justinian's declaration of papal supremacy went into effect. The church substituted the Roman Empire in the West and thus the beast (papacy) received its power from the Roman dragon (Rev 13:2). The papacy's claims to divine authority were depicted as the blasphemy of the little horn and of the beast (Dan 7:25; Rev 13:5–6); and their war against the saints, as well as the woman drinking the saints' blood, stood for the papacy's medieval persecutions (Dan 7:25; Rev 13:7; 17:6). The deadly wound of the beast marked the terminus of the 1260 years of papal supremacy, when in 1798 he who led into captivity was himself led captive (Rev 13:3, 10).

In their study and presentation of the historical fulfillment of the foretold career of the Antichrist, Adventists focused on the political and chronological aspects of the papacy (though these overlapped with religious matters, such as the issues of church, state, and religious freedom). When it came to the history of the papacy, Adventists focused mostly on the topics of Sunday-keeping, immortality of the soul, papal infallibility, and the pagan roots of Catholicism.[68] Some of Luther's interests – such as justification by faith vs. salvation by works – were often conspicuously missing as independent themes, thus it depended on the author whether these categories of religious and political history served as Adventist jars for Lutheran wine, or whether the drink had any Reformation flavor at all.

Adventists' usage of the papal past also differed from Luther's. Luther used theology to expose the Antichrist, but Adventists did so with history. Reading history and prophecy together became Adventists' prime method of exposing the enemy, though the wording is not as straightforward in recent publications.[69] In fact, Adventists read

68   Bruinsma, *Adventist Attitudes toward Catholicism*, 148–157.
69   In Adventists' official fundamental beliefs, the Antichrist is not mentioned. Art. 13, entitled "The Remnant and Its Mission," only states that "in the last days, a time of widespread apostasy," the remnant will proclaim the message of "the three angels of Revelation 14." *Seventh-day Adventists Believe: A Biblical Exposition of Fundamental Doctrines*, 2nd ed. (Silver Spring, MD: Ministerial Association of the General Conference of Seventh-day Adventists, 2005), 181. That the papal Antichrist is part of this end-time apostasy is clear when one reads the explanations of the Fundamentals (ibid., 182–189, 195–197). Two other examples of this more guarded wording are Stefanovic's commentary on Revelation, which is used at many Adventist university seminaries, and the Andrews Study Bible. On Revelation 13, Stefanovic identifies the beasts sparingly. Once he has marked the first beast as the "Roman papacy," he adds apologetically: "Although such an interpretation seems harsh and unfair in these modern days characterized by ecumenism and religious tolerance, the presence does not erase historical realities" (Stefanovic, *Revelation of Jesus Christ*, 420). The Andrews Study Bible identifies the harlot in Revelation 17 indirectly by its note that she is

their prophetic emphasis back into the Reformation and came to think that it was mainly apocalyptic prophecy that had convinced Luther of who the Antichrist was.[70]

Despite usage of other apocalyptic passages and their different historical emphasis, Luther and Adventists shared the same understanding of the big picture of the Antichrist's past. They agreed that the apostasy had begun in the apostolic age and that it had resulted in the establishment of the papacy in the sixth century. Both believed that the devil was behind the rise of the Antichrist. Unable to stop the church with persecutions, the prince of this world led her to compromise the gospel with paganism[71] by offering her the world:

> Satan once endeavored to form a compromise with Christ. He came to the Son of God in the wilderness of temptation, and showing Him all the kingdoms of the world and the glory of them, offered to give all into His hands if He would but acknowledge the supremacy of the prince of darkness. Christ rebuked the presumptuous tempter and forced him to depart. But Satan meets with greater success in presenting the same temptations to man. To secure worldly gains and honors, the church was led to seek the favor and support of the great men of earth; and having thus rejected Christ, she was induced to yield allegiance to the representative of Satan – the bishop of Rome.[72]

Adventists also shared Luther's pessimism about any undoing of this apostasy. But, unlike Luther, they believed that the worst – the worst by far – was yet to come in the history of the Antichrist.

## In the Future

Adventists did not adhere to Luther's extended papal decline until the Last Day. In fact, they did not see 2 Thessalonians 2:8 as delineating the two phases of the Antichrist's decay and destruction, but rather as two synonymous phrases for the latter

---

"a counterfeit end-time religious system ... the heir of the medieval union of church and state" and that "the medieval church produced many martyrs." Otherwise it does not identify the power in the traditional Antichrist passages. *Andrews Study Bible: Light. Depth. Truth* (Berrien Springs, MI: Andrews University Press, 2010), 1122–1128, 1135, 1576–1577, 1675–1676, 1680–1681.

70 The belief that prophecy rather than theology was the main factor in the Reformer's identification of the papal Antichrist is at least as old as LeRoy Edwin Froom's monumental work on the history of prophetic interpretation. He wrote that "it was the profound conviction springing from the great outline prophecies and the inescapable conclusion that the Papacy was the predicted Antichrist that impelled separation and gave courage to battle the great apostasy" (Froom, *Prophetic Faith of Our Fathers*, 2:245). Many more examples could be furnished, but one will have to do: An official share-book from the turn of the century affirmed that Daniel 7 was the "prophecy that convinced the Reformers about the antichrist." Martin Weber, *Millennimania* (Nampa, ID: Pacific Press, 1998), 59.
71 Ellen G. White, *Great Controversy*, 42–45.
72 Ibid., 50.

only. They did agree that the papacy had declined in power towards the end of its 1260 year reign until it was struck by a fatal blow in 1798. Yet this was not the end of its reign. Adventists envisioned a new penultimate act in the career of the Antichrist, which would play out before his ultimate destruction by the brightness of the returning Christ. This apocalyptic framed the mission of the Adventists, for their three angels' gospel message sounded the warning against the rise of the Antichrist. This new chapter in the Antichrist's future was found in Revelation 13.[73] The beast healed from its deadly wound with all the world following after it meant that the papacy would rise again to its former supremacy (v. 3). During its healing pro-

73 It seems that the Revelation 13 scenario did not *clearly* include the resurgence of the papacy even as late as the 1870s. See Damsteegt, *Foundations of Message and Mission*, 192–242. This changed in the 1880s. See Ellen G. White, *Spirit of Prophecy*, vol. 4 (1884), 380–410; Alonzo Trévier Jones, *Ecclesiastical Empire* (Battle Creek, MI: Review and Herald, 1901), 867–874; and Haskell, *Seer on Patmos* (1905), 232–233.
  Bruinsma has pointed out that two trends ran through the late 19th century: The Roman Catholic Church grew in numbers and influence in America, and a resurrected papacy became part of Adventist apocalyptic. He suggests that the former explains the latter (Bruinsma, *Adventist Attitudes toward Catholicism*, 131, 139). It is easy to see the connection between the two: Protestants feared that growing Catholic influence in the United States could end, due to Roman opposition to democracy, in Catholic America, and Adventists shared this concern. In that vein, an 1870 article in the Review stated that "the one aim of Catholicism in this country is to secure political ascendancy" (ibid., 167–168). By the 1870s, Adventists believed that Protestants in America would adopt Catholic principles to such an extent that they would legislate the papal Sunday. (In hindsight, this implied a resurgent papacy, for would not the pope arise to power once America would enforce the sign of papal authority?) The worry of growing Catholic influence in America fit right into that prophetic scenario: If Catholics themselves were becoming politically strong in America, this meant that not only would Protestants apostatize to the point of making Catholic dogma a law, but Catholics might enable that endeavor. Furthermore, since Catholics were loyal to the papacy, once they had enough political clout, America might be brought under the domain of the Holy See. This would mean that the beast of Revelation 13 (the papal Antichrist) would reign again.
  It is a point worthy of further research that, unlike Bruinsma's suggestion that Adventists developed the Revelation 13 scenario in response to historical developments in the 1880s, this apocalyptic had already received its last component (the resurgence of the papacy) in the decade before. An early example is Uriah Smith's comment in 1874: "The people are to be called upon to make an image *to* the beast, which expression doubtless involves the idea of some deferential action toward, or concessions to, that power; and the image, when made, is an image, likeness, or representation *of* the beast. Verse 15. The beast from which the image is modeled, is the one which had a wound by a sword and did live, or the papacy. From this point is seen the collusion of the two-horned beast with the leopard or papal beast. He does great wonders in the sight of that beast; he causes men to worship that beast; he leads them to make an image to that beast; and he causes all to receive a mark, which is the mark of that beast. These palpable evidences of co-operation with the papal power, led Eld. J. Litch, about 1842, to write concerning the two-horned beast thus: – 'I think it is a power yet to be developed or made manifest, as an accomplice of the papacy in subjecting the world.'" Uriah Smith, *The United States in the Light of Prophecy; or, An Exposition of Rev. 13:11–17* (Battle Creek, MI: Steam Press of the Seventh-day Adventist Pub. Assn., 1874), 103.

cess, Protestantism, centered in the United States (the other beast) would complete its own apostasy: While having the lamblike appearance of a Christian nation, the States would eventually speak – that is legislate – like a dragon (v. 11). As America would repudiate all the principles of the Reformation, the road it would travel would lead it inexorably back to Rome, and the prophecies showed by what process. America would undo the separation of church and state and thus become a religio-political power, similar to the medieval papacy, and thus an image of the former beast (vv. 14–15). America's apostasy would culminate in nationwide blue laws. Since the papacy claimed the Sunday Sabbath as its seal of authority, it would gladly help America in enforcing the laws, and thus America would unwittingly play into the hands of the papacy. The supremacy the See had lost in Europe it would regain through the United States, the most powerful nation on the earth, ready to do its bidding. The enforcement of Sunday-keeping would constitute the mark of the beast (vv. 16–17), all nations would follow America's example in papal allegiance, and eventually the mark would be backed up by a death decree (v. 15). False miracles would be wrought to substantiate the apostasy (vv. 13–14; 2 Thess 2:9–10), great tribulation would ensue (Dan 12:1), and then Christ would come to destroy the Antichrist and save his people (2 Thess 2:8; Rev 19:19–20).

The main similarity in the future Adventists and Luther envisioned for the Antichrist was that he would remain to the end and be destroyed by Christ. Apart from this, the differences were great. Luther was waiting for Antichrist's continuing decline and destruction; Adventists warned against the resurgence of the Antichrist to world dominance. This new addition to the acts of Antichrist was still connected to Luther. While it had not been part of his apocalyptic, it resembled his history. The resurrection of the Antichrist would be a global reenactment of all that Adventists knew about the history of the papacy and the Reformer. It would blend together endtime Reformers, a great revival, the false miracles of the Antichrist, and medieval-style persecution. Like Luther, the Adventists would wrestle through their *Anfechtungen* ("the shaking")[74] to the light of the gospel. And like the Reformer they would preach the restored gospel to backslidden Christendom. Like Luther's, their message would raise the ire of the Antichrist. But all these similarities remained a projected future. While Luther had shaken all of Europe, Adventists were, despite their massive missionary project, but one of many young denominations, and were met mostly with indifference. Their newfound truths also did not lead to the final revival.

Yet there always remained one strand of history that Adventists believed showed that the dim future act was indeed unfolding, and that was the activities of the present papacy. While Adventists have deemed it pertinent to word their prophetic interpretation more carefully, the shadow of the looming papal Antichrist has length-

---

74  Ellen G. White, *Spiritual Gifts,* vol. 1, 183–188.

ened in their apocalyptic. Standing on their watch post, Adventists continue to follow the activities of the papacy in the light of the setting sun of what is to come.[75]

## Concluding Remarks

Antichrist has traditionally been understood as the great final enemy of Christ. This means that Antichrist is largely the antithesis of what people believe the gospel and the church to be. Thus, Antichrist could be identified in the same way (as the same entity or person) but for different reasons. This can be seen in how Luther and the Adventists (even among themselves) focused on different aspects of the same adversary.

Adventists believe that the enemy of the Reformer will one day give them the battle. Yet while the future struggle will supposedly be caused by the same factors as the Reformation, Adventists have shown surprisingly limited interest in some of the very themes that to Luther defined the gospel as truth, and the Catholic hierarchy as apostate. The largest topic here would be justification by faith. Adventists themselves tacitly confess that they do not have the same grasp on this vital truth as Luther did. They self-identify as Laodicea – the true church in the last days, yet apathetic to Christ and the gospel. Adventist discourse on Antichrist continues to be lacking in this respect. They have not probed into the theological connections between inner and outer evil. To most Adventists, the statements by Luther (and White) that there is a direct affinity between one's own self-righteousness and the Antichrist, would sound startling. Unlike Luther, the unsaid assumption in Adventism is that doctrinal knowledge is protection enough against falling into the ranks of the enemy. Here is where Adventist understanding of evil – despite White's penetrating insights into the great controversy – tends to be surprisingly superficial.

A survey of Adventists' view on the papal Antichrist reveals deficiencies in their study and knowledge of the papacy and Catholicism. Using the most outrageous claims of the papacy from the past, while ignoring the realities of present Catholicism, is untenable. A more comprehensive and updated Adventist understanding of the papacy is overdue. In this light, Bruinsma's conclusion on Adventist attitude towards Catholicism is an appeal that remains to be answered: "It seems to me that Adventists must enter into some sort of dialogue with Roman

---

75 Adventists have for a long time covered the history of their contemporary papacy. The following is a representative list: 1929 Lateran Treaty: Alonzo L. Baker, *The Pope King Again: Is the "Deadly Wound" Healing?* (Mountain View, CA: Pacific Press, 1929); 1962–1965 Vatican II: Bert Beverly Beach, *Vatican II: Bridging the Abyss* (Washington DC: Review and Herald, 1968); 1965 Pope Paul VI visit to the United States: E. L. Cardey, *Hands across the Gulf* (Atlanta, GA: School of Bible Prophecy, 1966); 2015 Pope Francis' visit to the United States: Christopher Hudson, "LEOPARD VISION (VOL. 1)," YouTube video, 1:26:14, posted by "TheForeRunner777," December 3, 2017, https://goo.gl/ UCf2XP (May 22, 2017). For Adventist reaction to the Roman Catholic Church, see Bruinsma, *Adventist Attitudes toward Catholicism*, 114–119, 163–165, 245–273.

Catholics, both on the individual and corporate level, if they want to arrive at a fair appraisal of present-day Roman Catholicism."[76] But there is more at stake here theologically than "knowing your enemy." That military maxim is transcended by Christ's command: "Love your enemies." The greater the enemy, the more urgent this principle. It is given additional weight by the fact that Adventists are strong proponents of free will, and thus (in theory) opponents of fatalism. If Adventists will continue to hold to the identification of the Antichrist as the pope, is it not their duty to warn him and his fellow-believers of their danger, and, if possible, to help them, all the time being remindful that their own hearts are inclined to the very same errors? It seems that humble self-examination and sympathy for one's opponents are the main Christian practices one can draw from apocalyptic applications, lest they become mere "divine labeling" of one's opponents.

---

76   Ibid., 301–302. A dialogue in the early 2000s quickly died out. See Ángel Manuel Rodríguez, "Conversations between Adventists and Catholics," *Reflections* no. 4 (October 2003): 2–3 (https://goo.gl/sFshvT); and "Roman Catholic Dialogue with the Seventh-day Adventists," Berkley Center for Religion, Peace & World Affairs, https://goo.gl/g0B1IA (Dec. 3, 2017).

*Christian Lutsch*

# Martin Luther's View of the Scripture Principle

## Abstract

Hermeneutics can be considered the mother of all theological disciplines. All else is influenced by it. A discussion of the *Sola Scriptura* principle is in essence a discussion of hermeneutics. Luther's view of the Scripture Principle is no abstract theorem. Rather, it arose from his confrontation with the thinkers and the thought of his day, which were shaped by church tradition. Luther's struggle was not primarily directed against the church, but against the irreverent treatment of Holy Scripture. For Luther, the Scriptures are God's Word that is still speaking and calling people to repentance. Those who listen to it are entering into a dialogue with God. No human authority or tradition is permitted to step between the sinner and his Savior, speaking through the Bible. For those in whom the Word awakens faith, the principle of *Sola Scriptura* has reached its goal.

## Introduction

*Sola Scriptura* – Scripture alone. Much has been said and written about this Reformation principle. It has become something of a war cry in interchurch discourse. Those who like the Seventh-day Adventist Church confess *Sola Scriptura* in their *Credo* appear to be standing on solid ground. Still, in order to arrive at an accurate understanding of the so-called Scripture Principle, its historical place in the sixteenth century[1] must be considered. The expression "the Scriptures alone" by itself does not reveal much – except one's own state of mind.[2] To speak of *Sola Scriptura* while neglecting the history of Luther and of the Reformation is like wanting to assemble a puzzle by using only a single piece.

Of course, there are limitations: For starters, the hermeneutical circle is inescapable – but it must be considered.[3] A further limitation lies in the virtual impossibility of proofing the Scripture Principle – or any doctrine about Scripture – biblically, "since one seeking to prove this (that is, the canonical authority of the

---

1 Volker Leppin, "Biographie und Theologie Martin Luthers – eine Debatte und (k)ein Ende? Ein Nachwort," in *Spätmittelalter, Humanismus, Reformation,* vol. 53, ed. Volker Leppin and Dietrich Korsch (Tübingen: Mohr Siebeck, 2010), 314.
2 Hermann Sasse, *Sacra Scriptura. Studien zur Lehre von der Heiligen Schrift* (Erlangen: Verlag der Ev.-Luth. Mission, 1981), 322. In light of this statement, it seems reasonable to use many secondary sources; to limit oneself to Luther's writings means to be alone with him and with oneself, i.e., with one's own preconceived ideas ("vorgefassten Auffassungen").
3 The "hermeneutical circle" implies that a researcher always interprets historical data through the lens of his own contemporary history and worldview. Ultimately, only approximations are possible.

Scripture), must approach it as already having recognized it."[4] This paper offers one of many possible interpretations of *Sola Scriptura* and requires examination and scrutiny. You are invited to do just that!

## Presuppositions

### Martin Luther – A Pastoral Theologian

Martin Luther: student, monk, doctor, reformer, husband and songwriter. All through his life, he was pursuing some goals, facing even the highest authorities of the time because of it. Whatever the subject at hand, he tended to be radical: either – or![5] No compromises. Still, shaped by a sharp dialectic, Luther could also answer some questions with both – and.[6]

Luther's theology emerged, not primarily from the desk, but from daily life. He "put the Scriptures into practice, lived by them and with them."[7] There is no formulated dogma *De Sacra Scriptura*. For Luther, theology concerns the experience of human beings. He was not a withdrawn ecclesiastic or philosopher, but a pastor.

In addition, Luther found himself in the context of several intellectual currents and teachers that had great influence on the philosophy and theology of the time.

### The Intellectual Matrix at Luther's Time – The Catholic "Scripture Principles"

#### Augustine

Among the church fathers, Aurelius Augustinus (354–430) stands out. In his work *De Consensu Evangelistarum* he describes the authors of the four Gospels as "tools" in God's hand.[8] Apparent contradictions between the Gospels were overcome through an "allegorical-mystical explanation."[9] This shows the influence of

---

4   Gerhard Ebeling, "Wort Gottes und Tradition. Studien zur Hermeneutik der Konfessionen," in *Kirche und Konfession. Veröffentlichungen des Konfessionskundlichen Instituts des Evangelischen Bundes*, vol. 7, ed. Heinrich Bornkamm et. al., 2nd ed. (Göttingen: Vandenhoeck & Ruprecht, 1966), 105: "da ein solcher das zu Beweisende, nämlich die kanonische Autorität der Schrift, ja schon als anerkannt voraussetzen müsste."
5   "*Characteristic of Luther is 'the decisive alternative, the exclusive either-or.'*" Hans-Martin Barth, *The Theology of Luther: A Critical Assessment* (Minneapolis, MN: Fortress Press), 4.
6   For example, the tension between faith and reason, spirit and letter, law and gospel, faith and works. Luther sees these opposites as interwoven.
7   Jörg Baur, *Luther und seine klassischen Erben: Theologische Aufsätze und Forschungen* (Tübingen: Mohr Siebeck), 60: "[Er] nahm die Schrift in den Brauch, lebte aus ihr und mit ihr."
8   Sasse, 252.
9   Ibid., 257.

the philosophical notion of truth on the Latin church father that entails a logical-rational understanding of inerrancy.

## *Via Antiqua* – Scholasticism

The most prevalent intellectual current of the time was Scholasticism, which remained the prevailing method of thought throughout the Middle Ages – the *via antiqua*. One of the most significant exponents of High Scholasticism was the Dominican Thomas Aquinas (1225–1274). He is considered the "principal witness to Catholic truth."[10] In his writings, long before Luther, can be found this momentous formula: *"sola canonica Scriptura est regula fidei."*[11] Holy Scripture alone is the standard of faith! By contrast, church tradition is a sort of commentary on the Bible.

For Scholasticism, however, logical contradictions are by no means permitted in theology. Therefore Holy Scripture and church tradition must be in agreement, since tradition emerges from the Scriptures. They are formally distinct, but in the end, belief in certain statements of truth *(fides quae creditur)* and the foundation of faith *(fides qua creditur)* are identical.

## *Via Moderna* – Nominalism

An important conceptual development within late Scholasticism came in the form of Nominalism. In Nominalism, the empirical understanding of reality appeared alongside logic: Personal experience of God became more important. Scholasticism, the foundation of medieval theology, began to quake – with Nominalism, the *via moderna* was born. One influential proponent of Nominalism was the English scholar William of Ockham (1288–1347).

Ockham distinguished theology from philosophy and taught the preeminence of Holy Scripture over church tradition, which was greatly shaped by philosophy. Nevertheless, he also believed that the church was in agreement with the Scriptures.[12]

Martin Luther, however, rejected the thought "that the teaching of Scripture and the teaching of the Roman Church were necessarily identical."[13]

---

10 Stephan H. Pfürtner, "Das reformatorische 'Sola Scriptura' – theologischer Auslegungsgrund des Thomas von Aquin?" in Sola Scriptura. Ringvorlesung der theologischen Fakultät der Philipps-Universität, ed. Carl-Heinz Ratschow (Marburg: N.G. Elwert, 1977), 53 (48–80): "Kronzeuge katholischer Wahrheit."
11 Cited in ibid., 55, 57.
12 A. Skevington Wood, Captive to the Word. Martin Luther: Doctor of Sacred Scripture (Grand Rapids, MI: Eerdmans, 1969), 119. Hermann Sasse claims that Ockham did in fact consider contradictions between the Scriptures and the church possible, if only in ethical questions (p. 329). The Ockhamist school in Erfurt, the town where Luther studied, recognized the pope and not the councils as the doctrinal authority of the church.
13 Wood, 120.

At the time, a commentary by Gabriel Biels (1415–1495) on the four *Sentences* of Peter Lombard (ca. 1100–1160) was "the fundamental textbook of theology."[14] Ultimately, "in the time before Luther, the Scriptures were understood within the framework of the all-encompassing tradition of the Church and along the lines of the doctrinal formulations of the Church."[15]

## Humanism

Another influential development in the history of ideas during that period was Humanism. One of Humanism's principles of research would become very important for dealing with the Holy Scriptures: *ad fontes* – to the sources! Older is better. This explains the great interest in biblical manuscripts in the original languages. Luther received much support from humanists in his teaching and Bible translation; still, he clearly distanced himself from staunch humanists.[16]

# The Development of Luther's "Scripture Principle"

## *The Scholar Dr. Martinus*

It is from this context, then, that in the course of time Luther's Scripture Principle emerged. After his undergraduate studies, his time in the Augustinian monastery in Erfurt, and his theological studies at the University of Wittenberg, Luther returned to Wittenberg as Doctor of Theology where he taught *Lectura in Biblia* (Bible Interpretation). From that time forward, his entire life and work was situated in the context of the interpretation of the Bible.[17]

---

14 Siegfried Raeder, "Luther als Ausleger und Übersetzer der Heiligen Schrift," in Leben und Werk Martin Luthers von 1526–1546. Festgabe zu seinem 500. Geburtstag, Bd.1, ed. Helmar Junghans (Berlin: Evangelische Verlagsanstalt, 1983), 253 (253–278).
15 Bernhard Lohse, Martin Luther. Eine Einführung in sein Leben und Werk (Berlin: Evangelische Verlagsanstalt GmbH, 1983), 174. Cf. Barth, 431.
16 Heinz Liebing, "Sola Scriptura – die reformatorische Antwort auf das Problem der Tradition," in *Sola Scriptura. Ringvorlesung der theologischen Fakultät der Philipps-Universität*, ed. Carl-Heinz Ratschow (Marburg: N.G. Elwert, 1977), 83 (81–95); Bernhard Lohse, *Luthers Theologie in ihrer historischen Entwicklung und in ihrem systematischen Zusammenhang* (Göttingen: Vandenhoeck & Ruprecht, 1995), 38. For more on Luther's dissociation from Humanism, see below the section "The Conflict with Erasmus von Rotterdam (1524–1525)." For further influences in the history of ideas upon Luther, see Lohse, *Luthers Theologie*, 35–40.
17 Lohse, *Martin Luther. Eine Einführung*, 105; cf. Liebing, 82.

## The First Lectures on the Psalms (1513–1515)

During his first lectures in Wittenberg (on the Psalms), Luther still cited Augustine frequently. While these citations are to an extent placed in a new context, Luther nevertheless shows himself deeply rooted in medieval interpretation. "Whatever is said literally concerning the Lord Jesus Christ as to His person must be understood allegorically ... And, at the same time, it must be understood tropologically."[18]

Luther is still adhering to the "fourfold sense of Scripture" principle of interpretation, according to which each Biblical statement has (1) a literal-historical, (2) an allegorical-theological, (3) a tropological-moral-ethical, and (4) an anagogical-eschatological meaning. Originally, the fourfold sense of Scripture served to limit the many interpretations of Scripture to just a few. However, this type of interpretation often gave opportunity to get around the plain text, should its message be unpleasant.

Luther searched for the exact meaning of the original text of the Psalms. In this process, he noticed that even in the literal sense of the text, the words present a double form: letter and Spirit. God's Word does not speak either law or gospel – as it had been understood until then – but rather both at the same time. The *letter* startles the hearer of the Word of God and calls to repentance (law), while simultaneously the *Spirit* grants him comfort amidst his trial (gospel).[19]

This recognition was a hermeneutical change of direction. In view of this double form of God's Word as letter and Spirit, for Luther, the fourfold sense of Scripture increasingly lost its significance.

## The 95 Theses (1517)

The nailing of the 95 theses on October 31, 1517, in Wittenberg is unequivocally *the* event of the Reformation and celebrated to this day as "Reformation Day."[20] The widely held view that in the theses Luther set the authority of the pope against the authority of Christ speaking in the Scriptures needs further clarification. Luther actually cites the Scriptures only once at the very beginning: "Repent!" (Matt

18 LW 10:7. All citations are from *Luther's Works,* American Edition, 55 vols., edited by Jaroslav Pelikan and Helmut T. Lehman (Philadelphia: Muehlenberg Press and Fortress Press; and St. Louis: Concordia, 1955–1986). German original in WA 55 I, 8 *(Vorrede der 1. Psalmenvorlesung; 1513–1515)*: "Quicquid de domino Ihesu Christo in persona sua ad literam dicitur. Hoc ipsum allegorice ... intelligi. Idemque simul tropologice debet intelligi ..." All citations are from *Weimarer Ausgabe: D. Martin Luthers Werke, Kritische Gesamtausgabe,* 127 vols. (Weimar: H. Böhlau, 1883–2009). It is grouped into Schriften/Werke [Writings] (WA), Tischreden [Table talks] (WA TR), Deutsche Bibel [German Bible] (WA DB) and Briefwechsel [Exchange of letters] (WA BR).
19 Lohse, *Luthers Theologie,* 77ff.
20 The fact that the real turn toward the reformatory convictions for Luther first occurred in 1518 is often overlooked. The nailing of the theses was no more than the opening of a series of public disputations, but in no way the conclusion of his reformatory discoveries.

4:17).²¹ That is his Biblical basis for the disputation. In his 95 theses, Luther primarily turns against the sale of indulgences, which impart a false (repentance-avoiding) sense of security. Luther places sinful, penitent humans directly under the law and grace of God, not under the clergy. His criticism thus only indirectly strikes the authority of the pope.

Luther's critics appeal to church authority,²² but Luther permits only "reason" or "scriptural grounds" as valid arguments (thesis 18).²³ The fact that Luther plays off the Holy Scriptures against church authority "meant a break, because for Scholasticism and for the Church hierarchy the Church and Scripture could not be in conflict with each other." ²⁴

## *The Bull of Leo X. Threatening Excommunication (1520)*

The 95 theses on indulgences marked the starting point of a series of, at times, very intense disputes Luther had with representatives of the church. Luther was indicted and henceforth needed to defend himself publicly, for escalation was impending.²⁵

As Pope Leo X threatened excommunication in 1520, Luther wrote several articles in which he revealed a "new understanding of Scripture."²⁶ The issue was more complex than merely Scripture and tradition put against each other.²⁷ Luther did not turn away from every form of tradition. Wherever in his estimation tradition harmonized with Scripture, there was no problem. What he reproved, however, was the binding of Scriptural interpretation to tradition. This indicates that the Scripture Principle did not constitute the basis for Luther's conflicts with the church, but rather was a result of this conflict.²⁸

21  In the 78ᵗʰ thesis, Luther cites a portion from 1 Corinthians 12, but here the Scripture is more a side-note than an argument.
22  Sasse, 325.
23  See https://goo.gl/nkkPBO (November 29, 2017).
24  Lohse, *Luthers Theologie*, 205: "bedeutete einen Bruch, da Kirche und Schrift für die Scholastik und für die Kirchenleitung nicht in Gegensatz zueinander treten konnten." Gerhard Ebeling notes that in scholastic theology, one "hardly meets the word *traditio* and … one was not aware of the possibility of tension between the two [Scripture and Tradition]" (92): "… das Wort *traditio* kaum begegnet und … man sich der Möglichkeit einer Spannung zwischen beidem [Schrift und Tradition] nicht bewusst war." Consequently, Luther's opponents claimed the Holy Scriptures as their own, even if on a different level, that is, Scripture in light of the church, to which Scripture was entrusted by God for interpretation (Ebeling, 112f.). In the course of the Counter-Reformation, a "two-source theory" emerged, which validated church tradition as authority alongside Scripture (Liebing, 82). But whether tradition is understood only as *interpretation* of Scripture or as *supplement* to Scripture – in both instances Scripture stands *under* the judgment of the church. From 1517 onward, Luther could no longer teach this.
25  Ebeling, 93.
26  Lohse, *Martin Luther. Eine Einführung*, 58.
27  Wood, 128.
28  Liebing, 85; Ebeling, 122.

## The Conflict with Erasmus of Rotterdam (1524–1525)

In the mid-1520s, Luther exchanged correspondence with the renowned humanist Erasmus of Rotterdam (1466–1536). In this context, statements were made regarding their respective understanding of Scripture.

Erasmus divided the biblical texts into categories of "clear" and "unclear." He relegated the "unclear" passages to the *deus absconditus* (the hidden God), while the "clear" passages proceeded from God as *deus revelatus* (the revealed God). He wanted to defer only to the "clear" passages; where the Scripture by itself remained "unclear," there he trusted in church tradition, which could provide for clarity.[29]

Luther was convicted that "the Bible is 'clear' in essential matters, and not ambiguous."[30] In contrast to Erasmus, the "unclear" passages appeared to him also clear in light of the "clear" passages.[31] Only a tiny few remained truly "unclear." "God and the Scripture of God are two things, no less than the Creator and the creation are two things. That in God there are many things hidden, of which we are ignorant, no one doubts."[32]

Of course, a part of God remains hidden, for God is not identical with the Scriptures. Luther considered preoccupation with the *deus absconditus* to be pointless. At the center of Scriptural understanding is the *deus revelatus* in Jesus Christ and with Him the clear Scripture passages. Christ is the center of Luther's hermeneutic.[33] Erasmus also called Christ "the center of Scripture," but by this he did not mean to delineate a hermeneutical principle, but rather a moral demand: Christ our Example.[34]

Both Erasmus and Luther claim the Holy Scriptures for themselves. However, they use it in different ways. For Luther it is "ultimately about something else than for Erasmus: not about the rational or biblically justifiable morality of God and man, but rather about the certainty of man concerning God's Word and Work."[35]

---

29 It is notable that Erasmus of Rotterdam, a staunch humanist who considered human beings to have free will and thus tremendous power, was reserved towards the "unclear" passages. This testifies to a fundamentally humble position. Cf. Bernhard Lohse, *Lutherdeutung heute* (Göttingen: Vandenhoeck & Ruprecht, 1968), 51ff., and Wood, 123.
30 Lohse, *Martin Luther. Eine Einführung*, 80.
31 Liebing, 90; herein lies the "wesentliche Unterschied zwischen Erasmus und Luther" ("fundamental difference between Erasmus and Luther.") Lohse, *Luthers Theologie*, 213.
32 LW 33:25; Latin original found in WA 18, 606 *(De servo arbitrio; 1525)*: "Duae res sunt Deus et Scriptura Dei, non minus quam duae res sunt, Creator et creatura Dei. In Deo esse multa abscondita, quae ignoramus, nemo dubitat."
33 Luther's hermeneutical approach, which solidified in the course of time, was in the centuries after the Reformation, especially in Protestant orthodoxy, increasingly displaced by the verbal inspiration view "as if suddenly everything the Reformation had taught on this subject was forgotten" (Sasse, 260).
34 Wood, 172.
35 Liebing, 88: "... letztlich um etwas anderes als Erasmus: nicht um die rational oder biblizistisch begründbare Moralität Gottes und des Menschen, sondern um die Gewissheit des Menschen über Gottes Wort und Werk." The notion that Luther and Erasmus entirely

## The Disputation on Communion with Zwingli (1524–1529)

The certainty concerning God's Word and Work was ultimately the core issue in the disputation between Luther and the Swiss Reformer Ulrich Zwingli on communion. "This *is* my body" (1 Cor 11:24; Vulgate *"Hoc est corpus meum."*). Luther rejected the doctrine of transformation of bread and wine into the body and blood of Christ, but adhered to the real presence of Christ in bread and wine. Zwingli saw the real presence of Christ manifest through the Holy Spirit. He understood "is" as symbolic, Luther, on the contrary, as literal.

Yet Luther was not concerned here with how literal the Holy Scriptures are to be understood, but with the real presence of Christ in His church at the Lord's Supper. Under no circumstances should it be spiritualized or in any other way toned down.[36]

Luther accepted several methods of interpretation as valid – literal, allegorical, historical, etc. – just as long as they did not water down the gospel of Christ.

## Luther's Bible Translation (1521–1534)

Arguably, Luther's greatest contribution in connection with his understanding of Scripture was his translation of the Bible into German. It was based, not on previous translations, but on manuscripts in the original languages. Luther's way of working on the translation was a mirror of his understanding of Scripture and his attitude towards the church. He had several collaborators – interpretation is a task for the entire church of believers, not for lone individuals. Soon after translating the New Testament Luther said in a sermon: "Would to God that my exposition and that of all doctors might perish and each Christian himself make the Scriptures and God's pure word his norm. You can tell by my verbosity how immeasurably different God's words are in comparison with any human word."[37]

---

talked past one another and misunderstood each other must be rejected in light of Luther's radical teaching on sin and grace, which was at stake in the discussion with Erasmus. For more on this, see Christian Lutsch, "Sola Gratia. Die Entwicklung der Gnadenlehre und das Verständnis von Gnade bei Martin Luther," term paper, 2013, 24f.

36  Lohse, *Martin Luther. Eine Einführung*, 87: "Out of the Scriptures sprang a new paradigm directing the central aspect of faith and doctrine. In the communion disputation, Luther, however, emphasized the literal sense of the Eucharistic formula. Of course, he did not resort to biblicism in this." ("Von der Schrift her war es zu einer Neuprägung der zentralen Aspekte von Glaube und Lehre gekommen. Im Abendmahlsstreit hingegen betonte Luther den buchstäblichen Sinn der Einsetzungsworte. Freilich verfiel er dabei keinem Biblizismus."). Accusing Luther of Biblicism in the communion disputation misjudges the core issue of the dispute. The concept of a verbally inspired Bible and a strictly literal understanding of Scripture are totally foreign to Luther.

37  LW 52:286; German original in WA 10 I, 1, 728 *(Kirchenpostille 1522. Evangelium am Tage der heiligen drei Könige. Matthäus 2,1–12)*: "O das gott wollt, meyn und aller lerer

The traditional view that the correct interpretation of Scripture is the sole prerogative of the church through the clergy is radically called into question here. This struggle was intensified by Luther's theology that became clear in his Bible translation.[38]

## Luther's "Sachkritik" during Canon Formation and Bible Translation

### Approach to the Apocrypha

In the process of translating the Bible, Luther wanted to remain true to the Hebrew, Aramaic, and Greek manuscripts and was thus inevitably confronted with the question as to which writings he should consider part of the biblical canon and which not.[39] To answer it, certain internal and external criteria needed to be applied. Luther found external criteria in the humanistic principle *ad fontes*. Realizing that the Hebrew canon did not contain the Old Testament apocrypha, he concluded, "Apocrypha: these books are not held equal to the Scriptures but are useful and good to read."[40] The most ancient witnesses take precedence over tradition.[41] This estimation of the Apocrypha is an "important step forward in the direction towards the soon-to-be-formulated principle of Luther, '*Sola Scriptura*.'"[42] But the biblical writings themselves are a part of tradition.[43] Is tradition then put against tradition? Luther does not take the bait:

---

außlegung untergiengen, unnd eyn iglicher Christenn selbs die blosse schrifft und lautter gottis wortt fur sich nehme! Du sihest yhe auß dissem meynen geschwetz, wie unmeßlich ungleych gottis wortt sind gegen aller menschen wortt."

38   Lohse opines that Luther's "Bible translation must be viewed from the standpoint of its defining theological motivation." (Lohse, *Evangelium in der Geschichte. Studien zu Luther und der Reformation* [Göttingen: Vandenhoeck & Ruprecht, 1988], 195: "Bibelübersetzung im entscheidenden von ihrer theologischen Motivation her gesehen werden [muss].") This will be examined in more depth in the following sections.

39   For example, the Septuagint (LXX) and its Latin translation, the Vulgate, contain more writings than the Hebrew canon. For more on Luther's approach to the canon, see Lohse, *Evangelium in der Geschichte*, 211–236.

40   LW 35:337 n. 1; German original in WA DB 12, 2 *(Bibel 1534. Titel und Register der Apokryphen)*: "Apocrypha. Das sind Bücher: so nicht der heiligen Schrifft gleich gehalten: und doch nützlich und gut zu lesen sind."

41   The role of human authorship is by no means undermined. On the contrary, it is thus clarified: The canon is about more than tradition and humanism, i.e., it is about God's Word. External criteria are insufficient.

42   Lohse, *Evangelium in der Geschichte*, 221: "wichtiger Fortschritt in Richtung auf den wenig später von Luther formulierten Grundsatz des 'Sola Scriptura'." To what extent Luther himself formulated the principle *sola scriptura* is debatable.

43   Barth, 430; cf. Ebeling, 98f.

Therefore it should be known, in the first place, that the notion must be given up that there are four gospels and only four evangelists ... On the contrary, it is to be held firmly that just as the Old Testament is one book in which are written God's laws and commandments, together with the history of those who kept and of those who did not keep them, so the New Testament is one book in which are written the gospel and the promises of God, together with the history of those who believe and do not believe them.[44]

Luther is somewhat inconsistent in using external criteria for canonicity. The Apocrypha were not accepted into the canon *because of* their questionable authorship, that is, their tradition. The other books remained preserved in the canon *despite* their tradition. But for Luther, tradition history is no exclusive criterion for dealing with biblical writings.[45] Rather, Luther's "biblical criticism" is based on the conviction that God and not a human being is speaking in the Holy Scriptures.[46] The internal criteria were more important than the external ones.[47]

---

44 LW 35:357–358; German original in WA DB 6, 2 *(Vorrede zum Neuen Testament, 1522)*: "Darumb ist auffs erste zu wissen, das abtzuthun ist der wahn, das vier Euangelia und nur vier Euangelisten sind ... Sondern festiglich zu halten, das gleych wie das allte testament ist eyn buch, darynnen Gottis gesetz und gepot, da neben die geschichte beyde dere die selben gehallten und nicht gehallten haben, geschrieben sind, Also ist das newe testament, eyn buch, darynnen das Euangelion und Gottis verheyssung, danebe auch geschichte beyde, dere die dran glewben und nit glewben, geschrieben sind."
45 In critical scholarship in recent decades, the use of the method that reads biblical writings in the light of their tradition history has declined. Instead, the emphasis is placed again on the text in its final form. What at first seems like a purely methodological question, is ultimately a hermeneutical decision: Can I trust the biblical text the way it stands before me? Or is an investigation of the evolution of the text necessary in order to understand the Bible?
46 Armin Wenz, *Das Wort Gottes – Gericht und Rettung. Untersuchungen zur Autorität der Heiligen Schrift in Bekenntnis und Lehre der Kirche*, Forschungen zur systematischen und ökumenischen Theologie, vol. 75, ed. Wolfhart Pannenberg and Reinhard Slenczka (Göttingen: Vandenhoeck & Ruprecht, 1996), 40. The Bible often says "The Word of the LORD came to ..." (e.g., Jer 1:2; Jonah 1:1; Hag 1:3; Zech 4:8).
47 Luther's confrontation with enthusiastic movements particularly made the question of the inner criteria for dealing with the Bible more urgent: "If Luther first had considered the Bible translation to be essential for the disputation with Rome, in order to hold up the pure Word of God against the words of men, then the conflict with the so-called enthusiasts proved the necessity of providing Bible readers with help in understanding it." (Lohse, *Evangelium in der Geschichte*, 201: "Hatte Luther zunächst die Bibelübersetzung in der Auseinandersetzung mit Rom für notwendig gehalten, um das lautere Gotteswort den Menschenworten entgegenzustellen, so erwies der Konflikt mit den sogenannten Schwärmern die Notwendigkeit, den Bibellesern Verstehenshilfen zu geben."). For Luther, the Holy Spirit did not stand in opposition to Scripture, rather He manifested Himself therein as the Word of God (Wood, 161). Interestingly, against the enthusiasts and heretics of his day, Thomas Aquinas held up church tradition as the only valid interpretational framework.

## Sola Scriptura – *The "Subject Matter" of Scripture*

In the first edition of the New Testament in the German language, Luther had already revealed the inner criterion he applied to the biblical canon.

> All the genuine sacred books agree in this, that all of them preach and drive [*treiben, promote*] Christ. And that is the true test by which to judge all books, when we see whether or not they drive Christ ... Whatever does not teach Christ is not yet apostolic, even though St. Peter or St. Paul does the teaching. Again, whatever preaches Christ would be apostolic, even if Judas, Annas, Pilate, and Herod were doing it.[48]

It must be emphasized that, in the disputation with Luther, the church did not fight against the doctrine of Christ or the testimony of Christ! What bothered the church authorities was that Luther was questioning the church's prerogative of interpretation. The hierarchical church viewed itself responsible for handing down the Scriptures and the doctrine of the apostles. For Luther, however, Christ is the true subject matter of Scripture. And as "the head of the body, the church" (Col 1:18), He is not dependent upon the church.

"What drives Christ" *(Was Christum treybet)*. This is, in short, Luther's decisive criterion for his biblical criticism.[49] His hermeneutic is a radical new method of interpretation, one in which human beings are placed directly under the Scriptures, the Word of God and of Christ. The meaning of the biblical text is not – as in the fourfold sense of Scripture – to be sought *behind*, but rather *in* the meaning of the words, because Christ Himself speaks therein to us humans.[50] In this respect "the Holy Scriptures ultimately are not that which needs to be illuminated, but rather are themselves the source of enlightenment."[51] "The Scriptures deserve to raise their voice as judge, which is impossible if we have not given the Scriptures the preeminent

---

48  LW 35:396; German original in WA DB 7, 384 *(Vorrede auff die Episteln Sanct Jacobi unnd Judas, 1522)*: "Und daryn stymmen alle rechtschaffene heylige bucher uber eyns, das sie alle sampt Christum predigen und treyben, Auch ist das der rechte prufesteyn alle bucher zu taddelln, wenn man sihet, ob sie Christum treyben, odder nit, ... Was Christum nicht leret, das ist nicht Apostolisch, wens gleich Petrus odder Paulus leret, Widerumb, was Christum predigt, das ist Apostolisch, wens gleych Judas, Annas, Pilatus und Herodes thett."
49  Baur, 75f. Regarding Luther's approach to the Apocrypha it can be said that "it is therefore ultimately a form of subject matter criticism which led Luther to his reservations regarding the Old Testament Apocrypha." (Lohse, *Evangelium in der Geschichte*, 232: "Infolgedessen ist es letzlich eine Sachkritik, die bei Luther zu seiner Reserve gegenüber den alttestament-lichen Apokryphen führt.") This is also the reason why the epistle to the Hebrews, the epistle of James, and the epistle of Jude, as well as the book of Revelation, are placed at the end of Luther's Bible.
50  "For a thousand years the Church had buttressed its theological edifice by means of an authoritative exegesis which depended on allegory as its chief medium of interpretation. Luther struck a mortal blow at this vulnerable spot" (Wood, 164). However, if Jesus is better testified to and acknowledged by an allegorical interpretation, then Luther would let it stand (Barth, 444; cf. Raeder, 260).
51  Ebeling, 124.

position ... so that they themselves through themselves, most certainly, most effortlessly, most plainly are unveiled, [being] their own interpreter."[52]

Here is made clear what the *"Sola"* in *Sola Scriptura* stands for. It does not mean, as is often wrongly assumed, the reduction of the Christian faith to the Bible alone,[53] as if tradition per se was something wrong. Rather, it is about the fact "that Scripture ... does not first need approval or empowerment by another institution."[54] Scripture itself possesses the highest authority in the interpretation of Scripture, for God, the Highest, speaks in it and speaks to the individual, "The creative, life-giving faculty of Scripture – its auctoritas causativa – evidences and establishes ... its authority as auctoritas normativa."[55] Notwithstanding this – or perhaps even because of this – careful exegesis is essential, so as not to pass by the subject matter of Scripture. Because Luther found Christ in the Scriptures, he was to an extent liberated from the literal wording of the biblical text. The important thing is that Christ is permitted to speak and make the text "clear."

## Claritas Scripturae – *The Twofold Clarity*

> "What more sublime thing can remain hidden in the Scriptures, now that the seals have been broken, the stone has been rolled from the door of the sepulcher, and the supreme

---

52 "Es gebührt sich nämlich für die Schrift, als Richterin ihre Stimme abzugeben, was unmöglich ist, wenn wir nicht der Schrift den ersten Platz gegeben haben ..., das ist, damit sie selbst durch sich selbst ganz gewiss, ganz mühelos, ganz enthüllt sei, ihr eigenerAusleger ..." Latin original in WA 7, 97 *(Assertio omnium Articulorum M. Lutheri per Bullam Leonis X. Novissimiam damnatorum, 1520)*: "Oportet enim scriptura iudice hic sententiam ferre, quod fieri non potest, nisi scripturae dederimus principem ... hoc est, ut sit ipsa per sese certissima, facillima, apertissima, sui ipsius interpres ..."

53 The early Sabbath-keeping Adventists followed the motto: "No creed but the Bible." They did follow certain church traditions, but this statement is an excessive interpretation of the *Sola Scriptura* of Luther, who came in conflict with church tradition and practiced a more nuanced criticism.

54 Lohse, *Luthers Theologie*, 207–208: "dass die Schrift ... nicht erst der Bestätigung oder Inkraftsetzung durch eine andere Institution bedarf." Gerhard Ebeling (p. 119) defines the principle of *Sola Scriptura* in this way: "The Holy Scriptures are the sole source of their own interpretation." ("Die Heilige Schrift ist die alleinige Quelle ihrer Auslegung.") In other words: "To interpret Scripture by Scripture is simply to let the Holy Spirit do His own work." (Wood, 161); cf. Wenz, 104.

55 Baur, 63: "Das schöpferische, lebendige Vermögen der Schrift – ihre *auctoritas causativa* – erweist und begründet ... ihre Autorität als *auctoritas normativa*." At the same time, Scripture transcends our experience. For example, it speaks of God the Father, God the Son, and God the Spirit, without explaining the transcendental reality of God. For more on this, see below the section on "Reason and Faith." The extent to which Luther's understanding of Scripture was formed by his own experience with God will be taken up again in the section "*Sola Scriptura* and the Deeper Conflict."

mystery has been brought to light, namely, that Christ the Son of God has become man ... Take Christ out of the Scripture, and what will you find left in them?"[56]

For Luther to present the Word of God from the Scriptures with clarity to the common people, it must first have become clear to him through Christ.[57] To be sure, this Word would be quickly discarded as unclear by the natural mind of humans (Rom 8:7). Thus Scripture can simultaneously be "clear" (in our grasping it [*Begreifen*]) and "unclear" (in its grasping us [*Ergreifen*]). This tension between the clarity of Scripture, on the one hand, and the lack of clarity for the reader and hearer, on the other, is unfolded by Luther "as the doctrine of the twofold clarity of Scripture."[58]

Scripture becomes truly clear to its hearers only once "the Holy Spirit presses home the externally clear truth of Christ against human beings and causes it to become internally clear in the heart."[59] While the external clarity *(claritas externa)* of the Holy Scriptures is simply given through its subject matter, it continues to remain unclear in those hearers of the Word whom the Holy Spirit cannot reach. By contrast, when the external clarity leads to internal clarity *(claritas interior)* through the Holy Spirit, then even unclear passages of Scripture cannot overthrow it.

In the discussion of the twofold clarity of Scripture, a frequently overlooked hermeneutical aspect of *Sola Scriptura* comes into play – the Holy Spirit. "The result is a hermeneutics that does not teach how to understand in a distanced and cognitive sense but is intended to create an inner joining of Christ and the reader or hearer."[60]

## Viva Vox Evangelii – *The Proclaimed Word of God*

For Luther, the Word of God only comes alive existentially when it is preached. If God still speaks through Scripture to human beings, then it is His living Word: the

---

56 LW 33:25–26; German original in WA 18, 606 *(De servo arbitrio, 1525)*: "Quid enim potest in scripturis augustius latere reliquum, postquam fractis signaculis et voluto ab hostio [*sic*] sepulchri lapide, illud summum mysterium proditum est, Christum filium Dei factum hominem, ... Tolle Christum e scripturis, quid amplius in illis invenies?"
57 Logically, "as the interpretation and explanation of the Scriptures, the sermon presupposes them as being clear" (Rudolf Hermann, *Von der Klarheit der Heiligen Schrift. Untersuchungen und Erörterungen über Luthers Lehre von der Schrift in* De servo arbitrio [Berlin: Evangelische Verlagsanstalt, 1958], 34: "setzt die Predigt als Interpretation und Erklärung der Schrift diese eben als klar voraus.")
58 Ebeling, 126: "als Lehre von der doppelten Klarheit der Schrift."
59 Baur, 111: "der Heilige Geist die äußerlich klare Christuswahrheit gegen den Menschen durchsetzt und sie an ihm zur inneren Herzensklarheit werden lässt."; cf. Bernhard Rothen, *Die Klarheit der Schrift*. Part 1: *Martin Luther Die wiederentdeckten Grundlagen* (Göttingen: Vandenhoeck & Ruprecht, 1990) 86; Wood, 160.
60 Barth, 444.

*viva vox evangelii.*[61] It must be spoken, and it must be heard. "This is why Christ himself did not write anything but only spoke. He called his teaching not Scripture but gospel, meaning good news or a proclamation that is spread not by pen but by word of mouth."[62]

In view of this statement of Luther, "the 'sola scriptura' is only properly understood in relation to the 'solo verbo' of the act of proclamation."[63] *Sola Scriptura* is thus no doctrine, but rather describes the process by which the clear, pure Word of God through Jesus Christ is heard and believed as well. God's Word needs no human authority to interpret it. It speaks *sola* – out of itself. This means that biblical interpretation can never be completed. That would be to silence God.[64]

## Reason and Faith[65]

The sharp distinction between Scripture and other authorities is very idealistic. But "there is no such thing as Sacred Scripture 'alone'; it always stands within the context of a particular socio-cultural constellation.[66] Luther's interpretation is in fact *his* interpretation – and he was aware of this. In 1521, when he was summoned to recant his critical views on the church before the Diet of Worms, Luther said:

> Unless I am convinced by the *testimony of the Scriptures* or by *clear reason* (for I do not trust either in the pope or in councils alone, since it is well known that they have often erred and contradicted themselves), I am bound by the Scriptures I have quoted and my *conscience* is captive to the Word of God. I cannot and I will not retract any-

---

61 Liebing, 86; cf. Heb 4:12. "As living and life-giving testimony of Christ in law and Gospel, Scripture is the proclaimed Word, address, influence and assurance of God. For precisely this reason the written Word presses for the public and audible proclamation of the message set forth therein. God wants his Word to be audible." (Wenz, 36: "Als lebendiges und Leben schaffendes Christuszeugnis in Gesetz und Evangelium ist die Schrift gepredigtes Wort, Anrede, Wirkung und Zuspruch Gottes. Gerade aus diesem Grund drängt sie über die Schriftlichkeit hinaus zur öffentlichen und mündlichen Verkündigung der in ihr aufgezeichneten Botschaft. Gott will, dass sein Wort laut wird.") The original testimony of Christ (the Scripture) empowers that of the present (the sermon).
62 LW 35:123; German original in WA 10 I, 1, 17 *(Kirchenpostille 1522. Ein kleiner Unterricht)*: "Darumb auch Christus selbs nichts geschrieben, ßondern nur geredt hatt, und seyn lere nit schrifft, sonder Euangeli, das ist eynn gutt botschafft odder verkundigung gennet hatt, das nitt mit der feddernn, ßondern mit dem mund soll getrieben werden."
63 Ebeling, 129: "... das 'sola scriptura' nur recht verstanden in Ausrichtung auf das 'solo verbo' des Verkündigungsgeschehens." Gerhard Ebeling here counts the sacraments (baptism and the Lord's Supper) as proclamation.
64 Lohse, *Evangelium in der Geschichte*, 204.
65 For further thoughts on this complex topic, see Lohse, *Luthers Theologie*, 214–223.
66 Barth, 430.

thing, since it is neither safe nor right to go against conscience. I cannot do otherwise, here I stand, may God help me, Amen (emphasis added).[67]

Three criteria forced Luther to hold fast to his convictions as he had formulated them: (1) the testimony of Scripture; (2) sound reason; and (3) his own conscience. God does not work past human beings, but on and in them – with everything that entails.

## Deus Absconditus – *Scholarly Reason and Proofs for God*

How did Luther view reason? He highly valued reason as the ability to understand and to make judgments *(ratio)*. Here, to him, lies the major difference between humans and animals. Luther believed that before the Fall, man could optimally know God through his reason.[68] But after the Fall, reason only led to false and appalling conceptions of God. Through sin, human reason is fundamentally questioned.[69] "For through this [nature], God cannot be reached, and in quick succession one makes this God and another makes a different God."[70]

---

67 LW 32:112–113; Latin original found in WA 7, 838 *(Verhandlungen mit D. Martin Luther auf dem Reichstag zu Worms, 1521)*: "Nisi convictus fuero testimoniis scripturarum aut ratione evidente (nam neque Papae neque conciliis solis credo, cum constet eos et errasse sepius et sibiipsis contradixisse), victus sum scripturis a me adductis et capta conscientia in verbis dei, revocare neque possum nec volo quicquam, cum contra conscientiam agere neque tutum neque integrum sit. Ich kan nicht anderst, hie stehe ich, Gott helff mir, Amen."
68 Lohse, *Luthers Theologie*, 215.
69 The conflict Luther had with human reason also is evident in the debate over the will with Erasmus of Rotterdam. Luther sharply opposes the idea of a free will with his notion of the sin-enslaved will. Likewise, he opposes a "rational" knowledge of God to sin-enslaved reason. "Sin manifests itself even in the attempt to know God." (Lohse, Martin Luther. Eine Einführung, 179: "Die Sünde äußert sich auch in dem Versuch der Gotteserkenntnis.") – sStephan Pfürtner views Luther as standing in the same tradition as the Scholastic Thomas Aquinas. Similar to Luther, he also ruled out a "rational" knowledge of God (Pfürtner, 62). Even his "proofs for God" do not contradict this: "Seen from the conditions in which we find ourselves, God is simply inaccessible ... This basic presupposition of the Thomistic doctrine of God should precede any discussion on so-called natural proofs for God." (ibid., 60). Despite this reading of Thomas Aquinas in a Luther-like fashion, the question remains whether the mere idea of a "natural" or "rational" knowledge of God takes the radicalness of sin seriously enough.
70 "Denn durch diese [Natur] kann Gott nicht erreicht werden, und gleich darauf macht sich der eine sozusagen diesen und der andere jenen Gott." Latin original in WA 9, 448–449 *(Predigten Luthers gesammelt von Joh. Poliander, 1519–1521)*: "Nam per eas deum assequi non potest, et subinde aliud quiddam atque aliud sibi deum facit."

## Deus Revelatus – *Theological Reason and Faith*

Reason can even exist without a relationship to God. By contrast, faith, brought about through Christ in the Scriptures, leads the entire person into an existential experience that transcends reason, because it is of divine origin (cf. Phil 4:7). *Sola Scriptura* does *not* permit itself to be proven or explained by human reason, but can only be believed. In this sense "the verdict 'sola scriptura' [is] an act of confession. It ultimately refers to the *testimonium spiritus sancti internum* as the means by which the 'subject matter' of Scripture asserts itself."[71] Dealing with Scripture involves not only Scripture itself, but faith in God.

For Luther, human reason has a bad and a good side. The bad: reason wants to know God but cannot, because it is depraved through sin; the good: reason can step back and submit to God![72] That is reasonable faith.

## *Sola Scriptura* and the Deeper Conflict

After all that has been said, one may suspect Luther and his view of Scripture being involved in an even deeper conflict.

During Luther's time, the distinction between divinity and humanity was formally very clearly emphasized,[73] but in reality marginalized. Scholasticism with its claim of preserving divine doctrine, as well as Humanism, ultimately made human *reason* the judge of the reality of God's revelation. Man was elevated to sovereign "scholar" while God lost increasingly more of His sovereignty. Against this view, Luther maintained: God is exalted above everything human.[74] Because God and man are so radically different, God must reveal Himself. The means of doing this is His Word – revealed in the Holy Scriptures. There God meets man in Christ humanly. This Word can only be believed in humility. It is not about "whether or not, or to what extent one can dogmatically verify an exegetical proposition with biblical passages. Only when a better, clearer, and more joyful

---

71 Ebeling, 106 ("[ist] das Urteil 'sola scriptura' Bekenntnisäußerung. Sie bezieht sich letztlich auf das testimonium spiritus sancti internum als die Weise, wie sich die Sache der Schrift Geltung verschafft").

72 Christoph Türcke, *Heilige Hure Vernunft. Luthers nachhaltiger Zauber*, 2nd ed. (Lüneburg: Klampen, 1991), 58. Christoph Türcke sees two dimensions in Luther's relationship to reason. On the one hand, reason is a "holy whore" that can give human beings certainty; on the other hand, it is an "unholy whore of the devil" that strives to explain and know everything – ultimately to be God.

73 This is especially evident in the sale of indulgences and in the concept of a purgatory that purifies from all evil. Man must first be made ontologically fit to stand before God *[gotttauglich]*. This was even more evident in the language of *deus absconditus*, the hidden, i.e., distant, non-human God.

74 This is especially evident in the doctrine of justification by faith in Jesus Christ alone. Human beings with all their works can in no way eclipse divinity. They remain radically distinct from God (Cf. Isa 64:5; Hos 11:9).

testimony of Christ is evoked is evidence of truth delivered."[75] Luther himself said: "Although the knowledge of the words comes first, nevertheless the knowledge of the subject matter is of greater importance. When the subject matter changes, the words also change to another meaning and a totally new grammar applies."[76]

The external clarity, Christ, transforms the Word and leads to inner clarity, to faith, which recognizes God's Word in the Scriptures. The Word of God can only be correctly understood by faith. Thus the supposition arises that, ultimately, behind Luther's entire understanding of Scripture stands his own experience of Christ. Yet, "faith does not constitute God's Word, but rather the proclaimed Word of God constitutes faith."[77] The existential experience with God's Word is crucial for a correct understanding of Scripture. Thus, the deeper conflict was not so much about the "true doctrine" but rather about allowing God to be God in the face of the hubris of man.

In this sense, Luther could say: "Scripture cannot be taken to mean anything, except that man is nothing, and Christ alone is everything."[78] This hermeneutical principle, by which humans submit themselves to Christ uncompromisingly and allow Him to speak through Scripture, may indeed be considered the "mother" of all theological disciplines. All else is influenced and determined by it.[79]

---

75  Barth, 19.
76  "Wenngleich nämlich das Verständnis des Wortes [Pl.] den ersten Rang hat, ist dennoch das Verständnis der Sache [Pl.] noch wichtiger. Denn durch die verwandelte Sache [Pl.] wird auch das Wort [Pl.] verwandelt in einen anderen Sinn, sodass es eine völlig neue Grammatik sei." LW 1:264; Latin original in WA 42, 195 *(Vorlesungen über 1. Mose von 1535–1545, 1. Mose 4,5–7)*: "Etsi enim verborum cognitio ordine prior est, tamen rerum cognitio est potior. Nam mutatis rebus etiam verba mutantur in alium sensum et fit plane nova Grammatica."
77  Wenz, 41: "nicht der Glaube konstituiert das Wort Gottes, sondern das verkündete Wort Gottes konstituiert den Glauben." Cf. Rom 10:17. Jörg Baur sees a weakness of *sola scriptura* in this: "The danger of this subjective-theoretical construct lies however in that Scripture does not remain strictly prior to faith, but becomes correlative to the autonomy of faith." (Baur, 54: "Die Gefahr dieses subjektivitäts-theoretischen Konstruktes liegt allerdings darin, dass die Schrift dem Glauben nicht streng vorgeordnet bleibt, sondern zum Korrelat der Autonomie des Glaubens wird.")
78  "Die Schrift darf nicht anders 'gedeut werden,' als dass der Mensch nichts sei, und alleine Christus alles." Latin original in WA 15, 527 *(Predigten des Jahres 1534. Predigt am Ostermontag Nachmittag. 28. März)*: "Scriptura non debet aliter gedeut werden, quam quod homo nihil sit, et solus Christus omnia,"
79  Luther's understanding of Scripture is closely connected to other theological views that indicate what *Sola Scriptura* really says: "The Reformation principle of *sola scriptura* can only be understood properly when one adds to it *sola gratia, sola fide*, and, above all, *solus christus*." (Lohse, *Martin Luther. Eine Einführung*, 197: "Der reformatorische Grundsatz des *sola scriptura* wird erst dann recht verstanden, wenn man das *sola gratia, sola fide* und vor allem das *solus christus* hinzunimmt.").

## A Look Forward

Luther's Scripture Principle was the result of many years of engagement with the Bible in conflict with circumstances in society and the church that were hindering God's Word.[80] Later, *Sola Scriptura* became a theorem about Holy Scripture, and through the practice of verifying doctrinal issues simply by quoting various Bible texts, the original intent of Luther was weakened. Wherever Christ is not acknowledged as its true subject matter, Holy Scripture – even if it is used – is robbed of its content and becomes an empty word.

Today, Protestant Christians stand before the never-ending task of utilizing the biblical canon. It is not enough to adopt the views of some individuals on certain questions of doctrine. The ever-relevant discussions on revelation, inspiration, and authority demand new answers in new contexts to the old question of the authority of Scripture.[81] The Scripture Principle can never come to completion. A confession of *Sola Scriptura* is simultaneously a confession of an open interpretation of Scripture. What does God still have to tell us? Let us not harden our hearts!

Martin Luther's *Sola Scriptura* principle is a kind of theological method. It rests upon a basic attitude of faith in which a person condemned in sin gives expression to his/her radical openness to God's Word that alone can save him/her. He who Himself is the subject matter of Scripture, Jesus Christ, gets to the heart of it: "If any man will do his [God's] will, he shall know of the doctrine, whether it be of God, or whether I speak of myself" (John 7:17).

---

80  Pfürtner, 70.
81  Hans-Martin Barth honors the legacy of Luther critically when he refers, on the one hand, to his understanding of Scripture and, on the other hand, to current hermeneutical issues. "Lutheran theology and churches will have need, in the present time, for biblical translations of all sorts designed for different groups of readers, but they will repeatedly turn to Luther's Bible as a standard that makes it clear whether a translation really does justice to the Gospel as the Reformation understood and preached it" (Barth, 447f.).

Sully Sanon

## *Sola Scriptura* as *Devotio*:
## An Appeal to Theological Dialogue[1]

> *Every genuine artist must be regarded as one who is protecting something acknowledged as sacred, which he intends to propagate with thoughtfulness and with care. But every age, in its own way, tends towards what is secular, striving to make what is sacred common, what is difficult easy, what is serious amusing: and nothing could be said against this, were it not for the fact that sincerity and humour are thereby utterly destroyed.* J. W. Goethe (1749–1832)[2]

### Abstract

The "one source theory" versus "two source theory" dispute is obsolete; few proponents of *sola scriptura* today would deem other sources of theological authority trivial. This paper considers some historical and theological factors that keep the phrase viable: its polemical (political) nature, its unintended confessional developments, and its appeal to dialogue. As *devotio* (commitment to give Scripture primal authority) *sola scriptura* defines a timeless Protestant theological ethos that promotes Scripture's material sufficiency for salvation, on the one hand, and fosters an appeal to theological dialogue in an *ecclesia semper reformanda* perspective, on the other hand. Therefore, a proper defense of the primacy of Scripture reverses inadequate fights over the best theological method and accepts theologies as "metatext," that is, dialogue about and at the service (of the text) of Scripture.

### Introduction

From its inception, *sola scriptura* has been controversial. The Protestant Reformation particularly used it as a rallying cry for theological protests replacing ecclesial authority with the ultimate authority of Scripture. Seventh-day Adventists have displayed a clear appropriation of the *sola scriptura* slogan. Yet, how Adventists perceive the meaning of the phrase in the context of the Protestant Reformation is contentious. Past and present Adventist understandings of the Scripture Principle need to be scrutinized as the hermeneutical underpinnings of *sola scriptura* directly affect Adventist thinking and theology. A good starting point for such revisions is found in the historical and theological context of the sixteenth-century Reformation,

---
1   This paper constitutes the reflective part of my MTS (Master of Theological Studies) thesis that discusses the meaning of *sola scriptura* from a Seventh-day Adventist perspective.
2   Letter to the composer Carl Friedrich Zelter (1758–1832), Weimar, March 18, 1811; trans. by Lorraine B. Bodley in *Goethe and Zelter: Musical Dialogues* (Burlington, VT: Ashgate, 2009), 146.

which is barely considered in Adventist readings of *sola scriptura*. This article seeks to stimulate interest in discussions and dialogues in Adventist circles by reflecting upon the history and theology behind the phrase.

## Preliminary Remarks

Proponents of *sola scriptura* often associate the phrase with the concern of safeguarding the authority of Scripture – a fight for the primacy of the Scriptures over other sources of theological authority. Yet, Christian theology has always been concerned with maintaining the primacy of Scripture. Few Protestant scholars would deny the Scriptural Word a *norma normans non normata* status. Observably, theological polemics in the name of *sola scriptura* are not concerned with safeguarding the primacy of Scripture per se; rather they seek to end theological fights over the proper interpretation of Scripture with the help of Scripture as final arbiter. Before Luther, the church establishment judged private opinions over the proper meaning of Scripture with the theological consent of the Magisterium aided by state or ecclesiastical power. After Luther, the individual's conscience became the ultimate judge of what is to be believed from the written text. In this context, the church was expected to become a community of faith where a continuous conversation with the text of Scripture prevails, i.e., the willingness to change former views when a clearer understanding of the text is found. *Ecclesia reformata semper reformanda*. Outside this context, the *sola scriptura* slogan is void.

Today, most defenses of *sola scriptura* are still concerned with the obsolete "one-source theory" versus "two-source theory" debate while the hermeneutical nature of the phrase is being lost over continuous debating of doctrinal differences. The *ad litteram* hermeneutic of the one-source theory failed, its Christocentric allure underdeveloped. Ironically, evangelical traditions, longtime proponents of tradition-free readings of Scripture, have turned up seeking a magisterium to safeguard their rather brief theological history. A return to the hermeneutical concern of *sola scriptura* is necessary. However, this search is vain outside context. This reflection focuses on three aspects that any search for the viability of *sola scriptura* should consider: the polemical (political) nature of the phrase, its occasioned hermeneutical chaos, and its appeal to dialogue.

## The History and Theology behind *Sola Scriptura*

### Sola Scriptura *and Political Hermeneutics*

Martin Luther did not originate the hermeneutics of *sola scriptura* but contributed to its politics.[3] Up to the sixteenth century, *sola scriptura* as a nominative predicate

---

3  On Luther's hermeneutics in the early context of the Reformation, see Heiko A. Oberman, "Luther and the *Via Moderna*: The Philosophical Backdrop of the Reformation Break-

– i.e., Scripture as the ultimate authority for faith and practice – was a medieval consensus.[4] Heiko A. Oberman observes that Luther and the other mainstream Reformers were not concerned with introducing a new hermeneutic of Scripture against the tradition of the fathers. To him, the real matter at stake was "the clash between two concepts of tradition."[5] In the "Tradition 1" or the "coincidence view" of Scripture and tradition, the church was not seen as the "maker" *(innovatio)* of Scripture but rather as its witness or its guardian.[6] In this sense, Irenaeus' concept of the *regula fidei* [7] ("what is in Scripture and what is in

through," *The Journal of Ecclesiastical History* 54, no. 4 (2003): 641–670. Although Luther was distant from scholastic hermeneutics, he did not invent a new way of reading Scripture. Instead, he was defending the tradition of the fathers. He wrote to Trutfetter: "I simply believe it is impossible to reform the church, unless the canons, decretals, scholastic theology, philosophy, logic, as we now have them, be eradicated completely and other studies substituted; and I proceed accordingly in that conviction, when I pray that this may happen immediately, and the purest study of the Bible and the holy fathers be recalled. You think I am no logician, and perhaps I am not, but this I know, that I fear no one's logic in defending this conviction." WA BR 1, 170. All citations are from *Weimarer Ausgabe: D. Martin Luthers Werke, Kritische Gesamtausgabe,* 127 vols. (Weimar: H. Böhlau, 1883–2009). It is grouped into Schriften/Werke [Writings] (WA), Tischreden [Table talks] (WA TR), Deutsche Bibel [German Bible] (WA DB) and Briefwechsel [Exchange of letters] (WA BR).
4   James R. Ginther, "The Concept of Sola Scriptura in Medieval Theology," (paper given to the Hull & District Theological Society, Department of Theology, University of Leeds, February 21, 2001, https://goo.gl/1yanq7 [November 30, 2017]). The understanding of *sola scriptura* in this sense was very present in almost all theological circles. Edward Farley and Peter C. Hodgson notice that "until recently, almost the entire spectrum of theological opinion would have agreed that the scriptures of the Old and New Testaments, together with their doctrinal interpretations, occupy a unique and indispensable place of authority for Christian faith, practice, and reflection. But this consensus now seems to be falling apart." Edward Farley and Peter C. Hodgson, "Scripture and Tradition," in *Christian Theology: An Introduction to its Traditions and Tasks,* 3rd ed., eds. Peter Hodgson and Robert King (London: SPCK, 2008), 61.
5   Heiko A. Oberman, "Quo Vadis? Tradition from Irenaeus to a *Humani Generis,*" *Scottish Journal of Theology* 16 (1963): 225 (225–255).
6   "Sola Scriptura, the sole authority of Scripture over church and creed, represents, then, a consensus of the several confessional families of the Protestant Reformation. At best, the church is to be seen as, in the words of The Thirty-Nine Articles of the Church of England, 'a witness and a keeper of the Holy Writ,' which is not to be put on a level with Holy Scripture" (Jaroslav Pelikan, *Credo: Historical and Theological Guide to Creeds and Confessions of Faith in the Christian Tradition* [New Haven, CT: Yale University Press, 2003], 138).
7   See D. B. Reynders's study of tradition and how he demonstrates the novelty of its usage in Irenaeus, "Paradosis: Le Progrès de l'idée de tradition jusqu'à saint Irénée," *Recherches de théologie ancienne et médiévale* 5 (1933): 155–191. Cf. Everett Ferguson: "The emphases in Ireneaus that the tradition derives from the apostle, that it is maintained in the church, and that it is transmitted orally (as well as in Scripture) were dictated by the polemic against Gnostics, who claimed their teaching came to them from the apostles in a secret oral

Tradition is the same"[8]) constituted the theological foundation to maintain the Christian faith as "an *obiectum* or a *depositum*, a fixed quantity"[9] received from God. Therefore, the Protestant Reformation is to be understood as a call to return to the deposited content of the Christian faith in Scripture and in the tradition of the fathers. Thus, *sola scriptura* was claimed not against tradition as such but against the violation of the primacy of Scripture when *Menschensatzungen* (traditions of men) were given authority as they were claimed necessary for salvation. The process of identifying what was traditions of men, on the basis of the Scriptural text, was both a question of hermeneutics (nothing new so far) and politics.

Luther developed his concept of *sola scriptura* around the polemics of the Reformation. The emphasis on Scripture alone *(allein Gottes Wort)*[10] as sufficient for salvation became primarily a hermeneutical principle, an ablative of means, pointing to how something must be done, as Luther had to further develop his theology without the support of the church establishment. His *theologia crucis*[11] was made a new hermeneutical paradigm that moved from the medieval *quadriga* hermeneutics to *sacra scriptura sui ipsius interpres*.[12] This Christ-centered hermeneutic is indeed the *innovatio* of the Protestant Reformation, an Augustine-based *sola fide* reading of Scripture. Interestingly, Wilhelm Dilthey understood this

---

tradition." Everett Ferguson, "*Paradosis* and *Traditio*: A Word Study," in *Tradition and the Rule of Faith in the Early Church: Essays in Honor of Joseph T. Lienhard, SJ.*, eds. Ronnie J. Rombs and Alexander Y. Hwang (Washington, DC: Catholic University of America Press, 2010), 12.

8  Ferguson, "Irenaeus consistently identifies tradition with what was delivered by the apostles and maintains that it was preserved in the churches," "*Paradosis* and *Traditio*," 13.

9  Gillian Rosemary Evans, *Problems of Authority in the Reformation Debates* (Cambridge: Cambridge University Press, 1992), 72.

10  WA 15, 118.

11  Hans-Martin Barth argues: "Luther's whole theology is, we might say colored by and soaked in the blood of the Crucified and the suffering of the world" (Hans-Martin Barth, *The Theology of Martin Luther: A Critical Assessment* [Minneapolis, MN: Fortress Press, 2013], 79). Interestingly, he observes that Luther's *theologia crucis* rests primarily on two New Testament passages, (1 Cor 1:18–25, Rom 1:18–23) plus one reference from the Old Testament (Exod 33:18–23). He, however, quickly contends that "it would be a mistake to see Luther's *theologia crucis* as having a biblicist foundation. His concern is rather with taking the cross of Christ, which cannot be slotted into human categories of wisdom and strength, with the utmost seriousness," ibid.

12  Alister E. McGrath, *The Intellectual Origins of the European Reformation* (Malden, MA: Blackwell, 2004), 149. Luther's attachment to Scripture may suggest that he developed his theology from the literal reading of Scripture. But although medieval humanism contributed to Luther's *ad litteram* exegesis, it is "especially through the study of the anti-Pelagian Augustine" that Luther got his radical theology of sin, grace, and the human nature; that is, the originality of his theology. See Athina Lexutt, "Die Genese der Theologie Martin Luthers," *Glaube und Lernen* 30:1 (2015): 43–47.

shift in the interpretation of Scripture as against the principle of *sola scriptura* itself. Gadamer observes: "Ultimately asserting the Protestant creedal formulae as guides to the scriptural principle of the unity of the Bible, [Protestantism] too supersedes the scriptural principle in favour of a rather brief Reformation tradition."[13]

Unsurprisingly, Luther's fight to free Scripture and tradition from the traditions of men turned against him when the Swiss Reformers and the Radical Reformation challenged his canon-within-the-canon hermeneutics *(was Christum treibet)*. A hermeneutical chaos became pervasive in Protestant circles. The medieval consensus was broken, introducing what Jürgen Moltmann later described as a search for the "political hermeneutics" of the Gospel.[14] The Bible reader stands alone confronting the text of Scripture with "a strong revolutionary freedom which undermines prejudice against novelty in the future."[15]

*Sola scriptura* functions fully as polemics.[16] The commitment to the text of Scripture develops a polemical attitude as no external authority can judge the proper meaning of the text.[17] While the Reformation's *ecclesia semper reformanda* motto fosters a spirit of continual reformation, *sola scriptura* adherents, in the Radical Reformation tradition, tend to "transpose Reformation debates and issues into our present time, as if history did not exist, ... creating small fundamentalist factions who fight one another and the rest of the world, each residing in an isolating bubble of timelessness."[18] For Pietist theologian John Owen, argues

13 Hans-Georg Gadamer, *Truth and Method*, trans. Garrett Barden and John Gumming (New York, NY: Continuum, 1994), 177.
14 For Jürgen Moltmann this "political hermeneutics" situation starts in Reformation times with "unmasking the authoritarian myths of the contemporary powers of Church and state. Then in the name of comprehensive and many-faceted truth, it turned its attention to the scriptures in order to undermine the Church's claim to authority." (Jürgen Moltmann, "Toward a Political Hermeneutics of the Gospel," *Union Seminary Quarterly Review* 23:4 [1968]: 303).
15 Ibid.
16 G. C. Berkouwer, *Holy Scriptures: Studies in Dogmatics* (Grand Rapids, MI: Eerdmans, 1975), 299.
17 Ibid., 306.
18 Jens Zimmermann, *Recovering Theological Hermeneutics: An Incarnational-Trinitarian Theory of Interpretation* (Grand Rapids, MI: Baker Academic, 2004), 112. Wayne Grudem's *Systematic Theology: An Introduction to Biblical Doctrine* is often considered as a typical example of such hermeneutical assumptions. According to McGrath, in Grudem "interpretation takes the shape of reconciling apparently contradictory passages. Biblical passages are treated as timeless and culture-free statements that can be assembled to yield a timeless and culture-free theology that stands over and above the shifting sands of our postmodern culture." Alister McGrath, "Evangelical Theological Method: The State of the Art," in *Evangelical Futures: A Conversation on Theological Method*, ed. John G. Stackhouse Jr. (Grand Rapids, MI: Baker Books [Inter-Varsity Press, Regent College Publishing], 2000), 30–31. Although a number of evangelical scholars support the epistemological claims behind Grudem's methods, recent treatments tend to follow Kevin J. Vanhoozer taking hermeneutics with a far greater seriousness in evangelical circles. That is, "constantly reexamine our

Zimmerman, these "acrimonious interpretive conflicts" are due to human pride. For others, a hermeneutic of charity, of humility, or of tolerance[19] may help when tackling the contours of power struggles in the act of interpreting Scripture.

According to Brad Gregory, "the shared commitment to *sola scriptura* entailed a hermeneutical heterogeneity that proved doctrinally contentious, socially divisive, and sometimes (in the German Peasants' War, the Anabaptist Kingdom of Münster, and the English Revolution) politically subversive."[20] In other words, there are power plays both in the interpretative act of Bible readings and in the receptive act of such readings in the community of faith. Yet, as Gregory puts it, "There is no intrinsic, necessary, or logical connection between enjoying political support and rightly interpreting God's word."[21] Thus, when politics around clashes over the proper interpretation of Scripture supersede the focus on the text of Scripture itself, *sola scriptura* vanishes. For Berkouwer, the Scripture principle "will only have significance when it is not used in terms of a theoretical axiom for polemics, but when it takes on visible and concrete forms, showing to what extent the entire church is prepared to take every objection captive to obey Christ (II Cor. 10:5)."[22]

## Sola Scriptura *and its Unintended Hermeneutical Chaos*

With *sola scriptura*, reformation polemics shifted the interpretative power from the church establishment to the individual.[23] Accordingly, some critics argue that the phrase is a recipe for pluralism. However, Luther's appeal to individual conscience was not a new *regula fidei*. Jens Zimmermann observes that for Luther conscience was not seen as "pure and unerring."[24] Rather, one has to distinguish between "a conscience informed by atrophied tradition and one reformed by biblical study."[25] Still, however captive the conscience is to the Word of God, the reading of

---

ideas and values against Scripture and avoid the complacency and laziness of thinking that the parrot-like repetition of the past ensures orthodoxy" (ibid.).
19 According to Zimmermann's study of Owen, the belief in the power of God's word requires the insistence on the interpretive humility, ibid., 115.
20 Ibid., 92.
21 Brad S. Gregory, *The Unintended Reformation: How A Religious Revolution Secularized Society* (Cambridge, MA: Belknap Press, 2012), 151.
22 Berkouwer, 326.
23 Berkouwer argues this "sola" shift of the Reformation to be "exclusive and radical." In other words, understanding *sola scriptura* demands a look at the "wider context, embracing the polemic against all additions that influence the life of the church, even where the *sola Scriptura* is not an issue at all." (302, 305).
24 Zimmermann, 108.
25 Ibid. Cf. Ebeling arguing that "man is ultimately a hearer, someone who is seized, claimed, and subject to judgment, and that for this reason his existential being depends upon which word reaches and touches his innermost being," *Luther: An Introduction to His Thought* (Philadelphia, PA: Fortress, 1970), 119–120.

Scripture remains contextual. In this sense, *sola scriptura* is not a prerequisite for doctrinal unity. On the contrary, it fosters different theological opinions, and thence fuels hermeneutical chaos.

The post-enlightenment reaction to the hermeneutical chaos in the name of *sola scriptura* was a call for the end of the principle. Joseph Cardinal Ratzinger (Benedict XVI) puts it in the following way: "Anyone who reads attentively the ever-growing number of ecumenical agreed statements gets the ever-clearer impression that the classic criterion of *sola scriptura* is seldom applied nowadays and that instead a new formal principle seems to be developing that I would tentatively like to describe as *traditionibus*."[26] This current consensus of accepting the "other" with an epistemology void of any absolute truth whatsoever renders the task of theology to "be merely a form of diplomacy, of politics."[27] Ratzinger reminisces: "Our quarrelling ancestors were in reality much closer to each other when in all their disputes they still knew that they could only be servant of one truth that must be acknowledged as being as great and as pure as God intended it for us."[28]

In the same vein, Ulrich Duchrow puts Luther's view in dialogue *(Gespräch)* with present contextual interpretations and concludes that *sola scriptura* is not a hegemonic principle but a central element of a *Gegenkultur* (counterculture).[29] Thus, he no longer seeks the "center of Scripture," but rather tries to understand *die große Erzählung* (the grand narrative) of the scriptures. Paying attention to the political and social conflicts of Scripture in their concrete contexts, he concludes that the righteousness of God is the central theme of the Bible in view of human history.[30]

Thus, *sola scriptura* without an agreed framework of understanding, an agreed epistemology, or an agreed center of Scripture will relegate the interpretation of the text to the hands of the most powerful in the community of faith. In this sense, the *ecclesia semper reformanda* motto is overlooked and every tradition becomes a medieval Catholicism in miniature.[31]

26 Joseph Cardinal Ratzinger (Pope Benedict XVI), *Church, Ecumenism, and Politics: New Endeavors in Ecclesiology*, trans. Michael J. Miller et al. (San Francisco, CA: Ignatius Press, 2008), 96.
27 Ibid.
28 Ibid., 98.
29 Ulrich Duchrow, "'Nur die Schrift'. Hegemoniales Prinzip oder Gegenkultur?" in *Schriftgemäß. Die Bibel in Konflikten der Zeit*, eds. Carsten Jochum-Bortfeld and Rainer Kessler (Gütersloh, München: Gütersloher Verlagshaus, 2015), 207–228.
30 Ibid., 228.
31 George Karamanolis does not read consensus among the so-called "Fathers of the Church." In his view, the Fathers did not secure theological disputes with a consensus. Rather, the formation of the teaching office – the decision of the assembly of bishops – after the Council of Nicaea "invented a criterion that decides and settles doctrinal disputes" up to the 16th century, a criterion "largely political in nature" (George Karamanolis, *The Philosophy of Early Christianity* [London and New York: Routledge, 2013], 27).

For *sola scriptura* to be workable without political forces, Anabaptists and Puritans opted for a free church. Still, shifting the interpretive power from the church establishment to the individual did not put an end to the issue. In fact, the matrix became more complex, with omnipresent frictions and tensions within every Protestant congregation. Is this the only way for *sola scriptura* to be workable?

## Sola Scriptura *as an Appeal to Dialogue*

According to McGrath, "The historical origins and intellectual foundations of Protestantism are such that diversity and tension have been essential aspects of its identity from the beginning."[32] In other words, when the essentials of faith are agreed upon, the non-essentials remain open for dialogues. Woodrow Whidden suggests a similar approach in order to accommodate tensions among Adventists. "If one affirms the essentials," he advances, "there ought to be room enough to discuss, even vigorously dialogue about, controverted progressive issues."[33]

*Sola scriptura* is therefore an appeal to dialogue. Luther started his Reformation with Bible reading followed with a call for dialogue. The Swiss Reformers and the Anabaptists promoted theological dialogues around an open Bible. At the core of these practices was the principle of the clarity of the Scriptures and the belief that Bible readers are at best, in Luther's words, "witnesses, disciples, and confessors of Scripture."[34] Under *sola scriptura*, these roles are performed within the community of faith in dialogue. Yet, there was no clear warranty of unity of mind but only the willingness to come together and search the Scriptures for clarity. With such a commitment, Bible readings, far from remaining an individual act, push the community of faith toward mutual hearings and dialogues *with* and *about* Scripture.

---

32 Alister E. McGrath, *Christianity's Dangerous Idea: the Protestant Revolution; A History from the Sixteenth Century to the Twenty-First* (San Francisco, CA: HarperOne, 2007), 9.

33 "One of my deepest longings is that those who call themselves historic Adventists will answer my appeal affirmatively and that believers who do not share their particular burdens will be open, charitable, accepting, and patient in Christian respect." Woodrow Whidden, "Essential Adventism or historic Adventism?" *Ministry*, October 1993, 7–9.

34 In his *Lectures on Galatians 1535* (LW 26:58, all citations are from *Luther's Works*, American Edition, 55 vols., edited by Jaroslav Pelikan and Helmut T. Lehman (Philadelphia: Muehlenberg Press and Fortress Press; and St. Louis: Concordia, 1955–1986), Luther made this point clear. Scripture is a "queen that must rule and everyone must obey, and be subject to, her." Hence, "The pope, Luther, Augustine, Paul, an angel from heaven – these should not be masters, judges, or arbiters but only witnesses, disciples, and confessors of Scripture," ibid. Here Luther affirms the ultimate authority of Scripture. However, in confessional tone, he later concurs that "the supreme worship of God, the Sabbath of the Sabbaths, is true godliness, *to hear and read the Word*. On the other hand, nothing is more dangerous than to become tired of the Word. Therefore anyone who is so cold that he thinks he knows enough and gradually begins to loathe the Word has lost Christ and the Gospel" (LW 26:64; emphasis added). Further, he advanced that "we are to believe neither the pope nor the fathers nor Luther nor anyone else unless they teach us the pure Word of God" (LW 26:67).

Petr Pokorný provides a helpful definition of what dialogue means in this context. For him the interpretative corpus of Scripture (verbal commentary, notes to a critical edition, monographs, commentaries, homilies, meditation on the text, etc.) constitutes a "metatext," which is "a substitute for dialogue." Thus, to him dialogue has a "critical and cognitive function and challenges what had been accepted as a fixed tradition."[35] In other words, because tradition or sedimented history "becomes a part of our linguistic world," thus "the buttress of our praxis and our thinking," dialogue should be acknowledged as a "stabilizing force," one that "determines the rules without which communication with the surrounding world would be impossible."[36] Hence the interpretative task becomes a dialogue not in the sense of a vicious circle but as a spiral.[37] He further explains:

> The unique character and otherness of the text as a partner of the dialogue must be respected unconditionally. If the text were open to any interpretation, than [sic] no dialogue would be possible. The silent text remains the counterpart and norm of all interpretations. A reader who fails to respect this and adjusts the text to his or her own views loses the possibility of authentic dialogue.[38]

In the end, Pokorný interprets Luther's *Scriptura sui ipsius interpres* not as "a summary of exegetic methods ... but an expression of the experience ... of the text interpreting the life of the interpreter."[39] Here the dialogue starts with the individual allowing the text to rule over his conscience. As Calvin has observed, this dialogue demands also a "public test" of the individual experiences with the Scriptures.[40]

---

35  Petr Pokorný, *Hermeneutics as a Theory of Understanding*, trans. Anna Bryson-Gustová (Grand Rapids, MI: Eerdmans, 2011), 70.
36  "We already know that, without knowledge of what is older, what is 'sedimented,' it is impossible to express what is new" (ibid., 82).
37  "From a part of the text we proceed to the 'spirit' of the whole, and from the latter we can then understand the individual part; we are proceeding from questioning to the text and back again," ibid., 90–91.
38  Ibid., 91. In this, he subscribes to Ricoeur's view that "a good interpretation of a text is one that is able to determine, express, and evaluate its pragmatics. The originality of the text is founded on its 'point,'" Paul Ricoeur, *Du texte à l'action* (Paris: du Seuil, 1986); for an English translation see, *Text to Action* (Evanston, IL: Northwestern University Press, 1991), 124, quoted in ibid., 98.
39  Ibid., 131.
40  "If everyone has the right and liberty to make judgements, nothing will ever be settled as certain, and the whole of religion will falter. Yet I reply that there is a twofold test of doctrine – private and public. The private test is that by which each individual settles his own faith, and rests securely in that teaching which he knows comes from God ... The public test relates to the common consent and *politeia* of the church. For since there is a serious danger of fanatics rising up and presumptuously declaring that they are endowed with the Spirit of God, it is a necessary remedy that believers should meet together and seek a way of godly and pure agreement." *Comm.* 1 John 4:1, *Calvin's Commentaries*, vol. 5 (Edinburgh: Saint Andrews Press, 1961), 285, quoted in Anthony N. S. Lane, *John Calvin: Student of Church Fathers* (Edinburgh: T&T Clark, 1999), 37–38.

Interestingly, Calvin recognizes that such a "public test ... relates to the common consent and *politeia* of the church."[41] In the medieval context, the material sufficiency of Scripture for salvation constituted the basic consent of the church aided with a magisterium, the *politeia*. Today, this "common consent" is vanishing since the polemics about the proper interpretation of Scripture shifted the individual search of the Scriptures to sophisticated systematic formulations that only a select group in the church can understand – the theologians.

## *Sola Scriptura* as *Devotio*

*Sola scriptura* as *devotio* postulates that both defenders and critics of the phrase share the *commitment* to embrace the task of reading Scripture with the utmost seriousness *(devotio)*. Post-Reformation developments evidence *sola scriptura*'s sensitivity toward trends, *zeitgeist* or cultural change;[42] that is, *sola scriptura* implies not only a dialogue of the individual with Scripture but also of individuals about the content of Scripture. Thus, whether as *prima scriptura*, something close to the Wesleyan Quadrilateral, or "the Bible only" as some would prefer, hermeneutics of *sola scriptura* are void without the willingness of every reader to "subordinate" their private readings to the "rule of the word" and agree to learn from one another.

Every tradition would wish to remain true to its own identity (tradition) in doing theology, which is understandable and almost inescapable. Thus, *sola scriptura*'s developments within a given tradition hold a certain legitimacy. Consequently, a reflection upon *sola scriptura* beyond traditional boundaries seeks to outline a common thread, a red line, where the concerns of both proponents and critics correlate. *Devotio* serves as capturing the main trust in such an endeavor.

### Devotio: *A Framework*

As an ancient Latin word, *devotio* underwent considerable change of meaning. Originally, the phrase meant (1) "to vow, devote, to devote one's self to death, to sacrifice one's self,"[43] and it was associated with the idea of nemesis or fate. In the Roman imperial age, *devotio* meant "the willingness to sacrifice oneself for the

---

41  Ibid.
42  For the current evangelical debate, see Stanley J. Grenz and John R. Franke, *Beyond Foundationalism: Shaping Theology in a Postmodern Context* (Louisville, KY: Westminster John Knox Press, 2001); and Millard J. Erickson, Paul Kjoss Helseth, and Justin Taylor, eds., *Reclaiming the Center: Confronting Evangelical Accommodation in Postmodern Times* (Wheaton, IL: Crossway, 2004); this is just to mention the main positions. For a more recent review of the evangelical debate see, D. A. Carson, ed., *The Enduring Authority of the Christian Scriptures* (Grand Rapids, MI: Eerdmans, 2016), 3–42.
43  *A Latin Dictionary* (1879), s.v. "devotio." Edited by Charlton T. Lewis and Charles Short. Oxford: Clarendon Press, 1879.

wellbeing of a group or a major cause."[44] This resonates with the Old Testament accounts of Abraham's sacrifice of Isaac (Gen 22) or Jephthah's daughter episode (Judg 11:29–40). As evidenced by the translation of *devotio* in Acts 23:12, 21[45] – the only references of the phrase in the Latin Vulgate – some Roman authors used the phrase referring to (2) "a cursing, curse, imprecation."[46] In other words, as a "solemn oath" *devotio* tolerates both a positive and a negative connotation.

In classical Latin, *devotio* denotes loyalty, fidelity and respect. Medieval uses subscribe to the Roman Christian authors' sense: devoutness, piety, respect of authority. For instance, the fourteenth-century spiritual reform movement – *Devotio Moderna,* a clear demarcation from medieval scholasticism – demanded from its members (The Brethren of the Common Life) a consecration *hic et nunc* under the *imitatio Christi.*[47] Interestingly, Luther's thought and theology has been influenced by the *Devotio Moderna* especially during his stay at Magdeburg.

In this *devotio* framework, *sola scriptura* stands as a "solemn oath" to take Scripture seriously. The Reformers' experience demonstrates that such a pledge includes a willingness to martyrdom for the sake of one's conviction over the meaning of the Scripture. Moreover, as Mark Noll suggests, this "commitment" to take Scripture as final authority works both as a blessing and as a curse.[48] That is, faith commitments that helped spread Christianity to the ends of the earth, on the one hand, and hermeneutical chaos that kept Protestantism in theological disunity, on the other. Therefore, the reflection on *sola scriptura* (from a theological perspective) within this framework envisions to consider the main aspects of the phrase, outlining its "power plays," and shows its openness to both hermeneutical blessings and theological chaos.

## *Scripture Alone is Sufficient to Lead to Salvation in Christ*

Aquinas struggled in his *Summa Theologiae* with the central question as to whether the study of *sacra doctrina* through Scripture is "necessary for salvation."[49] He

---

44 Jan Willem van Henten and Friedrich Avemarie, *Martyrdom and Noble Death: Selected Texts from Graeco-Roman, Jewish, and Christian Antiquity* (London: Routledge, 2002), 19–21.
45 The text reports the Pharisees' plot to kill Paul. In both instances the Latin uses *devoverunt* [Greek: ἀνεθεμάτισαν] which some versions translate "an oath" (KJV, NKJV, NRSV, NIV, among others), others a "curse" (GNV, ERV, DBT, among others) or "a bound" (NAS).
46 *A Latin Dictionary,* s.v. "devotio."
47 See John Van Engen, *Sisters and Brothers of the Common Life: The Devotio Moderna and the World of the Later Middle Ages* (Philadelphia, PA: University of Pennsylvania Press, 2008); R. R. Post, *The Modern Devotion: Confrontation with Reformation and Humanism* (Leiden: Brill, 1968).
48 Mark A. Noll, "Chaotic Coherence: *Sola Scriptura* and the Twentieth-Century Spread of Christianity" in *Protestantism after 500 Years,* eds. Thomas Albert Howard and Mark A. Noll (New York, NY: Oxford University Press, 2016), 258–282.
49 *ST* I q.1.a.1.

argues: "it is necessary, if man is to fulfil the purpose for which he was made, that God should make certain things known to him by revelation, which his reason would not otherwise be able to discover."[50] In this sense, Scripture was viewed as the unique text where salvation in Christ is revealed. Thus, the idea that Scripture contains all that is necessary for salvation in the Reformation context was nothing new. The criticism was that of the medieval church adding "human traditions" as necessary for salvation.[51] *Sola scriptura* was then the blessed slogan that reminded Bible readers that "the official pronouncements of the Church had gone too far, in adding to Scripture, in imposing unnecessary rituals upon the faithful, and above all in claiming that these were necessary for salvation."[52]

Still, the hermeneutics that would extract from Scripture the necessary "content" for salvation was elusive. For Calvin, "nothing is necessary to salvation which is not in Scripture."[53] Such a position fit the Radical Reformers' focus on the literal words of Scripture rejecting any other authorities. The theologians of Paris, however, wrote in 1544 that "it is certain that many things must be believed which are not expressly and individually handed down *(tradita)* in the Holy Scriptures. We must accept as certain what is drawn out *(elicitum)* by the finely tuned reasoning of learned men from the text of Scripture."[54] The same is said in the Thirty-Nine Articles of the Church of England: "What is implicit in Scripture carries the same authority as what is explicitly stated there."[55] Thus, *sola scriptura* as necessary for salvation does not stand as a substitute for exegesis, rather "a certain way of reading Scripture, implying a continual turning toward the gospel as the saving message of Scripture."[56] In this sense, *sola scriptura* does not entail the rejection of past ecclesial readings of Scripture.[57]

---

50  Quoted in Evans, 75.
51  For Berkouwer, "this was the background for *sola Scriptura*," 302.
52  Evans, 74. Cf. William Chillingworth in his classic defense of *sola scriptura*: "things necessary to be believed are evidently contained in Scripture; and what is not there evidently contained cannot be believed" (William Chillingworth, *The Religion of Protestants a Safe Way to Salvation. Or an Answer to a Booke Entitled Mercy and Truth, or, Charity Maintain'd by Catholiques, which Pretends to Prove the Contrary* [Oxford: Leonard Lichfield, 1638], 115).
53  Paris Articles 20, 1544. Quoted in Evans, 75.
54  Ibid.
55  Ibid.
56  Berkouwer, 306.
57  Cf. Berkouwer, "the decisive question that the Reformers considered and answered in the affirmative was as follows: Had not tradition in the Roman Catholic Church become an independent and in fact a normative authority, valid in itself, through a gradual historical process? The Reformers wished to protest against that independence and its range of influence. The sentiment was not that of an antihistorical revolt but that of a desire for preservation and continuity" (Berkouwer, 303).

The idea of scripture alone as necessary for salvation is still present in some theological sources and certain Protestant confessions of faith.[58] A recent glossary of an evangelical editor defines *sola scriptura* as "a Latin phrase meaning 'Scripture Alone,' pointing to the Bible as the primary authority for all things necessary to know, believe, and observe for salvation."[59] Although most evangelicals often find themselves operating under an alleged epistemology where Scripture is believed to be "the only rule of *all things* which in this life may be done by men,"[60] most of their articles of faith are concerned primarily with the "saving purpose of scripture." The Church of the Nazarene's article of faith number four on the Holy Scriptures states: "We believe in the plenary inspiration of the Holy Scriptures, by which we understand the 66 books of the Old and New Testaments, given by divine inspiration, inerrantly revealing the will of God concerning us in all things necessary to our salvation, so that whatever is not contained therein is not to be enjoined as an article of faith."[61] Although Seventh-day Adventists' Fundamental Belief number one does not endorse "plenary inspiration" nor "inerrancy," it states that "in this Word [the Holy Scriptures, Old and New Testaments], God has committed to humanity the knowledge necessary for salvation."[62]

*Sola scriptura* shares the concern that "all truths that were in any sense necessary to salvation were those given publicly and directly in Scripture, or that could be directly inferred from that same Scripture" – thus acknowledging "Christian theology" to be "essentially the exegesis of Scripture within the context of the church."[63] This core of Christian theology is being less emphasized today partly because post-Reformation polemics were mostly concerned with the "metatext"

---

58 Jaroslav Pelikan observes a shift from the normal draft of confessions of faith from the Reformation onwards. He writes "almost every Reformation confession that does not lead off with *The Shema* and the Trinity devotes its opening article to the authority of Holy Scripture," *Credo*, 138 (emphasis added). In addition, most of them emphasize the sufficiency of Scripture for faith and practice, i.e., for salvation and moral conduct. See ibid., 139–157.
59 David S. Dockery and Timothy George, eds., *The Great Tradition of the Christian Thinking: A Student's Guide* (Wheaton, IL: Crossway, 2012), 108.
60 Alexandra Walsham, "'Frantick Hacket': Prophecy, Insanity and the Elizabethan Puritan Movement," *Historical Journal* 41 (1998): 27–66; Nicholas McDowell, "Self-Defeating Scholarship? Antiscripturism and Anglican Apologetics from Hooker to the Latitudinarians," in *The Oxford Handbook of the Bible in Early Modern England, 1530–1700*, eds. Kevin Killeen, Helen Smith, and Rachel Judith Willie (Oxford: Oxford University Press, 2015), 237–256.
61 Church of the Nazarene, Manual 2013–2017 (Kansas City, MO: Nazarene Publishing House, 2013), 29. For further reading see Michael Lodahl, *All Things Necessary to Our Salvation: The Hermeneutical and Theological Implications of the Article on the Holy Scriptures in the Manual of the Church of the Nazarene*, Monograph Series 4 (San Diego. CA: Point Loma Press, 2004).
62 *Seventh-day Adventists Believe...: An Exposition of the Fundamental Beliefs of the Seventh-day Adventist Church*, 2nd ed. (Washington, DC: Ministerial Association, General Conference of Seventh-day Adventists, 2005), 11.
63 McGrath, *The Intellectual Origins*, 138–139.

*about* Scripture instead of the content (the text) of Scripture itself. Maintaining *sola scriptura* as a timeless reminder that salvation is deposited in the content of the Scriptures alone would constitute a theological blessing since the *function* of Scripture is primarily to make "wise unto salvation." However, hermeneutical chaos has been observed as theological conversations *about* the text of Scripture ("metatext") eschewed the *sacra scriptura sui ipsius interpres* principle, thus, losing the *object* of Scripture in the interpretative act – i.e., confront the reader or the hearer of the Scriptures with the salvific transforming power of the Word.

## Sola Scriptura *as Theological Ground*

While the primacy of Scripture is acknowledged in nearly every theological approach, albeit not with the same propensities, recognized theological sources or models that relate sources of authority to Christian theology do not avoid hermeneutical chaos as they all face the challenges of the hermeneutical circle. Evidently, theologians operating under similar hermeneutical patterns may eventually differ in their interpretations as no one can predict the fusion of the horizons.[64] In this sense, the question as to whether operating under one or more theological sources makes a difference or not is pertinent. Apparently, the hermeneutical principle *sola scriptura* appears irrelevant in this context.

Perhaps it is helpful distinguishing between the *source of theology* and *sources of authority* for Christian theology. Until recently, the source of Christian theology was undoubtedly Scripture, the Word of God. Today, this consensus is under serious jeopardy, as the text of Scripture is believed to be written in a specific cultural context that thus must be viewed instead as "a witness"[65] among other "witnesses" to the Word of God.[66] Those who operate under this inference are quick

---

64 Grant R. Osborne, *The Hermeneutical Spiral: A Comprehensive Introduction to Biblical Interpretation*, rev. ed. (Downers Grove, IL: InterVarsity, 2010), 469.
65 Karl Barth, "'What stands there,' in the pages of the Bible, is the witness to the Word of God, the Word of God in this testimony of the Bible," *Evangelical Theology. An Introduction* (Grand Rapids, MI: Eerdmaans, 1963), 36. He recognizes the authority of the community as "secondary witnesses, the society of men called to believe in, and simultaneously to testify to, the Word in the world," ibid., 37. In this sense, "Theology is a service in and for the community and springs from the tradition of the community," ibid. For further readings on Barth's doctrine of Scripture, see, G. W. Bromiley, "The authority of Scripture in Karl Barth," in *Hermeneutics, Authority and Canon*, ed. D. A. Carson and J. D. Woodbridge (Leicester: InterVarsity, 1986), 271–294.
66 For example, Friedhelm Hartenstein sees the biblical texts not to be read as poetry or historiography but in their respective contexts as credible witnesses of experienced salvation ("glaubwürdige Zeugnisse erfahrener Rettung") ("Autorität der Religionsgeschichte – Polyphonie der Theologien?" in *Säkularität und Autorität der Schrift*, ed. Michael Meyer-Blanck, Veröffentlichungen der Wissenschaftlichen Gesellschaft für Theologie Band 45 [Leipzig: Evangelische Verlagsanstalt, 2015], 65). Cf. Robert W. Jenson who shifts the attention not to the "polyphony of testimonies" in Scripture but recognizes the canon of Scripture as "the

to give equal weight to any other authoritative theologizing source. On the other hand, (some) evangelicals who counter with the claim that Holy Scripture *is* the Word of God often belittle the relevance of other authoritative theological sources as the necessity to preserve the ultimate authority of Scripture becomes primordial. For the theologian performing under this assumption, *sola scriptura* is portrayed, of course, as theological ground. A. N. Williams puts it this way:

> The theologian of *sola scriptura* proclivities wishes to do just that: only scripture, being the record of divine self-disclosure, can ground true theological assertions and presumably to the extent that these assertions merely render divine self-disclosure in other language, they are indubitable. Nevertheless, proponents of a *sola scriptura* approach tend also to have a high doctrine of faith: we do not know doctrines to be correct because they have been reached by a process of correct argumentation; rather, we know teachings to be true because we have faith and in faith need holy scripture, trusting it to be the word of God.[67]

Williams captures the often less-emphasized confessional nature of all *sola scriptura* claims. In this sense, the legitimacy of other theological sources must not be necessarily the concern to make faith reasonable. Early Christians cultivated philosophical thinking mainly for apologetic reasons.[68] In other words, they were supposed to "always be ready to give a defense to everyone" (1 Pet 3:15, NKJV) who asks about the "rationality of faith."[69] Hence, "The truthfulness of Scripture is not a given but a case that the Christians need to make."[70] That is the task of Christian theologians to preserve the truthfulness of Scripture as a *depositum*. While the early Christians used philosophy to make such a case, the sixteenth-century *sola scriptura* postulates against the Hellenized medieval theological system. Thus, seeking faith

---

*norma non normata* of gospel-speaking and not directly of faith in the gospel or of theology about the gospel" (*Systematic Theology*, vol. 1: *The Triune God* [Oxford: Oxford University Press, 1997], 28). That is, "distinguish between Scripture's authority as living word of God and its authority as a norm used in the church's theological effort to speak that living word," ibid.

67 A. N. Williams, *The Architecture of Theology: Structure, System, and Ratio* (Oxford: Oxford University Press, 2011), 83.
68 According to Karamanolis, it is "for three main reasons: (a) in order to articulate, specify and justify the claims that occur in Scripture; (b) in order to settle disputes within Christianity about how scriptural claims are best to be understood; and (c) in order to defend the possibility of Christian faith and the attainability of knowledge by the Christians against the challenges of scepticism" (Karamanolis, 12).
69 Pope Benedict XVI shares this particular concern. In his view, "Theology rightly belongs in the university and within the wide-ranging dialogue of sciences, not merely as a historical discipline and one of the human sciences, but precisely as theology, as inquiry into the rationality of faith," "Faith, Reason and the University: Memories and Reflections," A Lecture given at Aula Magna of the University of Regensburg, September 12, 2006, https://goo.gl/3qMH3T (November 30, 2017).
70 Karamanolis, 11.

*in fontibus*, or as originally found in the biblical Word, the reformers posited Scripture alone as theological ground void not of rationality but of philosophy or "scholastic reason" as theological source.

Still, there is no room to argue that the Reformers discarded all other sources of authority. Tradition was recognized as a "source of knowledge or doctrine" but in necessary dependence on Scripture.[71] As far as reason is concerned, it may suffice to say that since the postmodern episteme rejects "absolute reasoning," the rationality of the Christian faith as argued in Enlightenment-based systematic textbooks may need to be given more local or contextual tone in the current "experiential" framework. This does not necessarily jettison the truthfulness of Scripture; instead, it seeks to confirm it.

As stated by Ellen T. Charry, "Formal recognition of experience as a source of knowledge of God is relatively new for theology as well as for philosophy."[72] It started with Schleiermacher who attempted a response to the Enlightenment in his *On Religion*. His main contention that "man is born with religious capacity" is contentious.[73] However provocative and excellent his explanation may have been, contemporary critics acknowledge the limits of his liberal agenda describing an "attitude of awe" as *the* religious experience.[74] Still, the provocative fact is that scholars often define experience as theological authority in Schleiermacher's sense. Not in the sense of

> experiences available to everyone, either through common or special Christian scriptural revelation, but to immediate, individual, private or semi-private experiences of divine illumination, visions, epiphanies, or flashes of clarity, insight, or understanding that are claimed to be personally transforming, often as moments of conversion from nominal Christianity to evangelical faith.[75]

Insofar as Charry is right arguing that "experience for theology can only be Christian Theological Experience," that is, "experiences of the God of the Christians, shaped by interactions with revelation, scripture, tradition, worship, and Christian thought

---

71  A. N. Williams, *Architecture of Theology*, 84–85. Cf. Hans Burger's recent Reformed appreciation of the Catholic view. "Without the Scriptures," he writes, "the church will disappear. That is the truth of *sola scriptura*. Without the church, the Scriptures cannot play a formative role. That is the truth of the catholic position," "A Soteriological Perspective on Our Understanding," in *Correctly Handling the Word of Truth: Reformed Hermeneutics Today*, eds. Mees te Velde and Gerhard H. Visscher (Eugene, OR: Wipf and Stock, 2014), 202.

72  Ellen T. Charry, "Experience," in *The Oxford Handbook of Systematic Theology*, eds. John B. Webster, Kathryn Tanner, and Iain Torrance (Oxford: Oxford University Press, 2007), 414.

73  Ibid., 421. Jenson makes the same remark (Robert W. Jenson, *Systematic Theology*, vol. 1, *The Triune God* [Oxford: Oxford University Press, 1997], 9).

74  The criticism is that every religious experience remains the product of a specific historical context. Charry, 421.

75  Ibid., 417.

itself,"[76] one may subscribe to Luther's "*Sola experientia facit theologum*,"[77] not in the sense that experience per se makes a theologian, but "the experience of agonizing struggle in the context of wrestling with Scripture."[78]

Christian theology can be content to have its core deposited in the scriptures. Yet, its function is to witness to this very content by passing its message from one generation to the other. This is performed at a crossroad where linguistics, stories, experiences, reasoning and philosophy meet. A proper commitment to *sola scriptura* will not ignore them; instead, they are all accepted as the broader context within which the witness to the Word is possible.

## Sola Scriptura *as Commitment to Theological Dialogue*

Commitment to *sola scriptura* when properly understood can be "happy science" in the Barthian sense of the term: "The theologian is bound, beyond all mere wonderment and concern, to knowledge and confession of his proper object."[79] Indeed, Barth's concern for the object or content of theology helps the case proposed in this essay. It is my contention that *sola scriptura* is a commitment to foster theological dialogue.

The first objection to this would be the claim that dialogue is another catchy slogan for pluralist agendas. This is partly true as models of dialogues, trialogues, tetralogues, etc. dominate the current theological discourse. Still, in its original sense of "*dia-logos*" (through-word, discourse), theology has always been a dialogue, confessional and contextual. Thus, "recent clamor for 'contextual' theology is of course empty."[80] *Dialogos* is used here not as an appeal to exchange opinions. That is the clash of "monologues." *Dia* does not entail a conversation of two: "Two monologues [or more] do not make a dialogue."[81] Here dialogue is acknowledged as "a conversation with a center, not sides."[82] People are expected to "think together in relationship," which means that no one's position is final.[83] In David Bohm's words, dialogue fosters "a *stream of meaning* flowing among and through and

76 Ibid., 421.
77 WA 50, 657–661.
78 Ronald K. Rittgers, "How Luther's Engagement in Pastoral Care Shaped His Theology," in *The Oxford Handbook of Martin Luther's Theology*, eds. Robert Kolb, Irene Dingel and L'ubomir Batka (Oxford: Oxford University Press, 2014), 469 (462–470).
79 Karl Barth, 86. Cf. Jenson, "Neither Scripture nor creed nor liturgy nor teaching office, nor yet their ensemble, can as historical structures guarantee the fidelity of our proclamation and prayer to the apostolic witness, … the church's tradition sustains the community's self-identity through time only in that it sustains witness to a particular event, the Resurrection" (Jenson, 25).
80 Jenson, ix.
81 Commonly attributed to Jeff Daly.
82 William Isaacs, *Dialogue and the Art of Thinking Together: A Pioneering Approach to Communicating in Business and Life* (New York and London: Currency, 1999), 19.
83 Ibid.

between"[84] the partners in conversation. Thus, in dialogue the goal is not "to analyze things, or to win an argument, or to exchange opinions." Rather, it is the commitment "to suspend your opinions and to look at the opinions – to listen to everybody's opinions, to suspend them, and to see what all that means."[85] In this sense, *sola scriptura* as dialogue does not promote pluralism; rather it acknowledges its possibility and works beyond its limitations.

The second objection would probably be the question, how does this work with *sola scriptura*, a radical and exclusive principle in nature. The answer is twofold and captures the core argument of this paper, that is, *sola scriptura* as a call for a dialogue *with* the text of Scripture, and *about* its meaning. It is becoming clear that such a definition seeks to reconcile both the positive and the negative aspects of the principle.

On the one hand, *sola scriptura* is a call to dialogue *with* the text of Scripture. The individual reader does not analyze, scrutinize, or exchange opinions with the text. Instead, he allows himself the experience of the word reading his life. In this sense, Scripture is not a metaphysical entity from above void of any experiential element but constitutes an historical event in dialogue with humans in history. In addition, the individual recognizes that Scripture does not necessarily read individual lives similarly. Thus, one's private experience with Scripture does not establish a final meaning of the text since Scripture remains in continuous conversation with the other. Thus, private readings contribute only to the conversation *about* Scripture (the "metatext") but not *for* Scripture. *Sola scriptura*, in this sense, remains sufficient to lead to salvation and needs no external element to make its own case, aside from the commitment of the individual readers to refrain themselves from reading the text but allow the text to read their lives, their faith experiences.[86] Obviously, text in this sense is not limited to the letter but includes the object of Scripture, the Living Word, or the center that allows the possibility of dialogue.

On the other hand, *sola scriptura* is a call to dialogue *about* the text of Scripture. Here too, text means the holy Word, the object of Scripture. It has been observed above that such a dialogue is often polemical, political, pluralist, chaotic, etc., thus jettisoning the viability of *sola scriptura*. This alleged impossibility is due to the long focus on the nature of Scripture rather than on its object. If theologies are to maintain "a cheerful openness toward the spirit of the times,"[87] it is rather the commitment to the content of Scripture that must bind all theological discourse. In the words of Karl Barth, "obedience to the spirit of the age" would

---

84   David Bohm, *On Dialogue* (London and New York: Routledge Classics, 2004 [1996]), 30.
85   Ibid.
86   Consider for instance Clement of Alexandria's theory of truth about Scripture. He argues that finding the truth cannot be carried out successfully "unless one receives the rule of truth *[ton kanona tēs alētheias]* from the truth itself." He then suggests the scriptures to be interpreted "on the basis of the spirit of Scripture itself" (Clement, *Stromata* 7.16.6 [*ANF* 2: 552]).
87   Karl Barth, 91.

render theological endeavor monotonous, predictable, and culturally dependent.[88] Hence, the dialogue that is expected here is not a particular hermeneutical choice of sources of authorities that decide how one should talk *about* the content of Scripture. It is a willingness to "think together in relationship" (no matter one's hermeneutical choice) about communal experiences of the object of Scripture. The best success in this sense is, perhaps, the worship experience, particularly in songs, where all power struggles in the community are nullified as the focus is given to the worshiped Word. When all aspects in the "metatext" reach such a goal, theology moves from being a discourse *about* the Word to become a discourse *in the service* of the Word. Therein lies, at least, a viability of a hermeneutical *sola scriptura*.

## Conclusion

As *devotio, sola scriptura* is concerned with the following: First, the primacy of Scripture is as old as Christianity and can be preserved only in dialogue with ears open to the voice of the Holy Spirit *within* the believing community. Second, *sola scriptura*'s ecclesial polemical history depicts the *devotio* (commitment) of Protestant theologies to be conversant with the (Spoken, Living) Word *through* the scriptural Word; this must be preserved. Third, the current hermeneutical chaos of Protestant theology created by naïve *sola scriptura* hermeneutics can be reversed by a return to *sola scriptura* itself, that is *devotio* (a pledge) to accept theologies as "metatext" – dialogue *about* and *at the service* of the text of Scripture. Only in this sense is *Ecclesia reformata semper reformanda* viable.

Thus, any theological hermeneutic – whether radical Anabaptism's Tradition 0, mainstream Protestantism's Tradition 1, *prima scriptura*, a Wesleyan Quadrilateral, a hermeneutical triangle, or any other – must allow Scripture its primacy, that is, the authority of guiding, judging and correcting. In other words, all traditions (including one's own) and all possible hermeneutical models must recognize that they *serve* the object of Scripture in allowing individuals to read privately their experience of salvation in the scriptural Word or through other means that the Holy Spirit may deem appropriate for those who do not have access to the written text. The task of theologies is to facilitate a dialogue within the community *about* Scripture and *for the sake* of the object of Scripture.

---

88   Cf. ibid., 90–91.

# Part II

# Perspectives on the Magisterial and Radical Reformation

*Michael W. Campbell*

# Martin Luther, Seventh-day Adventism, and the Lord's Supper

## Abstract

The Lord's Supper is a vital church ordinance with rich meaning for Martin Luther and Seventh-day Adventism. Although some four centuries apart, a comparison of the two is fruitful for understanding Adventist theology. Luther's Reformation discovery was first of all a hermeneutical insight. In turn, this led to his rejection of transubstantiation – the idea that the elements become the body and blood of Jesus. Protestants – although they agreed in their rejection of transubstantiation – were not united about the meaning and observance of the Lord's Supper. Adventists, as self-perceived heirs, who view themselves as within the trajectory of the Protestant Reformation, inherited this ambiguity about the meaning and interpretation of the Lord's Supper even as they appropriated this sacred rite in new and creative ways.

## Introduction

One of the most sacred Christian ordinances is that of the Lord's Supper or Eucharist.[1] Instituted by Jesus, it is a lasting ordinance that has various understandings in terms of meaning, purpose, and results. The Roman Catholic Church articulates a view called *transubstantiation*, which since the Fourth Lateran Council (1215) contends that the elements of the bread and wine are changed into Christ's body and blood. The bull *Unam Sanctam* (1302), possibly the greatest assertion of Roman Catholic spiritual supremacy ever issued by the papacy, featured Pope Boniface VIII who stated: "There is one holy, Catholic and apostolic church ... and that outside this church there is no salvation or remission of sins."[2] In contrast to earlier periods, the mystical body of Christ *(corpus mysticum Christi)*, as understood through the sacrament of the Eucharist, was meant to signify the church as a whole. The conflation of meaning was important because it signals just how important the Eucharist became during medieval Christianity. The Church was not

---

1  A variety of names are used to describe the Lord's Supper including the preferred term of the medieval period, "Mass" (a term retained by Luther); but Protestants have been reluctant to use this term, preferring instead "the bread," "communion," "the memorial" (or "remembrance"), or "Eucharist" among other variations. This paper utilizes the terms "Eucharist" in the context of Reformation discussions of the 16th century, and the "Lord's Supper" as the preferred term by Protestants in the 19th century, although the terms obviously overlap.
2  Quoted by C. Scott Dixon, *The Church in the Early Modern Age*, The I. B. Tauris History of the Christian Church (London: I. B. Tauris, 2016), 68.

*like* the body of Christ; it *was* the body of Christ. Thus the Eucharist or Mass became "the central sacrament of the middle ages."[3]

The rise of Protestant Christianity challenged the claims of Latin Christianity. Fine theological distinctions led to divisions within Christianity. Even though medieval Christianity was far from being united in terms of a theology of the Eucharist, it was generally agreed that it was the main sacrament. Christ was present in substance and all other sacraments without it had no meaning. It thus became a reenactment of Christ's sacrifice. Martin Luther and other Reformers "completely redefined Christian thinking on the sacrament and how the body of Christ should be understood in relation to the community of the faithful."[4]

Luther wrote about the Eucharist in a figurative and symbolic sense. Later on, he became more conservative in his stance, particularly as he became embroiled in debates with others. His view, described as *consubstantiation*, contends that bread and wine do not become Christ's actual body and blood, but that they are truly present "in, with, and under" the elements. Finally, other Reformers viewed the Lord's Supper as the *spiritual presence* of Christ. Bread and wine are not empty symbols. They are a sign that Christ is actually present.[5]

The development of Luther's view of the Lord's Supper is well-documented.[6] A study of the Eucharist during the Reformation, particularly as related to Luther, is especially useful for understanding on-going debates within the Adventist church. While Adventists have not had the in-depth debates over the Lord's Supper (the preferred term within Adventism), some of the underlying issues do relate with current debates about women's ordination.[7] What is more is that despite many differences between various Protestant factions, they were generally aligned in their common rejection of the Roman Catholic understanding of transubstantiation, the mediatorial role of the priest in transforming the emblems into the body of Christ, and the need to allow everyone access to both symbols (the bread and the wine) in kind.[8] A brief review of both Luther and Adventism on this topic can prove instructive for the present.

3   Ibid.
4   Ibid., 70–71.
5   Gregg R. Allison, *Historical Theology: An Introduction to Christian Doctrine* (Grand Rapids, MI: Zondervan, 2011), 635.
6   A recent example is Lee Palmer Wandel, ed., *A Companion to the Eucharist in the Reformation*. Brill's Companions on the Christian Tradition (Leiden: Brill, 2013).
7   The issue of the Lord's Supper is a church ordinance and so relates more broadly to a theology of church ordinances. The practice of ordination, although not held fully as a church ordinance, does relate to a general theology of church ordinances. Nicholas P. Miller observes a parallel between Reformation debates over the Lord's Supper and the on-going debates within Adventism over women's ordination. He cautions that Adventists could learn from these Reformation debates over the Lord's Supper. See Nicholas P. Miller, *The Reformation and the Remnant: The Reformers Speak to Today's Church* (Nampa, ID: Pacific Press, 2016), 89–99.
8   Allison, *Historical Theology*, 635–636.

## Martin Luther and the Lord's Supper

Luther wrote extensively on the Eucharist.[9] His "writings on the sacraments are vast" and "constitute one of his finest contributions to Christian theology."[10] Approaches range from evaluating the development of his understanding, to comparisons of Luther with other Reformers. Most scholars follow the lead of Friedrich Gräbke (1908) whose study identified four distinct chronological stages in the development of Luther's understanding of this sacrament.[11] In the earliest stage, Luther focuses on the Word, which gives assurance and forgiveness, but does not discuss the meaning of the sacramental elements. In the second stage, beginning in 1525, Luther identifies the body and the blood as the means for forgiveness. Third, after 1526, Luther combines the first two stages so that the body and blood, along with forgiveness, become the focal point. Finally, after the Marburg Colloquy of 1529, Luther argues for a sacramental union between Christ, the elements, and the proclamation of forgiveness for sins. Although scholars have adapted, modified, and condensed this scenario, most notably by Susi Hausammann in 1969, most of the scholarship pertains to how Luther defined himself against his opponents.[12]

Naturally, Luther's earliest writings about the Lord's Supper reflected the medieval tradition, but this quickly changed. In 1518, Luther published a *Sermon on the Proper Preparation of the Heart for the Sacramental Reception on the Eucharist*[13] that expressed his pastoral concern toward the issue. The following year he published another treatise, *The Blessed Sacrament of the Holy and True Body of Christ and the Brotherhoods*[14] that reflected his interpretation of Augustine between the outward sign *(signum)* of bread and wine, which points to the community of

---

9 Gordon A. Jensen, "Luther and the Lord's Supper," in *The Oxford Handbook of Martin Luther's Theology*, ed. Robert Kolb, Irene Dingel, and Lubomír Batka (New York, NY: Oxford University Press, 2014), 323.
10 *The Cambridge Companion to Martin Luther*, ed. Donald K. McKim (Cambridge, UK: Cambridge University Press, 2003), 50.
11 Friedrich Gräbke, *Die Konstruktion der Abendmahlslehre Luthers in ihrer Entwicklung dargestellt* (Leipzig: Deichert, 1908). For a discussion see *Oxford Handbook of Martin Luther's Theology*, 322–323.
12 Susi Hausammann, "Realpräsenz in Luthers Abendmahlslehre," in *Studien zur Geschichte und Theologie*, Festschrift für Ernst Bizer, ed. L. Abramowski and J. F. G. Goeters (Neukirchen-Vluyn: Neukirchener Verlag, 1969), 157–173. See also modifications by John Alfred Faulkner, "Luther and the Real Presence," *The American Journal of Theology* 21 (1917): 225–239; Ralph W. Quere, "Changes and Constants: Structure in Luther's Understanding of the Real Presence in the 1520s," *Sixteenth Century Journal* 16 (1985): 45–78.
13 WA 1, 329–335. All citations are from *Weimarer Ausgabe: D. Martin Luthers Werke, Kritische Gesamtausgabe*, 127 vols. (Weimar: H. Böhlau, 1883–2009). It is grouped into Schriften/Werke [Writings] (WA), Tischreden [Table talks] (WA TR), Deutsche Bibel [German Bible] (WA DB) and Briefwechsel [Exchange of letters] (WA BR).
14 WA 2, 742–758; LW 35:45–74. All citations are from *Luther's Works*, American Edition, 55 vols., edited by Jaroslav Pelikan and Helmut T. Lehman (Philadelphia: Muehlenberg Press and Fortress Press; and St. Louis: Concordia, 1955–1986).

believers *(communion)*, and the importance of the inward faith of the believer. At this stage, the spiritual body supersedes the natural body in the sacrament.[15] Although Zwingli took the same idea from Augustine to use it against Luther, Luther worked to connect the two together. His emphasis upon faith led him to question the idea of the sacrament justifying a person by the mere action of the sacrament *(ex opere operato)* since this would contract the emphasis on faith. Instead, Luther highlights the action of the one acting in faith *(opus operantis).*[16]

A significant shift occurred in 1519 with the publication of *The Lord's Supper, A Treatise on the New Testament, that is, the Holy Mass.*[17] He explored the Lord's Supper as a testament or will, given by Christ to the community of believers as a seal or sign expressed through the bread and wine. "This shift in understanding begins to open the floodgates to Luther's critiques of multiple Eucharistic practices," observes Gordon A. Jensen.[18] His primary critique had to do with the sacrifice of the mass as related to how people offer something to God. Instead, the Lord's Supper should be viewed as a testament, a gift of promise, given by the testator to the heirs. It is not a "benefit received [by God] but a benefit conferred" by God to us.[19] The central theme is that of God's promise. In turn, this led him to criticize masses for the dead (as "works" used to reduce time in purgatory), the practice of priests "mumbling" words of institution into the cup (because it prevented the heirs from hearing what was in the will), and communion in only one kind, the sacraments as magic to ward off evil, and the commercialization of the sacrament (in private or for the dead). All of these practices detracted from the foundational understanding of God's gift. While faith was still necessary, he emphasized the life-giving Word in the sacrament that strengthens and creates faith.

The most significant attack by Luther on the doctrine of transubstantiation is found in his 1520 *The Babylonian Captivity of the Church.*[20] He did not outright reject transubstantiation (he retained a commitment to protect the real presence), but did not consider it correct doctrine either. In fact, such a view was at best unhelpful, and at worst, illogical. Although he disagreed with transubstantiation, he felt the "real presence" should not be abandoned either. Both transubstantiation and consubstantiation explained the *how* by using philosophical categories that drew attention away from the much more important purpose of the meal: the forgiveness of sins. Such forgiveness could only happen if Christ was truly present in the Supper.

*The Babylonian Captivity of the Church* also decried the practice of withholding the cup from the laity – a direct violation of Christ's command in Matthew 26:27 ("Drink of it, all of you"). He attacked the mass as a sacrifice or good work. Instead, the focus must always be on the benefits God gives, not on what humans

15  WA 2, 752; LW 36:62.
16  WA 2, 751; LW 36:63–64.
17  WA 6, 353–378; LW 35:79–112.
18  *Oxford Handbook of Martin Luther's Theology*, 324.
19  WA 6, 364; LW 36:93, cited in *Oxford Handbook of Martin Luther's Theology*, 324.
20  WA 6, 497–573; LW 36:3–236.

can offer. Luther addressed this issue in a series of follow-up treatises: *The Misuse of the Mass* in 1521[21] and in *The Adoration of the Sacrament* in 1523.[22] Luther contrasts sacrifice and promise. A sacrifice is something we present to God; a promise is God's word that expresses His mercy and grace. "This becomes the focus of his theology of the Lord's Supper, intimately connected to God's Word of promise."[23] Thus, the primary shift for Luther was away from the actions of the priest, to God's saving activity in the sacrament. In contrast, Zwingli, Bucer, and other Reformers emphasized the faith of the recipient. Either way, the focus shifted upon the ability of the priest or upon the recipient to properly believe.[24] Either extreme deemphasized God as the subject of the action. Luther, however, saw the sacraments as signposts to the promise of the proclaimed Word, and not as important as God's actual Word of promise.

A significant shift occurred after Luther perceived a series of religious extremes, pertaining also the Lord's Supper, which forced him to leave his Wartburg castle retreat in late 1521. This illustrates Luther's pastoral concern. Initially he had argued that receiving the cup was possible, yet not mandatory. By January 1523, Luther was willing to offer the cup to all. The use of the altar then became reserved for the Lord's Supper (carrying over a strong proclivity among Protestants to decorate the table with a depiction of the Lord's Supper).[25] From approximately 1525 to 1528 Luther was pushed by those in South Germany and by the Swiss to clarify what he meant by "real presence." It is clear that this became a decisive shift in which his attention turned from attacks against Roman Catholic abuses to attacks leveled against him by other Protestant Reformers. Luther responded in a series of three major articles: *The Sacrament of the Body and Blood of Christ – Against the Fanatics in 1526*;[26] *That These Words of Christ, "This is My Body," etc, Still Stand Firm Against the Fanatics* in 1527[27] and the *Confession Concerning Christ's Supper* in 1528.[28]

In yet another treatise, *Against the Heavenly Prophets in the Matter of Images and Sacraments* in 1526,[29] Luther connected Christ's forgiveness on the cross with the forgiveness bestowed in the sacrament. Karlstadt charged that Luther taught that it was "a piece of bread" that forgave sins, but Luther refused to distinguish between obtaining forgiveness as a one-time event and the sacrament itself. He stated: "Christ has achieved [forgiveness] on the cross, it is true. But he has not distributed

21 WA 8, 506–637; LW 36:162–198.
22 WA 11, 431–456; LW 36:275–305.
23 *Oxford Handbook of Martin Luther's Theology*, 325.
24 Ibid.
25 *The Cambridge Companion to Martin Luther*, ed. Donald K. McKim (Cambridge, UK: Cambridge University Press, 2003), 29–30.
26 WA 19, 482–523; LW 36:329–361.
27 WA 23, 64–283; LW 37:3–150.
28 WA 26, 261–509; LW 37:151–372.
29 WA 18, 62–125, 134–214; LW 40:73–223.

or given it on the cross. He has not won it in the supper or sacrament. There he has distributed and given it through the Word, as also in the gospel, where it is preached."[30]

Such a distinction is crucial for understanding Luther's emphasis upon the word "distribute." It moved the sacramental action away from the bread and wine to become the body and blood of Christ to one that focuses on the benefit *given* by Christ. "The distribution of forgiveness, rather than the adoration of a transubstantiated host, makes it a means of grace."[31]

Challenges to Luther's understanding of the Eucharist came from two directions: first from within Wittenberg itself, and then, later, from Reformers in Switzerland. According to the sixteenth-century biography of medieval theologian Wessel Gansford (the *Wesseli Groningensis*), in 1521, Hinne Rode, rector of the Brethren of the Common Life in Utrecht, arrived in Wittenberg with a manuscript on the Lord's Supper.[32] The supposed author was Cornelius Henricxz Hoen (d. 1524), an affluent court lawyer from The Hague. It is unclear whether he wrote the actual tract or not, but the fact is that the tract was extremely influential both in Wittenberg and for Zwingli and others in Switzerland. His *Epistle on the Eucharist* was the first systematic defense of the symbolic interpretation of the sacrament to surface during the Reformation. He argued that the phrase "this is my body" should be interpreted in a symbolic or figurative manner. It was effectively a pledge of forgiveness, in the same way that a token or ring represent a pledge or a promise. According to the *Vita* the manuscript fell into Luther's hands around 1521, which he promptly read and rejected (and wrote against).[33]

Others like Andreas Karlstadt reacted differently. He followed Luther in rejecting the Roman Catholic notion of sacrifice and transubstantiation, but over time moved toward Hoen's position in his *Epistle*. Karlstadt became the first to publish against Luther. Of note was his emphasis upon a typological interpretation (or "ardent remembrance") that stressed the subsequent words "given for you" rather than the real presence. For Karlstadt the Eucharist was not a recreation of the New Testament supper, but rather something that could only be experienced in a symbolic or typological sense.[34]

Similarly Huldrych Zwingli was also influenced by Hoen's *Epistle*, which had been published anonymously in Worms and Strasbourg in 1525, and that had clearly reached him years earlier, since he mentions both the work and its author by

---

30  WA 18, 203; LW 40:213–214; cited in *Oxford Handbook of Martin Luther's Theology*, 326.
31  *Oxford Handbook of Martin Luther's Theology*, 326.
32  Dixon, *The Church in the Early Modern Age*, 72; Alister E. McGrath, *Reformation Thought: An Introduction*, 4th ed. (Oxford: Wiley-Blackwell, 2012), 177–179.
33  Dixon, *The Church in the Early Modern Age*, 72.
34  Ibid., 72–73.

name.[35] Zwingli, like Karlstadt and Hoen, clearly emphasized the memorial aspect of the Lord's Supper using the same symbolic mode of interpretation.

Luther was reluctant to let go of the "real presence." First, he argued against any tendency to split the physical versus the spiritual presence of Christ. Whereas Karlstadt, Zwingli, and Oecolampadius each insisted that Christ was only spiritually present in the Lord's Supper,[36] Zwingli had gone even farther by equating the symbol as figuratively representing the church.[37] Luther objected that if there was a problem with the physical presence, then the physical incarnation of Christ would also similarly not make any sense. In a similar way the incarnation could not be separated. Christ's body was given not "in the same form or mode but in the same essence or nature."[38]

Second, Luther addressed attempts to separate the bread and wine from the body and blood of Christ in the words of Jesus, "This is my body." Karlstadt argued that "this" does not refer to the bread; Zwingli insisted that the words were representative; and Oecolampadius interpreted it as "This is a figure of my body." Luther, on the other hand, maintained that the words should speak for themselves. He viewed Zwingli's argument (along with Hoen and Karlstadt) as both theologically and grammatically suspect. Such a plain meaning should not be so readily dismissed.

The third argument put forth by Zwingli was that since Christ is at the right hand of God he could not also be at the Supper at the same time. Luther responded by stating that God is present everywhere because of his omnipotence, and is active in the world. For Luther, Christ was present in the bread and the wine. He explained this "mystery" as *unio sacramentalis* (sacramental union) between the bread and the wine, and the body and blood of Christ. He refused to explain *how* this actually happened. Such theories could only serve to distract from the spiritual benefits that are to be received.

Finally, after the Marburg Colloquy, Luther continued conversations with Bucer. Bucer did come around and accept Luther's position of the "real presence" in terms of sacramental presence. Yet, there were two remaining issues that separated them. Bucer objected to the preposition used to describe the bread and body of Christ. Whereas Luther was flexible, Bucer insisted that the preposition "with" be used on a "parallel" plane to the body and blood, without mixing them together. It was this preposition that was inserted into the Wittenberg Concord of May 1536. Luther and Bucer also continued to debate who ate the body of Christ in the meal. Luther argued, based upon 1 Corinthians 11:29, that the person who partakes of the sacraments eats the body of Christ. The faith of the godly or ungodly did not affect what was received. Luther does not allow for any obedience to cause Christ's body and blood to be present. Bucer insisted that faith was crucial in the reception of the

35 Ibid.
36 See chapter 38 by Burnett on this topic.
37 Gregg R. Allison, *Historical Theology*, 650.
38 WA 26, 299; LW 37:195; cited in *Oxford Handbook of Martin Luther's Theology*, 327.

sacrament. The impasse was finally resolved when Luther, following the lead of Wittenberg pastor Bugenhagen, proposed a third category of "unworthy." Thus, ultimately, the Wittenberg Concord stated that "the body and blood of the Lord are truly extended also to the unworthy, and that the unworthy receive, where the words of institution of Christ are retained."[39]

One final Reformation development was the views of John Calvin, who steered a middle course between those in Wittenberg (i.e., Karlstadt and Oecolampadius) and Zurich (Zwingli). He maintained that the Eucharist was an external symbol in which the finite and physical were used to reveal invisible truths. This growth in understanding was a lifelong project, and remained a mystery *(arcanum)* that extended beyond human reason. He did teach Christ was substantially present for those with proper faith. Thus he comprehended two realities at once: "physical signs" that expressed invisible/spiritual truths.[40]

What is clear is that among the Reformers there was a clear *evangelical* or Protestant understanding of the Eucharist that developed. While there was still some variety, including the development, nuancing, and polarization among various Reformers, together they believed it was God's life-changing presence and action that reached troubled people. As for Luther, his views "underwent considerable development."[41] Yet what did not change was his pastoral concern against the Roman Catholic abuse of the Eucharist. Luther was consistent by emphasizing God's grace and gift expressed through the sacrament. "Thus by the mid-sixteenth century, Protestant Christianity understood the Eucharist, and with it Christ and his relationship to the Church, in radically different terms to Catholicism."[42]

## The Lord's Supper in America

Protestant attacks upon the Roman Catholic notion of *transubstantiation* meant that in general, Protestants deemphasized the importance of the Lord's Supper, particularly within an American context.[43] This can be seen in the importance of the *weekly* proclamation of Scripture through the sermon, and the resulting periodic (often *monthly* or *quarterly*) celebration of the Lord's Supper. Theological controversy further lessened its significance. The 1559 Settlement of Religion by the English Parliament both affirmed the "real presence" in the elements while leaving room for the bread and wine as symbols.[44] The middle ground meant that Protestant observance of the Lord's Supper, especially in an American milieu, was extremely rich and varied. Some, such as the late-nineteenth-century Salvation Army, com-

39  WA BR 12, 207, 209; cited in the *Oxford Handbook of Martin Luther's Theology*, 329.
40  Dixon, *The Church in the Early Middle Age*, 74–75.
41  *The Cambridge Companion to Martin Luther*, 50.
42  Dixon, *The Church in the Early Modern Age*, 75.
43  James F. White, *The Sacraments in Protestant Practice and Faith* (Nashville, TN: Abingdon, 1999), 73, 85.
44  Hans J. Hillerbrand, *A New History of Christianity* (Nashville, TN: Abingdon, 2012), 195.

pletely abandoned the practices of the Lord's Supper and baptism altogether. The presence of Roman Catholicism in the Americas meant that in former French colonies (what is today Quebec and Maryland) traditional forms of the Mass, as the ordinance is known within Catholicism, continued, and also across a series of missions that spanned from Mexico to California. Protestants were well-represented in the New England and Mid-Atlantic colonies (what is today Maine to South Carolina). It was along this eastern seaboard that many traditional Protestant divisions occurred within an American religious context. In order to appreciate the Seventh-day Adventist perspective, it is helpful to briefly review these developments.

Puritans emphasized preaching above sacrament. Even the arrangement of benches around the pulpit reinforced this distinction. The Lord's Supper was celebrated with plain vessels and plates, often with a common cup. The practice of the Lord's Supper was especially significant in terms of religious conformity. Early Anglicans in Virginia, for example, passed laws during the 1630s that mandated that individuals participate in Communion at least three times a year, with fines imposed for unexcused absences. Despite such laws, early Colonial leaders struggled to maintain the status quo. The most famous example was the infamous Half-Way Covenant that dealt with a new kind of church member – the one who did not profess conversion but still showed up at church. Jonathan Edwards (1703–1758) refused to compromise by not baptizing or offering the cup to unconverted members. Edwards emphasized the importance of conversion, and later the Half-Way model fell into disuse after the American Revolution. During this Colonial period, Protestant ministers generally celebrated Communion four times a year, modeled upon the Anglican practice of celebrating Communion on or near the principal festivals of the church (Christmas, Easter, and Ascension). Some enthusiastic clergy celebrated it as often as six to eight times per year.

The American Revolution significantly changed American religion. Egalitarian assumptions can be seen in the democratization of American Christianity. The notion of the priesthood of all believers meant that ordinary citizens could read and study the Bible without the aid of an elite clergy. American society shifted from one that was predominantly rural and agrarian to one that was increasingly urban and industrialized. Revivalism helped tame religious chaos. In the midst of democratic self-sufficiency, Americans during the nineteenth century realized that they needed to reassert the power of sacraments. Thus, the Lord's Supper began to be celebrated more regularly among new revivalist groups, especially the Baptists and the Methodists. It was also during the nineteenth century that the term "Communion" became a conventional way of referring to the Lord's Supper. Traditional divisions among Protestants (stemming back to the diversity that existed toward the end of Luther's life) continued, but now they existed with even more variety. Some of the most frequent sources of division centered around who was allowed to participate in the Lord's Supper. Whereas some religious groups became more open, others grew more exclusive. Some encouraged footwashing, but that practice – with the exception of certain Baptist groups – generally fell into disuse. The variety reflected the rich tapestry within the American religious marketplace.

## Seventh-day Adventism and the Lord's Supper

The Lord's Supper within Seventh-day Adventism evolved from one of passive adoption to active engagement. The earliest stage occurred during the formative period during and after the Millerite revival and continued up through the 1860s. A second discernible stage is also evident from the 1870s forward, during which the practice became well-established.

### Formative Development

Early Sabbatarian Adventism evolved out of the Millerite revival of the 1830s and 1840s. The movement was largely a "one doctrine" movement centered upon the Second Advent of Jesus Christ. As a result, differences in theology and practice were minimalized. It is clear that Wm. Miller himself, as a Baptist minister, observed the Lord's Supper.[45] Yet the topic was generally not a source of contention, with the exception of some extremists who mingled footwashing between the sexes (something that went against notions of propriety). Yet overall, the background of early Sabbatarian Adventist leaders demonstrates that a wide variety of influences contributed to their beliefs and practices, Restorationism (through the Christian Connexion) and Puritanism being two primary influences. In addition, with the bulk of early members and ministers coming out of Methodist and Baptism backgrounds, Sabbatarian Adventists largely borrowed the practice during this early formative period. It appears that it was largely carried over, which may also explain its quarterly observance.

The emphasis by early Sabbatarian Adventism upon restoring God's law, a creative expression of Restorationism, meant that they would view the Lord's Supper in such a manner. The earliest Sabbatarian Adventists generally believed in "closed communion" so that only committed and baptized believers were allowed to observe the Lord's Supper. As part of their view of eschatology they affirmed, like their Protestant counterparts, that these sacred symbols "had been supplanted by the idolatrous sacrifice of the mass" within the Roman Catholic Church.[46] It appears that, most likely as a result of the Baptists, early Sabbatarian Adventists adopted the rite of footwashing, too, in contrast to other Advent groups after the Great Disappointment. For example, Joshua V. Himes in the 1849 Albany Conference condemned "the act of promiscuous feet-washing" as both "unscriptual" and

---

45 Cf. William Miller, Diary for 1846, Aurora University, Jenks Collection.
45 Ellen G. White, *The Great Controversy Between Christ and Satan: The Conflict of the Ages in the Christian Dispensation* (Boise, ID: Pacific Press, 1950 [1911]), 33, 59.

"subversive."[47] Josiah Litch, in 1858, joined Himes in condemning the washing of feet.[48]

Among Sabbatarian Adventism footwashing was largely carried over from other Protestant churches. It appears that the emphasis upon Restorationism made them especially receptive to this practice. It does not appear to have been a very controversial practice – with the exception of "promiscuous" footwashing. In actuality, it does appear that Joseph Bates, one of the three co-founders of Seventh-day Adventism, held regular communion services – with both footwashing and the Lord's Supper – as a part of his revival meetings. Similarly, Ellen White reflects on an early Bible Conference in Volney, New York, at which they partook of the sacred emblems of the Lord's Supper. When someone objected that he "had no faith in what we were about to do" because he believed in the annual observance of the Passover, he was quickly rebuked.[49]

The first significant theological statement on the Lord's Supper appeared by James White in the first issue of *The Present Truth* (1849). He explained that the meaning of the Sabbath as a symbol between Christ and his church is the same as that of the Lord's Supper, for "communion of the body and blood of Christ was given for a memorial to the Church, that we may not forget the sufferings and death of the Lamb of God."[50] The most enthusiastic adherent of the Lord's Supper was Joseph Bates, who referenced celebrating the rite in almost every church he visited. The earliest known reference to a communion service by Ellen White comes from a letter in which she urges that the ordinance "should be more frequently practiced by us." She opined that it was fanaticism connected to footwashing that caused some hesitancy and confusion. She made it clear that men should not wash the "sisters" feet or vice versa.[51] It appears that this squelched any further objections and allowed for the continuation of both footwashing and the Lord's Supper.

During the 1850s and 1860s, the number of references to the Lord's Supper or Communion increases exponentially. Various theological attributes are used to describe this ordinance. Most often, the Lord's Supper is described in commemoration of the sufferings of Christ. His suffering may have reflected their own identification with suffering and isolation as God's end-time (remnant) church. It also appears that, at least early on, most Adventists were against "open communion." This was

46  *Proceedings of the Mutual Conference of Adventists, Held in the City of Albany, the 29th and 30th of April, and 1st of May, 1845* (New York, NY: Joshua V. Himes, 1845), 20.
47  Josiah Litch, "Feet-washing" *The Advent Herald*, August 7, 1858, 254.
48  For this story, see James White and Ellen G. White, *Life Sketches: Ancestry, Early Life, Christian Experience, and Extensive Labors of Elder James White, and His Wife, Mrs. Ellen G. White* (Battle Creek, MI: Press of the Seventh-day Adventist Publishing Association, 1880), 247–248.
49  James White, "The Sabbath, a perpetual Weekly Memorial," *The Present Truth*, July 1849, 3.
50  Ellen G. White, Letter 9, 1853, to "Sister Kellogg" December 5, 1853. This letter was republished as part of *Experience and Views* (1854), and then later republished in *Early Writings*, 116–117, as Ellen White's first published reference to the communion service.

apparently a source of friction between Bates and Ellen White, as she strongly rebuked him for his view on closed communion.[52]

As Adventism developed a structure for church organization that included identifying and authorizing ministers who could administer the Lord's Supper, the practice of its quarterly observance was settled in conjunction with "quarterly meetings." This practice was the dominant form of church polity during the 1860s as Adventists, who tended to live in rural places, gathered together once a quarter for spiritual encouragement. Adventist pioneer J. N. Loughborough observed later on in life that in order to increase the effectiveness of these meetings it was decided to "celebrate the ordinances of humility and the Lord's Supper."[53] It appears that such an association appeared very early on because frequent reports in the *Review and Herald* describe these same meetings as "ordinance meetings."[54] Such visits were often the only times that church members saw one of the few early Adventist ministers. Sometimes the ordinances were not celebrated, and some groups had to wait several years in order to participate in the Lord's Supper.[55] In addition, the practice of observing the Lord's Supper was frequently connected to special holidays including New Year's Eve and the Fourth of July.[56] Since quarterly meetings generally spanned an entire weekend, most often the Lord's Supper and baptisms were conducted on a Sunday afternoon. It was not unusual for the Lord's Supper to be celebrated right after a baptism by a river or lake.[57] At other times, the Lord's Supper might be used as a way to conclude a church business meeting, and in one instance, was even conducted at a funeral.[58]

In terms of spirituality, the "rite of communion" was described often as a "refreshing season."[59] Frequently it was described in terms of a "covenant" by which God's commandment-keeping people profess to "make strait paths for our feet."[60] Clearly the Lord's Supper became a central part of Seventh-day Adventist identity,

51  Ellen G. White, Manuscript 14, 1850.
52  J. N. Loughborough, "Quarterly Meetings," *The Church Officers' Gazette*, August 1916, 1.
53  See, e.g., J. H. Waggoner, "In Ohio," *Review and Herald*, December 29, 1863, 38.
54  J. N. Loughborough, "Report from Bro. Loughborough," *Review and Herald*, May 10, 1864, 188. See also A. S. Hutchins, "Meetings in Vermont," *Review and Herald*, December 8, 1863, 13; and R. J. Lawrence, "Report from Bro. Lawrence," *Review and Herald*, March 8, 1864, 117.
55  A. S. Hutchins, "Report from Bro. Hutchins," *Review and Herald*, January 31, 1865, 78. See also the editorial commentary featured in *Review and Herald*, January 26, 1864, 72.
56  Joseph Bates, "Meetings in Mich.," *Review and Herald*, March 7, 1865, 106. See also, R. J. Lawrence, "Meetings in Mich.," *Review and Herald*, June 27, 1865, 32.
57  D. T. & A. C. Bourdeau, "Quarterly Meeting in Vt.," *Review and Herald*, January 10, 1865, 54; Joseph Bates, "Report from Bro. Bates," *Review and Herald*, January 19, 1864, 61. See also Joseph Bates, "Report from Bro. Bates," *Review and Herald*, September 6, 1864, 119.
58  William Russell, "From Bro. Russell," *Review and Herald*, March 7, 1865, 111. See also, Henry Gardner, "Monthly Meeting in N.Y.," *Review and Herald*, January 12, 1864, 53.
59  S. B. Whitney, "From Bro. Whitney," *Review and Herald*, August 15, 1865, 87.

through the continued commitment of Restorationism, coupled with the lasting influence of Puritanism. Believers were exhorted to live out the "solemn truths of the third angel's message."[61] During the 1860s the earlier pushes to exclusive communion gave way to a more open attitude. It appears that both "young and old" were allowed to participate. And although there continued to be occasional admonishments that such services should be held "away from the world," for some, most notably Bates, new interests were baptized as a consequence of participating during the Lord's Supper.[62]

Most significant during this early period was the Adventist appropriation of the Lord's Supper as an affirmation, not only of Christ's death in the past, but as a way of affirming their hope in the Second Advent of Christ. There is increasing frequency to the "Advent ordinance" in which Adventists affirm both the first and the second Advents. The sacred emblems "are to show for the Lord's death till he come."[63] Altogether, this meant that for early Adventists, the Lord's Supper was celebrated as an act of commemoration of the Lord's death that extended forward also to his Second Advent.

## Refining the Practice

If the Lord's Supper was equated in symbolic terms with the two Advents, then during the 1870s and 1880s questions about its proper observance were raised. They included question regarding footwashing, unfermented wine, and who may or may not administer the Lord's Supper.

The Lord's Supper was a "solemn" service characterized by genuine "heart-searching."[64] Adventists were admonished that when celebrating this ordinance they should contemplate the death of Jesus Christ on Calvary.[65] The two Advents remained integrally intertwined in numerous descriptions. Mary F. Maxson, a young woman who during the 1870s – before her tragic death from tuberculosis – was one of the most prolific authors in the *Review and Herald*, vividly described such a service: "Language fails to describe the precious season we here enjoyed. We felt that the blessed Jesus was walking through our midst, 'though unseen by human eye.' And by faith we heard him whisper, 'Peace I leave with you, my peace I give unto you'; and we realized that 'his peace' is not as the world giveth."[66] She described Jesus as a "heavenly flame" that perfects the church. Adventists must

60 Thomas Demmon, "From Bro. Demmon," *Review and Herald*, September 20, 1864, 135.
61 C. O. Taylor, "Note from Bro. Taylor," *Review and Herald*, August 29, 1865, 104; Joseph Bates, "Meetings in Michigan," *Review and Herald*, October 4, 1864, 149; William S. Ingraham, "Report from Bro. Ingramham," *Review and Herald*, December 29, 1863, 38; William Russell, "Quarterly Meeting in Wis.," *Review and Herald*, March 15, 1864, 126.
62 [James White], "The Conference," *Review and Herald*, May 24, 1864, 204.
63 Mary F. Maxson, "The Fast," *Review and Herald*, September 20, 1864, 133–134.
64 Ibid.
65 Ibid.

resist the powers of darkness. In the end she stated that the "victory" was gained as "a real triumph."

Thus, the Lord's Supper was seen as something that strengthened the believers' faith during a cosmic conflict between Christ and Satan, what Ellen G. White described as a "great controversy" struggle. In this way, the Lord's Supper was linked to the great controversy metanarrative. This idea is further reinforced in another description by C. H. Holcomb, a Sabbatarian Adventist living in Augusta Center, New York, who stated that there "were one or two that Satan tried to prevent from doing their duty" but in the end they finally participated in the Lord's Supper.[67]

During the 1870s, questions about the administration of the Lord's Supper occupied the attention of Adventists. Part of this may be due at least in part to the continued lack of qualified (i.e., ordained) ministers. In response to a query, Uriah Smith responded that local church elders can conduct the ordinances of baptism and the Lord's Supper in the absence of any higher officer.[68] Other questions concerned whether or not to use unleavened bread. One response to a query in the *Review and Herald* pointed to the fact that since the Lord's Supper is not a type of the Passover that any kind of bread is permissible.[69] Other questions concerned whether celebrating the ordinances was too much work for the Sabbath (which may also reflect an association that the Lord's Supper and baptisms were generally performed on Sunday). Smith stated that the Biblical evidence indicates that it was conducted during the evening and that there is no prescribed time as to when it may be performed.[70]

The most significant discussion about the Lord's Supper occurred as a series of articles by W. H. Littlejohn, a blind Adventist minister, who for many years served as the *de facto* pastor of the local church at Battle Creek, Michigan, with all of its affiliated institutions.[71] The flurry of questions about the proper observance, and even the meaning, of the Lord's Supper prompted a series of articles defending particularly the practice of footwashing coupled with a discussion of the Lord's Supper. It appears that the question of time and frequency continued to be an issue. Littlejohn supported Smith by asserting that the Lord's Supper can be celebrated anytime, and there is no prescribed frequency – which may be why Adventists continued with the time-honored tradition of celebrating it once a quarter.

*Perspective*

Seventh-day Adventists did not generally define the meaning of the Lord's Supper in intricate theological terms. As a general rule, Adventists were not concerned about

66  C. H. Holcomb, "From Bro. Holcomb," *Review and Herald*, March 29, 1864, 143.
67  See editorial comment found in *Review and Herald*, March 24, 1874, 120.
68  [Uriah Smith], "To Correspondents," *Review and Herald*, May 2, 1878, 144.
69  [Uriah Smith], "To Correspondents," *Review and Herald*, January 17, 1878, 21.
70  W. H. Littlejohn, "The Rejected Ordinance," *Review and Herald*, June 13, 1878, 185–186; June 23, 1878, 193–194; June 27, 1878, 1–2.

the controversies by the Reformers from the past. They were inheritors of Luther's commitment against the abuse of this sacrament. At the same time, there are some important points of intersection between Luther and Adventism. First of all, Luther's focus on the meaning of the emblems, particularly as they took on spiritual meaning, was also important for early Seventh-day Adventists. While Adventists, among the various Protestant groups, would retain an essentially Zwinglian/Calvinist view on Communion as a memorial of Christ's death, some early Sabbatarian Adventist accounts (such as Mary F. Maxson's) suggest that Christ's mysterious presence was an important aspect of the Lord's Supper. While the understanding was symbolic, the focus was on the mystical experience in which they imagined Christ being in their very midst.

Such examples make it clear that the ambiguity by early Protestant Reformers may have contributed to the fact that early Adventists were never very precise in defining their understanding of church ordinances, especially the Lord's Supper. While ordination is not generally considered a "church ordinance" to the same level as the Lord's Supper, they still are somewhat related and a theology of ordination is closely intertwined to a theology of the Lord's Supper (if for no other reason that during the medieval period, the priest carried on a mediatorial role in conducting the Mass, a point that Protestants emphatically rejected).

The pragmatic result is that most early Seventh-day Adventists, who came from a variety of Protestant traditions – chiefly Baptist and Methodist – simply carried over with them their understanding and practice of the Lord's Supper. During the formative decades of the 1850s and 1860s, early Sabbath-keeping Adventist believers observed this ordinance on a quarterly basis. What did make them stand out as unique was their adoption of the practice of footwashing, a question that associated them with Baptist (and therefore Anabaptist) tradition – something that Luther would have decried. Seventh-day Adventists remain the largest Protestant denomination to continue to practice footwashing in conjunction with the Lord's Supper.

The lack of theological precision among early Seventh-day Adventists meant that they have largely seen themselves as falling within the broader flow of the Protestant Reformation. While not necessarily precise about the Lord's Supper, they still accepted some of the basic Protestant tenants in communion of both kinds, and in rejecting transubstantiation and the mediatorial work of the priest. Instead, they saw the primary significance as pointing to the Lord's Supper as a memorial of Christ's death. Yet at the same time, they were willing to appropriate new meaning by focusing on Christ's promise to come again. In this way, the Lord's Supper became the "Advent ordinance" that took on special eschatological significance. The teaching and practice of the Lord's Supper was a part of their daily spiritual struggle in the conflict between the forces of good and evil. On this latter point, both Luther and Adventism most definitely agreed.

*Thomas Domanyi*

# John Calvin's Legacy in Seventh-day Adventist Belief

Abstract

> Comparing John Calvin's writings and Seventh-day Adventist Fundamental Beliefs reveals a conspicuous ideational relationship between the basic theological beliefs of the Geneva reformer and later Adventist teachings. To place the latter in their original historical setting sharpens their profile, and opens the way to a better understanding of these teachings. This is illustrated by selected points of faith.

## Introduction

If you ask Adventists what they see as the origin and identity of their community of faith, the classical answer will be: Seventh-day Adventists consider themselves as a Protestant independent (free) church of North American descent, rooted in the mid-nineteenth-century Millerite revival movement. Protestant – independent (free) – North American – how do these designations fit together? The Reformation had its starting point three centuries earlier in Europe, more precisely in Germany and Switzerland.

Closer examination will inevitably lead one to the name of John Calvin. Between 1541 and 1564, in continuation of ecclesial reformation endeavors, he transformed the Republic of Geneva into a "Jerusalem of Protestantism" (John Knox), a second center of the Reformation movement after Wittenberg. Calvinism succeeded in entering regions such as France, Holland, England, and Scotland, countries which initially remained closed to Lutheranism. When, in 1620, the Mayflower with the Pilgrim Fathers set sail from Plymouth, the spirit of Calvin was on board with them. The English Dissenters, who left their homeland for their faith's sake, were dedicated Calvinists. To them, North American Protestantism owes its Calvinist imprint. The Fundamental Beliefs of Seventh-day Adventists give evidence to this fact.

In order to substantiate my proposition, I will pick as an example certain fundamental beliefs where Calvin's influence is easily observable. In this brief overview, we will have a closer look at the following issues:

- Calvin's perception of the church
- Calvin's Biblicist approach to theology
- Calvin's principle in dealing with the Scriptures
- Calvin and the Old Testament
- The secret operations of the Holy Spirit

It would also be possible to address:

- Calvin and the *sola scriptura* principle
- Calvin's understanding of the Lord's Supper

However, in order to prevent overlapping with other contributions in this symposium, I forego to elaborate on these items.[1]

## Calvin's Perception of the Church

Generally, John Calvin is considered the great Systematic theologian among the Reformers. This is why some historians have tried to portray him against the backdrop of his fundamental literary work "Institutes of the Christian Religion" *(Institutio Christianae Religionis).*[2] This point of view, however, misses the mark. On a level of equal importance with the "Institutes" are the "Geneva Catechism" and the "Geneva Church Order," works for which Calvin would have been willing to die. These two volumes demonstrate that Calvin's main concern was not the theoreticcal explanation of the biblical-reformatory doctrine, but rather the formation and preservation of the church. The persecuted Reformed churches in his French homeland should be supported and enabled to stand their ground in a diaspora environment. It is proper, therefore, to begin by exploring Calvin's understanding of the church.

The church is the focal point of Calvin's theology. To him, the church is a visible community of pardoned sinners. In attributing such significance to the church as a community of believers, Calvin distinguishes himself from Luther, who favored the invisible church over and against the visible church, as well as from certain Anabaptist circles, who wanted to define church as a community of sinless believers. For Calvin, the church owes its existence not to human excellence, but to divine grace. The hallmark of the true church, therefore, is not the moral perfection of its members, but the proclamation of the pure and undistorted gospel, and the faithful administration of the sacraments (baptism and Lord's Supper).

Within the church there are not only true believers, but also hypocrites. However, since we are unable to actually discern these two groups, there is a visible and an invisible church. These two cannot be separated from each other. Thus, it

---

1   Basic literature: John Calvin, *The Institutes of the Christian Religion (Institutio Religionis Christianae),* 1559, trans. by Henry Beveridge 1845, https://goo.gl/56GHFB (November 28, 2017); https://goo.gl/dBDcCj (November 28, 2017); *Seventh-day Adventists Believe: A Biblical Exposition of Fundamental Doctrines,* 2nd ed. (Silver Spring, MD: Ministerial Association of the General Conference of Seventh-day Adventists, 2005). See also Bryan W. Ball, *The Puritan Roots of Seventh-day Adventist Belief,* 2nd ed. (Cambridge: James Clarke), 2014.
2   *Institutio Religionis Christianae,* 1559; Christian Classics Etheral Library; https://goo.gl/UzNQkk (December 3, 2017).

would be a mistake to abandon the church because of its moral deficiencies in order to find a pure church.

The visibility of the church is displayed in its order of worship. Church order is the basis for the worship service, as well as for the entire life of the church. This order is intended to foster the worthy reception of the sacraments. An exceptional position in the church order is assigned to the office-holders, such as pastors, doctors, elders and deacons. To receive the Lord's Supper worthily presupposes the presence of a pastor legitimately called by the assembled congregation *(rite vocatus minister)*.

Despite the fact that Calvin justifies the establishment of church offices with the New Testament, his high appreciation of offices and of church order is grounded not in his Biblicism, but in his foundational religious convictions, namely the *Christus resurrexit* and his *Credo in Spiritum Sanctum*. Because of Christ's resurrection, the church of Jesus Christ exists. Because the Holy Spirit exists, he calls his church into his presence and guides it. Christ lives within the church, the Holy Spirit is at work in the church. This is why the existence of a visible community of believers is inevitable.

Nevertheless, according to Calvin, the real essence of the church remains legally and outwardly inaccessible, since the community of faith exists by means of the word of promise. Communion with God can be grasped only by faith in the divine promise (Matt 28:20). Therein lies the invisible nature of the church. By the power of the Word of God and the Holy Spirit, the church acquires a visible form among men. The essence of the church consists not only of its inner spirit, but also of its bodily form. Because the corporeality of the church is demanded by Christ, Calvin is so serious about it. Christ is the Lord of the order of worship. Wherever this order becomes distorted by unbiblical ceremonies or by an immoral lifestyle, the right of Christ as the Lord of the church is subverted. This view of the church is the basis for Calvin's high esteem of ecclesiastical functions and positions.

How close Calvin's and the Adventist views are in this respect, is demonstrated by article 12 of the *Fundamental Beliefs:*

> The church is the community of believers who confess Jesus Christ as Lord and Saviour. In continuity with the people of God in Old Testament times, we are called out from the world; and we join together for worship, for fellowship, for instruction in the Word, for the celebration of the Lord's Supper, for service to humanity, and for the worldwide proclamation of the gospel [i.e., the church is visible and recognizable]. The church derives its authority from Christ, who is the incarnate Word revealed in the Scriptures [Christ is the Lord of the church]. The church is God's family; adopted by Him as children, its members live on the basis of the new covenant. The church is the body of Christ, a community of faith of which Christ Himself is the Head. The church is the bride for whom Christ died that He might sanctify and cleanse her. At His return in triumph, He will present her to Himself a glorious church, the faithful of all the ages, the purchase of His blood, not having spot or wrinkle, but holy and without blemish.[3]

3  *Seventh-day Adventists Believe,* 163.

## Calvin's Way of Doing Theology

From his early years as a student until his death, Calvin considered himself a disciple of the Holy Scriptures. The fact that he also was an outstanding instructor of the Bible is demonstrated by his commentaries on all the books of the Bible (with the exception of the book of Revelation). This explains why in his theological approach he was incredibly biblical. This fact begs attention: Do not Adventists like to call themselves "the people of the Book"?

Calvin had systematically thought through and written down his comprehensive theological insights in his main literary work of almost 1,000 pages entitled *Institutio Religionis Christianae*. To this day, this presentation of Protestant theology is one of the most valuable to read. In order to handle the abundance of materials he is processing, Calvin used the methodology we nowadays call "Biblicist," which means: The religious convictions presented are explained historically and philologically, verified with quotations from the literature of the Church Fathers, and supported by logical arguments. Still, the final and most frequently cited authority behind all doctrine is the Bible. To Calvin, a correctly quoted Bible text is the uppermost and ultimate criterion.

Accordingly, Calvin's *Institutio* has nothing else in mind than serving as a guide to and through the Holy Scriptures. Just as God and Christ occupy the center of Holy Scripture, so Calvin's theological approach is theocentric. It leads from the knowledge of God to the knowledge of man. The compelling thing about this method is its view from top down, that is, the "view with the eyes of God." Everything human becomes secondary. The glory of God is all that really counts. This trait in Calvin's theology "bestows a rigid, but at the same time noble character upon the French Protestantism."[4]

## Calvin's Principle in Dealing with the Scriptures

Those knowledgeable in Adventist history know the famous statement of J. N. Loughborough on the question whether or not Adventists should formulate a fixed creed. It was in 1861, when in the context of the organization of the first local conference, the framing of a creed and a constitution was discussed. On this occasion Loughborough expressed what he called "the five steps to apostasy":

> "The first step of apostasy is to get up a creed, telling us what we shall believe. The second is, to make that creed a test of fellowship. The third is to try members by that creed. The fourth to denounce as heretics those who do not believe that creed. And, fifth, to commence persecution against such."[5]

---

4   Max Geiger, University of Basel, Faculty of Theology, Lecture WS 1973, author's transcript.
5   "Doings of the Battle Creek Conference," Review and Herald, October 8, 1861, 148 (emphasis added).

The reluctance to write up a fixed creed as expressed in 1861 had a lasting impact on Adventist history. To this day, the Seventh-day Adventist Church avoids referring to a creed or confession; instead the expression "Fundamental Beliefs" is used. They possess no constitutive relevance, but a declarative one, that is, they have informative significance or function, and can be revised and voted on again every five years at the occasion of a General Conference session. In the *Preamble of the Fundamental Beliefs*, approved and voted at the session of 2015, it is stated: "Revision of these statements may be expected at a General Conference Session when the church is led by the Holy Spirit to a fuller understanding of Bible truth or finds better language in which to express the teachings of God's Holy Word."[6]

In contrast to the dogmas of the Roman Catholic Church and the Lutheran Augsburg Confession of 1530, the Adventist Fundamental Beliefs – following the example of the Reformed confessional documents – forego the claim to constitute fixed statements of faith. Adventists are well aware of the limitation, subjectivity, and progression of all human knowledge, as well as the exclusivism and schismatic dynamics inherent in any dogma or confession declared to be "final." Instead of binding future generations to certain perceptions of faith and expressions of belief, they signal openness for new theological insights and discoveries in the future, trusting in the secret operation of the Holy Spirit (John 3:8; 1 Cor 12:11). Only the Spirit of God conveys final certitude in matters of biblical faith. This is why a rigid confession-tied interpretation of Scripture jeopardizes the liberty of Scripture, and thus, the *sola scriptura* principle.

The young Calvin stood at the beginning of the skeptical attitude towards creeds in the Reformed tradition. To him, the confessions of the ancient church had become a problem in his exegetical involvement with the Bible. This is demonstrated by his heated controversy with the former Sorbonne-theologian Pierre Caroli. The latter came to favor the Reformation movement and in 1535 travelled to Basel. From there, he accused a co-worker of Calvin, William Farel, of adhering to Arianism. Later – after a short pastoral employment in Geneva – he went to Lausanne, where in March 1537, he succeeded in organizing a synod against Calvin and Farel. In this assembly he required the Geneva clergy to endorse the confessions of the early Christian church (Apostolicum, Nicaenum, Athanasianum). Calvin agreed with the chief contents of the early church confessions, yet he refused to comply with Caroli's demand because to him such an indorsement implied an assault on the "liberty of Scripture."

Adventist theology is well advised to distinguish carefully between the Scriptures as *norma normans*, and the Bible-based support tools of a believer's faith as *norma normata*. This applies also to relationship between the Bible (as the essential and authoritative source of Christian faith) and the literature of Ellen G. White (as a genuine spiritual gift), or when the prime authority of the Bible is confused with the secondary role of Fundamental Beliefs as useful tools of communication.

6  *Seventh-day Adventists Believe*, v.

Calvin's position was unheard of at the time, but the synod of Lausanne accepted him. Calvin was acquitted, whereas Caroli was convicted. Not long afterwards Caroli returned to the fold of the Catholic Church.

## Calvin and the Old Testament

Adventist theologians not only bear in mind the *sola scriptura* principle, but they also follow the rule of *tota scriptura*, that is, the Bible in its entirety. This is documented in the first sentence in article 1 of the Fundamental Beliefs: "The Holy Scriptures, Old and New Testaments, are the written Word of God."[7]

This equation – the Bible equals the Old and New Testament – may seem obvious and self-evident, but in the historical context of the Reformation it was not so. While the Roman Catholic Church at the Council of Trent included some of the deuterocanonical scriptures into its compilation of fundamental doctrines, the Reformers restricted the source of divine revelation concerning issues of Christian faith and life to the canonical scriptures, consisting of the Old and New Testament. But contrary to Luther who prioritized the New Testament over against the Old and who postulated a "canon within the canon" (based on the differing Christocentric focus of Bible books), Calvin believed in the equality of the Old and the New Testament. In his opinion, they jointly constitute the Holy Scriptures that are authoritative for the Christian faith. "It is true, indeed, that if we choose to proceed in the way of arguments, it is easy to establish, by evidence of various kinds, that if there is a God in heaven, the Law, the Prophets [OT], and the Gospel [NT], proceeded from him."[8]

For Calvin, the Old and the New Testament are of equal importance, and complement each other in many ways. The continuity of salvation history is foremost in connecting them to each other. Without the Old Covenant one could not speak of the new covenant. God's dealings with mankind started at creation, and will end with our glorification. There are two decisive points between creation and consummation: the fall of man and the incarnation of Christ. The fall caused man to lose his free will; ever since he has been a slave of sin. He owns his redemption solely to Christ, who is the focus in the Old and New Covenant. The thrust of the Old and New Testament is the same, as the first heralds the promise, the latter announces the fulfillment. Furthermore, the new covenant, as opposed to the old, addresses not only Jews but also Gentiles.

The complementary relationship between the Old and New Testament can also be deduced from the word-pair "law and gospel." The law is rooted in the covenant God made with the Fathers. Here Calvin distinguishes between the ceremonial law and the moral law. The ceremonial law has been done away with by the sacrifice of Jesus; the moral law however is still binding. It has a threefold function:

7  *Seventh-day Adventists Believe*, 11.
8  John Calvin, Inst I.7.4.

Firstly, it is a *mirror* that makes us aware of our guilt and of our need for grace *(usus peadagogicus legis)*. Secondly, it serves as a *rule* that regulates public life and is the basis of civil legislation *(usus politicus legis)*. Thirdly, it serves as *seal* and rule of life of a believer; he obeys it in grateful appreciation of his redemption and as sign of his rebirth *(usus in renatis)*.

The reference to the law as the rule for public life and the basis of civil legislation shows that Calvin is interested in the Old Testament not only with regard to salvation history. To him it serves just as well in determining the attitude of a Christian citizen towards the political and societal order outside the realm of the church. The Anabaptists with whom Calvin was disputing on this point were, in disregard of the Old Testament, advocating an attitude of uncompromising political abstinence, and accordingly wanted to achieve reformation without or even against the existing civil order. Calvin, on the other hand, understood public authority to be a gift of God to ensure justice and humaneness *(humanitas)* among the people. Public authority is not an emergency order to be taken care of only by unbelievers.

Furthermore, the messianic prophecies and ceremonial regulations of the Old Testament do not mean that the civil order, which is essential for public life, should be revoked. In this regard, the Israel of the Old Covenant still is a model for everything the term "people" implies. Though the legal system – just as man – is not sinless; what makes it a gift from God is not the perfection Anabaptists were striving for, but the political order. "Humans may be wrong; God's directives we have to love."[9]

"Even if Christians live in a perishing world, they are – in both the Old and New Testament – called by God to act in solidarity with this world's civil duties and hardships. It is this dimension of the world as well, which rests in the hand of God and participates in the work of his Spirit."[10]

The Reformed churches have internalized these theological perspectives of Calvin in a most profound way, and in doing so secured for the Old Testament a permanent place in the Protestant tradition. Thus, initiated by Calvin, a hermeneutical basis has been set in motion without which Adventist theology would be hardly conceivable.

## The Secret Operation of the Holy Spirit

As one of the main leaders of the Geneva church, educated in legal and theological matters, it was Calvin's desire to share with his congregation speedily and clearly *(perspicua brevitas)* what he understood to be the essentials of Christian belief. It did not escape him that in the attempt to fathom the basics of faith in a rational

---

9  Decree Sacro Sancta Oecumenica, April 8, 1546, Calvini Opera 52, 266, on 1 Tim 2:2: „Et certe non effigit hominum pravitas quominus amanda sit Dei institutio."
10 Hans Scholl, „Der Geist der Gesetze – die politische Dimension der Theologie Calvins, dargestellt besonders an seiner Auseinandersetzung mit den Täufern," in *Calvin im Kontext der Schweizer Reformation* (Zurich: TVZ, 2003), 111 (93–125).

manner, one always arrives at one's limits. While Luther struggled all his life with the hiddenness of God, Calvin – in view of the incomprehensible dealings of God – demands of the believer a *sacrificium intellectus* and points him to God's awe-inspiring majesty. Still, he does not stop here resignedly; instead he praises the secret operations of the Holy Spirit in God's creative and redemptive acts. If God's absolute sovereignty is valid and indisputable, then the laws of logic and the demands of reason have to make way for confidence in his providence *(providentia)*.

> If, then, we would consult most effectually for our consciences, and save them from being driven about in a whirl of uncertainty, from wavering, and even stumbling at the smallest obstacle, our conviction of the truth of Scripture must be derived from a higher source than human conjectures, Judgments, or reasons; namely, the secret testimony of the Spirit.[11]

> The Spirit is called an earnest and seal to confirm the faith of the godly, for this very reason, that, until he enlightens their minds, they are tossed to and fro in a sea of doubts.[12]

> A simple external manifestation of the word ought to be amply sufficient to produce faith, did not our blindness and perverseness prevent. But such is the proneness of our mind to vanity, that it can never adhere to the truth of God, and such its dullness, that it is always blind even in his light. Hence without the illumination of the Spirit the word has no effect; and hence also it is obvious that faith is something higher than human understanding.[13]

This Spirit is God himself in the form of the third person of the Trinity. His self-disclosure to man is founded solely in his free will. This is why the function of the Spirit cannot be limited or tied to a sacrament or otherwise be exploited. In this sense, the work of the Holy Spirit is beyond any human disposal. His activities generally include the whole of creation, but in particular human beings and the church. This results in the comforting realization that an individual does not exist in a causally determined cosmic sequence of events, but is continuously taken care of and watched over by God. A person learns this by way of the Word, and God employs his Spirit to make it understandable.

By being at work in the divine Word and the human mind the Spirit binds man solely to himself and, at the same time, sets him free from all other authorities and bonds: "Since by means of this privilege of liberty which we have described, believers have derived authority from Christ not to entangle themselves by the observance of things in which he wished them to be free, we conclude that their consciences are exempted from all human authority."[14]

11   Calvin, Inst I.7.4.b.
12   Calvin, Inst I.7.4.h.
13   Calvin, Inst III.2.33.
14   Calvin, Inst III.19.14.

When this statement is thought through to its conclusion, the claim for freedom of conscience is inevitable. For God is the only witness of Himself, and if his Word becomes sealed within humans exclusively by means of the internal testimony of his Spirit, then every coercion in matters of faith or belief is denied any legitimacy.

Admittedly, still bound by the spell of the dawning enlightened absolutism, Calvin was unable to implement this radical consequence of his theology in society and civil politics. This breakthrough was the merit of his adherent Roger Williams who, in 1663 – as the first one in recent history –, succeeded to enforce liberty of faith and freedom of conscience as a law in the constitution of Rhode Island. Williams justified his historical achievement by arguing that the Holy Spirit's role in divine election and spiritual rebirth predisposes religious liberty.[15] That the Adventist pioneers in North America were in full agreement with this tradition is well known.[16]

## Conclusion

The comparison of some of John Calvin's foundational views with several Seventh-day Adventist *Fundamental Beliefs* reveals a striking relationship between the faith convictions of the Geneva reformer and the doctrines of the Seventh-day Adventist Church, which were formulated three centuries later. Placing the latter within their historical-theological framework sharpens their profile, and may also open the way for better understanding. This was demonstrated by a selection of common teachings. To this could be added several others, like the doctrine of the Trinity, or the belief in the priestly office of Christ upon his ascension. The affinity existing between Reformed theology and Adventist teaching has bridge-building potential and facilitates the church's endeavor to promote tolerance, freedom of conscience and religious liberty. By making use of this legacy, the Seventh-day Adventist Church contributes in a small measure to much-needed world peace.

---

15 Roger Williams, RGG, 3rd ed., vol. 6, col. 943.
16 The term "Holy Spirit" occurs 19 times explicitly, and 10 times implicitly in the 28 Fundamental Beliefs of Seventh-day Adventists.

Reinder Bruinsma

# The Sixteenth-Century Reformation and Adventist Ecclesiology

Abstract

Seventh-day Adventist ecclesiology originated in a mid-nineteenth century American Protestant milieu. It did not so much evolve from a careful study of biblical and historical sources, but developed as a response to the practical and organizational issues the movement was facing. The Adventist model of church governance is indebted to the various traditions from which the early Adventist leaders came, in particular Methodism and the Christian Connexion. However, these traditions were, in turn, deeply influenced by the Calvinist roots they shared with a substantial part of American Protestantism. They also show some influence of Lutheranism and, especially, of the free church tradition that was much indebted to the Radical Reformation.

What connections are there between the sixteenth-century Reformation and Adventist ecclesiology? How consciously did Adventism, as it emerged from the Millerite movement and developed into a substantial denomination, borrow elements from the various Reformation ecclesiologies for its doctrine of the church and its practical choices regarding church governance? That there are connections will become clear from this paper, but it will also become clear that the borrowing from these various ecclesiologies did not result from in-depth study and careful comparison of the underlying biblical and theological data, and was far from systematic or consistent.

Right from the start it needs to be stated that, even though the Seventh-day Adventist Church developed an intricate and strong governance structure, for a long time its ecclesiology was underdeveloped. At first other doctrines demanded more urgent attention.[1] In fact, only recently the doctrine of the church has come into sharper focus.[2] And as Adventism developed, the emphasis was mostly prag-

---

1   For a concise but useful survey of the development of the Adventist doctrinal system, see George R. Knight, *A Search for Identity: The Development of Seventh-day Adventist Beliefs* (Hagerstown, MD: Review and Herald, 2000).
2   See Raoul Dederen, "The Church," in *Handbook of Seventh-day Adventist Theology*, ed. Raoul Dederen et al. (Hagerstown, MD: Review and Herald, 2000), 538–581; Reinder Bruinsma, *The Body of Christ: A Biblical Understanding of the Church* (Hagerstown, MD: Review and Herald, 2009); Gerald A. Klingbeil, "Ecclesiology in Seventh-day Adventist Theological Research, 1995–2004," in *Andrews University Seminary Studies* 43:1 (2005): 11–29; and two publications of the Biblical Research Institute: *Toward a Theology of the Remnant: An Adventist Ecclesiological Perspective*, Studies in Adventist Ecclesiology, vol. 1

matic. The focus was on what the church *does* or must *do*, rather than on what the church *is*. The main questions were: How does the church most effectively fulfill its mission and how does the church remain united as it goes about its missionary task?

Another preliminary remark concerns the fact that Adventism did not originate or develop in a vacuum. The church was born and grew in the context of mid-nineteenth-century America. Thus, though it undoubtedly had roots (in common with many other Protestant denominations) in the sixteenth-century Reformation, early Adventism was already some centuries removed from Reformation times, and in the meantime many developments had taken place in Protestantism, notably also in the United States.

The fact that the Adventist church originated in America is an important aspect to remember. In the introduction to his book *The American Mind,* Henry Steele Commager writes that the nineteenth-century American was, above anything else, "practical about politics, religion, culture, and science."[3] He goes on to say that the American of that era was "incurably utilitarian."[4] His religion, "notwithstanding its Calvinist antecedents, was practical."[5] A cursory look at the domain of philosophy in the United States reveals immediately how utilitarianism clearly dominated the approach to everyday life and to the world at large.[6] This, to a large extent, explains the eclectic approach of Adventism in its appropriation of ecclesiological elements from the various streams of Protestantism. To the extent that they were not prohibited by the Bible, Adventists adopted elements from different traditions and sources, if they found them useful for their own situation.

## Various Ecclesiologies from Reformation Times

It seems appropriate to provide a summary sketch of the ecclesiologies of Lutheranism, Calvinism, the Radical Reformation, and such movements as Methodism.[7]

---

(Silver Spring, MD: Biblical Research Institute, 2009); and *Message, Mission, and Unity of the Church*, Studies in Adventist Ecclesiology, vol. 2 (Silver Spring, MD: Biblical Research Institute, 2013).

3 Henry Steele Commager, *The American Mind: An Interpretation of American Thought and Character since the 1880's* (New Haven & London: Yale University Press, 1950), 7.
4 Ibid., 8.
5 Ibid., 9.
6 See the second part of Bruce Kuklick, *A History of Philosophy in America, 1720–2000* (Oxford: Clarendon Press, 2001), 95–178 ("The Age of Pragmatism").
7 There is a great number of books and scholarly articles that deal with the history of the doctrine of the church and with the details of the ecclesiologies of the various traditions that emerged from the Reformation. There are also many useful summaries and comparisons of these various views. I have found the summary provided by Veli-Matti Kärkkäinen especially helpful: *An Introduction to Ecclesiology: Ecumenical, Historical and Global Perspectives* (Downers Grove, IL: InterVarsity, 2002), 17–91. See also Raoul Dederen, 569–575; Justo L. González, *A History of Christian Thought*, vol. 3 (Nashville, TN: Abingdon, 1987), 61–

## Luther

Several pre-cursors of the Reformation had already, for some considerable time, been protesting against erroneous ideas about the church in the Roman Catholic "mother church" with its hierarchical and sacerdotal structure and its serious abuses. But it was Martin Luther (1483–1546) who was bold enough to eventually cut all ties with the Church of Rome. Through his study of Paul's Letter to the Romans, Luther became convinced that man is saved on the basis of grace and is justified by God through faith. This had profound consequences for his view of the church. He returned to the Augustinian thesis that the church is always a mixed community, with justified sinners in various stages of spiritual growth.[8] Confronted with the heresy of Donatism, the church father forcefully rejected the idea of a pure church. The communion of the saints is always simultaneously a communion of sinners. This is in line with Luther's soteriological maxim that the believer is *simul iustus et peccator* – simultaneously righteous and sinful.

The church, Luther maintained, is where the Word of God is purely preached and heard and where the sacraments – i.e., baptism and communion – are properly administered. These are the only two *notae ecclesiae* or marks of the church.

Luther placed great emphasis on the New Testament key principle of the priesthood of all believers (over against the sacerdotal system of Catholicism). However, he recognized a special role for those who are called to preach and who are ordained for public service. It is the task of the pastors and the bishops to regard every diocese as a hospital where the church members receive the treatment they need.

The church is both visible and invisible. For Luther both aspects were important. He stressed the non-institutional aspect of the church and preferred the terms *Sammlung* (gathering) or *Gemeinde* (community), over the word *Kirche* (church). Baptism is linked with faith, but faith does not have to precede baptism. Luther defended infant baptism and rejected the necessity of believers' baptism. His view of the Lord's Supper was a compromise between the Roman Catholic doctrine of transubstantiation and the view of other contemporary Reformers who defended a symbolic meaning. Luther's concept is referred to as *consubstantiation*.

Another important aspect to be mentioned is Luther's doctrine of the two kingdoms – both are created by God, but with different roles. Though the church and the state have their own spheres, Luther did not want total separation.

---

69, 79–85, 161–174; Alister E. McGrath, *Historical Theology: An Introduction to the History of Christian Thought* (Malden, MA, and Oxford, UK: Basil, 1998), 200–207; and Mark Husbands and Daniel J. Treier, *The Community of the Word: Towards an Evangelical Ecclesiology* (Downers Grove, IL: InterVarsity, 2005), 23–40.

8 McGrath, 34; Jaroslav Pelikan, *The Emergence of the Catholic Tradition (100–600)*, in *A History of the Development of Doctrine*, vol. 1 (Chicago, IL: University of Chicago Press, 1971), 302–312.

## Zwingli

Before we go on to John Calvin, we need to say a few words about another prominent Reformer: Huldrych Zwingli (1484–1531). Some of his ideas were to have a significant influence on the Radical Reformers, and thereby on developments in the free churches, also in North America. But for our present purpose, Zwingli is less important than either Martin Luther or John Calvin.

Zwingli was more radical than Luther in rejecting the traditions of the medieval church. Like Luther he recognized the existence of an invisible as well as a visible church. The latter must be kept as pure as possible. The local church must therefore play an important role in providing the necessary discipline. Like Luther and Calvin, Zwingli defended infant baptism. He differed from Luther in his views on the Lord's Supper, which he regarded as purely symbolic. Zwingli saw a very close connection between church and state which came close to a form of theocracy.

## John Calvin

McGrath points to the fact that the first generation of reformers was particularly preoccupied with the question of *grace*, while the representatives of the second generation had to address the question of the *church*, as they came under increasing pressure to develop a coherent ecclesiology that would justify the break with Rome. Where Luther was especially occupied with the doctrine of grace, Martin Bucer and John Calvin were, in particular, responsible for the development of the Protestant understanding of the church.[9]

A significant portion of Calvin's *Institutes of the Christian Religion*[10] was devoted to his views on the church. Like Luther, Calvin proposed a minimalist definition of the church: The church is where the Word of God is purely preached and heard and where the sacraments are administered according to Christ's instructions. However, Calvin did not, to the extent that Luther did, refer to the continuity with the historical church through the ages. Calvin also more clearly differentiated between the perfect invisible church of all the elect, and the visible church, where both the elect and the reprobate are members. It is not the condition of the members but the presence of the authorized means of grace that determines whether it is the true church. The visible church is a sign of the invisible. Calvin strongly emphasizes the need for discipline, which is to be administered by the pastor.

One of the most important points to keep in mind in the context of this study is that Calvin believed that the Bible teaches a four-fold church order: pastor, teacher, elder, and deacon. He insisted that the church must return to the organizational model of early Christianity. Luther accepted things that were not expressly forbidden by Scripture; Calvin only accepted what was clearly taught by the Bible.

9   McGrath, 168.
10  John Calvin, *Institutes of the Christian Religion*, transl. Henry Beveridge (Peabody, MS: Hendrickson Publishers, 2012), Book iv, 669–988.

Nonetheless, he defended – like the other Reformers – infant baptism. He argued that, if faith must precede baptism, it becomes a kind of work and is no longer a symbol of true grace.

Calvin's view of the Lord's Supper was somewhere between that of Luther and that of Zwingli. He did not believe in the real presence of Christ in the bread and the wine but regarded Zwingli's view of mere symbolism as too meager. He argued that the bread and the wine are signs, which in a very pregnant way show us how the blood and body of Christ are available to us.

Calvin defended an integral relationship between the church and the state. During his Geneva years, he saw the church and the state as parallel entities, with a common goal, providing mutual support and collaboration. In later years, he described the church and the state as two aspects of one single reality that cannot be identified. The state is subject to the church and Christian statesmen are to defend true doctrine.

Calvinism developed a theory of a just war and of resistance against tyranny, provided some clear conditions are met,[11] and defended the use of the death penalty. If necessary, the state was to assist the church in disciplining its members. The emphasis on severe discipline, no doubt, was a factor in stimulating a legalist undercurrent in much of Calvinism, as it sought "to implement specific and rather ascetic norms of Christian conduct."[12] Calvin placed more emphasis on correct faith and an upright Christian life than Luther did.

Calvin's view of church governance was based on the principle that authority should arise from the church's base. At the local level, pastors, teachers (as distinct from the office of the pastor),[13] elders, and deacons were to care for the well-being of the congregations. Delegates from the lower levels were to elect the members of higher ecclesial bodies – a method that became very influential in the widespread Presbyterian model of church governance.

## Radical Reformers

Some reformers were more radical than Zwingli, Luther, Calvin, and their associates. The Anabaptists were the most important wing of the so-called "Radical Reformation."[14] They rejected the kind of close association between church and state that would lead to the establishment of state churches or established churches

---

11 See Reinder Bruinsma, "The Calvinistic Theory of the Right of Resistance and its Influence on the Dutch Revolt against Spain," unpub. MA thesis (Andrews University, 1966).
12 Kärkkäinen, 51.
13 Calvin, *Institutes*, Book IV, chapter 3, sections 4 and 5; Travis Fentiman, "Introduction to the Biblical Office of Teacher," https://goo.gl/4wTD2x (November 28,2017).
14 A good guide to the Radical Reformation is still George H. Williams, *The Radical Reformation* (Philadelphia, PA: Westminster, 1962); see also William R. Estep, *The Anabaptist Story: An Introduction to Sixteenth-Century Anabaptism*, 3rd ed. (Grand Rapids, MI: Eerdmans, 1996).

in a number of European countries. The Radical Reformation provided the roots for such movements as the Mennonites, the Quakers, and the Baptists. In many ways, modern evangelicalism (including Adventism) can trace some of its major ideas to the Radical Reformation.

The Anabaptists insisted that believers' baptism was the only valid mode of entrance into the church, which they conceived of as a visible community of committed Christians. They saw themselves as the true church of God – as an assembly of the righteous, rather than a mixed body of sinners in various stages of their Christian development.

The Radical Reformers were opposed to the territorial system of the Lutherans (*cuius regio, eius religio*, a concept agreed upon in the Augsburg peace agreement of 1555); they stood for total separation of church and state. They also opposed any participation in warfare and the swearing of oaths.

## *The Christian Connexion and Methodism*

Two other Christian movements must be mentioned. One has become global, the other was strictly American, remained small and rather quickly disappeared from the religious scene. These movements had a major impact on the thinking of the Adventist pioneers. Some of the early Adventist leaders had belonged to the *Christian Connexion*, an early nineteenth-century reform movement that originated when Christians with a mixed denominational background wanted to return to a version of faith that would be true to the New Testament model.[15] It was a branch of the wider movement of so-called primitivism and restorationism. The Connexionists tended to be extremely biblicistic and claimed that they had no other creed than the Bible. Two of the three founders of the Adventist Church – James White and Joseph Bates – had been Connexionists.[16] For the early Connexionists, any form of organization was associated with the devil. Yet, practical considerations forced them to somewhat mitigate this initial anti-organization stance, and by 1830, state conferences were formed that met each year.[17]

Methodism originated within the Church of England, but became a separate movement as time went on.[18] It was a latecomer on the American religious scene,

---

15 For a discussion of the main theological convictions of the Connexionists, such as their anti-Trinitarian position and their acceptance of conditional immortality, see George R. Knight, *Joseph Bates: The Real Founder of Seventh-day Adventism* (Hagerstown, MD: Review and Herald, 2004), 38–41.

16 George R. Knight, "Christian Connexion," in *The Ellen G. White Encyclopedia*, ed. Denis Fortin and Jerry Moon (Hagerstown, MD: Review and Herald, 2013), 702–703.

17 Andrew G. Mustard, *James White and SDA Organization* (Berrien Springs, MI: Andrews Univ. Press, 1987), 29–33; George R. Knight, *Organizing to Beat the Devil: The Development of Adventist Church Structure* (Hagerstown, MD: Review and Herald, 2001), 16–17.

18 See Richard P. Heitzenrater, *Wesley and the People Called Methodists* (Nashville, TN: Abingdon, 1995), especially chapter 4ff; John H. Wigger, *Taking Heaven by Storm:*

but eventually cornered a major portion of the American religious market. In 1776, there were only 65 Methodist churches (with an estimated average size of circa 70 members) in the American colonies, out of a total of over 3,200 Protestant congregations.[19] However, by 1850 one in every three American Protestants was a Methodist.[20] American Methodism split over the years into many different denominations.

Methodism never developed a detailed ecclesiology. Gradually it came to embody elements from Anglicanism (e.g., its hierarchical structure), along with elements from the free-church tradition, with its roots in the Radical Reformation.

Methodist influences on Adventism are, in particular, noticeable in the area of church organization. Methodism used conferences as umbrella organizations for local groups and churches, with a so-called "General Conference" as its highest ecclesial body. The conferences *as institutions* grew out of the annual conventions (referred to as "conferences"), which dealt with questions of doctrine and polity.

In line with John Wesley's view, American Methodism regarded no form of church governance as fully right or wrong.[21] The focus, it was maintained, should not be on polity but on the spiritual fruits in the lives of the believers.

## The Mid-Nineteenth Century Religious Milieu in the USA

In colonial times, the American religious landscape looked very different from what it would be in the mid-nineteenth century. However, it is important to remember that, from its inception, American Protestantism had a distinctly Calvinist flavor. Most settlers in the Mid-Atlantic region and in New England were Calvinists, including the English Puritans, the French Huguenots, and the Dutch settlers of New Amsterdam (later New York), as well as the Scotch-Irish Presbyterians of the Appalachian backcountry. Most nonconforming Protestants, such as the Puritans and other English dissenters, who had not been satisfied with the degree of reformation in the Church of England, also held Reformed (i.e., Calvinist) views. The Congregationalists, who emphasized the autonomy of the local church, were the largest church family in the late eighteenth century, followed by the Presbyterians. The other major players were the Baptists, the Episcopalians, the Quakers, and the Dutch and German Reformed. Most of these had Calvinist roots, while the Lutherans accounted for only five percent of the population.[22]

---

*Methodism and the Rise of Popular Christianity in America* (Urbana and Chicago, IL: University of Illinois Press, 2001).
19 Roger Finke and Rodney Stark, *The Churching of America 1776–1990: Winners and Losers in our Religious Economy* (New Brunswick, NJ: Rutgers University Press, 1992), 25.
20 Ibid., 55.
21 Heitzenrater, 153.
22 Finke and Stark, 25.

These churches, which were a growing force in America and elsewhere in the world, owed much of their spiritual heritage to the Radical Reformation. As believers' churches, they tended to opt for a participative model of church configuration, with significant autonomy for the local church. The Baptists were foremost among these, but at the time, the Quakers with their informal church services lacking any sacraments also had a significant presence. The free churches emphasized holy living, strong discipline, and missionary witness as the raison d'être of the church.[23] Having frequently experienced the oppression from traditional Christian forces, it is not surprising that they maintained a strong focus on religious liberty and on separation between church and state.

By 1830–1840, the strength of the Congregationalists, the Presbyterians, and the Episcopalians had much declined, leaving the Baptists and the Methodists as the great winners (while gradually Roman Catholicism also became a force to be reckoned with). [24] One significant factor is, undoubtedly, that America had been greatly affected by two powerful waves of revivals. This had a significant effect on Calvinist thinking, in particular with regard to the doctrine of predestination. This proved to be a very contentious teaching.[25] Arminian influences that had come from Europe had already convinced many that this basic Calvinist tenet was not correct, and the revivalist preaching, which emphasized free will in an often very popular manner, also did its work.

Nonetheless, Calvinism had in many ways left its enduring imprint on America. It may be that Loraine Boettner (1901–1990) was overstating his case when he wrote that "history is eloquent in declaring that American democracy was born of Christianity and that that Christianity was Calvinism." [26] But many church historians do agree that the Calvinist roots of the population of the colonies was a significant, if not decisive factor, in the struggle for national independence and democracy.[27] Others such as, for example, Nicholas Miller, a scholar at Andrews University, maintain that radical, dissenting Protestants played a key role in this process.[28]

---

23 Kärkkäinen, 59–67, 90–91.
24 Reinder Bruinsma, *Seventh-day Adventist Attitudes toward Roman Catholicism, 1844–1965* (Berrien Springs, MI: Andrews University Press, 1994), 15–19.
25 As expressed in the title of an important book on the history of the idea of predestination in North America: Peter J. Thuesen, *Predestination: The American Career of a Contentious Doctrine* (Oxford: Oxford University Press, 2009).
26 Loraine Boettner, „Calvinism in America," *Studies in Reformed Theology* 8 (1998): 16, https://goo.gl/RDLvrZ (November 28, 2017).
27 See, e.g., Mark A. Knoll, *A History of Christianity in the United States and Canada* (Grand Rapids, MI: Eerdmans, 1992), 115–122.
28 Nicholas P. Miller, *The Religious Roots of the First Amendment: Dissenting Protestants and the Separation of Church and State* (New York, NY: Oxford University Press, 2012).

## Reformation and post-Reformation Influence on Adventist Ecclesiology

Luther, by and large, received a much more extended press in the Adventist church than Calvin, even though Calvinism was a much stronger force in American nineteenth-century religion than Lutheranism. Perhaps the clearest proof for this is found in the way the two Reformers are treated in Ellen White's book *The Great Controversy*.[29] Not only did she devote far more pages to Luther than to Calvin, but she also appears to be much more positive about Luther than about the Genevan reformer.

With regard to Calvin, Ellen White states: "For nearly thirty years Calvin labored at Geneva, first to establish there a church adhering to the morality of the Bible, and then for the advancement of the Reformation throughout Europe. His course as a public leader was not faultless, nor were his doctrines free from error."[30]

A little further in the same book she spoke in no uncertain terms about the "monstrous" Calvinist doctrine of predestination.[31] Compare this with the glowing accolade to Martin Luther: "Foremost among those called to lead the church from the darkness of popery into the light of a purer faith stood Martin Luther. Knowing no fear but the fear of God, and acknowledging no foundation for faith but the Holy Scriptures, Luther was the man for his time."[32]

And when referring to Luther's appearance before the Diet of Worms, Ellen White comments: "Thus stood this righteous man upon the sure foundation of the word of God. The light of heaven illuminated his countenance. His greatness and purity of character, his peace and joy of heart, were manifest to all as he testified against the power of error and witnessed to the superiority of the faith that overcomes the world."[33]

### Lutheran Influence

Even though Lutheranism was in a minority position in the USA, Luther was admired by Adventist believers and certainly exerted a strong influence. His courage to confront the church of his day with accusations of theological error and ecclesial abuse found an enthusiastic reception among the increasingly anti-Catholic Adventist believers of the nineteenth century. His insistence on the principle of *sola scriptura* and the New Testament idea of justification by faith, rather than by works, and his view of the priesthood of all believers, were also warmly welcomed.[34]

---

29  Ellen G. White, *The Great Controversy* (Nampa, ID: Pacific Press, 2005).
30  Ibid., 236.
31  Ibid., 261.
32  Ibid., 120.
33  Ibid., 160.
34  Adventists certainly agreed with the Lutheran re-discovery of justification by faith and its insistence on *sola scriptura*, but in actual practice often found it difficult to live up to these essential Protestant principles, as is attested by Adventist history. Adventism has suffered –

Whether or not they were aware of it, Adventists were like the Lutherans in their preference for terms as community, gathering, or meeting over the word "church." As already noted, Luther had a strong preference for *Gemeinde* (community) over the term *Kirche* (church). The Adventists did, however, probably take this practice from other, more contemporary religious groups. And in a number of important areas, Adventism chose a route that differed significantly from Luther's ideas.[35]

Adventists defined the church more narrowly than Luther, who saw the church as invisible and visible, and regarded the visible church as a communion of the saints as well as a school for sinners – or even a hospital for the spiritually sick. Adventists were much more inclined to stress the importance of the visible church as a community of committed Christians, who had entered the church through believers' baptism rather than through infant baptism. Adventists would, to a large extent, agree with Luther's definition of the church as a place where the Word is purely preached and the sacraments are administered properly, but would place more emphasis on the *true* church – which they would usually refer to as the *remnant* church – i.e., as the community of those who keep God's commandments and recognize "the spirit of prophecy" in the ministry of Ellen White.[36]

Luther's view of consubstantiation was seen by Adventists as a compromise with the Roman Catholic practice of the mass that was totally unacceptable, as was Luther's doctrine of two kingdoms, and the close relationship between the state and the church. It should be further added that Adventists opted for a different system of church governance than was to be found in Lutheranism.

## Calvinist Influence

There is no evidence that the early Adventists made any in-depth study of Calvinism as they were establishing and organizing their new denomination.[37] As already mentioned, the major Calvinist denominations had been significantly reduced by the middle of the nineteenth century, but many elements of the Calvinist heritage continued to play an important role. The strongest influence of Calvinism on Adventism – albeit mostly indirectly, through such movements as Methodism and the Christian Connexion – was in the area of the offices in the local church, and of the structure of church governance. Although the Adventists would not recognize a separate office of teacher in the same way as original Calvinism did, its emphasis on the role of ministers, elders, and deacons is similar. Also, the Adventist system of electing the various echelons in the denominational structure – delegates from lower organization electing the personnel at the higher organization – has a Calvinist flavor.

    and this is even true today – from a tendency towards legalism and has not always practiced the principle of full equality between all believers, male and female.
35  Dederen, 569–570; González, 61–69.
36  The texts usually referred to are Rev 12:17, 14:12, 19:10, and Joel 3:1–5.
37  Dederen, 570–571; González, 161–174.

## Influence from Anabaptism

Early Adventism owed many of its ideas to its Anabaptist roots through some of the free churches that emerged from these same roots. It shared its view of the church as a believers' church, in which the members enter through believers' baptism, and in which holy living and commitment to mission are of paramount importance. Indirectly, such convictions as the symbolic view of the Lord's Supper – with a rediscovery of the value of foot washing[38] – also stem from the Radical Reformation, as does the insistence on a full separation between church and state.[39]

## Influence from Methodism and the Christian Connexion

The influence of the free-church tradition, which was rooted in the sixteenth-century Radical Reformation, was channeled into Adventism mainly through Methodism and the Christian Connexion.[40] A very significant number of the leaders in the Millerite movement had come from these two movements and from the Baptists. Research has shown that 44 percent of the Millerite preachers were Methodists and 27 percent were Baptists, while 8 percent came from the much smaller group of Connexionists.[41] Ellen White had been a Methodist before joining the Advent movement while James White and Joseph Bates, two other prominent leaders in early Adventism, came from a Christian Connexion background.

Some practices of the Methodists and, even more so, of the Connexionists, were adopted, seemingly without much reflection, by the emerging Sabbatarian Adventist movement. The continued validity of the ordination that ministers had received when still in the service of their former denominations was apparently no issue. These ministers could also, by virtue of their own ordination, ordain others. Thus,

> the practice of ordination entered the Seventh-day Adventist Church mainly as a practical initiative in order to safeguard the unity and mission of the church ... The theology of ordination was not built on a thorough study of ordination in the Bible as a whole in the original languages. It was heavily influenced by the evangelical church traditions on ordination which the Sabbatarians were accustomed to.[42]

---

38 Reinder Bruinsma, "Christ's Commandment of Humility," *Ministry*, July 1966, 24–26.
39 It should be noted that in many parts of the world current views about the relationship between church and state have, over time, significantly developed. See Ronald Lawson, "Church and State at Home and Abroad: The Evolution of Seventh-day Adventist Relations with Governments," *Journal of the American Academy of Religion* 64:2 (1996): 279–311.
40 See Mustard, 232–237, for a comparison of the main features of the forms of church governance that were adopted by Congregationalists, Presbyterians, Baptists, and Methodists.
41 See Everett N. Dick's unpub. PhD dissertation, "The Adventist Crisis of 1843–1844" (University of Wisconsin), 232.
42 Bertil Wiklander, *Ordination Reconsidered: The Biblical Vision of Men and Women as Servants of God* (Bracknell, UK: Newbold Academic Press, 2015), 25.

Early on, the Sabbatarian group that was to develop into the Seventh-day Adventist Church adopted the practice of appointing local elders and deacons as leaders of the local church. The earliest references to this practice in the available literature date from the early 1850s.[43] Ministers were also often referred to as elders,[44] but they were initially referred to as "traveling elders."[45] This, of course, reminds us of the itinerant ministry of the "circuit riders" among the Methodists that was standard practice in mid-nineteenth-century American Methodism.[46]

The first steps toward the organization of the local church reflect the influence of the covenantal or federal theology of Puritanism. The earliest Adventist churches in the first decades after 1844 organized themselves on the basis of a "covenant" between the members. Such covenants had become rather common in more or less congregationally organized churches and could, therefore, also be expected to emerge in the Adventist faith communities.[47]

Creating umbrella organizations was a controversial issue in Sabbatarian Adventism in the first two decades after 1840. Much of the anti-organizational sentiment of the Christian Connexion had been transferred to the emerging Adventist movement. However the Connexionist movement slowly started to introduce a measure of supra-local organization, and the Adventist leaders also saw the need for some further structuring of their movement. George Knight sums it up as follows:

> We should recognize that by the early 1850s the Sabbatarians had largely replicated the organizational structure of the Christian Connexion from which James White and Bates had migrated. Throughout the 1850s the Sabbatarian movement would consist of a loose association of congregations and individuals united through the agency of periodicals and 'conferences,' or general meetings, of believers. Thus, whether they realized it or not, the Sabbatarians were operating with the same type of church order as that of the Connexionists and the Millerites.[48]

Originally, the conferences referred to in this quotation lacked organizational structure and authority. From the mid-1850s onward James White gradually changed his mind and no longer adhered to the non-organizational attitude he had inherited from the Connexionists. In time he would become the most important promoter of organization. He eventually adopted the view that for a further organizational structuring of the church, practical needs and common sense should be the basis, as long

---

43 "Church Elder" and "Deacons," in *Seventh-day Adventist Encyclopedia* (Hagerstown, MD: Review and Herald, 1996), vol. 1, 366–367, 446.
44 This is still the case in the Seventh-day Adventist Church in some English-speaking areas in the world.
45 Knight, *Organizing to Beat the Devil*, 31–41.
46 Heitzenrater, 102, 278.
47 Mustard, 154.
48 George R. Knight, *Organizing for Mission and Growth: The Development of Adventist Church Structure* (Hagerstown, MD: Review and Herald, 2006), 33.

as these did not lead to elements that were expressly forbidden by the Bible.[49] Between the mid-1850s and 1861, the concept of "conference" transformed itself in White's mind "from a gathering of believers, who wished to confer with one another, to the permanent operating organization of a group of churches, somewhat equivalent to an Episcopal diocese or a Methodist conference."[50] From 1861 onward, state conferences would be formed – the first one in Michigan – following largely the Methodist model and nomenclature.

The next step in the organizational development was the organization of a General Conference, also in line with the Methodist model. This "marked the end of an era in Adventist history. Sabbatarian Adventism had moved from a virtually unstructured beginning to a mildly hierarchical form. The transition was much greater for James White, who had come out of the anti-organizational Christian Connexion, than it was for his wife, who had belonged to the highly structured Methodist Church."[51] In adopting major elements of the Methodist form of church governance, Adventists did not, however, adopt the title of "bishop" for their leaders, as became customary in Methodism since bishop Francis Ashbury in the late 1700s acquired that title.

Perhaps it should be added that the manifestation of the prophetic gift in the ministry of Ellen White was also facilitated by the Methodist frontier environment in which Sabbatarian Adventism originated. In early nineteenth-century American Methodism, (female) prophets and "exhorters" played a significant role.[52]

## Conclusion

In many ways early Adventism has been inspired, directly and indirectly, by the Christian and, in particular, Protestant traditions of its time, and this is certainly also true of its ecclesiological views. The various forms of Protestantism have been influential to different degrees, usually more subconsciously than as the result of careful study. Factors such as its origin in the Millerite movement with all its diversity, and the spiritual roots of its leaders, have played an important role. As we look at the relevance for our present topic, we must remember that the Adventist form of church governance has been the result of a very eclectic process, in which pragmatism was a key factor.

The Adventist church of the twenty-first century must, I believe, continue to be pragmatic in the further development of its organizational structure. It must not forget that its form must always be mission-driven. It appears, however, that much

49  Knight, *Organizing to Beat the Devil*, 63.
50  Ibid.
51  Ibid, 61.
52  Heitzenrater, 97–146; Howard A. Snyder, "John Wesley Redfield: A Study in Nineteenth-Century American Methodist Revivalism," *Wesleyan Theological Journal* 41:1 (2006): 205–222; and Ann Tavis, "Visions," in *Ellen Harmon White: American Prophet*, ed. Terrie Dopp Aamodt et al. (Oxford: Oxford University Press, 2014), 33–38. See also Wigger, 151–172.

of the adaptability of the past has been lost and that it has become more and more difficult to effect the reorganizations that may be needed or desirable, as the world around us changes. We also would do well to remember our original aversion to a strongly hierarchical system and to ask ourselves whether or not the church of today is moving too much in a direction contrary to its own tradition.

It is presently, and shall continue to be important to remember that, with all its peculiarities and "unique" ideas, Adventist theology and practice – including in the domain of ecclesiology – is firmly embedded in the Christian past and that we may, with gratitude, look back to its direct and indirect Reformation roots.

*Timothy J. Arena*

# The Soteriology of Philip Melanchthon and the Importance of Its Legacy for Seventh-day Adventists

Abstract

> Philip Melanchthon's soteriological legacy is of exceptional significance for Seventh-day Adventists. Through its echoes in Arminius, Wesley, and Ellen White, it is connected to the historical stream of thought which stems from the fountainhead of the Protestant Reformation. This paper examines Melanchthon's thought on three essential soteriological doctrines: (1) hamartiology/anthropology – the fall, depravity, and the nature of graced freedom; (2) justification – by grace through faith resulting in forensic imputation; and (3) sanctification – the third use of the law and good works. If the findings of this study are correct, Adventists can and should essentially appropriate this soteriological legacy as their own.

## Introduction

The soteriological thought of Philip Melanchthon is of lasting and exceptional significance for Seventh-day Adventists. The fundamental aspects of his thought that they have appropriated provide for them a direct link with the fountainhead of the most influential period of the Reformation – when those who rejected Rome's formulations on soteriological questions were systematically framing their own.

This paper will examine Melanchthon's conception of three essential doctrines that comprise the essential core of the soteriological cluster: (1) hamartiology/ anthropology – the Fall and its effects, the nature of the will, the Holy Spirit, freedom, and God's grace; (2) justification by grace through faith and the imputed righteousness of Christ; and (3) sanctification – the importance of the third use of the law and the role of the Holy Spirit in transformation.

Melanchthon's soteriology resonates through and has an impact upon later theological history in that his views had a significant influence on Jacob Arminius, whose soteriological views were embraced by John Wesley – two of Adventism's most significant theological forbearers – and this legacy had an eventual direct point of contact with the Seventh-day Adventist church through the writings of Ellen G. White. While it is not known whether she read Melanchthon widely (she did write approvingly of him in several places),[1] this paper will examine how her writings on

---

1 E.g., "God's providence sent Melanchthon to Wittenberg. Young in years, modest and diffident in his manners, Melanchthon's sound judgment, extensive knowledge, and winning eloquence, combined with the purity and uprightness of his character, won universal

salvation evince a deep connection with his thought in regard to all three of the soteriological doctrines examined here.

## Melanchthon's Hamartiology and Anthropology

### The Fall and Its Effects

Throughout the scope of his writings, Melanchthon maintained a strong view of original sin, over against Pelagian or semi-Pelagian conceptions. In the earliest 1521 version of his *Loci Communes,* he wrote that original sin was "propagated upon all posterity by Adam."[2] He did not generally dwell on the mechanism by which Adam's sin was passed along to his posterity, but he did refer to both "imputation"[3] of his guilt as well as the passing along of a sinful nature through birth.[4]

Melanchthon's views regarding the effects of sin upon the total human organism in regard to the incapacity of human beings to be saved without the divine initiative through the Holy Spirit also remained consistent. He regularly maintained that without conversion, "the soul being without celestial light and life

admiration and esteem. The brilliancy of his talents was not more marked than his gentleness of disposition. He soon became an earnest disciple of the gospel, and Luther's most trusted friend and valued supporter; his gentleness, caution, and exactness serving as a complement to Luther's courage and energy. Their union in the work added strength to the Reformation and was a source of great encouragement to Luther." Ellen G. White, *The Great Controversy Between Christ and Satan* (Mountain View, CA: Pacific Press, 1888/1907), 134. White's writings are available online at egwwritings.org.

2   Philip Melanchthon, *The Loci Communes of Philip Melanchthon – with a Critical Introduction by the Translator,* trans. Charles Leander Hill (Boston, MA: Meador Press, 1944), 82. This translation is of the first, 1521 edition of *The Loci Communes.*

3   This concept was the core of what later became known as the "Federal View" of original sin, in which Adam's sin, because he was our representative, is counted against humanity by imputation (rather than actual personal participation with Adam in Eden, as in Augustine), analogously to how the righteousness of Christ is imputed to us. See Charles Hodge, *Systematic Theology,* reprint, 3 vols. (Grand Rapids, MI: Eerdmans, 1940), 2:194–205; John Wesley, "Justified by Faith," in *The Essential Works of John Wesley,* Alice Russie, ed. (Uhrichsville, OH: Barbour Publishing, 2011), 285; see also the discussion of Wesley's view below. For a study of the various views of original sin, with a case for the outlines of the Federal View, see Timothy Arena, "The Person and Work of Christ as Representative Rectification: The Soteriological and Theodical Implications of The Roles of The Two Adams Examined in Theological Canonical Exegesis of Romans 5:12–21," term paper presented at the 2016 Scholarship Symposium in Berrien Springs, MI, USA, https://goo.gl/7Qm77S (November 28, 2017). It should be noted that the view I express regarding the fate of those who die as infants in this present paper (see below, footnote 61) is different from – and an intended improvement upon – the one presented at the end of the aforementioned term paper.

4   Philip Melanchthon, *Commentary on Romans,* trans. Fred Kramer (St. Louis, MO: Concordia Publishing, 1992), 132–133.

is in darkness, it most ardently loves itself, seeks its own desires and wishes nothing but carnal things and despises God."[5] The inbred sinful nature, according to Articles II, V, and XVIII of the *Augsburg Confession*,[6] is sin itself, and prevents anyone from turning to God without the aid of the Holy Spirit. "Because of it [original sin], human nature is not able truly to obey the Law of God, but has defects and lust against the Law of God."[7] In the 1555 edition of the *Loci*, Melanchthon (citing Scriptures such as Gen 8:21; Ps 51:5; Jer 17:9; Rom 8:3; 1 Cor 2:11; Eph 2:3) wrote concerning the effects of the Fall: "All good virtues toward God in the heart and will were also lost ... God is not received where the Holy Spirit has not first enlightened and kindled the understanding, will, and heart. Without the Holy Spirit ... the miserable human heart stands like a desolate, deserted, old and decaying house, God no longer dwelling within."[8] There is "total depravation" of the "original righteousness" with which humans were created.[9] "The knowledge of original sin is necessary. For the magnitude of the grace of Christ cannot be understood – no one can heartily long and have a desire for Christ for the inexpressibly great treasure of divine favor and grace which the Gospel offers, unless our diseases be recognized."[10]

## *The Response of the Human Will to God's Grace*

It was in regard to Melanchthon's view of the relationship between the divine initiative and the human response of the will in conversion that his views most significantly changed. It is also in this area that his most unique contribution to the Reformation can be seen, and as such it is worthy of somewhat more space and explanation than will be devoted to the other issues.

At the time of the first edition of the *Loci Communes*, Melanchthon exhibited a thoroughly deterministic conception, akin to Luther in his *De Servo Arbitrio*,[11]

---

5 Melanchthon, *The Loci Communes* [1521], 83.
6 Philip Melanchthon, *Augsburg Confession*, https://goo.gl/LmS4aH (November 28, 2017). See also Philip Melanchthon, *Melanchthon on Christian Doctrine: Loci Communes 1555*, trans. and ed. by Clyde L. Manschreck (Grand Rapids, MI: Baker, 1964), 79; Melanchthon, *Commentary on Romans*, 24–25, 133.
7 Melanchthon, *Commentary on Romans*, 133.
8 Melanchthon, *Melanchthon on Christian Doctrine*, 52.
9 Philip Melanchthon, *Confessio Doctrinae Saxonicarum Ecclesiarum scripta Anno Domini MDLI ut Synodo Tridentinae exhiberetur*, quoted in *Evangelical Free Will: Philip Melanchthon's Journey on the Origins of Faith*, Gregory B. Graybill (New York, NY: Oxford University Press, 2010), 261. Melanchthon, *Melanchthon on Christian Doctrine*, 76.
10 Philip Melanchthon, *Apology to the Augsburg Confession*, Part I, "Of Original Sin," trans. F. Bente and W. H. T. Dau, https://goo.gl/WktCWk (November 28, 2017).
11 Martin Luther, *De Servo Arbitrio*, xii, trans. Henry Cole, https://goo.gl/czWgaa (November 28, 2017).

and Calvin in his *Institutio*.[12] "All things that happen, happen necessarily according to divine predestination, there is no freedom of the will." While there seemed to be a freedom of the will in secular matters and in appearances of good works, this exterior freedom was ultimately illusory, since they are controlled by the sinful "affections."[13]

While most Melanchthon scholars agree that his theology changed considerably on the role of the will in human affairs generally as well as in justification specifically,[14] there is some disagreement as to when and why this took place. Certainly Melanchthon was able to consider the matter of the human will deeply during the dispute on the subject between Erasmus and Luther in 1524–1526. Some suggest that Melanchthon followed Erasmus, and that this is what led to the change in his thought on the will; others suggest that he followed Luther.[15] More accurately, it could be said that while he came to disagree with certain aspects (and certainly the tone) of what Luther wrote, the best way of describing the situation is that "Melanchthon strongly agreed with Luther's basic position that humans had no ability to seek God on their own power."[16] But he had, by this time, developed a two-tier conception of the human will. It was free in relation to all matters in the temporal realm, but it was bound in all matters in the spiritual realm. Only the Holy Spirit could change the human will.

This was a distinct modification from his deterministic view in the early *Loci* as well as Luther's *De Servo Arbitrio*.[17] His refined position was cogently argued in his 1527 *Dissertatio* on Colossians. "I do not make God out to be the author of sin. Rather, he is the one who preserves nature, and who imparts life and motion …

---

12 For example, John Calvin, *Institutes of the Christian Religion*, trans. Henry Beveridge, 2 vols. (Grand Rapids, MI: Eerdmans, 1957), 2:231–232 [3.23.7].
13 Melanchthon, *The Loci Communes*, 72–80.
14 See e.g. Graybill, *Evangelical Free Will;* John M. Drickamer, "Did Melanchthon Become a Synergist?" *Springfielder* 40:2 (September 1976): 95–101. ATLA Religion Database with ATLASerials, EBSCOhost; Clyde Leonard Manschreck, *Melanchthon: The Quiet Reformer,* (New York, NY: Abingdon, 1958), 293–302; J. A. O. Preuss, "Translator's Preface to the First Edition" in *Loci Praecipui Theologici*, xxxiii; Manschreck, "Preface" in *Loci* 1555, xiii–xiv; Timothy J. Wengert, "Philip Melanchthon and the Origins of the 'Three Causes' (1533–1535): An Examination of the Roots of the Controversy over the Freedom of the Will" in Irene Dingel, Timothy J. Wengert, Nicole Kuropka, and Robert Kolb, *Philip Melanchthon: Theologian in Classroom, Confession, and Controversy* (Göttingen: Vandenhoeck & Ruprecht, 2012), 183–208.
15 For a discussion of the various views, see Graybill, 125–131 where he argues based on his letters that Melanchthon supported Luther primarily, but not exclusively.
16 Graybill, 129.
17 Melanchthon wrote in 1530 in his *Ratio Discendae Theologiae*, "I would … order the reading of my *Loci* [of 1521], but they contain much that is yet crude which I have decided to alter," quoted in Clyde L. Manschreck, *Melanchthon: The Quiet Reformer* (New York, NY: Abingdon, 1958), 298.

which the devil and godless people do not use aright."[18] "Holy Scripture grants to the human will a certain freedom in social activities," yet even this freedom is hindered by the weakness of human flesh due to original sin, as well as the activity of Satan.[19] In regard to spiritual matters, however, "the human will has no freedom ... What need would there be for the Holy Spirit, if the human will could by its own abilities fear God, trust God, put down concupiscence, love the cross?"[20]

Yet, even here there is a possible hint of his later forthright assertion of the human capacity to respond to God after the Spirit has awakened it: "What is it but arrogance, not to seek the Holy Spirit's help, when Christ promised, indeed commanded it, and instead seek help in our own abilities?"[21] In the 1530 *Augsburg Confession*, and later *Apology* to the *Confession*, similar assertions and ambiguities appear. In Article XVIII on Free Will, it is asserted that

> Of free will they teach that man's will has some liberty to choose civil righteousness, and to work things subject to reason. But it has no power, without the Holy Ghost, to work the righteousness of God, that is, spiritual righteousness; since the natural man receiveth not the things of the Spirit of God, 1 Cor. 2:14; but this righteousness is wrought in the heart when the Holy Ghost is received through the Word.[22]

In Article V it is asserted that "whenever and wherever it pleases God, this ministry [the Word and Sacraments] creates faith in those who hear the gospel."[23] Perhaps the wording here is deliberately flexible enough to entertain either a predestinarian particularity reading as well as one which could include the idea that it is the pleasure of God to create faith in those who freely ask for Him to do so. In the 1531 *Apology*, Melanchthon asserted that "it is *assent* to the promise of God that in Christ remission of sins and justification are freely offered (emphasis added)."[24]

However, all ambiguities were laid aside in 1532 in the *Commentary on Romans*. As Gregory Graybill notes in his important 2010 study on Melanchthon's theology of grace, *Evangelical Free Will*, this commentary was the clearest articulation of his new conception. In his comments on Romans 5 and 9, Melanchthon was now willing to say that the promises are "universal" and that while the mercy of

---

18  Philip Melanchthon, *Paul's Letter to the Colossians*, trans. D. C. Parker (Sheffield: Almond, 1989), 39.
19  Ibid., 41.
20  Ibid., 40.
21  Ibid.
22  Melanchthon, *Augsburg Confession*, XVIII, https://goo.gl/LmS4aH (November 28, 2017).
23  Ibid.
24  Melanchthon, *Apology to the Augsburg Confession* "Article IV: Of Justification" https://goo.gl/h9CaA8 (November 28, 2017), quoted in Clyde L. Manschreck, "Reason and Conversion in the Thought of Philip Melanchthon," in *Reformation Studies: Essays in Honor of Roland H. Bainton*, ed. Franklin H. Littell (Richmond, VA: John Knox Press, 1962), 172 (168–180).

God was the cause of election, "there is some cause in the one accepting, insofar as one does not refuse the offer of the promise."[25]

His position was strengthened further in the 1532 *Loci*, where he made it clear that while the Holy Spirit must take the initiative in conversion, there are nevertheless three causes of this event: "the Word, the Holy Spirit, and the will, not indifferently, by all means, but resisting our infirmity."[26] In his 1540 *Commentary on Romans*, while citing Scripture passages such as Matthew 11:28; Romans 3:22; 10:12,17; and 1 Timothy 2:4, he wrote, "God truly wants to accept also the unworthy, and that he offers grace to all, asking only that they believe the promise." "The Word ... offers grace to all, even though not all accept it." "The promises are universal." "Resistance is an act of the will, since God is not a cause of sin." "The elect do not resist the calling."[27]

In the 1555 *Loci*, the Reformer wrote, "We should not think that a man is a piece of wood or a stone, but as we hear the Word of God ... we should neither despise nor resist it." Noting that "outside of God's word we should not invent a single thought about his nature and will,"[28] Melanchthon again cited the above Scriptures (as well as others) to point out that "since the divine promises proffer grace to *all* who are terrified, we should include ourselves in the *all*, and we should reflect that the greatest sin is not willing *to believe in the Lord Christ*, and not willing to receive His grace."[29] He specifically rejected Luther's concept of the *deus absconditus* and *deus revelatus*[30] or any possible notions of compatibilism when he wrote, "We should not put contradictory wills in God, *contradictorius voluntates*. To *all* who tremble before his wrath and seek comfort in Christ, *to each and every*

---

25 Philip Melanchthon, *Commentary on Romans* [1532], *Melanchthons Werke in Auswahl*, ed. R. Stupperich, 7 vols. (Gütersloh: Gerd Mohn, 1951–1975), 5:253–254, quoted in Graybill, 207–209.
26 Philip Melanchthon, *Corpus Reformatorum: Philippi Melanthonis opera quae supersunt omnia*, ed. K. Bretschneider and H. Bindseil, 28 vols. (Halle: Schwetschke, 1834–1860), quoted in Graybill, 221.
27 Melanchthon, *Commentary on Romans*, 20–21, 139, 187–188.
28 Melanchthon, *Melanchthon on Christian Doctrine*, 60.
29 Ibid., 187.
30 Interestingly, Luther, who before his death knew about the change in Melanchthon's views, continued to support and recommend his writings. "There is no book under the sun in which the whole of theology is so completely presented as in the *Loci Communes* [1535 version with Melanchthon's changed views] ... No better book has been written after the Holy Scriptures than Philip's." "Substance and words – Philip. Words without substance – Erasmus. Substance without words – Luther. Neither substance nor words – Karlstadt." (Martin Luther, *Luther's Works*, vol. 54, ed. Theodore G. Tappert and Helmut T. Lehmann (Minneapolis, MN: Fortress Press, 1967), 245, 440, quoted in Heinz Scheible, "Philip Melanchthon," in *The Reformation Theologians*, ed. Carter Lindberg [Malden, MA: Blackwell Publishers, 2002], 71–72). Manschreck, *Melanchthon: The Quiet Reformer*, 300–302, even suggests that Luther himself changed his views to agreement with Melanchthon's.

The Soteriology of Philip Melanchthon

*one,* grace and blessedness are offered and promised."[31] In the 1559 Loci, he wrote that

> the free choice in man is the ability to apply oneself toward grace, that is, our free choice hears the promise, tries to assent to it and rejects the sins which are contrary to conscience ... Since the promise is universal and since in God there are not conflicting wills, it is necessary that there is some cause within us ... Since our souls rest in the Son of God who is shown to us in the promise, this will cast light upon the connection of the causes which are the Word of God, the Holy Spirit, and the will of man.[32]

"Just as the preaching of repentance is universal and accuses all ... so also the promise of grace is universal, as many passages testify [he then quotes Matt 11:28; John 3:16; Rom 3:22; 10:12; 11:32)." He then cites Isaiah 53:6; Acts 10:43; 13:39; 1 Timothy 2:4; Acts 10:34; and Deuteronomy 10:17 and comments, "He treats all equally: He convicts us of sin, yet he receives all who flee to the Son."[33] "It is certain that the cause of reprobation is the sin in men who do not hear or receive the Gospel or who reject the faith." It is "their sin and their human will. For it is a completely true statement that God is not the cause of sin and does not will sin."[34] "We must cling to this comfort regarding the effect of election: God wills that the entire human race not perish, and He always calls through mercy for the sake of His Son. He draws and gathers the church and receives those who assent."[35] Finally, to demonstrate the complete reversal from the 1521 Loci, there is a letter to the elector of Saxony in 1559, in which Melanchthon wrote, "Both during Luther's lifetime and also later I fought against the stoical and Manichaean delusion which led Luther and others to write that all works whether good or evil, in all men whether good or bad, take place of necessity."[36] In logical consonance with his view on a graced freedom, Melanchthon held (at least since the *Augsburg Confession* of 1530) that believers could fall from grace and be lost if their faith is not maintained and nurtured.[37]

---

31 Melanchthon, *Melanchthon on Christian Doctrine,* 189. Given the evidence examined, I cannot concur with the suggestion that Melanchthon believed that "man can cooperate with God apart from grace" in soteriological matters (Alister McGrath, *Iustitia Dei,* 2 vols. [New York, NY: Cambridge University Press, 1986, 1991], 2:30).
32 Melanchthon, *The Chief Theological Topics: Loci Praecipui Theologici* 1559, trans. J. A. O. Preus (St. Louis, MO: Concordia Publishing House, 2011), 62–63.
33 Ibid., 326–327.
34 Ibid., 327.
35 Ibid., 331.
36 *Corpus Reformatorum* 9:766, quoted in Harry Buis, *Historic Protestantism and Predestination* (Philadelphia, PA: The Presbyterian and Reformed Publishing Company, 1958), 81.
37 "They condemn the Anabaptists, who deny that those once justified cannot lose the Holy Ghost. Also those that contend that some may attain to such perfection in this life that they cannot sin" (Melanchthon, *Augsburg Confession,* XII, https://goo.gl/LmS4aH [November 28, 2017]). In the 1540 *Commentary on Romans,* he refers to "sins against conscience" when one "violates the commandments of God contrary to his conscience; or indulges in a

Graybill claims for Melanchthon the title of founder for the concept of "evangelical free will."[38] Whether or not one accepts this appellation will depend on how the word "evangelical" is defined. As Graybill himself notes, there were "one or more of the early radicals" that embraced free will, but they tended to lack the doctrine of forensic imputation of Christ's righteousness in justification[39] – which would be considered by many (myself included) to be a non-negotiable concept for being evangelical. "Grace is for the Radical Reformers not so much a forensic change in status before God as it is an ontological change within the believer himself."[40] It is also true that a number of them taught a universal legal justification

---

depraved desire and does not fight against it. People who commit such transgressions lose grace, grieve and drive out the Holy Spirit, and cast of faith." They will be lost "unless they repent and return again to faith." He then lists fifteen texts that support this position (Melanchthon, *Commentary on Romans,* 48–50): Rom 8:13; Matt 12:45; Matt 13:22; 1 Cor 6:9; 1 Cor 10:8; Gal 5:22; 1 Tim 5:8; Heb 3:4; 2 Pet 2:20; Matt 10:33; Matt 24:13; 25:41; 1 Cor 13:2; 1 John 3:10; John 8:44. In commenting on 1 Cor 6:9, he notes, "He [Paul] is speaking to those who had previously received the benefits of Christ. He commands that they should be careful lest they lose them" (ibid., 49). In the 1555 *Loci,* the same position was maintained: "Some sins grieve and repel the Holy Spirit, causing some men to fall from grace, who, if not again converted, fall into eternal punishment" (Melanchthon, *Melanchthon on Christian Doctrine,* 183). When someone acts "consciously and willingly against the command of God, even though he had previously been holy and in God's grace, if he nevertheless grieves and repels the Holy Spirit, he is then not in God's grace, and if he is not again turned to God in this life, he will come to eternal punishment" (ibid., 183–184).

38  Graybill, 215.
39  Ibid. See also Alvin J. Beachy, *The Concept of Grace in the Radical Reformation* (Nieuwkoop: De Graaf, 1977), 29; Roger Olson, *The Story of Christian Theology* (Downers Grove, IL: InterVarsity, 1999), 425.
40  Beachy, 228. The outlines of the situation appear to be this: The radicals generally accepted the need for Christ's atonement and mediation to make up for lingering "imperfections" after conversion; they taught that the means of entering into a conversion experience involved faith, but also that this faith included works that "made" the believer righteous before God, due to the divine life being lived through them – an infused righteousness with panentheistic overtones.

It should be noted that Menno Simons avoided the most extreme aspects of this kind of theology. He referred to the need for Christ's atonement to make up for imperfections in "A Reply to Gellius Faber" in *The Complete Works of Menno Simons,* trans. Leonard Verduin, (Scottdale, PA: Herald Press, 1984), 654. But he also wrote that "The Lord commanded his gospel to be preached to every creature, so that all who believe and are baptized, may be saved. Where there is faith, which is called the gift of God, by Paul, there also are the power and the fruits of faith. Where there is an active, fruitful faith, there also is the promise; but where such a faith does not exist (we speak of adults), there also is no promise. For he that hears the word of the Lord, and believes it with the heart, manifests his fruit, and faithfully observes all things the Lord commanded him; for the Scriptures teach, the just shall live by faith, Heb 10:38. Then the remission of his sins is preached to him, as Peter teaches and instructs" (Menno Simons, "Foundation of Christian Doctrine," in Verduin, *The Complete Works,* 130–131). Thus the fruit appears to be part of the means of justification, not a concomitant but distinct outgrowth of being reconciled to God through forensic declaration of righteousness, as in Melanchthon.

Hubmaier wrote similarly that "faith *makes* us righteous before God" (emphasis added) and that such faith includes "all sorts of works of brotherly love," H. Wayne Pipkin, *Balthasar Hubmaier: Theologian of Anabaptism* (Scottdale, PA: Herald Press, 1989), 32. He also wrote that "mere faith alone is not sufficient for salvation" and "good deeds must be added to the faith" for salvation to take place (ibid., 526–527). While this could possibly mean that a true faith will be manifested in works, it more likely means that works, subsumed under the term faith, are part of the ground of salvation. Hubmaier also wrote that sin is only sin if it is willful, and that the sins of the flesh are not condemnable, since the flesh is bound in sin since Adam (ibid., 457) but also that God accepts imperfect obedience that needs forgiveness (ibid., 442). Olson posits Hubmaier as the "first evangelical synergist" (422), but as noted here, all things considered, the appellation "evangelical" is doubtful in light of this evidence.

Michael Sattler included "works of repentance" and "love" as being part of the faith that justifies. Michael Sattler, "Concerning the Satisfaction of Christ," trans. and ed. John C. Wenger, *Mennonite Quarterly Review*, October 1946, 245–246, quoted in Ronald David Rogers, "The Relationship between Soteriology and Ecclesiology in Sixteenth Century Anabaptism," ThD diss. (Mid-America Baptist Theological Seminary, 1986), 33–34. He also considered the "works" referred to by Paul in Romans to be only ceremonial ones – i.e., that Paul was not saying that no works at all justify, but only certain kinds (Sattler, "Concerning the Satisfaction," 113, quoted in Rogers., 34–35); and that works can justify because they are "God's works, not man's" (Sattler, "Concerning the Satisfaction," 116, quoted in Rogers, 36).

Dirk Philips wrote of the new birth and inner transformation without any connection to forensic justification, and that man must "amend himself" and be renewed to a "new divine being" before being baptized (Cornelius J. Dyck, William E. Keeney, and Alvin J. Beachy, ed., *The Writings of Dirk Philips* [Scottdale, PA: Herald Publishers, 1992]), 299, 295).

For Melchoir Hoffmann, salvation consisted of two justifications, and eventual divinization in which there is no need for an external law. For he who is "empowered by the Holy Spirit, the lawgiver, has the law removed from him" (Klaus Deppermann, *Melchoir Hoffmann*, trans. Malcom Wren, ed. Benjamin Drewery [Edinburgh: T & T Clark, 1987], 235f.).

The words of Peter Riedemann probably sum up the basic view of infused quasi-deifying righteousness of the Anabaptists: "We confess Christ to be our righteousness and goodness *because he himself worketh in us the righteousness and goodness through which we become beloved of God.* ... Many say of us that we seek to be good through our own works. To this we say, 'No,' for we know that our work, in so far as it is *our* work, is naught but sin and unrighteousness; but insofar as it is of Christ and done by *Christ in us,* so far it is truth." (Peter Riedemann, *Account of Our Religion, Doctrine and Faith* [1540–1541], trans. Society of Brothers (Woodcrest, Rifton, NY: Plough Publishing House, 1970), 35–36. This is justification by infused righteousness, not the alien righteousness of Luther and Melanchthon. Again, it is difficult to conceive of these kinds of soteriological formulations as "evangelical," in the sense of this term having as part of its historical definition the core principle of forensic justification and the imputed righteousness of Christ as understood by the early Reformers – including Melanchthon, Luther, Calvin, and Arminius.

doctrine – that everyone is born justified and no one is guilty of sin until actually choosing to embrace it.[41] I concur with Graybill's assessment that Melanchthon's views of grace and the will were unlike, in important respects, those of the other magisterial Reformers (Luther, Calvin, Zwingli, etc.) in regard to the power of God's grace to awaken a free choice of acceptance; unlike those of Erasmus and the Anabaptist radicals who relegated rather too much freedom to the natural will, underestimated the effects of the original sin and the Fall; and unlike those of the Catholics and radicals who underestimated the need for the imputed forensic righteousness of Christ in justification (which will be examined in the section on good works and the third use of the law below).

## *The Legacy of Melanchthon's Hamartiology and Views of a Grace-Freed Will*

Jacob Arminius held, in common with Melanchthon, a strong view of original sin and its results upon all human beings.[42] He also recognized the need for God's grace

---

41 Beachy, 39; Olson, 425. Menno Simmons wrote, "Even as we fell and became sinners in Adam, so we also believe and confess, that through Christ, the second and heavenly Adam, we are graciously helped to our feet and justified ... And therefore, we do truly believe, that they [all children] are in a state of grace, acceptable to God, pure, holy, heirs of God and of eternal life." ("A Foundation Plain Instruction of the Saving Doctrine of our Lord Jesus Christ," in *The Complete Works*, 130, 135.

Dirk Phillips wrote that "they are [all children], of course, descendants of a sinful Adam, yet original sin, as man calls it, is not reckoned to their account for the sake of Christ. For they are in this respect even as Adam and Eve were before the fall, in that they are innocent of either right or wrong and understand neither good nor evil" (Dirk Philips, *Vander Doope*, Bibliotheca Reformatoria Neerlandica, 74–75, quoted in Beachy, 39; cf. idem, "The Baptism of our Lord Jesus Christ," in *The Writings of Dirk Philips*, 77).

Hubmaier, while ostensibly accepting the idea of original sin (Pipkin, 540, cf. ibid., 284–285), claimed that it was only the soul and the flesh that were completely fallen after Adam, not the spirit. The soul needs prevenient grace, but the spirit retains its original righteoussness (ibid., 434, 437–438).

A similar view was held by Melchior Hoffmann. See Deppermann, *Melchoir Hoffmann*, 234. Melanchthon was aware of this and wrote, "Some simply take away original sin altogether; others imagine that after the resurrection of Christ no one is born with original sin. The passages cited from John [1:12–13; 3:3] fortify us against these fanatical opinions. But see how great is the madness of the Anabaptists! If there were no original sin, all men would live without sin and without death. Since this is clearly false, it is necessary that the cause remain, namely, original sin," Melanchthon, *Commentary on Romans*, 136.

42 "For in Adam 'all have sinned.' (Rom. v. 12.) Wherefore, whatever punishment was brought down upon our first parents, has likewise pervaded and yet pursues all their posterity. So that all men 'are by nature the children of wrath' (Ephes. ii. 3,) obnoxious to condemnation, and to temporal as well as to eternal death; they are also devoid of that original righteousness and holiness. (Rom. v. 12, 18, 19.) With these evils they would remain oppressed forever, unless they were liberated by Christ Jesus; to whom be glory forever" (Jacob Arminius,

to awaken the naturally depraved person,[43] and that this grace was resistible.[44] When he was challenged regarding his disavowal of determinism, he specifically cited Melanchthon as a notable precedent.

"Public Disputation 7: On the First Sin of the First Man," xvi, in *Works of James Arminius*, trans. James Nichols and Williams Nichols, 3 vols., [Grand Rapids, MI: Baker Book House, 1996], 2:156–157). Keith Stanglin and Thomas McCall, *Jacob Arminius: Theologian of Grace* (Oxford: Oxford University Press, 2012), 149–150, discuss to what extent Arminius emphasized punishment or guilt in his view of original sin. I would argue that he understood that the guilt (the condemnation of Rom 5) is what produces the punishment. He also affirmed the same "lack of original righteousness" as did Melanchthon. See Jacob Arminius, "Disputation XXXI: On the Effects of the Sin of Our First Parents," in *Works*, 2:374–375.

43 "In this state, the free will of man towards the true good is not only wounded, maimed, infirm, bent, and weakened; but it is also imprisoned, destroyed, and lost. And its powers are not only debilitated and useless unless they be assisted by grace, but it has no powers whatever except such as are excited by Divine grace." "As the very first commencement of every good thing, so likewise the progress, continuance and confirmation, nay, even the perseverance in good, are not from ourselves, but from God through the Holy Spirit" (Jacob Arminius, "Disputation XI: On the Free Will of Man and Its Powers," viii, xiv in *Works*, 2:192, 195).

44 "The primary efficient cause of repentance is God, and Christ as he is through the Spirit mediator between God and man. (Jer. xxxi. 18; Ezek. xxxvi. 25, 26; Acts v. 31; xvii. 30.) The only moving cause is the goodness, grace, and philanthropy of God our creator and redeemer, who loves the salvation of his creature, and desires to manifest the riches of his mercy in the salvation of his miserable creature. (Rom. xi. 5.) The outwardly moving cause, through the mode of merit, is the obedience, the death and the intercession of Christ (Isa. liii. 5; 1 Cor. i. 30, 31; 2 Cor. v. 21;) and, through the mode of moving to mercy, it is the unhappy condition of sinners, whom the devil holds captive in the snares of iniquity, and who will perish by their own demerits according to the condition of the law, and necessarily according to the will of God manifested in the gospel, unless they repent (John iii. 16; Ezek. xvi. 3–63; Luke xiii. 3, 5; Isa. xxxi. 6; Jer. iii. 14; Psalm cxix. 71; in the prophets passim; Rom. vii. 6, 7.) The proximate, yet less principal cause, is man himself, converted and converting himself by the power and efficacy of the grace of God and the Spirit of Christ. The external cause inciting to repent is the miserable state of the sinners who do not repent, and the felicitous and blessed state of those who repent" (Jacob Arminius, "Disputation XVII On Repentance," v, vi in *Works*, 238–239. "In this manner, I ascribe to grace the commencement, the continuance and the consummation of all good, and to such an extent do I carry its influence, that a man, though already regenerate, can neither conceive, will, nor do any good at all, nor resist any evil temptation, without this preventing and exciting, this following and cooperating grace. From this statement it will clearly appear, that I by no means do injustice to grace, by attributing, as it is reported of me, too much to man's free-will. For the whole controversy reduces itself to the solution of this question, 'is the grace of God a certain irresistible force?' That is, the controversy does not relate to those actions or operations which may be ascribed to grace (for I acknowledge and inculcate as many of these actions or operations as any man ever did) but it relates solely to the mode of operation, whether it be irresistible or not. With respect to which, I believe, according to the scriptures, that many persons resist the Holy Spirit and reject the grace that is offered" (Jacob Arminius, *A Declaration of the Sentiments of Arminius*, "IV. On the Grace of God" in *Works*, 1:664).

> This doctrine of Predestination has been rejected both in former times and in our own days, by the greater part of the professors of Christianity ... However highly Luther and Melancthon [sic] might at the very commencement of the reformation, have approved of this doctrine, they afterwards deserted it ... This change in Melancthon [sic] is quite apparent from his latter writings.[45]

Stanglin and McCall note that Arminius "appealed to Lutheran predecessors who taught a similar doctrine of predestination, especially Philip Melanchthon and Niels Hemmingsen, whose works appear in his personal library."[46]

John Wesley concurred on these matters of original sin, the total depravity of human beings, and the need for divine (resistible) grace. "By the sin of the first Adam, who was not only the father, but likewise the representative, of us all, we all fell short of the favour of God; we all became children of wrath; or, as the Apostle expresses it, 'judgment came upon all men to condemnation.'"[47] In discussing Christ and Adam he says, "Each of them being a public person, and a federal head of mankind. The one, the fountain of sin and death to mankind by his offence; the other, of righteousness and life by his free gift. . . . As the sin of Adam, without the sins which we afterwards committed, brought us death; so the righteousness of Christ, without the good works which we afterwards perform, brings us life: although still every good, as well as evil, work, will receive its due reward."[48] After the Fall, "God saw that the whole imagination of the heart of man was only evil ... In his flesh dwelt no good thing; all his nature was purely evil. It was wholly consistent with itself and unmixed with anything of an opposite nature."[49] All who deny original sin "are still but heathens."[50] Regarding grace, Wesley wrote, "How is it more for the glory of God to save a man irresistibly than to save him as a free agent, by such grace as he may either concur with or resist?" The glory of God was not displayed in reprobation and irresistible grace because it would reveal God to be deceptive in all of His numerous admonitions to repent and accept His grace.[51]

---

45 Ibid., "I. On Predestination," in *Works*, 2:642.
46 Stanglin and McCall, 44.
47 John Wesley, "Justification by Faith," in *The Essential Works of John Wesley*, ed. Alice Russie (Uhrichsville, OH: Barbour Publishing, 2011), 285 (283–293).
48 John Wesley, *Explanatory Notes on the New Testament* (London: Paternoster-Row, 1866), 224–225. Thomas McCall, in "But a Heathen Still" from *Adam, the Fall, and Original Sin: Theological, Biblical and Scientific Perspectives* (Grand Rapids, MI: Baker Academic, 2014), 150, discusses the disagreement among Wesleyan scholars concerning Wesley's beliefs regarding original guilt. What seems evident is that some of those who reject original guilt in their theology seek to make Wesley agree with their own view. McCall demonstrates the problems with their line of argumentation and shows that Wesley never denied original guilt. He simply maintained that Christ had provided atonement available to all.
49 Wesley, "Original Sin," in *The Essential Works*, 127.
50 Ibid., 133.
51 Wesley, "Predestination Calmly Considered," in ibid., 1103–1152.

## The Relevance of Melanchthon's Hamartiology for Seventh-day Adventists

Up to the present, many Seventh-day Adventists have rejected the idea of original sin, especially in regard to the idea of imputed guilt from Adam.[52] But contrary to what many have claimed, Ellen White affirmed original sin and guilt in some sense – not in the participatory, realist Augustinian sense, but rather imputed guilt in the "federal" sense of Adam being the representative of the human race.

> Adam was required to render perfect obedience to God, not only in his own behalf, but in behalf of his posterity. God promised him that if he would stand the test of temptation, preserving his allegiance to the Creator during the great trial to which he would be subjected, his obedience would insure his acceptance and favor with God. He would then be forever established in holiness and happiness, and these blessings would extend to all his posterity. But Adam failed to bear the test. And because he revolted against God's law, all his descendants have been sinners.[53]

"Adam sinned, and the children of Adam share his guilt and its consequences."[54] "Children received from Adam an inheritance of disobedience, of guilt and death." "Parents have a more serious charge than they imagine. The inheritance of children is that of sin. Sin has separated them from God. Jesus gave His life that He might unite the broken links to God. As related to the first Adam, men receive from him nothing but guilt and the sentence of death."[55] White also wrote in a number of places that Adam's sin resulted immediately in a "guilty race."[56] Regarding depravity,

---

52  See Norman Gulley, *Systematic Theology: Creation, Christ, Salvation*, vol. 3 (Berrien Springs, MI: Andrews University Press, 2012), 161, 167; John M. Fowler, "Sin," in *Handbook of Seventh-day Adventist Theology*, ed. Raoul Dederen (Hagerstown, MD: Review and Herald, 2000), 257; "Sin," in *Seventh-day Adventist Encyclopedia* (Washington, DC: Review and Herald, 1976), 1351; Gerhard Pfandl, "Some Thoughts on Original Sin," https://goo.gl/Biu8BU (November 28, 2017).

53  "The Sabbath was committed to Adam, the father and representative of the whole human family." Ellen G. White, *Patriarchs and Prophets* (Washington, DC: Review and Herald, 1890/1958), 48. Manuscript 126, December 10, 1901. "The relationship existing in the pure family of God in heaven was to exist in the family of God on earth. Under God, Adam was to stand at the head of the earthly family to maintain the principles of the heavenly family. This would have brought peace and happiness." *Testimonies for the Church*, 9 vols. (Mountain View, CA: Pacific Press, 1948), 6:236.

54  Ellen G. White, "Obedience is Sanctification," *Signs of the Times*, May 19, 1890, 290.

55  Ellen G. White, Letter 8, 1895 (February 9, 1896); *Child Guidance* (Washington, DC: Review and Herald, 1954), 475; "'Walk Even as He Walked'," *The Youth's Instructor*, November 8, 1894; *Patriarchs and Prophets* (Washington, DC: Review and Herald, 1958), 61; *Child Guidance*, (Washington, DC: Review and Herald, 1954), 475.

56  *Signs of the Times*, November 4, 1908; White, *The Great Controversy*, 347; see also *Signs of the Times*, January 39, 1879, where she refers to the "lost race" because of Adam and Eve's sin.

she wrote, "Selfishness is inwrought in our very being";[57] "Human nature is vile";[58] "The heart of man is by nature cold and dark and unloving."[59] It is only by accepting Christ through faith that this condition can be escaped. There is no evidence in her writings for "legal universal justification":

> Blessed is the soul who can say, "I am guilty before God: but Jesus is my Advocate. I have transgressed His law. I cannot save myself; but I make the precious blood that was shed on Calvary all my plea. *I am lost in Adam, but restored in Christ.* God, who so loved the world as to give His only begotten Son to die, will not leave me to perish while repentant and in contrition of soul. He will not look upon me, for I am all unworthy; but He will look upon the face of His Anointed, He will look upon my Substitute and Surety, and listen to the plea of my Advocate, who died for my sin, that I might be made the righteousness of God in Him" (emphasis added).[60]

These quotations raise the question of the state of infants who die. While Ellen White did not discuss this in detail, she did hint at the idea that they can and will be saved, (at least some of them).[61]

---

57 Ellen G. White, *Historical Sketches of the Foreign Missions of the Seventh-day Adventists* (Basle: Imprimerie Polyglotte, 1886), 138.
58 Ellen G. White, "The All-Important Lesson," *Signs of the Times,* November 15, 1883, 506.
59 Ellen G. White, *Thoughts From the Mount of Blessing* (Mountain View, CA: Pacific Press, 1955), 21. See also Woodrow Whidden, *Ellen White on the Humanity of Christ* (Hagerstown, MD: Review and Herald, 1997), 99–104.
60 Ellen G. White, *Sons and Daughters of God* (Washington, DC: Review and Herald, 1955), 120.
61 White wrote, "As the little infants come forth immortal from their dusty beds, they immediately wing their way to their mothers' arms. They meet again nevermore to part. But many of the little ones have no mother there. We listen in vain for the rapturous song of triumph from the mother. The angels receive the motherless infants and conduct them to the tree of life" (*Selected Messages,* vol. 2 [Washington, DC: Review and Herald, 1958], 260). While this might seem to imply the salvation of all infants, in another place, she wrote of the definitive role of parental faith (or lack of it) in regard to the salvation of infants. In reply to a direct question regarding the children of unbelieving parents, she first wrote that "this we should consider as one of the questions we are not at liberty to express a position or an opinion upon, for the simple reason that God has not told us definitely about this matter in His Word. If He thought it was essential for us to know, He would have told us plainly (Ibid., 3:314)." She then went on, though, to give some ideas that were relevant to the question: "the faith of the believing parents covers the children, as when God sent His judgments upon the first-born of the Egyptians ... The word of God came to the Israelites in bondage to gather their children into their houses and to mark the doorposts of their houses with blood from a lamb, slain. This prefigured the slaying of the Son of God and the efficacy of His blood, which was shed for the salvation of the sinner. It was a sign that the household accepted Christ as the promised Redeemer. It was shielded from the destroyer's power. The parents evidenced their faith in implicitly obeying the directions given them, and the faith of the parents covered themselves and their children. They showed their faith in Jesus, the great Sacrifice, whose blood was prefigured in the slain lamb. The destroying angel passed over every house that had this mark upon it. This is a symbol to show that the faith of the parents

extends to their children and covers them from the destroying angel." She then went on to contrast this situation with those parents who are neglectful toward their children, and that this might involve their children being lost as a result (Ibid., 314–315).

Melanchthon, while he did connect the guilt of original sin with the need for paedobaptism (baptism of infants), did not believe in *ex opere operato* efficacy in regard to the sacraments. "Infants are born with sin, and they are not made heirs of eternal life without the remission of sin. Now, God has established in the church the ministry of remitting sins and distributing remission through the sacraments ... Hence this benefit must be given to infants through baptism." *The Chief Theological Topics: Loci Praecipui Theologici 1559*, trans. J. A. O. Preus (St. Louis, MO: Concordia Publishing House, 2011), 267. But he also wrote in the *Augsburg Confession*, article XIII, "They therefore condemn those who teach that the sacraments justify by the outward act, and who do not teach that, in the use of the Sacraments, faith which believes that sins are forgiven, is required." https://goo.gl/LmS4aH (November 30, 2017). But how could an infant have such faith? Melanchthon attempts to answer this seeming inconsistency as follows: "It is certainly true that in adults repentance and faith are required. But it is sufficient to hold this regarding infants, that the Holy Spirit is given to them through baptism, and [He] affects in them new affections, new inclinations toward God in proportion to their condition." (*Chief Theological Topics: Loci 1559*, 268). In the end it appears that the basis of Melanchthon's advocacy for infant baptism was twofold – first, to affirm the corruption of the natural state of humanity in original sin over against Anabaptist objections (ibid., 265), and second, to affirm that infants must be regarded as being part of God's church, the primary place where God's grace is found. But he also held that continuing faith throughout a lifetime was necessary for salvation, such that one's baptism alone was no guarantee for continued grace (see above, n. 35).

By way of evaluation, the following can be noted: While baptism is associated with the repentance and faith that leads to salvation (John 3:5; Acts 2:38; 1 Pet 3:21; 1 Cor 12:13; Col 2:11–13; Acts 8:12; etc.), it is not given as the means *alone* by which a person is saved. It is never associated with a person who is not exercising faith. It is by grace through faith that we are saved (Rom 3–5; 10:8–10; Eph 1–2; John 3:16–18; Gal 3; Phil 3:8–15; etc.). Baptism, like the Lord's Supper, is a sign and strengthening of the grace we have received. Thus it is not the ritual in and of itself alone by which this grace is given, but only as it is mixed with true faith and repentance. Since no one is directly saved by the ritual alone (important, even necessary, as it is – all things being equal, as John 3:5 indicates), infants who die before being able to place their faith in Christ, would be saved by means of His atonement, appropriated by the faith of their parents. In the case of the infants who die with unbelieving parents, or the cases of those who have not been baptized (for various preventative reasons, though they have accepted Christ by faith), or who have never heard the Gospel, such persons could be saved on the basis of God's omniscience of unrealized future contingencies (known as "middle knowledge") – i.e., He knows if the person in question would or would not have accepted the Gospel or gotten baptized if they would have heard it or had the opportunity. Seventh-day Adventists can thus affirm Melanchthon's legacy (echoed by Ellen White) of original sin and its results without practicing infant baptism. They can also affirm his desire to view children as part of the church from birth, while heeding Ellen White's counsel concerning the importance of the role of parents in regard to their children's eternal salvation – both of which are highlighted through the practice of baby dedications, in which both parents and the church pledge their faith in regard to the infants being presented. The most important point is that Ellen White affirms (as did Melanchthon) that children are not

A denial of original sin has often led to a denial of imputed righteousness, something also common in Adventist history (but again not in Ellen White) since both are contingent upon the representative nature of Adam and Christ respectively. This denial has led to the idea that the sinful nature is not sin, and that sinless perfection is attainable in this life. However, if there is no initial sin in infants, then it logically follows that a person could successfully resist their ostensibly non-sinful nature and be sinless from the cradle to the grave, something that has been repeatedly claimed by those seeking theological consistency.[62] That Ellen White denied this possibility will be shown below in the section on justification.

White also carried on the Melanchthon, Arminius, Wesley tradition on a grace-freed will that could accept God's drawing. "The light shining from the cross reveals the love of God. His love is drawing us to Himself. If we do not resist this drawing, we shall be led to the foot of the cross in repentance for the sins that have crucified the Saviour. Then the Spirit of God through faith produces a new life in the soul."[63]

## Melanchthon on Justification

There is some disagreement among scholars regarding what degree of modification, if any, occurred during Melanchthon's career in regard to his views of the means, ground, and results of justification.[64]

In the first 1521 *Loci*, Melanchthon wrote, "We are justified ... when we cling to Christ nothing doubting but that the righteousness of Christ is our righteousness, that his satisfaction is our expiation, that his resurrection is ours." "If indeed such faith alone justifies us, there is plainly no respect for our merits or our works, but only of Christ's merits." This kind of language seems to embrace the idea of the imputed righteousness of Christ. Faith is the means by which the mercy of God through Christ is appropriated. "Faith is nothing other than reliance upon the divine mercy promised in Christ."[65] While the specifically forensic language of the later writings may be lacking, it does appear that the elements which account for it were

---

born sinless, or a blank slate, but rather are sinful, guilty, and in immediate need of a Savior – thus the importance of parental faith, baby dedications, and the careful nurturing of children in the Gospel to the end that they can eventually embrace the Gospel through their own faith.

62  See, e.g., the later E. J. Waggoner's suggestion that godly parents can have their children to be born as Christ was ("The Miraculous Birth," *Present Truth*, December 20, 1900, quoted in Woodrow Whidden, *E. J. Waggoner: From the Physician of Good News to Agent of Division* [Hagerstown, MD: Review and Herald, 2008], 265–266).

63  White, *The Desire of Ages* (Mountain View, CA: Pacific Press, 1940), 175.

64  See Timothy J. Wengert, *Law and Gospel: Philip Melanchthon's debate with John Agricola of Eisleben over Poenitentia* (Grand Rapids, MI: Baker Books, 1997), 179.

65  Melanchthon, *The Loci Communes* [1521], 171–172; 216; 196; 177.

already present (Christ's merits counted for us, and the faith that grasps them). Melanchthon was also clear that the faith that justifies is not "a mere historical opinion ... but productive always of good fruits";[66] such that "we of our own accord and joyfully do the law."[67] Yet these fruits were neither meritorious nor perfect, since "the works that follow our justification although they proceed from the Spirit of God ... are nevertheless of themselves unclean, because they are performed by a heart that is still impure. For our justification has just begun, and is not fully completed. We have received the firstfruits of the "Spirit," but not yet the "titles."[68]

The specifically forensic element of justification emerges in the *Apology* and the 1532 revised *Commentary on Romans*. In the *Apology* he wrote, "the imputation of the righteousness of the Gospel is from the promise; therefore it is always received by faith, and it always must be regarded certain that by faith we are for Christ's sake, accounted righteous."[69] "Therefore we must conclude that, being reconciled by faith, we are accounted righteous for Christ's sake, not for the sake of the Law or our works."[70] In the 1532 *Commentary on Romans*, he strengthened the forensic aspects by relating justification to the law court setting.[71] In the 1540 version of the *Commentary*, he reiterated this concept as well as clarified his thought regarding regeneration, effectively nullifying any case for misunderstanding possible ambiguities regarding what he had written in the *Apology*.

---

66   Ibid., 207.
67   Ibid., 177.
68   Ibid., 197. It is this kind of language that has led McGrath to suggest that justification in Melanchthon's early thought was "factitive," and still tethered to the Augustinian conception of infused righteousness (McGrath, *Iustitia*, 2:23). But Melanchthon's very point to the contrary seems to be that any works of human beings could not be considered righteous in the fullest sense, and that there was a later justification that took place at glorification, since the righteousness then would be perfectly actual.
69   Melanchthon, *Apology*, Part VI, article III, https://goo.gl/DqSnFQ (November 28, 2017).
70   Ibid. There has been some controversy over the following statement from the *Apology* (Part IV: "That faith in Christ Justifies" https://goo.gl/dFnYXS [November 30, 2017]): "We maintain this, that properly and truly, by faith itself, we are for Christ's sake accounted righteous, or are acceptable to God. And because 'to be justified' means that out of unjust men just men are made, or born again, it means also that they are pronounced or accounted just. For Scripture speaks in both ways. [The term "to be justified" is used in two ways: to denote, being converted or regenerated; again, being accounted righteous.] Accordingly we wish first to show this, that faith alone makes of an unjust, a just man, i.e., receives remission of sins." For a discussion of some of the various interpretations, see Lowell C. Green, *How Melanchthon Helped Luther Discover the Gospel* (Fallbrook, CA: Verdict Publications, 1980), 220–223. This statement is actually not inconsistent with others. What Melanchthon is conveying is that the new birth occurs at the same time as justification. What is crucial is that this renewal is not meritorious, and that the unjust becoming just is on the *basis* of the accounting of righteousness, and not on the renewal itself.
71   Wengert, 179.

> To justify is to pronounce or consider just ... But one must know that in the forgiveness of sins there is given at the same time the Holy Spirit ... Thus the gift of the Holy Spirit is connected with justification, which begins not only one virtue – faith – but also others ... But these virtues do not merit forgiveness of sins, nor are they the righteousness on account of which a person is accepted.[72]

According to McGrath, Melanchthon was the first major theologian in history to describe justification forensically. "The importance of this development lies in the fact that it marks a radical break with the teaching of the western church up to that point. From the time of Augustine onward, justification had always referred to both the event of being declared righteous and the process of being made righteous."[73]

The concept of the imputed righteousness of Christ is supported in the discussion of the Adam/Christ comparison in Romans 5: "This comparison powerfully illustrates both parts. It explains the matter of the merit, what each merited for others. Adam merited guilt for others; Christ merited reconciliation for others ... As others are guilty because of Adam, so others are righteous because of Christ."[74] In the 1555 *Loci*, all of the previous strands are compellingly drawn together, including a focus on Christ's mediation, something the *Apology* had also highlighted:

> The Mediator's entire obedience, from his Incarnation until the Resurrection, is the true justification which is pleasing to God, and is the merit for us. God forgives us our sins, and accepts us, in that he imputes righteousness to us for the sake of the Son, although we are still weak and sinful. We must, however, accept this imputed righteousness with faith ... As St. Paul says, Romans 5:19, 'By one man's (namely, Christ's) obedience many will be made righteous.' Thus we are clothed with a strange righteousness. Although our nature is still not uniform with God, nevertheless, as the Mediator Christ in his complete obedience is uniform with God and covers our sins with his righteousness, so we are justified, have forgiveness of sin, are pleasing to God, *for Christ's sake*, whose righteousness is accepted on our behalf. And this we must accept *with faith*.[75]

Melanchthon also reiterated the concept that the Holy Spirit begins renewal at the time of justification by faith, and that there are virtues that accompany his regenerating work that has begun. But these virtues are not "*causae justificationis;* they are not reasons why God accepts us."[76]

---

72 Melanchthon, *Commentary on Romans*, 25.
73 Alister McGrath, *Christian Theology: An Introduction* (Chichester: John Wiley and Sons, 2011), 362; McGrath, *Iustitia Dei*, 1:51.
74 Melanchthon, *Commentary on Romans*, 136.
75 Melanchthon, *Melanchthon on Christian Doctrine*, 161–162.
76 Ibid., 154, 166.

## Melanchthon's Legacy on Justification

Arminius embraced the doctrine of justification that the other Reformers did.[77] John Wesley also affirmed these doctrines, but he evinced some evolution on the issue of the imputed righteousness of Christ.[78] Initially, he felt that this doctrine would lead to antinomianism. "Least of all does justification imply ... that He [God] accounts them to be otherwise than what they are ... Neither can it ever consist in His unerring wisdom to think ... that I am righteous or holy because another is so."[79] But later he eventually came to embrace it. "If we take the phrase of imputing Christ's righteousness for the bestowing (as it were) the righteousness of Christ – i.e., in the privileges, blessings, and benefits purchased by it – so a believer may be said to be justified by the righteousness of Christ imputed."[80]

## The Relevance of Melanchthon's Views for Seventh-day Adventists

Ellen White embraced all of the aspects of justification espoused by Melanchthon that were discussed above. "By His perfect obedience He has satisfied the claims of

---

77 "It is a justification by which a man, who is a sinner, yet a believer, being placed before the throne of grace which is erected in Christ Jesus the Propitiation, is accounted and pronounced by God, the just and merciful Judge, righteous and worthy of the reward of righteousness, not in himself but in Christ, of grace, according to the gospel, to the praise of the righteousness and grace of God, and to the salvation of the justified person himself. (Rom. iii. 24–26; 3, 4, 5, 10, 11.)" Jacob Arminius, "Disputation 19: On the Justification of Man Before God," IV in *Works*: 2:254,). "I am not conscious to myself, of having taught or entertained any other sentiments concerning the justification of man before God, than those which are held unanimously by the Reformed and Protestant Churches, and which are in complete agreement with their expressed opinions ... I believe that sinners are accounted righteous solely by the obedience of Christ; and that the righteousness of Christ is the only meritorious cause on account of which God pardons the sins of believers and reckons them as righteous as if they had perfectly fulfilled the law. But since God imputes the righteousness of Christ to none except believers, I conclude that, in this sense, it may be well and properly said, to a man who believes, faith is imputed for righteousness through grace, because God hath set forth his Son, Jesus Christ, to be a propitiation, a throne of grace, [or mercy seat] through faith in his blood. Whatever interpretation may be put upon these expressions, none of our Divines blames Calvin or considers him to be heterodox on this point; yet my opinion is not so widely different from his as to prevent me from employing the signature of my own hand in subscribing to those things which he has delivered on this subject, in the third book of his Institutes; this I am prepared to do at any time, and to give them my full approval," Jacob Arminius, *A Declaration of the Sentiments of Arminius*, XI: "The Justification of Man Before God," in *Works*, 1:700.
78 See Woodrow Whidden, "Wesley on Imputation: A Truly Reckoned Reality or Antinomian Polemical Wreckage?" *The Asbury Theological Journal* 52:2 (1997): 63–70.
79 John Wesley, "Justification by Faith," in *The Essential Works*, 286.
80 Wesley, "The Lord Our Righteousness," in ibid., 301 (295–307).

the law, and my only hope is found in looking to Him as my substitute and surety, who obeyed the law perfectly for me. By faith in His merits I am free from the condemnation of the law. He clothes me with His righteousness, which answers all the demands of the law."[81] While she held that the imputed righteousness of Christ would not cover willful, "cherished sin,"[82] White asserted that it was sinners who needed it. "In ourselves we are sinners, in Christ we are righteous."

> Knowing himself to be a sinner, a transgressor of the holy law of God, he looks to the perfect obedience of Christ, to his death upon Calvary for the sins of the world; and he has the assurance that he is justified by faith in the merit and sacrifice of Christ. He realizes that the law was obeyed in his behalf by the Son of God, and that the penalty of transgression cannot fall upon the believing sinner. The active obedience of Christ clothes the believing sinner with the righteousness that meets the demands of the law.[83]

White never allowed for any basis of anything in human beings to merit justification. "If you would gather together everything that is good and holy and noble and lovely in man and then present the subject to the angels of God as acting a part in the salvation of the human soul or in merit, the proposition would be rejected as treason."[84]

> Let the subject be made distinct and plain that it is not possible to effect anything in our standing before God or in the gift of God to us through creature merit. Should faith and works purchase the gift of salvation for anyone, then the Creator is under obligation to the creature ... If man cannot, by any of his good works, merit salvation, then it must be wholly of grace, received by man as a sinner because he receives and believes in Jesus. It is wholly a free gift.[85]

> It was possible for Adam, before the fall, to form a righteous character by obedience to God's law. But he failed to do this, and because of his sin our natures are fallen and we cannot make ourselves righteous. Since we are sinful, unholy, we cannot perfectly obey the holy law. We have no righteousness of our own with which to meet the claims of the law of God. But Christ has made a way of escape for us. He lived on earth amid trials and temptations such as we have to meet. He lived a sinless life. He died for us, and now He offers to take our sins and give us His righteousness. If you give yourself to Him, and accept Him as your Saviour, then, sinful as your life may have been, for His sake you are accounted righteous. Christ's character stands in place of your character, and you are accepted before God just as if you had not sinned.[86]

---

81  White, *Selected Messages*, 1:396.
82  Ellen G. White, *Christ's Object Lessons* (Washington, DC: Review and Herald, 1941), 316.
83  Ibid., 394; White, *Youth's Instructor*, November 29, 1894.
84  Ellen G. White, *Faith and Works* (Nashville, TN: Southern Publishing Association, 1979), 24.
85  Ibid., 19.
86  Ellen G. White, *Steps to Christ* (Mountain View, CA: Pacific Press, 1956), 62.

Yet she also, as Melanchthon did, recognized that the new birth accompanies (though it is not the grounds for) justification. "God's forgiveness is not merely a judicial act by which He sets us free from condemnation. It is not only forgiveness *for* sin, but reclaiming *from* sin. It is the outflow of redeeming love that transforms the heart."[87]

Other Seventh-day Adventist writers have been reluctant to embrace forensic justification and imputed righteousness. E. J. Waggoner in his later writings held views essentially identical to those of Osiander, who viewed justification as essentially identical with inward transformation.[88] Others have embraced the universal legal justification model of the Anabaptists.[89] Ellen White's soteriological thought on depravity and justification is thus more integrally connected to the scriptural foundations of the Reformation as articulated by Melanchthon than has often been the case in other Adventist writings.

## Melanchthon on Good Works and the Third Use of the Law

Melanchthon's views on the role of good works and the "third use" of the law remained essentially consistent throughout his writings – concomitant with justification there begins the process of renewal, which includes good works and the keeping of the law. However, he always held that such obedience was tainted by sin, non-meritorious, and inadequate to fulfill the law perfectly.

In the 1521 *Loci*, he wrote of the "abrogation of the Law," but clarified his meaning: "Every right of the law to condemn and accuse us has been taken away." "Liberty does not mean that we do not do the law, but that we will and desire spontaneously from our hearts what the law demands." "The will of God is the law. And the Holy Spirit is but a living will of God and a motion. Wherefore when we have been regenerated ... we will already of our own accord, the very things which the law demanded." "The Spirit of God cannot be in the heart without expressing the decalogue *[sic]*."[90] As was noted above, however, he was always clear that this obedience to the law was neither perfect nor meritorious.[91]

---

87 White, *Thoughts from the Mount of Blessing*, 114.
88 See Calvin, *Institutes*, 2:36–59 [3.11] describing and refuting Osiander. Waggoner wrote, "[Justification] does not mean that Christ's righteousness which He did eighteen hundred years ago is laid up for the sinner, simply to be credited to his account, but it means that His present active righteousness is given to that man." "Being justified by faith, then, is simply being made a doer of the law by faith." "His obedience is not a substitute for our disobedience, but it is actually our righteousness ... He comes to walk over the same road in us" (E. J. Waggoner, "Being Justified," *Present Truth*, October 20, 1892, quoted in Whidden, *E. J. Waggoner*, 294, 296).
89 See, e.g., Ángel Rodríguez, "Some Problems with Universal Legal Justification," https://goo.gl/ZmxWGW (November 28, 2017.)
90 Melanchthon, *The Loci Communes* [1521], 221, 223, 228–229.
91 "Whatever is averse to the law of God is sin ... Let us confess therefore that it is a fact that sin is in our flesh." "Sanctification is not yet perfected in us ... The nature of the saints is

In the *Apology,* Melanchthon wrote of believers who receive justification "by faith alone, although, when the Holy Ghost is given, the fulfilling of the Law follows." "The Law ought to be begun in us, and be kept by us more and more – we are to keep the Law when we have been justified by faith, and thus increase more and more in the Spirit." Yet he was clear that this fulfillment was "inchoate."[92]

In the 1540 *Commentary on Romans,* Philip Melanchthon raised the question of "whether imperfect and contaminated obedience is acceptable to God, and how it is acceptable."[93] He then proceeded to list Scripture passages[94] that indicated that "sins remained in the saints," and after quoting 1 Peter 2:5, wrote that we must "believe that after we have been made sons by faith, and that the obedience which has begun is acceptable, not on account of our own purity or worthiness, but on account of Christ, the Mediator."[95] "Although ... works are not themselves fulfillment of the Law, nevertheless since they please because of Christ, they are, as it were, a certain fulfillment of the Law."[96]

In his commentary on Colossians, in its 1528 and 1534 revisions, Melanchthon developed the concept of the three uses of the moral law. These involved (1) restraint upon sinful society through the use of civil laws, (2) terrifying and humbling sinners – showing them their sinfulness and their need of Christ, and (3) guiding believers in their lives. God gave the law for three reasons: to "coerce the flesh, terrify the humble ... the third reason pertains to the righteous, that they may practice obedience."[97] As Wengert summarizes, even though the law has "lost its accusatory voice, being written on the hearts of all, including believers, that law continues to not only reveal the remnants of sin, but the will of God and the contours of Christian obedience."[98]

---

twofold: spirit and flesh, the new man and the old man, the inner man and the outer man" (ibid., 235, 234).
92  "Christ does not cease to be Mediator after we have been renewed. They err who imagine that He has merited only a first grace, and that afterwards we please God and merit eternal life by our fulfilling of the Law ... For our best works, even after the grace of the Gospel has been received, as I stated, are still weak and not at all pure." "Therefore we must conclude that, being reconciled by faith, we are accounted righteous for Christ's sake, not for the sake of the Law or our works, but that this inchoate fulfilling of the Law pleases on account of faith, and that, on account of faith, there is no imputation of the imperfection of the fulfilling of the Law, even though the sight of our impurity terrifies us" (Melanchthon, *Apology,* "Of Love Fulfilling the Law," Part 6, Article III, https://goo.gl/DqSnFQ [November 28, 2017]).
93  Melanchthon, *Commentary on Romans* [1540], 39.
94  Ibid., 41–42. See Ps 143:2; 1 John 1:8; Rom 7:23; 1 Cor 4:4; Matt 6:12; Luke 17:10; Ps 130:3; 19:12; 32:5; Job 9:20; Exod 34:7; Dan 9:7; Rom 11:32; 1 Cor 1:31.
95  Ibid., 43.
96  Ibid., 115.
97  Philip Melanchthon, *"Scholia in Epistolam Pauli ad Colessenes iterum ab authore recognita* XLVIII," quoted in Wengert, 196.
98  Wengert, 196.

In the 1555 *Loci,* Melanchthon again explained the three uses of the law. "The first use is civil" – to restrain evil and teach morality in external matters. "The second use of the law is more important; namely, to preach the wrath of God." The office of preaching will produce "terror and comfort" – terror by the law and comfort through Christ. "The third use ... is concerned with those saints who are now believers ... The Law in this life is necessary, that saints may know and have a testimony of which works please God."[99]

## Melanchthon's Legacy on Good Works and the Third Use of the Law

Arminius also embraced the three uses of the law.[100] He did, however, seem to have (as we will see also with Wesley) a greater optimism about the regenerated Christian, and even entertained the possibility of sinlessness and perfect fulfillment of the law in this life by the grace of Christ.[101] He (unlike Melanchthon and the other Reformers) viewed the man of Romans 7 as an unregenerate man, such that the experience of sin described there could not be one of a real Christian. In his treatise on this chapter, Arminius suggests that the reason for remaining sin in believers is the gradualness of regeneration, not the simultaneity of the "carnal" and "spiritual" due to the simultaneity and conflict of old and new natures,[102] as in Melanchthon.[103]

Wesley believed also in the three uses of the law.[104] There are some ambiguities in the writings of Wesley on the issue of sinless perfection and the entire fulfillment of the law. Space precludes dealing with all of the nuances here, but the following can be noted: Wesley could at times refer to the lingering sin in believers that needed Christ's intercession, and the lack of sinlessness in this life.[105] But at other times he wrote of sinless perfection in which no unholy "tempers" remained – that

---

99 Melanchthon, *Melanchthon on Christian Doctrine,* 123–127.
100 "The third use of the moral law is towards a man, as now born again by the Spirit of God and of Christ, and is agreeable to the state of grace, that it may be a perpetual rule for directing his life in a godly and spiritual manner: (Titus iii. 8; Jas ii. 8.)." Jacob Arminius, "Disputation 12: On the Law of God," V. in *Works,* 2:198–199.
101 "While I never asserted, that a believer could perfectly keep the precepts of Christ in this life, I never denied it, but always left it as a matter which has still to be decided ... [Augustine] thinks it possible for a man to be without sin, by means of the grace of Christ and free-will" (Jacob Arminius, *A Declaration of Sentiments* "On the Perfection of Believers in this Life," VII. in *Works,* 1:677–679).
102 Jacob Arminius, "A Dissertation on the true and Genuine Sense of the Seventh Chapter of the Epistle to the Romans," Verse the Fourteenth in *Works,* 2:512–517.
103 Melanchthon, *Commentary on Romans,* 160–161.
104 Wesley, "The Original Nature, Property and Use of the Law," in *The Essential Works,* 726 (717–729).
105 Wesley, "On Sin in Believers," in ibid., 341–351.

there was an "entire" sanctification that could take place (for some).[106] The former was, as we have seen, much closer to Melanchthon's conception, the latter would be in dissonance with it.

## The Relevance of Melanchthon's View on Good Works and the Law for Seventh-day Adventists

Ellen White maintained the same essential balance as Melanchthon did in affirming the necessity of keeping the law, the necessity of continued faith to avoid apostasy,[107] while also noting that all obedience was imperfect, non-meritorious, and in need of intercession.

> The religious services, the prayers, the praise, the penitent confession of sin ascend from true believers as incense to the heavenly sanctuary, but passing through the corrupt channels of humanity, they are so defiled that unless purified by blood, they can never be of value with God. They ascend not in spotless purity, and unless the Intercessor, who is at God's right hand, presents and purifies all by His righteousness, it is not acceptable to God. All incense from earthly tabernacles must be moist with the cleansing drops of the blood of Christ. He holds before the Father the censer of His own merits, in which there is no taint of earthly corruption.[108]

Many Adventists over the years, however, have posited the possibility of an unmediated righteousness and sinless state.[109] But White was actually closer to Melanchthon than Arminius and Wesley regarding the issue. While she always affirmed a perfection of committed consecration, she wrote that "sanctification is the work of a lifetime"[110] and that "those who are really seeking to perfect Christian character will never indulge the thought that they are sinless. Their lives may be irreproachable ... but the more they discipline their minds to dwell upon the character of Christ ... the more clearly will they discern its spotless perfection, and the more deeply will they feel their own defects."[111]

106 Wesley, "A Plain Account of Christian Perfection," in *The Essential Works*, 1031, 1047 (1025–1101).
107 Ellen G. White, in *The Seventh-day Adventist Bible Commentary: Ellen G. White Comments*, 7 vols. plus supplement (vol. 7A) ed. Francis D. Nichol (Washington, DC: Review and Herald, 1956/1980), 6:1114.
108 White, *Selected Messages*, 1:344.
109 This is largely based on a misunderstanding of a few Ellen White comments concerning the time "without a Mediator" (e.g., White, *The Great Controversy*, 425). What is missed in these interpretations are the references to the "blood of sprinkling" – a term related to atonement – that is completed before this time. That is to say that the final generation is *forgiven* before the close of probation; and that the sin nature that remains in their condition has been atoned for before glorification (see White, *Testimonies for the Church*, vol. 5 [Mountain View, CA: Pacific Press, 1948], 467–476).
110 Ellen G. White, *Christ's Object Lessons* (Washington, DC: Review and Herald, 1941), 65.
111 Ellen G. White, *The Sanctified Life* (Washington, DC: Review and Herald, 1956), 7.

## Conclusion

Because Melanchthon's views on the will were specifically rejected in Article II on free will (negative theses 4 and 8) of the *Formula of Concord*,[112] the influence of his soteriological thought in Lutheranism was made more ambiguous, and remains controversial to this day. Were it not for this rejection in the *Formula*, the evangelical free will adherents of Protestantism might have viewed Melanchthon rather than Arminius, as their namesake and fountainhead.

This study has been an attempt to survey the essential outlines of the soteriological thought of Philip Melanchthon, a comparison with selected writers of his time, and the legacy he left that was embraced by Arminius and Wesley. Most significantly, it has been shown that Ellen White, if not all other Adventists, embraced these essentials also. The continuing dispute regarding and lack of acceptance of some of these elements in Adventism underscores the need for continuing study of both the Reformation heritage through Melanchthon, Arminius, and Wesley, as well as an ongoing necessity for further engagement with Scripture as well as White's writings as a continuation and affirmation of this significant and continually pertinent soteriological legacy.

---

112 *Formula of Concord*, II. "Free Will or Human Powers" https://goo.gl/LmS4aH (November 28, 2017). Negative Theses 4 and 8, "Fourthly, the doctrine of the Synergists, who pretend that man is not absolutely dead to good in spiritual things, but is badly wounded and half dead. Therefore, although the free will is too weak to make a beginning, and to convert itself to God by its own powers, and to be obedient to God's Law from the heart, nevertheless, when the Holy Ghost makes a beginning, and calls us through the Gospel, and offers His grace, the forgiveness of sins, and eternal salvation, that then the free will, from its own natural powers, can meet God, and to a certain extent, although feebly, do something towards it, help and cooperate thereto, can qualify itself for, and apply itself to, grace, and apprehend accept it, and believe the Gospel, and can also cooperate, by its own powers, with the Holy Ghost, in the continuation and maintenance of this work." "Since also the youths in the schools have been greatly perplexed *de tribus causis efficientibus, concurrentibus in conversione hominis non renati*, that is, by the doctrine of the three efficient causes of the conversion of unregenerate man to God, as to the manner in which they, namely, the Word of God preached and heard, the Holy Ghost, and the will of man, concur, it is again manifest from the explanation above presented that conversion to God is a work of God the Holy Ghost alone, who is the true Master that alone works this in us, for which He uses the preaching and hearing of His Holy Word as His ordinary [and lawful] means and instrument. But the intellect and will of the unregenerate man are nothing else than *subiectum convertendum*, that is, that which is to be converted, it being the intellect and will of a spiritually dead man, in whom the Holy Ghost works conversion and renewal, towards which work man's will that is to be converted does nothing, but suffers God alone to work in him, until he is regenerate; and then he works also with the Holy Ghost [cooperates] that which is pleasing to God in other good works that follow, in the way and to the extent fully set forth above."

# Martin Rothkegel

## The Anabaptist Reformation Experience

### Abstract

Sixteenth-century Anabaptism has sometimes been seen as a predecessor of the modern believers' church traditions and, more generally, as a movement that anticipated the modern concept of a free church in a free society. John H. Yoder and other free church theologians have explored the theological significance of Anabaptism for the church of the present time. From a historical point of view, Anabaptism should be understood as an umbrella term for a diverse range of movements and groups including Sabbatarians, Austerlitz Brethren (with whom Pilgram Marpeck was affiliated), Hutterites, and Swiss Brethren, but also Italian Anabaptists and the Polish Brethren. Mediated by the denominational historiography of the Mennonites, the Anabaptist story became part of the denominational memorial cultures of many free churches including Baptists, Seventh Day Baptists, and Seventh-day Adventists.

### Approaches: Between Identification and Strangeness

In 2017, the German state and the Protestant Church in Germany *(Evangelische Kirche in Deutschland)* will celebrate [did celebrate (the editor)] Martin Luther not only as the iconic founding figure of Protestantism but also as a forerunner of the values of modern Western society.[1] What makes the Anabaptists a necessary component of this jubilee is the observation that the points of their conflict with the Magisterial Reformers of the sixteenth century anticipated some of those points in which modern democratic principles are in disagreement with the concepts of the classical Reformers like Luther, Zwingli, Calvin, and their followers.

The Magisterial Reformers all held to the idea of a Christian society in which affiliation with the dominant church is obligatory for all inhabitants – the Anabaptists advocated religious liberty and separation between church and state. The Magisterial Reformers approved of the use of violence including the death penalty against religious dissenters – the Anabaptists rejected the use of violence in religious matters altogether and held that the legitimate mandate of secular authorities is limited to maintaining public peace by punishing offenses against civil laws. The Magisterial Reformers maintained that inhabitants of a Christian country are born into membership of the Christian church without their individual consent

---

1 For a critical look at the 2017 Reformation Jubilee from a free church perspective, see Martin Rothkegel, "Reformation, Nonkonformismus, Freiheit. Freikirchliche Anmerkungen zum allzu deutschen Lutherjubiläum 2017," *Zeitschrift für Theologie und Gemeinde* 21 (2016): 157–173.

– the Anabaptists protested that faith is a free gift of God that cannot be automatically imparted by Christian parents to their children, hence baptism and membership in the Christian church are legitimate only for those who voluntarily confess their faith.

What the Anabaptists stood up for summed up to a radical, historically unprecedented call for the political disempowerment of the Christian religion. This radical challenge of traditional Christendom was not motivated by a secularist criticism of religion, but by the conviction that the rejection of coercion in matters of faith and that patient civil coexistence in a religiously diverse society are grounded in the message of the New Testament and therefore normative, obligatory marks of true Christianity. It is obvious that no Anabaptist of the sixteenth century intended to contribute to the rise of modern Western democratic values. In their contemporary context, the concerns of the Anabaptists were radically sectarian positions, and that is what they still were when they were partially adopted, modified and developed further by the English Dissenters of the seventeenth century, especially by the British Baptist movements and by early American radicals like Roger Williams. Anyway, as a result of subsequent developments, concepts rooted in radical religious dissent, including concepts inherited by the British Dissenters from the Anabaptist tradition, eventually *did* contribute to the rise of modern understandings of a free society in the American Revolution and in nineteenth-century Britain.

It is not surprising, then, that North American historiography has paid special attention to the dissenting, or radical, wing of the Reformation. This special interest has not been limited to researchers from believers' church backgrounds with pro-Anabaptist denominational biases. It was especially the impression that political mentalities rooted in the German Lutheran tradition contributed to the catastrophe of 1933 to 1945 which made the Anabaptist story appear attractive as an alternative Reformation narrative. Simply spoken, the implicit hypothesis was that if the Anabaptists had prevailed in Reformation Germany instead of Luther there would not have been Hitler. One can sense this kind of underlying counterfactual speculation on many pages of George Williams' famous synthesis *The Radical Reformation*.[2]

John Howard Yoder's *Politics of Jesus*, published in 1972, marks the rediscovery of the Anabaptist tradition for contemporary theology beyond the denominational boundaries of the Mennonite community.[3] In the context of the Cold War, Yoder's recourse to the pacifist Anabaptist tradition as a model for Christian ethics inspired Methodist and Baptist theologians like Stanley Hauerwas,

---

2   George H. Williams, *The Radical Reformation* (Philadelphia, PA: Westminster Press, 1962; 3rd ed. Kirksville: Truman State University Press, 2000). Other post Second World War contributions by American historians display a similar appreciation for the Anabaptist and radical movements of the Reformation, see, e.g., Roland H. Bainton, *The Travail of Religious Liberty: Nine Biographical Studies* (Philadelphia, PA: Westminster Press, 1951); Franklin H. Littell, *The Anabaptist View of the Church* (Chicago, IL: American Society of Church History, 1952).
3   John Howard Yoder, *Politics of Jesus* (Grand Rapids, MI: Eerdmanns, 1972).

James William McClendon, and Glen Stassen. On a more popular level, the label "Anabaptist" eventually became an umbrella or container term for a bundle of theological, ethical, social and ecological concerns. This connotation of the term has become familiar, for example, among British Baptist theologians.[4] But also the explicitly non-pacifist Southern Baptists claim – obviously for different reasons – the Anabaptist tradition as a component of their historical heritage.[5] It seems that the recourse to Anabaptism, a term that originally was a derogatory sect name, has become a common denominator and identity marker among theologians of the believers' church traditions, at least in the English-speaking world.

However, the amazing career of Anabaptism in theological discourse starting with Yoder's book of 1972 was based on an idealizing interpretation of Anabaptist history that was increasingly challenged by the historians since the early 1970s. Yoder's approach was inspired by the historiography of the Mennonite theologian Harold S. Bender. In his essay titled *The Anabaptist Vision* of 1944, Bender had identified Conrad Grebel and his tiny group of followers in Zürich who performed believers' baptism in January 1525 as the only legitimate founders of the Anabaptist movement.[6]

Although we have just a handful of texts produced by Grebel and his group, Bender claimed that the Zürich proto-Anabaptists developed a comprehensive vision of Christian doctrine and practice marked by Jesus-centered discipleship lived in believers' churches, pacifist non-resistance, keeping distance from state and politics, and stressing ethics rather than dogmatism, while firmly rooted in the theological foundations of the Swiss Reformation. Bender constructed a line of tradition leading from the Zürich group to the modern Mennonites which included Anabaptist individuals and groups that shared the marks of true "evangelical" Anabaptism. On the other hand, he marginalized or excluded all those figures which lacked these marks, like the non-pacifist Balthasar Hubmaier or the militant Anabaptists of Münster, apocalyptic and spiritualist thinkers like Hans Hut, Hans Denck and Melchior Hoffman – all these figures and their followers were classified as misled, or compromised, or fanatic, and, at most, semi-Anabaptist.

Starting with James Stayer's *Anabaptists and the Sword* of 1972, Bender's idealizing picture was subject to a thorough revision. Stayer challenged Bender's perception that the Zürich Anabaptists had a free church ecclesiology from the beginning and showed that apolitical nonviolence ethics was but a secondary development following the failure of the peasants' uprisings of 1525 in which quite a few of the earliest Anabaptists had been involved to some degree.[7] A number of critical contributions from both sides of the Atlantic followed, including Gottfried

4   See, e.g., Alan Kreider and Stuart Murray, eds., *Coming Home: Stories of Anabaptists in Britain and Ireland* (Kitchener, ON: Pandora Press, 2000).
5   See, e.g., Malcom Yarnell, ed., *The Anabaptists and Contemporary Baptists: Restoring New Testament Christianity* (Nashville, TN: Broadman & Holman, 2013).
6   Harold S. Bender, "The Anabaptist Vision," *Church History* 13 (1944): 3–44.
7   James M. Stayer, *Anabaptists and the Sword* (Lawrence, KS: Coronado Press, 1972).

Seebaß who rediscovered the significance of Hans Hut's apocalyptic mission movement for the dissemination of Anabaptism,[8] Werner Packull who examined the mystic-spiritualist strand within South German and Austrian Anabaptism,[9] and Klaus Deppermann who analyzed the life and thought of Melchior Hoffman, the initiator of the North German and Dutch Anabaptist movement that would have its tragic culmination in the Anabaptist kingdom of Münster in 1535.[10]

By 1975, Bender's apologetic construct of a continuous tradition of "evangelical" Anabaptism starting in Zürich and flowing into the Mennonite tradition was replaced by a polygenetic picture. A famous essay, *From Monogenesis to Polygenesis: The Historical Discussion of Anabaptist Origins* jointly authored by Stayer, Packull and Deppermann, described a plurality of Anabaptist movements arising between the 1520s and the 1530s in various places, with varying degrees of mutual contacts.[11] In a synthesis published in 1980, Hans-Jürgen Goertz gave a comprehensive account of the revised picture of Anabaptism.[12]

Since then, the Anabaptism referred to by Yoder and Yoder-inspired theologians has had less and less in common with the Anabaptism of the historians. There are some remarkable exceptions, however. Qualified efforts to bridge the gap between theological and historical perspectives include contributions by historian C. Arnold Snyder, whose historical research takes into account current concerns of Mennonite theology,[13] and by Mennonite theologians like John Rempel and Thomas N. Finger, whose Anabaptist-inspired theological contributions appreciate the diversity of sixteenth-century Anabaptism.[14]

Now, what have the historians of Anabaptism achieved since the late 1970s? It seems that the pluralistic picture recovered four decades ago still provides a valid base for the study of sixteenth-century Anabaptism. If you look at the *Companion to Anabaptism and Spiritualism*, a comprehensive collection of handbook chapters of

8   Gottfried Seebaß, *Müntzers Erbe: Werk, Leben und Theologie des Hans Hut* (Gütersloh: Gütersloher Verlagshaus, 2002), originally submitted in 1972 as *Habilitationsschrift* to the University of Erlangen.
9   Werner O. Packull, *Mysticism and the Early South German-Austrian Anabaptist Movement 1525–1531* (Scottdale, PA: Herald Press, 1977).
10  Klaus Deppermann, *Melchior Hoffman: Soziale Unruhen und apokalyptische Visionen im Zeitalter der Reformation* (Göttingen: Vandenhoeck & Ruprecht, 1979).
11  James M. Stayer, Werner O. Packull and Klaus Deppermann, "From Monogenesis to Polygenesis: The Historical Discussion of Anabaptist Origins," *Mennonite Quarterly Review* 49 (1975): 83–121.
12  Hans-Jürgen Goertz, *Die Täufer: Geschichte und Deutung* (München: Beck, 1980); English translation: *The Anabaptists* (New York, NY: Routledge, 1996).
13  One of his most recent publications is C. Arnold Snyder, "In Search of the Swiss Brethren," *Mennonite Quarterly Review* 90 (2016): 421–515.
14  John D. Rempel, *The Lord's Supper in Anabaptism: A Study in the Christology of Balthasar Hubmaier, Pilgram Marpeck, and Dirk Philips*, (Scottdale, PA/Kitchener, ON: Herald Press, 1993); Thomas N. Finger, *A Contemporary Anabaptist Theology: Biblical, Historical, Constructive* (Downers Grove, IL: InterVarsity, 2004).

various authors published in 2007 by John D. Roth and James Stayer, you will find that the outline of the book closely follows the lines drafted in the essay *From Monogenesis to Polygenesis* in 1975.[15] Anabaptism was no monolithic entity with a clearly defined theological message, and their beliefs, practices and religious expectations were probably extremely different from that of twenty-first-century people.[16] The manifold divisions within sixteenth-century Anabaptism do not mean that one group were the true Anabaptists and the others were misled, but the issues over which they divided reveal what were the crucial points of discussion amongst them, what had pivotal relevance for their religious identity.

New archival studies or the *relecture* of already published sources reveal a sometimes irritating distantness and strangeness of the sixteenth-century Anabaptist experience. I want to illustrate this in the following point by some short remarks on the present state of research on the group formation processes among the Upper German Anabaptists, that is, those movements in the geographical space in which Upper German dialects were spoken, spanning from Switzerland and Tirol in the south to the midst of Germany in the north, and from the Alsace in the west to Moravia in the east.

## Anabaptist Groups and Divisions: Remarks on Recent Research

Between 1525 and 1528, in almost all Upper German regions there was a rapid and largely ephemeral dissemination of rebaptism as an expression of dissent, in some places in opposition to local and territorial Reformations, in others in opposition to still prevailing pre-Reformation Catholicism. In some cases we have indications that these early Anabaptist groups and movements originally hoped to bring about a general change of the religious situation in their towns or territories, in others they started to form separate conventicles of an ecclesial character; and quite many early Anabaptists had no clear ecclesiological concepts at all because they were expecting the immediate end of the world.

By 1528, almost all of the prominent early leaders of the Upper German Anabaptists had fallen victim to the fierce persecution by both Protestant and Catholic authorities, or had turned away from Anabaptism. In some regions, clandestine Anabaptist conventicles survived for years or decades, and in some remote regions of South Germany and Switzerland even longer – generally under precarious conditions that did not allow the Anabaptist to fully act out their convictions and concerns.

---

15  John Roth and James Stayer, eds., *A Companion to Anabaptism and Spiritualism, 1521–1700* (Leiden: Brill, 2007).
16  For the sometimes irritating features of 16th-century Anabaptism see, e.g., Gary K. Waite, *David Joris and Dutch Anabaptism 1524–1543* (Waterloo, ON: Pandora Press, 1990); Anselm Schubert, *Täufertum und Kabbalah: Augustin Bader und die Grenzen der Radikalen Reformation* (Gütersloh: Gütersloher Verlagshaus, 2008).

The haven for persecuted Anabaptists from all Upper German Regions and from Silesia was Moravia, where tolerant nobles granted, to some extent, religious toleration or even active support. It seems that emigration to Moravia significantly contributed to the disappearance of Anabaptism in most of its neighbor countries. Moravia became the only region where Anabaptists had the opportunity to develop their concepts of church, their doctrine, and their way of life more freely. Anabaptist presence in Moravia took an abrupt end in 1622 when the political situation changed and all Anabaptists were expelled from the country. While the first Anabaptist congregations originated in Zürich, Switzerland, in 1525, it was in Moravia that Anabaptist groups developed clear denominational profiles, theologies, and structures.

## Sabbatarians

The first group to deal with is the Sabbatarians because their origins go back to the very beginnings of the dissemination of Anabaptism in Moravia, that is, to the local Reformation conducted in 1526/1527 by Balthasar Hubmaier in Nikolsburg, a town and dominion of the Lords of Liechtenstein at the southern border of Moravia. Readers of Ludwig Richard Conradi's *Geschichte des Sabbats* may remember that Conradi mentioned the Sabbatarians as an Anabaptist group located on the Nikolsburg dominion.[17] Conradi's narrative was based on a statement in a sixteenth-century Hutterite chronicle,[18] but there was consensus among most modern historians of Anabaptism that the Hutterite identification of the Sabbatarians with Hubmaier's followers in Nikolsburg must be a misapprehension.[19] Only recently several original Sabbatarian texts written between 1530 and 1535 were discovered that confirmed the validity of the Hutterite tradition.

The Anabaptist church of the Nikolsburg dominion had the character of a small territorial church; they worshipped in the existing parish churches and their preachers were recruited from former Catholic clergy. Hubmaier's activity in Nikolsburg lasted only one year. King Ferdinand of Habsburg exacted Hubmaier's extradition in the summer of 1527 and had him executed at the stake in Vienna the following spring. In 1531, a dispute arose among the Nikolsburg clergy on the validity of the Decalogue, and eventually they introduced some form of Saturday Sabbath observance. In 1535 a mandate of King Ferdinand forbade them to use the parish churches for worship, and most preachers were forced to leave the town and

---

17 Ludwig Richard Conradi, *Die Geschichte des Sabbats und des Ersten Wochentages im Lichte der Heiligen Schrift und der Geschichte von der Erschaffung der Welt bis auf die Gegenwart* (Hamburg: Internationale Traktatgesellschaft, 1912), 546–559.
18 Josef Beck, *Die Geschichts-Bücher der Wiedertäufer in Oesterreich-Ungarn, 1526–1785* (Wien: Gerold, 1883), 73.
19 Daniel Liechty, *Andreas Fischer and the Sabbatarian Anabaptists. An Early Reformation Episode in East Central Europe* (Scottdale, PA/Kitchener, ON: Herald Press, 1988); Jürgen Kaiser, *Ruhe der Seele und Siegel der Hoffnung. Die Deutung des Sabbats in der Reformation* (Göttingen: Vandenhoeck & Ruprecht, 1996).

villages of the Nikolsburg dominion. The Sabbatarians continued to exist as a small group in some places in Moravia. Different from the rest of the Anabaptist groups represented in Moravia, they approved of active involvement in secular authorities, of military service and of the death penalty. Dwindling remnant groups of the Sabbatarians existed until the 1560s.[20]

## Austerlitz Brethren

The Austerlitz Brethren were the first separatist Anabaptist group that formed an ecclesial structure in Moravia in 1528. The term "brethren" which occurs in this and several other Anabaptist group names goes back to the common usage in contemporary Czech to call sects or separatist groups "brethren" – in the small town of Austerlitz there already existed a congregation of the Bohemian Brethren, so the newcomers were called "German Brethren" or "Austerlitz Brethren" for sake of distinction. Different from the Sabbatarians that came from the local German-speaking population, most of the Austerlitz Brethren constituency consisted of refugees from the surrounding countries baptized by Hans Hut and his messengers, but also from the early Swiss Anabaptist tradition. The Hutterite chronicle contains a narrative of the origins of the Austerlitz Brethren, which has been thoroughly analyzed by Werner Packull in his monograph *Hutterite Beginnings* of 1995.[21]

Based on Packull's research and the availability of new sources it now seems probable that between 1528 and the 1550s the Austerlitz church functioned as the mother church of a denominational network of local Anabaptist churches and conventicles that spanned from Moravia to Switzerland, the Alsace and South Germany, trying to form one ecclesial body of the refugee groups in Moravia and the precariously persecuted remnant groups that had remained in the home countries. While they claimed to be a true church of Christ endowed with apostolic authority, it is not clear whether they actually claimed to be the only true church on earth. The letters exchanged between the churches of the Austerlitz network, part of which are preserved in the so-called *Kunstbuch* manuscript which is available in a critical edition and in an English translation,[22] contain much polemics against Sabbatarians, Hutterites and Swiss Brethren, the Schwenkfelders, and of course against the Catholics and Protestants. The Austerlitz Brethren mostly referred to

---

20 Martin Rothkegel, "Anabaptist Sabbatarianism in 16th Century Moravia," *Mennonite Quarterly Review* 87 (2013): 519–573; German original: "Die Sabbater. Täuferischer Sabbatarismus in Mähren im 16. Jahrhundert," in *Sabbat und Sabbatobservanz in der Frühen Neuzeit*, ed. Anselm Schubert (Gütersloh: Gütersloher Verlagshaus, 2016), 114–166.
21 Werner O. Packull, *Hutterite Beginnings: Communitarian Experiments during the Reformation* (Baltimore, MD/London: Johns Hopkins Press, 1995).
22 Heinold Fast and Gottfried Seebaß, eds., *Briefe und Schriften oberdeutscher Täufer 1527–1555: Das Kunstbuch des Jörg Probst Rotenfelder gen. Maler* (Gütersloh: Gütersloher Verlagshaus, 2007); John D. Rempel, ed., *Jörg Maler's Kunstbuch. Writings of the Pilgram Marpeck Circle* (Kitchener, ON: Pandora Press, 2010).

themselves as *Bundesgenossen*, "Fellows of the Covenant," a code name based on 1 Peter 3:16 where baptism is called a covenant. The whole network collapsed and dissolved soon after Pilgrim Marpeck's death in 1556.[23]

It seems plausible that during his career as an Anabaptist leader in Strasbourg and Augsburg from 1528 to his death in 1556, Marpeck was a messenger and elder of the Austerlitz Brethren, and the author of a considerable body of theological writings. He enjoys high popularity among Mennonite theologians today.[24] While Mennonite theologians tend to claim Marpeck as a Mennonite "church father," the historical Marpeck probably was the representative of an Anabaptist group that does not exist anymore and that has no direct links with the Mennonite tradition.

## *Hutterian Brethren*

The Hutterian Brethren originate from a split with the Austerlitz Brethren in 1531, subsequently they were called *Hutterische Brüder*, or "Hatmaker Brethren" because their first leader was the hatmaker Jacob Huter.[25] Huter claimed to be an apostle of Jesus Christ sent at the end of time with the mandate to gather the elect from all countries into the true church of God to Moravia which is the promised land of the latter days, or more exactly the place in the desert prepared by God for the woman clothed with the sun which is the church (Rev 12). As strange as this may sound, the Hutterites who called themselves the "Church of God in Moravia" became the most successful Anabaptist group between the 1530s and the expulsion of all Anabaptists from Moravia in 1622, with a membership of at least 20,000 around 1600, with a steady influx of new converts led to Moravia by a systematic mission to the Anabaptist remnant groups in South Germany, Austria, Switzerland, Silesia, the Rhineland, Hesse and North Italy. While the Sabbatarians and the Austerlitz Brethren ceased to exist after 1600, the Hutterite tradition continuously went on in changing places of exile, and is still alive today in the Hutterite groups that emigrated to North America in the late nineteenth century – albeit in a form that has been subject to fundamental changes since the sixteenth century.[26]

23  Martin Rothkegel, "Die Austerlitzer Brüder: Pilgram Marpecks Gemeinde in Mähren," in *Grenzen des Täufertums/Boundaries of Anabaptism. Neue Forschungen*, eds. Astrid von Schlachta and Anselm Schubert (Gütersloh: Gütersloher Verlagshaus, 2009), 232–270; idem, "Pilgram Marpeck and the Fellows of the Covenant: The Short History of the Rise and Decline of an Anabaptist Denominational Network," *Mennonite Quarterly Review* 85 (2011): 7–36.

24  Neal Blough, *Christ in Our Midst. Incarnation, Church and Discipleship in the Theology of Pilgram Marpeck* (Kitchener, ON: Pandora Press, 2007); Walter Klaassen and William Klassen, *Marpeck. A Life of Dissent and Conformity* (Waterloo, ON/Scottdale, PA: Herald Press, 2008).

25  Packull, *Hutterite Beginnings*, 224–235.

26  On Hutterite theology and community life, see Andrea Chudaska and Peter Riedemann, *Konfessionsbildendes Täufertum im 16. Jahrhundert* (Gütersloh: Gütersloher Verlagshaus, 2003); Astrid von Schlachta, *Hutterische Konfession und Tradition (1578–1619). Etab-

In sixteenth-century Moravia, the Hutterites developed a strictly regulated pacifist and communitarian lifestyle in autonomously administrated settlements and a very remarkable material and literary culture of urban character. At the heart of their identity was the conviction that they were the one and only true church of Christ: That their community, as the body of Christ, is nothing less than Christ's presence in this world and God's agent of salvation for fallen humankind. Evidence for this was, in their eyes, that their preachers were the carriers of the "Living Word," or inspired divine speech. The roots of the "Living Word" concept lay obviously in the mystic and spiritualist traditions of South German Anabaptism. One may wonder how Hutterite preaching sounded in practice and how the preachers learned and exercised to perform this skill. A recently published study of the "Living Word" concept in Anabaptism argues that the idea of charismatic speech as a mark of apostolic authority, whatever that meant in practice, is key to understanding sixteenth-century Hutterite religion.[27]

## Swiss Brethren

Besides the Hutterites, the Swiss Brethren are the only other sixteenth-century Upper German Anabaptist denomination that continued to exist into the seventeenth century and beyond. At the turn of the eighteenth century, the so-called Amish separated from the main branch of the Swiss Brethren, and from the 1720s on, a large portion of both the main branch Swiss Brethren and the Amish emigrated to Pennsylvania. In Europe as well as in North America, the mainstream Swiss Brethren gradually merged with the Mennonite tradition, which actually had a very different origin in North German and Dutch Anabaptism. Where does the Swiss Brethren tradition come from? For Harold Bender they were the direct successors of the first Anabaptist group founded by Conrad Grebel in Zürich in 1525.[28]

The problem is that in the vast body of sixteenth-century Anabaptist sources from Switzerland the "Swiss Brethren" are never mentioned (except for one document dating from 1588 that evidences Swiss Brethren presence near Basle).[29] Sixteenth-century documents that explicitly mention the "Swiss Brethren" as an Anabaptist sect locate them rather in Southwest Germany, in the Palatinate, in the Rhineland up to the Lower Rhine and the Eifel region, in Hesse, in the Alsace, but

---

*liertes Leben zwischen Ordnung und Ambivalenz* (Mainz: Philipp von Zabern, 2003); ead., *From the Tyrol to North America: The Hutterite Story Through the Centuries* (Kitchener, ON: Pandora Press, 2008).

27  Martin Rothkegel, "The Living Word: Uses of the Holy Scriptures among Sixteenth-Century Anabaptists in Moravia," *Mennonite Quarterly Review* 89 (2015): 357–403.

28  Cf. Harold S. Bender, *Conrad Grebel, c. 1498–1528: The Founder of the Swiss Brethren Sometimes Called Anabaptists* (Goshen, IN: Mennonite Historical Society, 1950).

29  For the latter, see Hanspeter Jecker, *Ketzer – Rebellen – Heilige: Das Basler Täufertum von 1580–1700* (Liestal: Verlag des Kantons Basel-Landschaft, 1998), 110.

also in Moravia. The earliest evidence for the label "Swiss Brethren" dates from the late 1530s and refers to a congregation in Württemberg. By the seventeenth century, for sure, most surviving Anabaptist groups on Swiss territory had also joined the denominational network of the Swiss Brethren, but there is no indication that the group had its first origins in Switzerland.

One clue leads back to the year 1535. The title page of a famous Anabaptist hymnal, printed in Frankfurt/Main in 1564, states that part of the songs were written by the "Swiss Brethren" that were imprisoned in Passau.[30] The story of this group of prisoners is well documented because their files and depositions are preserved. According to these sources, they were a group of Anabaptists from the Palatinate and neighboring regions that had lived for some time in Moravia, but decided to return to their home regions in 1535, when they eventually were arrested in the middle of the journey back home. After several years of imprisonment most of the prisoners were released. Some of them allegedly made their way to Moravia and settled down there. It is not altogether clear at what occasion the songs were brought out of prison and how they became the cadre of "Swiss Brethren" hymnology.[31]

While none of the Passau prisoners had direct connections to Switzerland, most of them originally came from Southwest Germany. So why were they later labeled "Swiss"? There are sixteenth- and seventeenth-century sources that claim that the "Swiss Brethren" were an Anabaptist sect named after one of its early leaders who was from Switzerland or who had the nickname Schweitzer, just as the Hutterian Brethren were called after their founder who was a hatmaker *(Huter)* by profession. This would mean that the Swiss Brethren had as much, or as little, to do with Switzerland as the Hutterites with hatmaking. I find this explanation plausible. I assume the "Swiss Brethren" were a denominational network that started in Southwest Germany in the late 1530s with the Passau survivors forming part of the original membership; that the label "Swiss Brethren" refers to a founding figure; and that they later succeeded in integrating additional Anabaptist circles in South Germany, Moravia and other regions including Switzerland. However, this interpretation has not found much support yet.[32]

## Enlarging the Picture, and the Survival of the Anabaptist Tradition

The Upper German territories were but one out of several regions of early modern Europe in which adult baptizing groups formed an important part of the sixteenth-

---

30 Galen A. Peters, ed., Robert A. Riall, trans., *The Earliest Hymns of the Ausbund: Some Beautiful Christian Songs Composed and Sung in the Prison at Passau. Published in 1564* (Kitchener, ON: Pandora Press, 2003).
31 Packull, *Hutterite Beginnings,* 89–98, 284–289.
32 Snyder, "In Search of the Swiss Brethren"; James M. Stayer, "Die 'Schweizer Brüder' – Auf der Suche nach einer neuen Definition," *Mennonitische Geschichtsblätter* 73 (2016): 7–18.

century Reformation dynamics. There were Anabaptist movements in non-Germanic countries like Italy and Poland, and there was, of course, the Low German-Dutch strand of Anabaptism which is the origin of the Mennonites who are the most important and most widely disseminated sixteenth-century Anabaptist tradition that has continuously survived to the present. Three short concluding remarks go to these Italian, Polish, and Low German-Dutch movements and their respective significance for subsequent developments.

## *The Italian Anabaptist Movement*

In the 1540s, there was a widespread Anabaptist movement in the capital and territories of the Republic of Venice, and in some other regions of Italy. It had its roots in the quite strong contemporary Italian philo-Protestant, or evangelical, movement from which it separated as a more radical wing. At some point in time, the clandestine local Anabaptist churches formed a supra-local ecclesial structure with four itinerant bishops, and in 1550 they held a synod in Venice during which most of the represented churches accepted an anti-Trinitarian doctrine. Starting in winter 1551/1552, the Roman inquisition conducted a systematic persecution of the movement, including many detentions and a number of executions. Some of the Italian Anabaptists escaped, some to the Ottoman Empire, others to Moravia where they merged with German-language Anabaptist groups. Anabaptist remnant groups and individuals were present on Italian ground until the 1570s.[33] The historical significance of the Italian Anabaptists lies in the fact that they, directly or indirectly, contributed to the rise of Socinianism and other forms of Evangelical Rationalism which would eventually contribute to the rise of the Enlightenment.[34] It is high time to rediscover Italian Anabaptism as a subject for Anabaptist research and to clarify its relation to the Anabaptist movements on the other side of the Alps.

## *The Polish Brethren*

In the 1560s, a radical wing separated from the Reformed Church in Poland. The articles under dispute were infant baptism and the doctrine of the Trinity. The separatists were called *Ecclesia minor* or "Polish Brethren" – again a group name formed in analogy with the Bohemian Brethren and the Anabaptist denominational labels. They introduced believers' baptism and adopted, with some modifications,

---

33 The sections on Italian Anabaptism in Williams, *Radical Reformation*, 3rd ed., 854–873, 885–892, still provide the most comprehensive treatment in English, but are partially outdated. The groundbreaking original contributions are by Aldo Stella, *Dall'anabattismo al socinianesimo nel Cinquecento Veneto: Ricerche storiche* (Padova: Liviana, 1967); idem, *Anabattismo e antitrinitarismo in Italia nel XVI secolo: Nuove ricerche storiche* (Padova: Liviana, 1969); idem, *Dall'anabattismo veneto al "Sozialevangelismus" dei Fratelli Hutteriti e all'illuminismo religioso sociniano* (Roma: Herder, 1996).
34 Luca Addante, *Eretici e libertini nel Cinquecento italiano* (Roma/Bari: Laterza, 2010).

the Anabaptist principles of nonviolence.[35] Around 1600, the Italian exile Fausto Sozzini became their leading theologian, hence they were called Socinians. They developed a very remarkable intellectual and literary productivity that blended Reformed, Anabaptist and Italian Evangelical Rationalist elements. Besides that there was clearly a strong Lutheran influence because many Polish Brethren or Socinian theologians of the late sixteenth century and of the seventeenth century originally had been German Lutheran clergy. In the middle of the seventeenth century the Socinian presence in Poland was violently brought to an end by the Counter-Reformation, but Socinian exiles played an important role in the early Enlightenment discourses in the Netherlands and England.[36] Socinianism exercised a strong influence on the Dutch Mennonites and part of the English General Baptist movement in the eighteenth century. The Anabaptist story is certainly incomplete if this remarkable strand of thought is neglected, which has often been the case due to the theological biases of historians of more orthodox backgrounds.

## *Dutch Mennonites, English Baptists, and the Incorporation of the Anabaptists into the Denominational Historiographies of the Modern Free Churches*

The Mennonite tradition originated in the years after the fall of the Anabaptist kingdom of Münster in 1535, when Menno Simons, a former Catholic priest, gathered part of the Low German and Dutch Anabaptist movement into a network of separatist congregations. Highly disciplined and strictly pacifist, the Mennonites outlived the persecutions of the sixteenth century and became the most significant Anabaptist tradition that has survived to the present.[37]

---

35   For a comprehensive, but partially outdated treatment, see Williams, *Radical Refomation*, 3rd ed., 1023–1061, 1079–1098, 1135–1175; for a very concise but up to date overview, see Mihály Balázs, "Antitrinitarianism," in *A Companion to the Reformation in Central Europe*, eds. Howard Louthan and Graeme Murdock (Leiden/Boston: Brill, 2015), 171–194. Selected sources in translation: George H. Williams, ed., *The Polish Brethren: Documentation of the History & Thought of Unitarianism in the Polish-Lithuanian Commonwealth and in the Diaspora, 1601–1685*, 2 vols., (Missoula, MT: Scholars Press, 1980).

36   Lech Szczucki, ed., *Faustus Socinus and His Heritage*, (Kraków: PAN, 2005); Martin Mulsow and Jan Rohls, eds., *Socinianism and Arminianism: Antitrinitarians, Calvinists and Cultural Exchange in Seventeenth-Century Europe* (Leiden: Brill, 2005); Sascha Salatowsky, *Die Philosophie der Sozinianer: Transformationen zwischen Renaissance-Aristotelismus und Frühaufklärung* (Stuttgart-Bad Cannstatt: Frommann-Holzboog, 2015); Piet Visser, ed., *Bibliographia Sociniana: A Bibliographical Reference Tool for the Study of Dutch Socinianism and Antitrinitarianism* (Hilversum: Verloren, 2004).

37   On Mennonite origins see the comprehensive synthesis published in Dutch by Samme Zijlstra, *Om de ware gemeente en de oude gronden. Geschiedenis van de dopersen in de Nederlanden 1531–1675* (Hilversum: Verloren 2000); Piet Visser, "Mennonites and Doopsgezinden in the Netherlands, 1535–1700," in *A Companion to Anabaptism and Spiritualism, 1521–1700*, eds. John Roth and James Stayer (Leiden: Brill, 2007), 299–345.

Mennonite influence contributed to the introduction of believers' baptism in early seventeenth-century English Separatist circles and the formation of the seventeenth-century Baptist movements. In the religio-cultural context of Puritanism, Anabaptism was chiefly associated with the ill-famed kingdom of Münster and other odious heresies; hence, seventeenth-century English Baptists were anxious to deny any direct connection with the continental Anabaptists. Anyway, beginning with the eighteenth century, the English-speaking Baptists started to claim the Anabaptist heritage in their denominational historiography.

Nineteenth-century Baptist historiography incorporated the Anabaptist story into their own historical narratives to the degree that they developed sectarian successionist theories according to which there had been "true believers" – which means Baptists in this case – in all centuries of history. Denominational successionist historiography was especially influential among the so-called Landmark movement in the South of the United States, and among the Seventh Day Baptists. The latter influenced, to some degree, early Seventh-day Adventist historical constructs like the above-mentioned work of Ludwig Richard Conradi.

*Trevor O'Reggio*

## The Radical Reformers (Anabaptists) and Seventh-day Adventism

### Abstract

Early Adventism, although not claiming direct Anabaptist roots, made similar claims as the Anabaptists about restoring the church to its New Testament roots. They understood the Reformation as only the beginning of that process, and they cast themselves as completing what the Reformers began. This involved the restoration of long-neglected truths. Many of these truths were taught by the Radical Reformers, in particular the Anabaptists. A cursory survey of Adventist doctrines reveals a striking resemblance with those taught by the Anabaptists. How influential then were the Anabaptists on Adventism? The purpose of this paper is to explore the extent and nature of that influence.

### Introduction

For almost 1,000 years the Roman Catholic Church held dominance over Christianity in the West, but at the beginning of the sixteenth century, its monopoly was broken with the rise of the Protestant Reformation. This movement consisted of four major strands – the Lutheran branch, under Luther and Melanchthon; the Reform movement through the efforts of John Calvin and Ulrich Zwingli; the English Reformation, comprising elements from Luther, Calvin and Zwingli; and finally, the so called "Radical Reformers" consisting of a variety of radical thinkers. The most well-known among the Radical Reformers were the Swiss Brethren rising out of Zwingli's inner circle and would come to be known as the Anabaptists.

Modern scholars view Anabaptism as a composite of many groups stemming from three main sources. The first of these is the movement of Swiss origins, biblicist and separatist in character. The second is the Dutch/Low German movement, which tended toward apocalypticism. And finally, the South German/Austrian movement, where medieval mysticism cross-fertilized with the sober biblicism of the Swiss.[1]

This paper explore the relationship of the Anabaptists to the Seventh-day Adventists in some of their key doctrines and the historical links of Adventism to the Radical Reformers, mediated through groups like the Christian Connexion, the Baptists and the Methodists. A cursory examination of the teachings of the Anabaptists and the Adventists reveals similarities in many of their doctrines and practices. Examples of these can be seen in the teachings on salvation, disciples' baptism, foot

---

1  Daniel Liechty, *Sabbatarianism in the Sixteenth Century: A Page in the History of the Radical Reformers* (Berrien Springs, MI: Andrews University Press, 1993), 12.

washing, Lord's Supper, holiness, pacifism and non-resistance, separation of church and state, the human will, separation from the world, and Christ's Second Coming. Indirect historical links can also be detected between Adventism and Anabaptism.

Since these groups were separated by over 300 years of history and thousands of miles in distance, what accounts then for these similarities in their doctrines and practices? How significant was the Anabaptist influence on Adventism? How was their influence exerted? Who were the intermediary groups and what was their role in mediating the influence? These are some of the questions explored in this paper.

The Radical Reformers, of which the Anabaptists were a substratum, were called "radicals" primarily in reference to the magisterial Protestant Reformers. Some equate this radicalism to a small group among them who took up the sword to violently overthrow the government, but these were the exception, for the vast majority of the radicals were non-violent pacifists who preferred death than defend themselves against their enemies. The attribution of radicalism was not only due to their behavior and practices but also their teachings.[2] So even the pacifists were still considered radicals and a threat to the established order, and were violently persecuted. The focus of this study is on the predominant pacifist element of the Radical Reformation.

## The Schleitheim Confession – Anabaptist Statement of Beliefs

The Anabaptists were not a homogeneous group and their beliefs had variations. The Schleitheim Confession penned by Michael Sattler expresses the common core beliefs of virtually all the early Anabaptists.[3] These are: baptism, ban, supper, separation, the election and role of pastors, sword and oath. In order to determine the level of similarity between Anabaptism and Adventism, the first four of these Anabaptist distinctive features will be elaborated on and compared to Adventist teachings along with their teachings on salvation, eschatology, and the Sabbath.

### Baptism

The subject of baptism lies at the very core of Anabaptists' identity. It was their rejection of infant baptism that gave them the name "Anabaptists" as they are known today.[4] Their views on baptism and communion were a strong expression of their

2 George H. Williams, *Radical Reformation* (Philadelphia, PA: The Westminster Press, 1952). Williams was the first person to coin the term Radical Reformation. He is also the first modern historian who made a serious effort to distinguish between pacifist and violent wings of the Radical Reformation.
3 The Schleitheim Confession was the most representative statement of Anabaptist principles, endorsed unanimously by a meeting of Swiss Anabaptists in 1527 in Schleitheim (Switzerland). See John H. Yoder, *The Schleitheim Confession* (Scottdale, PA: Herald Press, 1975).
4 *Anabaptizein* means in Greek to "rebaptize" or to "baptize again". Mostly because the early Anabaptists saw infant baptism as invalid and hence required all those who were baptized as infants to be rebaptized.

rejection of sacramental theology and sacramentalism. In spite of common belief, Anabaptists did not practice merely "believers' baptism" but instead the "disciples' baptism." A contemporary evangelical practice where one could experience a conversion in one church service and be baptized in the next was foreign to sixteenth-century Anabaptists. Only those who had demonstrated true conversion by choosing the self-sacrificing life of a disciple of Christ were qualified for baptism.[5]

Anabaptism like Adventism, in general, requires a thorough process of discipling before and after baptism. In most cases, an individual is required to be well acquainted with Adventist distinctive teachings as well as teachings that Adventism shares with other Christian denominations. One of the founder-figures of Seventh-day Adventism, Ellen G. White writes:

> The preparation for baptism is a matter that needs to be carefully considered. Bring the requirement of the gospel to bear upon the candidates for baptism. The new converts to the truth should be faithfully instructed in the plain, 'Thus saith the Lord.' The word of the Lord is to be read and explained to them point by point ... All who enter upon the new life should understand, prior to their baptism, that the Lord requires the undivided affections ... Before baptism there should be a thorough inquiry as to the experience of the candidate. Let this inquiry be made, not in a cold and distant way, but kindly, tenderly, pointing the new converts to the Lamb of God, who taketh away the sin of the world.[6]

Adventism and Anabaptism both view baptism as the rite by which one enters the church. It is a passage into a community to which an individual is held accountable. Most Anabaptists and Adventists regard the Christian life as communal life; all Christians are members of one body. Therefore baptism also involves the acceptance of the process of discipline, of mutual aid both spiritually and materially.[7]

Describing the nature of adult baptism, Anabaptist leader Konrad Grebel in Zürich wrote in a letter to Thomas Müntzer:

> The Scripture describes baptism for us thus, that it signifies that, by faith and the blood of Christ, sins have been washed away for him who is baptized, changes his mind, and believes before and after; that it signifies that a man is dead and ought to be dead to sin and walks in newness of life and spirit, and that he shall certainly be saved if, according to this meaning, by inner baptism he lives his faith.[8]

---

5 See James R. Payton, *Getting the Reformation Wrong* (Downers Grove, IL: IVP Academic, 2010), 161–162.
6 Ellen G. White, Manuscript 56, 1900 in *Manuscript Releases*, vol. 6. (Washington, DC: Review and Herald, 1975), 155.
7 See William Estep, *The Anabaptist Story: An Introduction to Sixteenth-Century Anabaptism* (Grand Rapids, MI: Eerdmans, 1996), 201–237.
8 Konrad Grebel, *Letter to Thomas Müntzer* (September 5, 1524) cited in Walter Klaassen, ed., *Anabaptism in Outline: Selected Primary Sources* (Kitchener, Ontario: Herald Press 1981), 162.

Grebel argues that baptism occurs after confession and repentance of all known sins. This repentance and forsaking of sin leads to a "change of mind" in which a person is "dead to sin" or to a desire to commit willful sin. Such person, who walks in "newness of life and spirit" according to Grebel, shall "certainly be saved" and ought to have a Christian assurance of salvation through Jesus Christ. Grebel is quick to point out that the outward baptism is only a symbol of "inner baptism."[9]

Ellen White, in a similarly radical fashion often focuses on a "renewed heart." She stresses that church membership is of little value without true conversion.

> All, high or low, if they are unconverted, are on one common platform. Men may turn from one doctrine to another. This is being done, and will be done. Papists may change from Catholicism to Protestantism; yet they may know nothing of the meaning of the words, "A new heart also will I give you." Accepting new theories, and uniting with a church, do not bring new life to anyone, even though the church with which he unites may be established on the true foundation. Connection with a church does not take the place of conversion. To subscribe the name to a church creed is not of the least value to any one if the heart is not truly changed.[10]

German Anabaptist leader Balthasar Hubmaier confirms that a candidate for baptism "is so minded, that he has already surrendered himself according to the Word, will, and rule of Christ to live henceforth for him, to regulate all his actions according to him, to fight under his flag unto death, and to allow himself to be baptized with *external* water in which he publicly confesses his faith and intention." A converted person seeking baptism, according to Hubmaier, has "decided and already *inwardly* given his intention that from this time on he will change and improve his life, and [now] he confesses this *openly* in the reception of the water."[11]

The theological views of baptism by Anabaptist and Adventists are similar but differ on the mode of baptism. It appears that only Swiss, Moravian and Polish Anabaptists practiced baptism by immersion. Other Anabaptists did not make an issue of the rite itself, usually practicing pouring.[12] In Adventism, the mode of baptism is more consistently tied to its theology. The symbolism of immersion represents the "death" of the baptized individual to the old way of life and rising in newness of life. It also symbolizes a participation in the death, burial and resurrection of Jesus.[13]

---

9   Ibid.
10  Ellen G. White, "The Truth as It Is in Jesus," *Review and Herald*, February 14, 1899, 97.
11  Balthasar Hubmaier, "The Sum of a Christian Life" (1525), in Klaassen, 165–166. Hubmaier confessed "three types of baptism: that of the Spirit given internally in faith; that of water given externally through the oral confession of faith before the church; and that of blood in martyrdom or on the deathbed" (Klaassen, 168).
12  Estep, 234.
13  Ministerial Association of the General Conference, *Seventh-day Adventists Believe…: An Exposition of Fundamental Beliefs of the Seventh-day Adventist Church*, 2$^{nd}$ ed. (Boise, ID: Pacific Press 2005) 215.

## Ban

In Anabaptism, those that are baptized place themselves under the authority of the community and willingly submit themselves to the communal discipline when they err, as outlined in Matthew 18. The Anabaptist ban was a result of the belief that a person could lose or forfeit his justification and if persistent in his downfall, must be separated from the flock to not influence the others.[14]

Similarly, Ellen White asserts: "Every sin must be renounced as the hateful thing that crucified the Lord of life and glory, and the believer must have a progressive experience by continually doing the works of Christ. It is by continual surrender of the will, by continual obedience, that the blessing of justification is retained."[15] By his disobedience, a person can forfeit justification and, if persistent, must be rebuked, first privately, and then publicly. At the same time, Ellen White warns against excessive rebuke and hardship upon fallen individuals. Efforts must be made to restore the person before he is publicly disfellowshipped:

> When a person comes to a minister or to men in positions of trust with complaints against a brother or a sister, let the minister ask, "Have you complied with the rules our Saviour has given?" And if he has failed to carry out any particular of this instruction, do not listen to a word of his complaint. In the name and Spirit of Jesus, refuse to take up a report against your brother or your sister in the faith. If members of the church go contrary to these rules, they make themselves subjects for church discipline, and should be under the censure of the church. This matter, so plainly taught in the lessons of Christ, has been treated with strange indifference. The church has either neglected her work entirely in the matter of correcting evil, or has done it with harshness and severity, thus wounding and bruising souls. Measures should be taken to correct this cruel spirit of criticism, of judging the motives of others, as though Christ had revealed to men the hearts of their brethren. The neglect of doing aright, with wisdom and grace, the work that ought to have been done, has left churches and institutions almost inefficient and Christless.[16]

## Supper

Anabaptists believed that only baptized and committed members can celebrate the Lord's Supper. Because of their strong rejection of sacramentalism, they repudiated the Catholic mass, the heart of Roman Catholic faith. Anabaptists saw the mass as "a manipulation of Christ and his sacrifice often for human gain."[17] They also rejected the Protestant's debate about the meaning of Christ's presence in the bread and wine. These discussions were considered useless for they saw the real presence of Christ not in the communion bread but in the body of believers.

14  C. Arnold Snyder, *Anabaptist History and Theology*, Abridged Student Edition (Kitchener, Ontario: Pandora Press, 1995), 158–159, 349–350.
15  Ellen G. White, *Selected Messages*, vol. 1 (Washington, DC: Review and Herald, 1958), 397.
16  Ellen G. White, "The Sinner Needs Compassion," *Review and Herald*, April 16, 1895, 242.
17  Klaassen, 190.

Similarly, Adventists have traditionally viewed the communion as a *memorial* of salvation rather than *means* for obtaining grace. This ritual is *commemorative* and *representative* and therefore, unlike the Catholic mass, which is sacramental in nature. It is a meal to remember the broken body of Christ, and is designed to encourage self-examination, unity and fellowship of the believers. Commenting on the Lord's Supper Ellen White writes:

> As He ate the Passover with His disciples, He instituted in its place the service that was to be the *memorial* of His great sacrifice ... The ordinance of the Lord's Supper was given to *commemorate* the great deliverance wrought out as the result of the death of Christ. Till He shall come the second time in power and glory, this ordinance is to be celebrated. It is the means by which His great work for us is to be kept fresh in our minds.[18]

Anabaptists avoided every ritual which would take a person away from the experience of inward regeneration and change of heart. They taught that the mass was something done by the priest, which did not really change a person from within – and hence as such, mass was rejected. Konrad Grebel expressed it this way: "Ordinary bread ought to be used, without idols and additions. For [the latter] creates an external reverence and veneration of the bread, and a turning away from the *inward*."[19] Hubmaier continues along the same line:

> Similarly, the wine is not the blood of Christ, but ... a *remembrance* that he has shed his blood on the cross for the cleansing from sin for all those who have faith even as the sign before the inn is not the wine, but a *sign* of the same. For it behooves us to remember what Christ has done for us, to announce it loudly and to be eternally thankful for it. From this follows and we clearly learn that the Last Supper is nothing else than a *remembrance* of the suffering of Christ, who has given his body for our sake and shed his red blood on the cross for the cleansing of our sins.[20]

Sattler rejected sacramentalism by asserting "that the real body of Christ the Lord is not present in the Sacrament" because the Scripture says: "Christ ascended into heaven and sitteth on the right hand of his heavenly Father, whence he shall come to judge the quick and the dead, from which it follows that, if he is in heaven and not in the bread, he may not be eaten bodily."[21] Jörg Volk describes the spiritual nature of the supper –

---

18   Ellen G. White, *The Desire of Ages* (Oakland, CA: Pacific Press, 1898), 652.
19   Konrad Grebel, "Letter to Müntzer" (1524), in George Williams, *Spiritual and Anabaptist Writers* (Philadelphia, PA: Westminster Press, 1954), 76–77.
20   Balthasar Hubmaier, "The Sum of Christian Life" (1525), in Klaassen, 193.
21   Michael Sattler, "Trial" (1527), in *Spiritual and Anabaptist Writers*, 140; Hans Schlaffer notices that the phrase "body of Christ" only appears in the context of the faithful community of believers (1 Cor 12:27; Eph 4:12. Col 1:18). He writes: "whoever eats of this bread in the Supper of the Lord, testifies that he desires to have fellowship with and to participate in all things with the body of Christ. That is, he commits himself to the community in all things,

He taught that the flesh and blood of Christ was not changed into bread ... It must be understood spiritually. The bread which he broke was the gospel. If he had not broken it, it would not have come into the whole world. When they have the Word, receive it, and hide it in their hearts as Christ taught, they are receiving the body of Christ spiritually.[22]

## Separation

The separation motif was a common feature of the Anabaptist life. They saw the world as degenerate, sinful, and controlled by the devil. They felt that their only choice was to separate themselves from the state and all of its activities. As they experienced greater and greater persecution, separation became even more necessary for survival. Konrad Grebel, one of the early followers of Ulrich Zwingli, urged his fellow reformers to avoid using the sword and the practice of usury.[23] Grebel and other Anabaptists firmly denied the use of force to preach the gospel. Zwingli rejected the Anabaptists' attitudes toward government and criticized their attempts to have a separate church calling it "separatism, sectarianism."[24]

Anabaptists saw the Kingdom of Christ (The Church) as characterized by peace, forgiveness, nonviolence and patience. The kingdom of the world or Satan was strife, vengeance, anger and the sword that kills. Although the civil government belonged to the kingdom of the world, the Anabaptists acknowledged that governments were allowed to rule by God and should be obeyed. However, they believed that a true Christian should not participate in government because a servant of Christ had no liberty to use coercion and vengeance or to kill – since that is contrary to the commandments of Christ.

Most Anabaptists rejected all participation in politics for the reasons mentioned above, and also because any Anabaptist in government in sixteenth-century Europe would soon find himself prosecuting the members of his own church. The nineteenth- and early twentieth-century Seventh-day Adventist pioneers had a very similar attitude towards the government, politics and usage of force. They saw military

---

in love and suffering, wealth and poverty, honor and dishonor, sorrow and joy, death and life, indeed, that he is ready to give life and limb for the brothers, as Christ gave himself for him" (Hans Schlaffer, "A Pleasant Letter of Comfort" [1527], in Klaassen, 196).
22 Klaassen, 197.
23 Konrad Grebel, letter to Thomas Müntzer, Zürich, September 5, 1524 (Stadtbibliothek St. Gallen, VB.XI.97), in Lelan Harder, *The Sources of Swiss Anabaptism: The Grebel Letters and Related Documents* (Scottdale, PA: Herald Press, 1985), 293; Jehchoon You, "The 'Separation from the World' Motif in Early Swiss Anabaptism and Early Seventh-day Adventism" (MA thesis, Andrews University, Seventh-day Adventist Theological Seminary, 2012), 22.
24 Konrad Grebel, "The Second Public Disputation on Baptism, Zurich, March 20–22, 1525," in *The Sources of Swiss Anabaptism*, 355. Jehchoon You, "The 'Separation from the World' Motif in Early Swiss Anabaptism," 23.

force and arms-bearing as a sign of Babylon. When the question of draft came for the Civil War in America (1861–1865), Ellen White wrote:

> I was shown that God's people, who are His peculiar treasure, cannot engage in this perplexing war, for it is opposed to every principle of their faith. In the army they cannot obey the truth and at the same time obey the requirements of their officers. There would be a continual violation of conscience. Worldly men are governed by worldly principles ... But God's people cannot be governed by these motives ... Those who love God's commandments will conform to every good law of the land. But if the requirements of the rulers are such as conflict with the laws of God, the only question to be settled is, Shall we obey God, or man?[25]

Adventists often exhibited their Anabaptist roots by abstaining from getting involved in partisanship, politicking, or voting for individuals that do not express Biblical principles. Although recognizing that some holy men of old such as Joseph and Daniel were able to exercise governmental roles, early Adventists were usually reluctant to cast their ballot, and if they did, they limited their vote to social issues such as abolition, alcohol prohibition and equality rights.[26] James White expressed a cautious attitude towards voting, "We are not prepared to prove from the Bible that it would be wrong for a believer ... to cast his vote. We do not recommend this, neither do we oppose. If a brother choose to vote, we cannot condemn him, and we want the same liberty if we do not."[27] James White was concerned about the believer becoming too engrossed in politics and "lose the spirit of the present truth and endanger his own soul."[28]

Like Adventists, many sixteenth-century Anabaptist leaders sensed a contradiction between the assertion that government was ordained by God (Rom 13) and the claim that no Christian could be a magistrate, with its corollary that no magistrate could be a Christian. Hans Denck, Pilgram Marpeck and Menno Simons either specifically allowed or implied that a Christian, in some circumstances, could be a magistrate.[29] Balthasar Hubmaier allowed for Christians serving in government and yielding sword as long as they serve justly.

---

25 Ellen G. White, *Testimonies for the Church*, vol. 1 (Battle Creek, MI: Seventh-day Adventist Steam Press, 1864), 361–362.
26 "God's people have been called out of the world, that they may be separated from the world. It is not safe for them to take sides in politics, whatever preference they may have. They are ever to remember that they are one in Christ. God calls upon them to enter their names as under His theocracy. He cannot approve of those who link up with worldlings. We are entirely out of our place when we identify ourselves with party interests. Let us not forget that we are citizens of the kingdom of heaven. We are soldiers of the cross of Christ, and our work is to advance the interests of His kingdom" (Ellen G. White, Manuscript 67, 1900, in *Manuscript Releases*, vol. 3 [Washington, DC: Review and Herald, 1972], 40).
27 James White, "Editorial," *Review and Herald*, August 21, 1860.
28 Ibid.
29 See Keith Graber Miller, *Wise as Serpents, Innocent as Doves; American Mennonites Engage Washington* (Knoxville, TN: University of Tennessee Press, 1996), 26–28.

Even a blind man can see that a Christian may with a good conscience be judge and a council member to judge and decide in temporal matters. Even though the contentious and the litigious sin, yet would they sin far more if they were to bring the matters before unbelieving judges. Now if a Christian may or ought to be a judge in his pronouncements in the power of the divine Word, so he may also be protector with the hand of justice and punisher of the unrighteous ... Thus also a Christian may according to the order of God bear the sword in God's stead against the evil doer and punish him. For it has been so ordered by God because of wickedness for the protection of the pious (Rom 13).[30]

Although Adventists and Anabaptists believe in separation from the world, they differ in the nature and degree of that separation. Anabaptists were far more radical, and included not just physical, but moral and spiritual separation.[31] Their physical separation can be explained by the religious context of their age where outwardly professing a religion not authorized by the state could lead to persecution and even death, so, for the Anabaptists, separation was a matter of survival. The Adventists faced no such challenge and their separation was more spiritual and internal rather than physical, since they lived in a society of religious freedom.

## Salvation

Anabaptists agreed with the Magisterial Reformers that believers are saved by grace through faith, but for Hubmaier and the Anabaptists, the faith that would lead to salvation was a faith that bore visible fruits in repentance, conversion, regeneration, obedience, and a new life dedicated to the love of God and neighbor by the power of the Holy Spirit. Righteousness was not simply imputed to the sinner for Christ's sake, as Luther had maintained, but rather being saved meant becoming righteous by the power of the risen Christ.[32]

Anabaptists believed that the process of salvation is initiated by God's gracious act in Jesus Christ. But they were equally adamant that man's cooperation with God was necessary in order to make their salvation effective. For that reason they rejected predestination and bondage of the human will. For them predestination made God the source of evil and robbed man of the liberty to make choices for and against God. Commenting on justification Hubmaier penned:

Faith alone and by itself is not sufficient for salvation. O yes, we believe that Jesus Christ suffered agony and death for us. Rather, faith must express itself also in love to God and the neighbor. Thus John teaches us when he says: Little children, let us not love in word or speech but in deed and truth. By this we shall know that we are of the truth (1 Jn.

---

30 Henry Clay Vedder, *Balthasar Hubmaier: the Leader of the Anabaptists* (New York, NY: G. P. Putnam's Sons 1905, 286–287.
31 Klaassen 248
32 Snyder, 76.

3). Faith must be active in love (Gal. 5). Therefore faith by itself alone is like a green fig tree without fruit, like a cistern without water, like a cloud without rain.[33]

Hubmaier also denied the bondage of the will:

> Whoever denies the free will of man and says that 'free will' is nothing but an empty and useless term without any reality, the same slanders God as a tyrant. He charges God with injustice and gives manifold cause to the wicked to remain in their sins. Indeed, he overthrows more than half of the Holy Scriptures, the proof of this article: If man were robbed of his free will, God could never justly condemn the sinner for his sins. For he condemns him for reasons about which man can do nothing. God forbid! Moreover Christ would be robbed of his just accusation, which he will bring against sinners on the last day saying: I was hungry and you did not feed me. I was sick and in prison and you did not come to me, etc. (Mt. 25).[34]

In order for a human being to respond and yield to the call in Christ to repentance and a new life, they must be free to respond. The Anabaptists therefore believed that humans were made free by God's grace to accept or not accept the call of God in Christ. Scholars have observed that on this point – i.e., the issue of free will – the soteriology of Anabaptists appeared to be more in harmony with late medieval teaching than with the Magisterial Reformers.[35]

However, the Anabaptists did not completely reject the idea of the bondage of the will. Hubmaier agrees that the human will was bound at Adam's fall but the fallen will was restored through Christ. "Although captive in the sinful and poisoned body," Hubmaier's point was that "the image or inbreathing of God is still in us ... and as a live spark covered with cold ashes is still alive and will steam if heavenly water is poured on it."[36]

Most Anabaptists appear to have believed that grace somehow "comes before" or *prevenes* repentance. Among the Swiss Brethren, Michael Sattler affirmed that "the willing and ability to turn to God are not of man but the gift of God through Jesus Christ our Lord."[37] According to Anabaptist scholar Kenneth Davis, the majority of Anabaptists would agree with Hubmaier's explanation that, after the fall, God placed in all men, a "latent grace," which is awakened when an individual hears the preaching of the Word, enabling the person to have *a choice* whether to accept salvation or not.[38]

Adventist soteriology is set within the framework of the great controversy between Christ and Satan. The central issue concerns the character of God and his law. Adventists believe that salvation "contains no thread of human devising," but its

---

33 Balthasar Hubmaier, "Justification," in Klaassen, 43–44.
34 Ibid., 44.
35 Snyder, 77.
36 Ibid.
37 Michael Sattler, "On the Satisfaction of Christ," in *The Legacy of Michael Sattler*, trans. and ed. John Howard Yoder (Scottdale, PA: Herald Press 1973), 116.
38 Kenneth Davis, *Anabaptism and Asceticism* (Scottdale, PA: Herald Press, 1974), 147–148.

effects lead to a new status and relationship of the sinner with God. At the core of this view is the understanding that Christ is both Savior and Lord. This means Christ offers us forgiveness for sin but also calls us to a life of obedient discipleship, walking in the spirit, manifesting the fruits of the spirit and loving service to God. White makes this point with great clarity, "Forgiveness has broader meaning than many suppose ... God's forgiveness is not merely a judicial act by which he sets us free from condemnation. It is not only forgiveness for sin, but reclamation from sin."[39]

The Adventist understanding of "righteousness by faith" encompasses both these elements. In other words, the ground of hope is the imputed righteousness of God called justification (our title to heaven), but we also must experience sanctification (our fitness for heaven). It is our union with Christ that brings about these two great soteriological realities. "The proud heart strives to earn salvation; but both our title to heaven and our fitness for it are found in the righteousness of Christ."[40]

Adventists and Anabaptists believe that although the human will is severely damaged, it is not dead but greatly weakened and can be made alive with the prevenient grace of God. Every man is free to choose what power he will have to rule over him.[41] Ellen White writes,

> Through disobedience, his [humanity's] powers were perverted, and selfishness took the place of love. His nature became so weakened through transgression that it was impossible for him, in his own strength, to resist the power of evil. He was made captive by Satan, and would have remained so forever had not God specially interposed.[42]

She goes on further to say, "His love is drawing us to Himself. If we do not resist this drawing, we shall be led to the foot of the cross in repentance ... Then the Spirit of God through faith produces a new life in the soul. The thoughts and desires are brought into obedience to the will of Christ ... The law of God is written in the mind and heart."[43]

Adventists and the Anabaptists strongly support the importance of the human will in responding to God's grace. White asserts,

> In the work of redemption there is no compulsion, no external force is employed. Under the influence of the Spirit of God, man is left free to choose whom he will serve. In the change that takes place, when the soul surrenders to Christ, there is the highest sense of freedom. The expulsion of sin is the act of the soul itself. True, we have no power to free ourselves form Satan's control but when we desire to be set free from sin, and in our great need cry out for a power out of and above ourselves, the powers of the

---

39 Ellen G. White, *Thoughts from the Mount of Blessings* (Melbourne: Signs Publishing, 1897), 114.
40 Ivan T. Blazen, "Salvation," in *Handbook of Seventh-day Adventist Theology* (Hagerstown: Review and Herald, 2000), 308 (271–313).
41 Ellen G. White, *The Desire of Ages*, 258.
42 Ellen G. White, *Steps to Christ* (Chicago, IL: Fleming Revell, 1892), 17.
43 White, *The Desire of Ages*, 176.

soul are imbued with divine energy of the Holy Spirit, and they obey His dictates of the will in fulfilling the will of God.[44]

## Eschatology

The Anabaptist views of the last days were shaped in large part by their suffering and persecution, which they regarded as preceding the Second Coming. While most Anabaptists agreed they were living in the last days, they disagreed in emphasis, specificity and especially regarding their own attitude towards, and participation in, the expected events.

Most Anabaptists agreed with Luther in identifying Rome as the Antichrist, the Babylonian harlot. The presumptuous claim of the papacy as the voice of God on earth and its claim of spiritual and secular power were identified as "abomination of desolation" from the book of Daniel.[45] Bernhard Rothmann wrote:

> This is the horn or beast with the three crowns, the pope, with his whole substance and nature. For he has elevated himself under the Roman Empire, taken his seat in God's place, given laws, and changed the time [Dan 7:25] according to his will. He has seated himself above everyone, that is, that he has brought under his feet the temporal power, God's order, the Roman emperor. He rules in pride to blaspheme God, boast of his power, and to suppress the saints and the truth. The prophet quite properly marveled at the proud scoffing of the horn until it perished with the beast and was cast into the fiery pit.[46]

Anabaptists believed that the papal Antichrist was soon to be overthrown, and thus, the end of the age should not be far off. Jakob Hutter comforted the brethren, "for the time of your deliverance is at hand. Lift up your head to God the Lord in Heaven and await your shepherd and king from heaven with meekness and great patience in righteousness and trust, in godly love with strong faith and confidence. For he who is to come will soon come in the clouds of heaven with great power and glory."[47]

Anabaptist eschatology was shaped by persecution; the early Adventists faced no such suffering, so although their perspectives were similar, they had different motivations. Much of Adventists' eschatology was based on their understanding of history and prophecy. They believed they were living in the very last days of earth's history and that all time prophecies in the Bible were fulfilled. They took the name "Adventists" to make the point about their fervent conviction about the imminent

44   Ibid., 466.
45   Estep, 136.
46   Bernhard Rothmann, "Concerning Earthly and Temporal Power" (1535), in Klaassen, 334.
47   Jakob Hutter, "The Fourth Epistle," in Klaassen, 325. Menno Simons assured his followers that "the desirable day of your release is at hand ... with this day in view all afflicted and oppressed Christians who now live under the cross of Christ are comforted in the firm hope of the life to come and they leave all tyrants with their heathenish mandate to God and his judgment" (Leonard Verduin, John C. Wenger and Harold S. Bender, ed., *The Complete Writings of Menno Simons* [Scottdale, PA: Herald Press, 1966], 613).

return of Jesus. They agreed with the Anabaptists on the identity of the Antichrist, the death and resurrection of the righteous and the wicked. Adventists, like the Anabaptists, had an apocalyptic consciousness that informed their ethics.

## Sabbath

Some Anabaptists accepted Saturday as the biblical Sabbath and rejected worshipping on Sunday. However, these Sabbatarians were a very small group among them. The Anabaptist leaders associated with the restoration of the biblical Sabbath were Oswald Glait and Andreas Fischer, both of whom wrote books defending their Sabbatarianism. Some of the essence of their arguments about the Sabbath is summarized in Caspar Schwenckfeld's refutation of the book *Concerning the Sabbath* by Oswald Glait. Here is a summary of some of their ideas:
1. Celebrating the Sabbath (Saturday) is a duty because it is the word, will, and commandment of God (Exod 20:8–11).
2. The Decalogue is the basis for the moral law; therefore, the Sabbath is a part of the moral law, which Christians are to obey.
3. There are ten commandments; we cannot say that some are to be followed while others can be forgotten.
4. The Sabbath commandment is one of the "strong" commandments.
5. God himself rested on the seventh day (Gen 2:1–4).
6. The Sabbath was celebrated by the patriarchs, even by Adam at creation (Exod 16).
7. The Greek phrase in Colossians 2:16 excludes from Paul's condemnation the biblical Sabbath.
8. Jesus clearly taught us to keep the commandments; he surely must have meant to include the Sabbath commandment.
9. The Day of the Lord (Rev 1:10) is not Sunday; Sunday worship was introduced by the popes.[48]

Similar arguments can also be gleaned from Valentin Krautwald's refutation of Andreas Fischer's book concerning the Sabbath.[49]

The Adventist understanding of the Sabbath followed a similar theological line, because they argued that Saturday is the seventh-day Sabbath and is to be kept as mandated by the Decalogue, which is still binding on all Christians. It was a day blessed, hollowed and a memorial of creation, symbol of redemption, sign of sanctification, kept by the patriarchs, apostles, and Christ himself. There was no divine mandate to change the day; this change took place over the Christian era and was supported by the Catholic Church. J. N. Andrews, eminent Adventist scholar on the Sabbath, noted that the ancient Sabbath was retained and observed by the Ana-

---

48 Liechty, 30–32.
49 Ibid., 36. Both volumes by Fischer and by Glait were destroyed and are lost to historical record. Their arguments can only be observed from the books written by their opponents.

baptists and a number of other Christian groups who refused to submit to Rome's authority.[50] Adventists differed from Anabaptists in the eschatological significance of the Sabbath and also its relationship to the sanctuary doctrine, but overall their arguments for the continual perpetuity of the Sabbath are strikingly similar.[51]

## Religious Liberty

The most profound influence of the Anabaptists on the Adventists was their teachings and practices on religious liberty and freedom of conscience. Although the Adventist pioneers lived in a land of religious liberty, they recognized that this did not happen by chance. They pointed back in history to the significant contributions of the Anabaptists in the establishment of this fundamental principle of American life. Although some of the theological links with Anabaptism and Adventism were indirect, this theological connection was recognized, and repeated references were made to it on numerous occasions.

In a number of articles written in the *Review and Herald*, *Signs of the Times*, and the *Youth's Instructor*, Charles Miles Snow, former associate editor of the *Review and Herald* and later editor of *Liberty Magazine*, traced the rise and fall of religious liberty in America. In these articles, he made repeated references to the role of the Anabaptists, who, unlike the other Reformers, were uniquely responsible for religious liberty in Europe and made it possible for the idea to come to America. Religious liberty and freedom of conscience was a trademark of the Anabaptists and their most important legacy to Protestantism.

Snow wrote that the first step out of spiritual bondage was the doctrine of justification by faith, the second was the notion of religious liberty. While the Anabaptists were often misunderstood and maligned, they were sustained by the doctrine of soul's freedom and became heralds of religious liberty in the old and the new world. For them freedom of conscience and worship were essential to spiritual growth. They taught that religion should be entirely exempt from the regulation and interference of civil power, "for a man's religion should not work for his disability."[52]

Snow attributed to Anabaptists the notion that each person has the freedom to worship God in his own way. Although viciously persecuted by both Catholics and Protestants, the shedding of their blood did not drain the vitality of the truths they held. It is estimated that over 50,000 of them fled to England in the sixteenth century. They were not received with open arms. James I threatened to make them conform or run them out of England. Henry VIII issued decrees against them threatening death or imprisonment. Their view that civil government has no concern with

50   J. N. Andrews, "Tracing the Sabbath during the Dark Ages," *Review and Herald*, May 12, 1862, 185.
51   *Seventh-day Adventists Believe* (Silver Spring, MD: Ministerial Association, General Conference of Seventh-day Adventists, 2005), 249–264.
52   Charles Miles Snow, "The Rise and Fall of Religious Liberty in America," *Review and Herald*, June 11, 1908, 4–6.

religion was noxious to governments at that time when the concept of religious liberty was totally foreign. The Anabaptist ideas on religious liberty were also picked up by English Puritans and merchants in Holland where the Dutch Anabaptists were well established.[53] These ideas of freedom were so associated with Anabaptism, that even Roger Williams, the father of religious freedom in America, was accused of being an Anabaptist.[54]

Quoting from Henry M. King in his book *Religious Liberty*, Snow noted, "As there were reformers before the Reformation, so there needed to be reformers after the Reformation, to take the work, painfully incomplete, on to its full completion."[55] Although not stated explicitly, Snow was implying that Adventists were the ones who would complete this reformation, especially as it pertained to religious liberty.

## Sabbatarian Adventism

In the mid-nineteenth century, America experienced a series of revivals known as the Second Great Awakening. The Millerite movement arose out of these revivals and focused primarily on end-time prophecies that would usher in the Second Coming of Jesus Christ. After a serious study of the Bible, specifically the books of Daniel and Revelation, William Miller concluded that Jesus would return at about the year 1843.[56] The key to this prophetic interpretation was Daniel 8:14. The phrase "the cleansing of the sanctuary" was understood to mean the earth as symbolized by the sanctuary. To Miller this meant that the earth would be cleansed by fire and Jesus would return. There was a great sense of excitement that surrounded Miller and his followers, as many sold farms and other possessions with the anticipation of the coming of Jesus. Their hopes would be shattered, their dreams destroyed, for Jesus did not come. It was out of this great disappointment that the Seventh-day Adventist Church was born. First known as Sabbatarian Adventists, they emerged along with other groups to forge a unique identity of their own.

The small group of Millerites who would form the core of early Sabbatarian Adventists began to coalesce as a group through a series of Bible conferences in Connecticut, New York, Maine, and Massachusetts. The purpose of these "Sabbath

---

53 Charles Miles Snow, "America and Religious Liberty," *Signs of the Times*, May 28, 1912, 3–5.
54 Abdiel, "Roger Williams, the Apostle of Religious Liberty," *Signs of the Times*, July 10, 1907, 3, 9.
55 Charles Miles Snow, "The Demoralizing Effect of Religious Intolerance," *The Youth's Instructor*, September 29, 1908, 12.
56 The most important biographies of William Miller and the Millerite movement are Sylvester Bliss, *Memoirs of William Miller* (Boston, MA: Joshua Himes, 1853 [New ed. by George R. Knight, Berrien Springs, MI: Andrews University Press, 2005]); Francis Nichol, *Midnight Cry: A Defense of the Character and Conduct of William Miller and the Millerites* (Washington, DC: Review and Herald, 1944); George R. Knight, *Millennial Fever and the End of the World* (Boise, ID: Pacific Press, 1993).

Conferences," as they were called, was to unify and clarify their understanding of the truths that had to be restored before Christ's Second Advent.[57]

Especially significant for early Sabbatarian Adventism was the new understanding of the prophecies in Revelation 10–14, culminating with the "three angels' messages" (Rev 14:4–14), warning the world of the imminent judgment of God. James White declared, "the work of uniting the brethren on the great truths connected with the message of the third angel commenced."[58] As a result, the Adventist message was systematically brought together and, by early 1848, Sabbatarian Adventists coalesced around four basic doctrinal pillars that would set them apart and provide them a sense of their unique identity:[59]

1. The personal, visible, premillennial return of Jesus.
2. The two-phase ministry of Christ in the heavenly sanctuary.
3. The perpetuity of the seventh-day Sabbath and its end-time importance.
4. Immortality is not inherent but comes only as a gift through Jesus Christ.[60]

As the Sabbatarian Adventist group consolidated their search for more biblical truth it would become evident that they had many doctrinal similarities with the Anabaptists. But how pervasive was the Anabaptist influence and where did it come from? These questions have been poured over but no conclusive answers have been given. Knight wrote that Adventism was heir to the Anabaptist restoration wing of the Reformation rather than the Lutheran or Calvinist, but he did not provide clear and explicit evidence except the indirect links through the Christian Connexion.[61]

Like their Anabaptist predecessors, the early Adventists were greatly concerned about restoring all the biblical teachings before the end times. Like them, they were not satisfied with the insights on the relationship between law and gospel as put forth by Luther in his reaction to medieval legalism. They wanted to construct a balanced theology of both the Sermon on the Mount and justification in Romans 3–5. Adventists concluded that the book of Romans was not against obedience but against the works of obedience outside of faith. In that sense, Adventists, like the Anabaptists and Wesley, advocated a life of faith working through love (Gal 5:6).[62]

This approach to justification and the pious life leads us back to the Anabaptist, Arminian, Pietist, and Wesleyan lineage of theology. Adventists, just like early Anabaptists sought to integrate justification and sanctification as a necessity of the Christian life and salvation. In some ways they were following Wesley who sought to balance the overreaction of the Protestant reformers to the works-oriented Roman Catholic view of salvation.

---

57 W. L. Emmerson, *The Reformation and the Advent Movement* (Washington, DC: Review and Herald, 1983), 206.
58 [James White], "A Brief Sketch of the Past," *Review and Herald*, May 6, 1852, 5.
59 Emmerson, 206.
60 Ibid., 74.
61 George R. Knight, *A Search for Identity: The Development of Seventh-day Adventist Beliefs* (Hagerstown, MD: Review & Herald, 2000) 30–35.
62 Ellen G. White, *Steps to Christ*, 67–75.

Sabbatarian Adventists would become the strongest of the post-Millerite groups who survived the Great Disappointment. The presence of Ellen White, considered a prophet, would prove decisive in the survival and organization of the group.

## Restorationist Roots

George Knight asserts that "while Anabaptism never made much of an institutional impact on early nineteenth-century American religion," broadly speaking and more specific to Adventism, the "spirit of Anabaptism literally permeated the evangelical denominations of the day."[63]

The movement known as Restorationism advocated restoring the teachings of the New Testament and sought to carry out completely the *sola scriptura* principle of the Reformation.[64] Restorationists felt that their task was to complete the Reformation that began in the sixteenth century. Joseph Bates and James White, two of the principal founders of Adventism, came from this group and brought in to early Adventism many Radical Reformation ideas via the Christian Connexion.

## Methodist Roots

Wesleyan Methodism is another important group which shaped Adventism. It was esteemed that 42 percent of the Millerite preachers came out of the Methodist Church.[65] Ellen G. White, considered the third founding member of Adventism, grew up in the Methodist Episcopal Church.[66] Methodism had an important influence in nineteenth-century American theology. Its emphasis on free will (in contrast with the Puritan/Calvinist mentality of predestination that dominated colonial American Christianity) was gaining wider acceptance rapidly especially in America where people's actions and choices had consequences specifically regarding their salvation.[67]

Wesleyan Methodism draws much of its theology from German Pietism, John Wesley himself was converted while attending a German Moravian prayer meeting. The Moravians, in the 1700s, were strong proponents of free will, assurance of

---

63 George R. Knight, *A Search for Identity: The Development of Seventh-day Adventist Beliefs* (Hagerstown, MD: Review and Herald, 2000), 30.
64 Hans Hillerbrand, *Encyclopedia of Protestantism* (New York, NY: Routledge, 2004), 122, 239–240.
65 Everett Dick, "The Adventist Crisis of 1843–1844" (PhD diss., University of Wisconsin, 1930), 232–233.
66 For more information on Ellen G. White and the Methodist connection with Adventism see Russell Staples, "Methodism," in *The Ellen G. White Encyclopedia*, ed. Denis Fortin and Jerry Moon (Hagerstown, MD: Review and Herald, 2013), 976–977.
67 Russell E. Richey, Jean Miller Schmidt, and Kenneth E. Rowe, *American Methodism* (Nashville, TN: Abingdon Press, 2012), 48–50.

salvation, sanctified life, and freedom of worship. These ideas were closely related to the German Anabaptist teachings.[68]

The exact relation of Anabaptism to Pietism has not yet been fully explored, both as to the possible influence of Anabaptism on the origins of Pietism, and their theological relationship. Friedmann and Roth theorized that Pietism was possibly influenced by Anabaptist ideas that circulated in Lutheran communities in seventeenth-century Germany.[69] Brown argued that Pietism flourished best on Anabaptist soil, especially in Anabaptist strongholds such as Württemberg. Brown also observed that Pietists read widely in *Das Geistliche Blumengärtlein*, which contained writings by Hans Denck, Hans Hut, Jörg Hauck and other Anabaptist leaders.[70] More recent studies conducted by Douglas Shantz seem to affirm the notion that early Pietism grew from and was directly immersed in Anabaptist ideas.[71]

Anabaptists and Pietists shared the belief in the restoration of the primitive church, the centrality of the "new birth" and the ethical motives of the "imitation of Christ." It is via Pietism that Anabaptist teachings influenced John Wesley and his Methodist movement. Seventh-day Adventism, in turn, embraced much of the Methodist and Restorationist understanding of justification and sanctification.

Another important Methodist teaching that draws its roots from Pietism and Anabaptism and directly impacted Adventism was Wesley's emphasis on "entire sanctification" or "Christian perfection." His view was not a monastic mystical deification but rather the Pietist notion of "perfect love." "Ellen White brought the Wesleyan/Methodist emphases on sanctification and perfection into Adventism."[72]

## Baptist Roots

The Baptists influence was also strong on Adventism. Everett Dick in his *Adventist Crisis* shows that almost 30 percent of Millerite preachers came from the Baptist

---

68 See Roger Olson and Christian T. Collins Winn, *Reclaiming Pietism* (Grand Rapids, MI: Eerdmans, 2015), 19–38.
69 Robert Friedmann, *Mennonite Piety through the Centuries*, Studies on Mennonite History no. 7 (Scottdale, PA: Herald Press, 1996); John D. Roth, "Pietism and the Anabaptist Soul," in *The Dilemma of Anabaptist Piety. Strengthening or Straining the Bonds of Community*, ed. Stephen L. Longenecker (Bridgewater, VA: Penobscot Press, 1997), 17–33.
70 Dale W. Brown, *Understanding Pietism* (Grand Rapids, MI: Eerdmans, 1978; rev. ed. Grantham, PA: Brethren in Christ Historical Society, 1996), 17–18, 35, 85, 102.
71 Douglas Shantz, *A Companion to German Pietism 1660–1800* (Boston, MA: Brill, 2015), 115–138. See also Douglas H. Shantz, *An Introduction to German Pietism: Protestant Renewal at the Dawn of Modern Europe* (Baltimore, MD: Johns Hopkins University Press, 2013).
72 Knight, *A Search for Identity*, 33.

denomination.[73] Miller himself was a Baptist, and the early Adventists accepted the seventh-day Sabbath from a Seventh Day Baptist missionary, Rachel Oakes.[74]

The Seventh Day Baptists were probably the first group of English Protestants who practiced Sabbath-keeping on Saturday instead of Sunday in colonial America. In 1664, some 40 years after the Mayflower landed in Plymouth, Stephen Mumford arrived in Newport, Rhode Island from England. Mumford and his family were Sabbath-keeping Baptists from England who taught the binding claims of the moral and immutable Ten Commandments on all Christians. They claimed that it was an anti-Christian power that changed the Sabbath from the seventh day to the first day of the week. Some members of the Baptist congregation in Newport, Rhode Island, responded favorably and separated themselves, forming the first Seventh Day Baptist church in America in 1671.[75] The Seventh Day Baptists became the early champions of the Saturday Sabbath in colonial America.

Besides the Sabbath doctrine, Adventism also inherited from the Baptists the idea of adult baptism by immersion and the notion of free will in the salvation process. One of the founders of the Baptist church, John Smyth, was directly influenced by the Anabaptist teachings in Holland.[76] Hence, it could be argued that Adventists received various threads of the sixteenth-century Anabaptism via the Baptist and the Methodist traditions. It appears that Methodism and the Baptist traditions were the strongest influences on Adventism and belonged to a distinctive type of Christianity profoundly different from Roman Catholicism and the magisterial state churches of Lutheranism, Calvinism and Anglicanism.[77]

The believers' church tradition reflects the views of a radical Protestant type of Christianity, which has its antecedents in medieval groups such as the Waldenses and the Czech Unity Brethren. Some scholars believe that the Anabaptists were the founders of the many movements that make up the radical Protestant tradition.[78] The Adventist pioneers identified with groups considered part of this tradition, although they made few references to any Anabaptist writings in their literature. Perhaps this can be explained by the fact that, in the age of the pioneers, the Anabaptists were given an unsympathetic treatment by historians because of the strong influence of Heinrich Bullinger, whose account of them was very negative. Recent scholarship has led to a thorough reassessment of the history and theology of

73  Dick, 232–233.
74  For an extensive treatment of Rachel Oakes and the Seventh Day Baptist connection to Adventism see Merlin Burt, *Adventist Pioneer Places* (Hagerstown, MD: Review and Herald, 2011), 94–96, 161–165.
75  Kenneth Strand, ed., *The Sabbath in Scripture and History* (Washington, DC: Review and Herald 1982), 241.
76  See Jason Lee, *The Theology of John Smyth; Puritan, Separatist, Baptist, Mennonite* (Macon, GA: Mercer University Press, 2003).
77  Charles Scriven, "Radical Discipleship and the Renewal of the Adventist Mission," *Spectrum*, December 1983, 12. Donald Durnbaugh, *The Believer's Church: The History and Character of Radical Protestantism* (New York, NY: Macmillan, 1968), 97–106.
78  Scriven, 12.

Anabaptism as scholars no longer rely on the writings of their adversaries to critique them, but now have access to the primary sources of notable Anabaptist scholars.[79]

## Conclusion

The spirit of Anabaptism permeated early Adventism, and it is hard to escape the conclusion that this Radical Reformation group had some influence on Adventism. The nature and depth of this influence is still undetermined. It is difficult to prove direct, explicit, and clear links because the Adventist pioneers rarely quoted from any of the Anabaptist scholars. Perhaps the absence of such scholarly writings or the disdain in which they were held in those days militated against their use. There is one area, however, in which the links seem more explicit, and that is in the area of religious freedom. Adventist scholars seem to attribute to the Anabaptist tradition the legacy of religious liberty which was not an idea championed by the Magisterial Reformers. What is incontrovertible is that the early Adventist pioneers emerged from the groups constituting the radical tradition of Protestantism that were influenced by the Anabaptists.

The debate on the extent and nature of the Anabaptist influence will continue on for some time. Nevertheless a cursory comparison of Anabaptist theology and practices show striking similarities with those of Adventism. The Anabaptist theological reasoning on doctrines like baptism, communion, salvation, Sabbath, eschatology, the human will, and separation from the world, finds a kindred spirit in Adventism. It is clear that Adventists did not follow the Magisterial Reformers like Luther and Calvin in many areas, especially in the key area of soteriology. It is not inconceivable that if Adventists had lived during the lifetime of these reformers, they might have been persecuted by them as were the Anabaptists. Adventism owes a debt of gratitude to the Radical Reformers for the rich tradition that has been handed down to them.

79  Ibid.

Charles Scriven

# The Radical Reformation and the Transformation of Adventism: The Legacy of James William McClendon, Jr.

Abstract

James McClendon († 2000) is Neo-Anabaptism's most important systematic thinker. He represents the third stream of Western Christian life, which is neither Protestant nor Catholic but Radical, and exemplified today in, e.g., Mennonite and Adventist communities. Recounting his scholarly perspective – concerning narrative in theology, relativism in a many-cultured world, the contemporary meaning of Radical Reformation thought – this paper shows how McClendon provides four leverage points for renewal in Adventism: his "transformational" definition of theology, his "practical" understanding of doctrine, his argument for Christocentrism, and his interpretation of the *present* significance of eschatology. All concern doctrine. First, doctrine is not only the content but also the practice of teaching; rightly conceived, it is community-transforming. Second, doctrine focuses on life; the point is not intellectual correctness but better discipleship. Third, doctrine's criterion is Christ; the Bible is a means to deeper understanding of creation's final victor. Fourth, doctrine must support earthly concerns, not withdrawal or escapism.

"Christianity is Christ."[1]

These words, and certainly this idea, appear repeatedly over the 3,000 or so book pages that constitute James William McClendon's lifework as a Radical Reformation theologian, and they summarize his perspective on teaching proper to the Christian Church. My purpose here is to show how that perspective offers crucial leverage toward faithful transformation of Adventism. The Radical Reformation embraced what Paul Tillich called the "Protestant principle," the view that any "absolute claim" such as may undergird "religious pride" and "ecclesiastical arrogance" must crumble under the realization of human finitude and sinfulness.[2] To that principle, however, the Radical Reformers conjoined a point of view powerful

---

1 I will refer often to James Wm. McClendon, Jr., *Ethics: Systematic Theology*, 2nd ed., vol. 1 (Nashville, TN: Abingdon, 2002), as well as to *Doctrine: Systematic Theology*, vol. 2 (Nashville, TN: Abingdon, 1994), and to *Witness: Systematic Theology*, vol. 3 (Nashville, TN: Abingdon, 2000). The short sentence quoted here is found in *Ethics*, vol. 1, 48, and in *Witness*, vol. 3, 313, 330.
2 Paul Tillich, *The Protestant Era*, trans. James Luther Adams (Chicago, IL: University of Chicago Press, 1948; Phoenix Books, 1957), 163.

enough to sustain a third main "stream"[3] of Western Christianity, one that is neither Catholic nor Protestant. This third stream, as it turns out, has produced relatively little "formal theology." McClendon suggests that this is in part due to hardships occasioned by the hostility of the other two, and in part due to distracting controversies such as that between modernists and fundamentalists. But the key reason is the failure of third-stream communities to "*see in their own heritage, their own way of using Scripture, their own communal practices, their own guiding vision*, a resource for theology unlike the prevailing tendencies around them" (emphasis his).[4]

Although the Radical Reformation involved several religious developments, the Anabaptist version is the one most pertinent here.[5] McClendon belonged to a circle of so-called Neo-Anabaptist thinkers that included John Howard Yoder, Richard Hays, Nancey Murphy, and Stanley Hauerwas.[6] By the time of his death in the year 2000, he had become the most formidable systematic thinker of the group, with assorted essays (now collected in a three-volume set) and two path-breaking monographs to his credit, and also a three-volume systematic theology.

McClendon grew up attending a Baptist Sunday school and church in Louisiana, served in the Navy just as World War II was ending, trained for, and briefly worked in, the Baptist pastorate, and spent the remainder of his life in a somewhat tumultuous academic career. His teaching, like his formal education in theology (ThD, Southwestern Baptist Theological Seminary), occurred mainly outside of the most renowned universities in the U.S. Twice his opposition to U.S. involvement in the Vietnam War led to separation from his employing institution, although it was not until he read Yoder's *The Politics of Jesus*, in 1975, that he took up a characteristically Anabaptist perspective on how the church should relate to the institutions and violence of the wider world.[7] McClendon eventually found permanent employment

3 McClendon, in his "A baptist [*sic;* on the small *b*, see below] Millennium?" in James Wm. McClendon, Jr., eds. Ryan Andrew Newson and Andrew C. Wright, *The Collected Works of James Wm. McClendon, Jr.*, vol. 1, with a foreword by Nancey Murphy (Waco, TX: Baylor University Press, 2014), 294–297, expresses his preference for the metaphor of "multiple streams" over the "'tree' model" of church history. The latter usefully suggests the common roots of Christian existence, but with its image of trunk and branches misleads by leaving the impression that followers of the third way are "at best latecomers" to the Christian scene. There were "multiple streams" early on, "well before a Catholic dominance suppressed most of the others." McClendon uses "baptist" with a small *b* to refer to the many communities in this stream, not just denominations using "Baptist" with a large *b* in their name.
4 McClendon, *Ethics*, vol. 1, 26.
5 On the varieties of Radical Reformation life and thought, the classic study remains George Huntston Williams, *The Radical Reformation* (Philadelphia, PA: The Westminster Press, 1962).
6 See, e.g., chapter 5, entitled "The Neo-Anabaptists," in James Davison Hunter, *To Change the World: The Irony, Tragedy, and Possibility of Christianity in the Late Modern World* (Oxford: Oxford University Press, 2010), 150–166.
7 For McClendon's own account of his life, see "The Radical Road One Baptist Took," "A Brief Narrative Account of My Professional Life and Work to the Present," and "A Decade

(1971–1990) at the Church Divinity School of the Pacific, an Episcopal seminary affiliated with the Graduate Theological Union in Berkeley, CA. During the final ten years of his life, he was distinguished scholar in residence at the Fuller Seminary in Pasadena, CA.

Despite his aptitude for physics (his training as a navy electronics officer involved study at both Harvard and MIT), McClendon early turned his attention to theology. Its questions concerned "life's most serious problems," and were, to him, more interesting than those addressed in the sciences or even in what he then understood of philosophy.[8] The latter discipline, especially in the work of John Austin, Ludwig Wittgenstein and Alasdair MacIntyre, did come, however, to shape his theological perspective. He sought full faithfulness to Christian Scripture, but at the same time engaged the best thinking – especially the best philosophical thinking – of the surrounding culture.

McClendon began publishing theological essays early in the 1960s. At first, he wrote on doctrinal themes for readers in his own Baptist denomination, evincing from the start the Christocentrism and concern with "total faith-response to God in Christ" that would characterize his thinking to the end.[9] But he was already pursuing philosophical study at Oxford University and at the University of California, Berkeley, and two articles published in 1966 reflected the precise language analysis he was learning from the philosophers at those institutions. Using that skill, he argued in one article that Trinitarianism expresses how Christ's ministry and resurrection illuminate the "action and presence" of the *one* God Christians worship. In another, John Austin's speech-act theory becomes a lever for understanding what baptism actually *accomplishes*. It is a sign by which candidate, congregation, and God *respond* to one another and so enter into deeper solidarity; the premise, as certainly for the candidate as for the congregation and God, is the *capacity for response*.[10]

McClendon's thinking continued to crystallize into lectures and articles on themes that, typically, would come to fuller expression in his books. By the late 1960s, McClendon was sensing that the Enlightenment's challenge to Christian faith could not be met by making arguments based on the Enlightenment's own questions and assumptions. That movement had tried to eliminate the relevance of traditions and stories, but what struck McClendon is that, in fact, traditions and stories under-

---

of Deeds and Dreams: My History Continued, 1969–1978 in McClendon, *Collected Works*, vol. 1, 17–25, 57–60 and 87–90.

8 See "Decade of Deeds and Dreams," McClendon, *Collected Works*, vol. 1, 18; and the essay "Biography as Theology," in James Wm. McClendon, Jr., eds. Ryan Andrew Newson and Andrew C. Wright, *The Collected Works of James Wm. McClendon, Jr.*, vol. 2, 154–155.

9 See, e.g., "Atonement, Discipleship, and Freedom," in McClendon, *Collected Works*, vol.1, 44 for the quote; 37–45 for the entire article; essays like this appeared in a magazine called *The Baptist Student*.

10 "Some Reflections on the Future of Trinitarianism" and "Baptism as a Performative Sign" appear consecutively in McClendon, *Collected Works*, vol. 1, 61–84.

gird all human conviction. It struck him further, as he would suggest in 1971 lectures at Goucher College, that one way for a community to challenge itself, and also to challenge competing points of view, is by attending to its own "compelling biographies." Within a particular tradition, the best lives – he spoke, e.g., of Martin Luther King – offer correction for those whose lives are less striking. When communities themselves disagree, the best lives in a particular tradition can strengthen the case for the one on which their own spiritual achievement depends. "The vindication of vision depends in part upon the quality of life that the vision evokes."[11]

The first of McClendon's two path-breaking monographs appeared in 1974 and grew out of the lectures delivered in 1971. Under the title *Biography as Theology*,[12] it makes three arguments. *One* is aimed at those who think ethics is fundamentally about deciding what to do in the face of moral quandaries. You start with moral principles, it is said, and from these think your way to a morally proper course of action. But, according to McClendon, this view overlooks the rock-bottom importance of character. People often act, and must act, without taking time for moral analysis; and even when they have time to think through what to do, habits and attitudes built up over time affect the outcome. The *second* argument is that character develops under the influence of particular communities and lives, and of the images and narratives that give these communities and lives their shape. You cannot completely step outside of the tradition you have grown up in; the story your tradition lives out and the stories it tells make you who you are. The *third* argument is that *singular lives* from a particular tradition are important sources of moral insight and inspiration. We do accumulate biases – it is the human *condition* to do so – and these biases do affect what lives we may be drawn to, but, for *embodying* a tradition's meaning in deep and surprising ways, such lives can still have transformative effect.[13]

Much of the book consists of life stories that illustrate these points. McClendon examines, for example, Dag Hammarskjöld, the Swedish diplomat, and Charles Ives, the American composer, as well as Martin Luther King and several others. In each case, he shows how Christian images and stories helped these individuals generate remarkable moral courage. He shows, too, how their life stories challenge the Christian community as to the "justification" of its present "way of life when held against theirs."[14] Thus biography can function as corrective, or transformative, theology.

11 Here see "Biography as Theology," in McClendon, *Collected Works*, vol. 2, 153–172; for the quoted phrase, 155, and for the paragraph-ending sentence, 171. Concerning McClendon's awakening with respect to the Enlightenment, see, e.g., "A Decade of Deeds and Dreams: My History Continued, 1969–1978," in McClendon, *Collected Works*, vol. 1, 87–89.
12 James Wm. McClendon, Jr., *Biography as Theology: How Life Stories Can Remake Today's Theology* (Nashville, TN: Abingdon, 1974).
13 On this latter point, see, too, the essay, "Theology, Language and Life," in McClendon, *Collected Works*, vol. 2, 182.
14 McClendon, *Biography as Theology*, 110.

The next year, in 1975, McClendon's *Understanding Religious Convictions*, co-authored with philosopher James M. Smith, came out.[15] This book builds on insights from Anglo-American philosophy in order to clarify what religious convictions are and how they may be justified. Convictions are *life-changing* beliefs, such that if you alter them you become a substantially different person. The book's primary question is how, in an age of relativism, such beliefs can be justified. Drawing inspiration from John Austin, the authors first show that speech expressing such beliefs must satisfy conditions obligatory for any use of human language. For example, it must abide by the rules of the language that speaker and hearer share. For another example, it must meet certain "representative" or "descriptive" conditions; insofar as a speaker assumes or states something to be the case, it must be so. If you ask someone to pass the salt but no salt is on the table, your speech-act fails; again, if you announce the resurrection, but Jesus remains in the tomb, your speech-act fails.

Some religious speakers may doubt whether even key elements of the story they tell need to reflect actual matters of fact; McClendon and his co-author make a counter-argument. But they realize – the "post-modern" sensibility is gaining traction as they write – that everyone speaks from a point of view and that no mere argument will settle major differences, especially in religion and morality, concerning what is true and what is not. Differences within religious traditions can be difficult; across sharp convictional divides even more difficult. The authors do consider non-relativism – the claim that by the use of reason you can just *show* that one perspective is right and another wrong – but remain convinced that it falls short. They also consider hard relativism, or the view that in such domains as religion and morality disagreements are irresolvable. Then they argue for a middle ground: Over time, and with the aid of certain broad commonalities among humans as to what is satisfying, minds can change. Evidence shows it to be so; minds *have* changed. So a kind of relativism is true, but it is "soft" relativism. Humans differ and their differences persist. Nevertheless, we are not prisoners of our perspective. So even if persuasion is hard and slow, it is worth attempting.

Like the essays appearing all along, these two books, one on narrative theology and one on convictions in a many-cultured world, bear on McClendon's three-volume systematic theology, which he conceived of around 1980 and worked on for "nearly twenty years." Significantly, he took the "heirs" of the Radical Reformation to be his "primary community of reference."[16] Along with Baptists, Brethren, and Mennonites, he specifically mentions Adventists as part of this third-stream community. The first volume, which appeared in 1986 under the title *Systematic Theology: Ethics*, explores how the church may truly *live*, and immediately emphasizes the importance of the Christian story and the reality of the church's disagree-

---

15  James Wm. McClendon and James M. Smith, *Understanding Religious Convictions* (Notre Dame, IN: University of Notre Dame Press, 1975); this book is now available as *Convictions: Defusing Religious Relativism* (Eugene, OR: Wipf & Stock, 2002).
16  McClendon, "The Radical Road One Baptist Took," in *Collected Works*, vol. 1, 23–24.

ment with those for whom this story has no central place. He continues the kind of analysis found in *Biography as Theology*, again examining particular Christian lives, including, for example, that of Dietrich Bonhoeffer. All this underscores the point that theology means "struggle." This struggle begins with the fact that "the church is not the world," and with the additional fact that the "temptation" to play down the Christian story in order to please the wider world remains always robust.[17]

Anabaptism attempted (not always successfully) to honor the Christian story and to resist the temptation to play it down. Near the beginning of *Ethics*, McClendon offers his take on Anabaptism's distinctive aspiration. The key aspects are *biblicism*, or the "humble acceptance of the authority of Scripture for both faith and practice"; *liberty*, or the freedom to respond to God "without the intervention of the state or other powers"; *discipleship*, or "life transformed into service by the lordship of Jesus Christ" and signified by "believers' baptism"; *community*, or "sharing together" in a life shaped by the Christian story; and *mission*, the responsibility to bear witness to Christ and to accept the suffering it may entail.[18] These are all, we may well note, features of what it means to *be* the church. For Anabaptists, theory about God and the world is not the point; although theory, or doctrine, has relevance, the point is *practice*, the actual living out of the life God's grace bequeaths.

My purpose here is to show how McClendon's theological perspective offers crucial *leverage* toward faithful transformation of Adventism. His story is now before us, and so, roughly, is the panorama he observes from his vantage point within two legacies: that of the Radical Reformation, and also that of twentieth-century Anglo-American philosophy. So how, we may now ask, does McClendon's theology open our eyes to the possible enhancement of our own faithfulness?

I will not here explore the full wealth of insight contained in his (elegant, if also densely argued) systematic theology. The first volume we have met. The second, entitled *Systematic Theology: Doctrine*, explores the main themes of Christian teaching, from creation, sin and salvation, for example, to Christology, ecclesiology and eschatology. The third, *Systematic Theology: Witness*, asks how followers of Christ may bear faithful witness among those who live by other lights. It assumes that even the church's "homelands" are now "mission fields," and in reflecting on all this deliberately defies the conventional expectation that Anabaptist sensibility comes down to irrelevant withdrawal. Considering how Christians may impart to others the gift they have received, McClendon bears the torch of *engagement* with the world, and in the process offers arresting commentary on science, literature, and music, as well as a three-chapter rumination on philosophy, which he calls the "world thinking itself" and describes, in colorful metaphor, as the "world's tall weather vane."[19] Volume 3, it turns out, is both a missiology *and* a theology of culture.

17 McClendon, *Ethics*, vol. 1, 17–18.
18 Ibid., 27–28.
19 McClendon, *Witness*, vol. 3, 185.

Again though, the point now is not detailed summary; it is finding leverage points useful for moving forward in our own shared life. A good starting place is with two key definitions, that of "theology" and that of "doctrine."

Theology, McClendon writes, "is the discovery, understanding or interpretation, and transformation of the convictions of a convictional community, including the discovery and critical revision of their relation to one another *and to whatever else there is.*"[20] This definition is general, not specific to the Christian faith; it distinguishes "any and all *theology* from other enterprises (emphasis his)."[21] What matters in particular, given our present concern, is the focus on *transformation*. The definition assumes a certain unawareness, or self-deception, regarding even what our convictions are, and so entails acknowledgement, for example, that official doctrinal statements are by no means fully accurate expressions of a community's *life-changing* beliefs. You discover *convictions* by taking note of how people's daily lives actually go. Furthermore, the definition assumes that convictions, once discovered, *require* revision because (as we may normally expect) they fall short of full authenticity, and fall short as well of full coherence with one another and with knowledge derived from other domains of intellectual endeavor. So, to repeat the point, the work of theology precisely *is* transformation; or more precisely still, *convictional* transformation. And if McClendon is right,[22] then his account of theology obviously does provide a leverage point for Adventists who are looking for community renewal.

Now consider "doctrine." Doctrine is "teaching," both the "thing taught" and the "practice" of doing the teaching.[23] This latter point is crucial. McClendon again and again considers what it is for something to be a "practice." Practices, he says, are complex social activities that "strive for some end beyond themselves," as when the practice of medicine embraces certain means and rules in order to foster health, not just achieve competence in diagnosis or drug prescription or surgical execution.[24] Christian doctrine is likewise an activity meant to be not an end in itself but a means to a higher end. McClendon assumes the notion of "practice" and pinpoints that higher end when he writes: Christian doctrine is "*a church teaching as she must teach if she is to be the church here and now* (emphasis his)."[25] Doctrine "constitutes communal existence";[26] ideally, genuine – as opposed to distorted – communal existence. Even Jesus' own teaching was not an end in itself. He "*summoned followers*" to enroll "*as students in his school*, where he led out in

---

20 McClendon, *Ethics*, vol. 1, 22–23.
21 Ibid.
22 For biblical perspective on human sin and self-deception, consider, e.g., Jer 17:9; for biblical perspective on human finitude, consider Isa 55:8–9 and 1 Cor 13:9, 12.
23 McClendon, *Doctrine*, vol. 2, 23, 29.
24 Ibid., 28.
25 Ibid., 24.
26 Ibid.

"*learn-by-doing ..., life-changing dialogue.*"[27] The school was not the point. The point was "*transforming discipleship* (emphasis his)."[28]

There is much talk in Adventism of the church's "message," or of its doctrinal distinctiveness. A disturbing amount of energy goes into quarreling over doctrinal niceties, and with this comes the danger of lapsing into obsessions that minimize or even eclipse the *point* of doctrine. Authentic followers of Christ cannot have "words" for a mission; they cannot shrink "evangelism" or the Gospel Commission into the mere promulgation of religious theory. The practice of teaching *serves* discipleship. Here again, then, McClendon offers crucial leverage for transformation in Adventism. Proper doctrine is undergirding for a particular kind of *life*. If there is a proper distinctiveness, it is, most importantly, a distinctiveness of *living*.

Teaching, or what McClendon calls the practice of doctrine, is for everyone. All members of the church, not just theologians, teach – by their living and by their sharing of Christian perspective in formal or informal settings. Doctrine as teaching is doctrine's "first-order task."[29] Doctrinal *theology*, on the other hand, takes up doctrine's "second-order" task, which is that of investigating and seeking to assist the church in the everyday teaching that is doctrine's first-order task.[30] Again, the business of theology is transformation. But now, thanks to the analysis of doctrine, theology's true end has become clearer: It is not better statements of belief; it is better lives. This emphasis provides another leverage point for the transformation of Adventism.

The theologian puts a question to the church: Your present convictions appear to be such and such; would it not be better, and for these reasons, to revise those convictions *thus*?[31] But how should the church respond? When reasons are offered, what counts toward the conclusion that they are good reasons?

Here we may return to key aspects of Anabaptist aspiration. McClendon's analysis, as we saw, casts a spotlight on biblicism, liberty, discipleship, community, and mission. The first of these, it turns out, is basic, is underpinning for the others. But here biblicism is not just high regard for Scripture; it is a particular kind of regard. The Bible is at once God's story and ours, each story "fully present" in the parts of the "indivisible" whole.[32] As such, it functions as "the doctrinal manual of the teaching church."[33] And just as the point of Jesus' teaching was discipleship, so is the point when Christians read the Bible. The book of Matthew, for example, tells about how, in the Galilean past, Jesus made a call to discipleship and explained its substance; decades later, the book's first readers took Matthew's message as a call to

27  Ibid., 32.
28  Ibid.
29  Ibid., 24.
30  Ibid., 34.
31  Ibid., 47.
32  Ibid., 476.
33  Ibid., 35.

*them*,[34] not just to their Lord's first followers. Nor was this way of reading new; it matched that of readers who had earlier immersed themselves in, for example, the book Deuteronomy – long after that book's story had taken place. The sixth chapter's instruction to parents to tell their children, "'We were Pharaoh's slaves,'" was instruction for these readers themselves, in their own here and now; it was not just a record about the past.[35] And it was the same when, according to the book of Acts, Peter broke into his Pentecostal homily. Listeners, struck by the disciples' strange abilities and enthusiasms, wonder if they might be drunk. Peter responds by saying that "*this is that* which was spoken by the prophet Joel," who had declared that in the "last days" God's spirit would pour out "upon all flesh," with sons and daughters prophesying, young men seeing visions, old men dreaming dreams, even male and female servants prophesying.[36]

*This is that* – this is that which was spoken by the prophet Joel. McClendon seizes upon this phrase, and makes it decisive. In the Bible, what happened in the past interprets what is going on today; the story addresses disciples now.

But there is one more thing. The Bible story points to a final end or goal. The approaching order, what will come into full blossom with the Second Coming, is one of "interactive love" – God loving humanity and humanity returning the love.[37] And, as always for McClendon, you must grasp the *story* in order to grasp the concept; you must recall how Jesus loved even his enemies, and ponder his death and resurrection. Through this latter event, God has made Jesus the definitive window on the nature of true love. Love is the character of Jesus, and his character is "the measure of human conduct."[38] As we might say in eschatological language, Jesus *lasts* – he is the final victor. It is no longer the conquering warlord who defines human excellence, but Jesus himself, the Lamb of God. As the picture of heavenly worship in Revelation 5 makes clear, the Lamb, still standing though once slain, is now the "master picture" by which we "learn to see" the truth about humanity.[39]

One way to summarize the proper Bible-reading strategy is to say: *this is that*; to say that we properly interpret the present by way of the past described in Scripture. But it is also important to say: *then is now*; to say that we properly interpret the present by way of the future described in Scripture. And if *this is that* is decisive, *then is now*, it turns out, is ultimately decisive. The way of life that suits the age to come *determines* what is right for the here and now. If the Bible is "God's Book, God's word to us," it is at the same time "a fully human story, human in its breadth and depth; human, too, in its foibles and failings."[40] So we

---

34 McClendon, *Ethics*, vol. 1, 217.
35 McClendon, *Doctrine*, vol. 2, 46.
36 McClendon, *Ethics*, vol. 1, 31–33. See Acts 2:16–18, KJV, quoting from Joel 2 (emphasis added).
37 McClendon, *Doctrine*, vol. 2, 67.
38 Ibid., 80.
39 Ibid., 96–101.
40 Ibid., 476.

must read it with a view to *where it goes*; the *then* guaranteed by the resurrection and arriving in fullness at the Second Coming elevates Christ, makes Christ the Bible's interpretive key. If we find anywhere in Scripture openness, say, to slavery or retributive violence, we need not stumble over that, and must not seize upon it to justify behavior or policy that conflicts with the measure of human conduct embodied in Christ. After all, and to invoke again the sentence earlier proposed as a summary of McClendon's thought, "Christianity is Christ." Scripture is our story, but "loyalty to Scripture" must "not compete with loyalty to Jesus Christ."[41]

We know enough now to make sense of the phrases McClendon uses to name the Anabaptist Bible-reading strategy. He calls it the "baptist vision," meaning by the small *b* to include all the heirs of the Radical Reformation, not just those in (large *b*) Baptist denominations. He also calls it "the prophetic vision," a phrase with special resonance for those who, like Adventists and the author of the Bible's last book, identify the "testimony of Jesus" with the "spirit" of the prophets.[42] The biblical prophets, as McClendon repeatedly suggests, do not just tell tales about the past or make predictions about the future; they *interpret the present*.[43] Consumed by what Martin Luther King famously called "the fierce urgency of Now,"[44] they construe what is going *today* – using eyes and ears formed by the long story that begins in the past and stretches to the ultimate future. King did this himself, and, as is worth noting, he thereby started a nation on its turn from racial lethargy.[45]

We have already identified two leverage points for the transformation of Adventism. One is McClendon's corrective, or transformational, understanding of theology. Another is his practical, or life-focused, understanding of doctrine. Now we may identify two more. One is that above all other authorities – individual, institutional, or written – God in Christ must be the criterion for doctrinal change. The second is that such change must address the "fierce urgency of Now." The temptation to treat the present as a parenthesis – a kind of bus stop where little happens but the waiting – threatens always to disable discipleship and turn hope into a rationale for withdrawal and escapism. But not if McClendon is our teacher.

As we have seen, Anabaptism espouses biblicism, liberty, discipleship, community and mission. These foci have shaped a Radical Reformation way of life that echoes and yet also differs from that of the Magisterial Reformation. Among its striking features is suspicion of violence-prone political power and refusal to align the church with the state. Just here we may consider a story McClendon tells – about Adventism. Late in life, while he is interim pastor for a Church of the Brethren congregation in Pasadena, CA, he is preaching a sermon on the book of

41  Ibid., 463.
42  I allude, of course, to Rev 12:17 and 19:10, both signature passages, as we might put it, for Adventist self-understanding.
43  Here consult, e.g., the following pages from McClendon, *Doctrine*, 69, 72, 234, 479.
44  From King's "I Have a Dream" speech, widely available in anthologies and on websites.
45  See again the "I Have a Dream Speech," and see also McClendon, *Biography as Theology*, 65–85.

Revelation as a clue to history's meaning. Revelation questions, he says, the notion that history's key players are the well-armed high and mighty, and defends the relevance of Jesus and of his sometimes-martyred followers. Then, as a kind of theology by example that recalls his *Biography as Theology*, McClendon tells the congregation about Adventists in Sarajevo who responded to conflict among Serbs, Croats and Muslims. They organized an informal postal system for delivering much-needed packages past the Serb-controlled outskirts of the city into its most isolated sectors. A newspaper reporter asked Milan Suslic, their leader, how Adventists could sustain the necessary cooperation and good will, and he replied that they were "'not part of any nationality or any side in the war … We are nobody's and everybody's.'"[46]

McClendon took this to be illuminating for his own congregation, as an example of Radical Reformation faithfulness. It was another evidence of his belief that the Seventh-day Adventist Church belongs to the community for which he was writing, and it underscores the question that I am raising here: Can we, on our own journey, embrace such leverage points toward transformation as this Neo-Anabaptist theologian has to offer? Are we open to the kind of Bible-centered self-criticism that he proposes?

If the answer is Yes, we may be about that very work. If it is No, we need to be clear about why it is No.

---

46 See "Apocalypse: A Christian View of History," in James Wm. McClendon, Jr., eds. Ryan Andrew Newson and Andrew C. Wright, *The Collected Works of James Wm. McClendon, Jr.*, vol. 3 (Waco, TX: Baylor University Press, 2016), 233–239.

# PART III

# THE IMPACT OF THE REFORMATION ON SEVENTH-DAY ADVENTISM

*Woodrow W. Whidden*

# The Groundbreaking General Conference of 1888: What Kind of Reformation Experience Was It About?

Abstract

The key thesis of this essay is that Ellen and James White were the key definers of the "triumph" of what can be called sixteenth-century Protestant Reformation emphases in Seventh-day Adventist soteriology, atonement theology, and Christology, not A. T. Jones and E. J. Waggoner. The latter two figures made a good start, but then descended into false views on the atonement, very subjective views of justification and extreme holiness concepts. And ultimately, both Jones and Waggoner were caught up in ethical scandal and false views on ecclesiology. For the Whites, the Protestant *solae* emerged as their predominant, shaping theological themes.

The phrase, "Minneapolis, 1888 and Righteousness by Faith" is one of the most legendary in Seventh-day Adventist history. Though the phrase has been haunted by decades of controversy and misunderstanding (based on a lot of facile assumptions), the issues involved in this historical "passage" and the debates which have swirled around it are certainly worthy of any effort to gain better perspective. This essay will not attempt a thorough review but will mainly focus on 1) *what* the historical event of 1888, its background and theological implications meant to Ellen White and to subsequent Adventist theological/spiritual development and 2) *how* these factors inform Adventism's indebtedness to its sixteenth-century Protestant Reformation heritage. Maybe it could be put this way: for White and her movement, what was the Protestant theological significance of 1888 and Minneapolis?

## Why Is Ellen White so Central?

As pointed out in another essay,[1] the "1888 experience" of Seventh-day Adventism was largely the fruitful result of the "vision" of Ellen G. White and her husband, James White, and not primarily the work of A. T. Jones and E. J. Waggoner. Clearly she saw Jones and Waggoner as key "messengers" of the important themes that were being highlighted during the late 1880s and the early 1890s. But she never ceded to them any sort of inspired "canonical" authority to define the theological

1  Woodrow W. Whidden, "The Definitive Interpreter of Minneapolis 1888," in *Adventist Maverick: A Celebration of George R. Knight's Contribution to Adventist Thought*, eds. Gilbert M. Valentine and Woodrow W. Whidden II (Nampa, ID: Pacific Press, 2014), 123–132.

meaning of the revival themes related to the "Christ and His righteousness" renewal. We have been largely indebted to Ellen White to convey to us the meaning of the 1888 phenomenon – including its troubling background, controverted aftermath and perceived theological legacy. In the light of such claims, further explanation is in order.

First of all, there would have been no 1888 and Minneapolis experience if it had not been for the initial theological and pastoral burdens of James White; but ultimately and most importantly, the "testimonies" of his aroused wife, Ellen White, became decisive. And furthermore, there is another sad fact of Adventist history: no matter how significant the contributions of Jones and Waggoner were, both at Minneapolis and in its aftermath, they both eventually fell into theological decline (ultimately, apostasy) and ethical/spiritual compromise. Thus, whatever their initial positive contributions were, their eventual, steady decline cries out for interpretation from the more authoritative and faithful Ellen White. There has to be some differentiation between the earlier, helpful teachings of Jones and Waggoner and important facets of their steadily unfolding false theology. As will be noted, this theological/ethical compromise would become most pronounced in the case of E. J. Waggoner. We will return to these issues, but first we need to briefly review the background for the rise of the 1888 phenomena.

## Historical Setting[2]

During the late 1870s both James and Ellen White had begun to sense that Adventism was moving into a state of theological and spiritual drift, even a dangerous misdirection. Most certainly Adventism had, by this time, experienced a number of positive advances: 1) it had largely defined its "present truth," or distinctively Adventist teachings, and 2) developed a growing institutional and organizational framework to support its expanding outreach in both North America and the beginnings of an international mission. But it still had not yet fully grasped the core of its broader Christian and Protestant heritage, especially when it came to the Trinity, the Holy Spirit, and the person and work of Christ as Savior and Lord. Emblematic of such theological deficits (and recovery possibilities) were "The Way of Life" prints which James White had been developing from 1873 to 1881.

The main significance of the changes in this succession of illustrative prints was not so much artistic, but theological. The marked change from the artistic prominence of the Ten Commandments (the law) to that of Christ on the cross reflected the concerns of both James and Ellen White that the Adventist message needed to be refocused in a more Christ-centered manner. Ellen White clearly sensed that

---

2   What follows is an overview that is largely drawn from my biography of E. J. Waggoner, entitled *E. J. Waggoner: From Physician of Good News to Agent of Division* (Hagerstown, MD: Review and Herald, 2008), 88–138, and my article, "Christ, The Way of Life Prints," in *The Ellen G. White Encyclopedia,* eds. Denis Fortin and Jerry Moon, (Hagerstown, MD: Review and Herald, 2013), 698–699.

there was widespread legalism, a lack of Christian piety and any genuine assurance of salvation. Speaking to the students at the General Conference Bible School in early 1890, she told of vows taken at her husband's deathbed to bring "an element [into] this work that we have not had yet."[3] Most certainly that "element" was a need to refocus on Christ and the central importance of His redeeming grace.[4]

It was during this period, following the death of James White, in 1881, that Ellen White commenced a more sustained emphasis on the primacy of Christ and His righteousness – a focus which comprehended converting, forgiving and transforming grace. Beginning with her public presentations at the 1883 Battle Creek General Conference session (afterward widely published in major Seventh-day Adventist periodicals in 1884), there would be a growing accent on justifying grace that featured her presentations which followed the Minneapolis General Conference of 1888, especially during the years from 1889 to 1893.

## What Did 1888 Mean to Ellen White?

Probably the most succinctly comprehensive statement that Ellen White would ever make about the meaning of Minneapolis, its theological and spiritual significance, and aftermath, is found in *Testimonies to Ministers and Gospel Workers*.

> The Lord in His great mercy sent a most precious message to His people through Elders Waggoner and Jones. This message was to bring more prominently before the world the uplifted Saviour, the sacrifice for the sins of the whole world. It presented justification through faith in the Surety; it invited the people to receive the righteousness of Christ, which is made manifest in obedience to all the commandments of God. Many had lost sight of Jesus. They needed to have their eyes directed to His divine person, His merits, and His changeless love for the human family. All power is given into His hands, that He may dispense rich gifts unto men, imparting the priceless gift of His own righteousness to the helpless human agent. This is the message that God commanded to be given to the world. It is the third angel's message, which is to be proclaimed with a loud voice, and attended with the outpouring of His Spirit in a large measure.[5]

This commentary was then augmented with such phrases as: "the uplifted Saviour" is to "appear in His efficacious work as the Lamb slain," dispensing "priceless

---

3 Cited from MS 9, 1890 in the *1888 Materials*, 540.
4 This Christ-centered emphasis was not anything new or novel to Ellen White, as she had for many years (at least since the 1850s) spoken of the "Matchless Charms of Christ." Cf. Peter M. van Bemmelen, "'The Matchless Charms of Christ': Theological Significance of This Phrase in Ellen White's Writings," in *Christ, Salvation, and the Eschaton: Essays in Honor of Hans K. LaRondelle*, eds. Daniel Heinz, Jiri Moskala, and Peter M. van Bemmelen (Berrien Springs, MI: Old Testament Department, Seventh-day Adventist Theological Seminary, 2009), 231–240.
5 Ellen G. White, *Testimonies to Ministers and Gospel Workers* (Nampa, ID: Pacific Press, 1923/1944/1962), 91–92. This statement is found in a letter to General Conference President, O. A. Olson, dated May 1, 1895.

covenant blessings, the benefits He died to purchase every soul who should believe on Him ... Christ is pleading for the church in the heavenly courts above, pleading for those for whom He paid the redemption price of His own lifeblood." White then continued on that this "message of the gospel of His grace was to be given to the church in clear and distinct lines, that the world should no longer say that Seventh-day Adventists talk the law, the law, but do not teach or believe Christ." She then concluded by speaking of the "efficacy of the blood of Christ [that] was to be presented to the people with freshness and power, that their faith might lay hold upon its merits"[6] – all presented in the setting of Christ's work as the believers' Intercessor, in His office as their "high priest," ministering His "blood" in the heavenly sanctuary.[7] In other words, the uplifted Christ was to be seen as both the sacrificial victim and the interceding High Priest in heaven, not just as soon coming Judge and ruling King.

What is to be made of this fervent theological presentation? Without a doubt, Ellen White was clearly accenting the importance of uplifting the person of Christ and His work of intercession, a vital work that would communicate the benefits of salvation through the ministry of the Holy Spirit and Christ's advocacy with the Father in the heavenly sanctuary – all to be carried out in conjunction with the proclamation of the distinctive doctrines of Adventist "present truth" teachings.

So what is it that is more distinctly Christian and Protestant in all of this emphasis? Maybe, for our purposes, the question could be rephrased this way: What were the key Protestant *solae* that were being set forth by the aroused Ellen White?

It appears that the primacy of *solus Christus* was leading the way to an aroused sense of the importance of experiencing the Trinitarian power of *sola gratia* and *sola fide*. Most certainly Seventh-day Adventists, with their strongly biblicist and Millerite background, did not need to be exhorted to renew their dedication to *sola scriptura*. Their intense work on the biblical basis for "present truth" had sealed them to their Bibles. But it was also quite apparent that they had somehow missed other important components of the biblical revelation of truth – especially the truths of the Trinity (including the full, eternal deity of Christ and the personhood of the Holy Spirit), and salvation by grace alone, through faith alone.

Maybe the case could be set forth this way: in pointing to the person and work of Christ, the Whites, especially Ellen, were reaping the benefits of not only a growing Trinitarian consciousness, but also of the love of the Holy Trinity (as a "Heavenly Trio") that was unfolding the winsomeness of the saving grace of Christ, not just as soon coming Lord and Judge, but as the merciful Jesus who is Lord of eternal salvation. Stated negatively, Adventist evangelists and writers had become so obsessed with biblical polemics in their defense of "present truth" that they had obscured the "eternal verities," especially the truths related to Christ and personal salvation from sin – via *sola fide and sola gratia*.

6   Ibid., 92.
7   Ibid.

So can it be said that the whole movement, from the late 1870s up to, and through the 1890s, clearly produced an Ellen White inspired, biblically supported understanding of justification by faith alone, through grace alone? Initially, let us simply address the "faith alone" witness of Ellen White. First of all, one only needs to re-read the previously cited passage from *Testimonies to Ministers,* where White says that "the most precious message" of 1888 "presented justification through faith in the Surety."[8] She then set forth the responsible grace qualifier, that when any true believer receives justifying grace, "the righteousness of Christ," it will be "made manifest in obedience to all the commandments of God."[9]

Carefully ponder the following: We begin with the compilation entitled *Faith and Works*[10] and the first selection entitled "Ellen White Clarifies the Issues."[11] Speaking of the "utter worthlessness of creature merit to earn the wages of eternal life," she went on to declare that "if you would gather together everything that is good and holy and noble and lovely in man and then present the subject to the angels of God as acting a part in the salvation of the human soul or in merit, the proposition would be rejected as treason."[12]

Furthermore, one does not need to go much further than the important compilation released in 1958, entitled *Selected Messages, Book 1* (Washington, DC: Review and Herald, 1958) and reflectively scan pages 300 to 400. In these revealing pages are found a group of statements which witness to a strong view of forensic justification by faith alone, including page 344 where Ellen White, in a clearly Trinitarian setting, speaks about "Christ, our Mediator, and the Holy Spirit," who are both "constantly interceding in man's behalf." She then clearly says that all the spiritual "fruit" of grace which "ascend from true believers" needs a special cleansing work by Christ in His role as Intercessor in heaven:

> They ascend not in spotless purity, and unless the Intercessor, who is at God's right hand, presents and purifies all by His righteousness, it is not acceptable with God. All incense from earthly tabernacles must be moist with the cleansing drops of the blood of Christ. He holds before the Father the censer of His own merits, in which there is no taint of earthly corruption ... Then perfumed with the merits of Christ's propitiation, the incense comes up before God, wholly and entirely acceptable ... Oh, that all may see that everything in obedience, in penitence, in praise and thanksgiving, must be placed upon the glowing fire of the righteousness of Christ.[13]

8   Ibid., 91ff.
9   Ibid., 92.
10  Ellen G. White, *Faith and Works: Sermons and Articles* (Nashville, TN: Southern Publ. Assn., 1979).
11  Originally listed as "Untitled Manuscript 36, 1890" and first published in the *Review and Herald,* February 24 and March 3, 1977.
12  Ibid.
13  Ellen G. White, *Selected Messages,* vol. 1 (Washington, DC: Review and Herald, 1958), 344.

We could go on citing statement after statement to reinforce this point of the primacy of justifying grace. But the key point to be made here is that, in this intercessory setting where the Trinity is active in behalf of God's faithful and loyal children, the primacy of justification by faith alone is abundantly on display. Such an experience, however, for any "true believer" will always bear the fruit of sanctifying grace. For White, "righteousness by faith" is always presented as justification by grace through faith alone, but the genuine faith that saves will never be "alone."

Not only was this notable revival of emphasis on grace and faith alone on display throughout the rest of her career (from the late 1880s and onward) in numerous published statements, but White would also embark on what became known as the "Life of Christ" project. This effort would become one of her key missions during the Australian years and would eventuate in the publication of *Thoughts From the Mount of Blessing* (1896, a commentary on the Sermon on the Mount and the Lord's Prayer), *Christ's Object Lessons* (1900, comments on the parables of Jesus), and then the release of the culmination of the "project," *The Desire of Ages* (1898).

It would be in this last publication that not only would her views on *sola fide, sola gratia* and *solus Christus* come to mature expression, but that she would also present the apex of her thought on the atoning death of Christ. When it comes to any classic expression of the doctrine of the atonement, the "Passion" chapters of *The Desire of Ages* (especially the chapters entitled "Calvary" [chap. 78] and "It is Finished" [chap. 79]) are prime exhibits of her firmly expressed convictions, unmistakably stated in terms of penalty, substitution and satisfaction. It is here suggested that with these atoning perspectives, the foundation had been laid for a forceful doctrine of justification by grace through faith alone. To put it in a bit of a different key, note the following: To deny the classic perspectives inherent in the models based on the images of penalty, substitution and satisfaction, would simply make the testimony of White descend into a bewildering theological incoherence.

So what can we say about Ellen White, 1888, and the Magisterial Reformers of the sixteenth century? It seems quite clear that not only is Ellen White the key exponent of what the theological meaning of 1888 should be for Seventh-day Adventists, but that her interpretation is basically in line with the soteriological consensus of Luther, Calvin and Melanchthon on the four great *solae – Christus, gratia, fide and scriptura* that were manifested in the sixteenth-century Protestant Reformation.

Once more, it is simply remarkable that Ellen White could emerge from her background of Wesleyan perfectionism, anti-Trinitarian influences and the Christless, law-centered, polemical and rationalistic theology of pre-1888 Adventism and yet manifest a theological exposition that was so Bible-based, Christ-centered, and grace-inspired – especially as manifested in her views on the atonement and applied soteriology (how sinners experience conversion, forgiveness, and growth in grace).

Thus it must be asked: Is it going too far to say that she was in essential agreement with the best expressions of the four sixteenth-century Magisterial Protestant *solae*? The answer here suggested is that she was indeed in essential agreement with these classic Protestant perspectives.

## What about Jones and Waggoner?

Can it truly be said that A. T. Jones and E. J. Waggoner were as reliably "Protestant" as Ellen G. White? The answer is a firm "Not so!" What follows is at the core of this negative claim.

While Ellen White did give strong support to these earnest and hard-working brothers in the Minneapolis (1888) revival of "Christ and His righteousness," they did eventually lose their way, both theologically and ethically. This is not to deny that they had made helpful, even path-breaking contributions to the whole "righteousness by faith" revival (from the late 1880s and on up to the early years of the twentieth century). But by 1893 they were both on a trajectory that would lead to their ultimate apostasy from the ministerial ranks and membership of the Seventh-day Adventist Church. The heart of their departures was based on theological confusion. Time and space do not permit an expansive tracing of these trajectories, but we can offer a few representative exhibits as to what were the core causes of their lapse into apostasy.

For Jones, the doctrinal aberrancy was not quite as theologically blatant as that of Waggoner. While Jones did reach Trinitarian clarity, Waggoner never really did. While Jones could talk a lot about justification by faith alone, he became so obsessed with "holiness," perfectionist themes and the so-called "post-fall" view of the humanity of Christ that he would essentially become a "holiness" Sabbatarian. For a more updated assessment of Jones' theological decline, turn to the latest edition of George Knight's biography entitled *Alonzo T. Jones: Point Man on Adventism's Charismatic Frontier* (Hagerstown, MD: Review and Herald, 2011), especially Chapters V ("The Meaning of Minneapolis") and XI ("The Nature of Christ: Seeds for the Twentieth-Century Replay of the Galatians Controversy"). There was simply not a lot that was of *sola fide* substance in Jones' soteriology.

With regards to the trajectory of E. J. Waggoner,[14] it is clear that he finally came to the point where it would be almost impossible to affirm that he had attained any truly clear teaching on *sola fide*, at least in any sense of a real affinity with the Magisterial Protestant view of justification by grace through faith alone. And this was most likely based on his almost complete rejection of any perspectives on the atonement that affirmed the basic conceptions of the penalty, substitution and satisfaction models of the atoning work of Christ. By 1893, he had pretty much embraced an essentially "subjective" view of the atonement that was tinged with "mystical" overtones. For him, the panentheistic Christ, through the mystical, alleged internal workings of the Holy Spirit, so effectively makes the believer righteous and just before God, that God can then declare the believer to be justified because of a righteousness that has been manifested as the fruit of sanctifying grace. An apt sample or two of this sort of interpretive strategy will illustrate the point.

---

14 What follows is selectively drawn from my biography of Waggoner, especially from chapter XI entitled "The Theological Divide Clarifies," 261–312.

## Waggoner on Justification

As Waggoner's thought unfolded during the years 1892 and 1893, there was a noticeable shift to a concept that featured being "made righteous," which involved more than the inevitable *fruit* of the genuine *root* of a "faith that works." Waggoner had obviously evolved to a subjective understanding of justification in which faith subjectively produces a righteousness that makes the believer actually just before God. Thus the just demands of God's righteousness are met in the victorious, obedient lives of the faithful believers. This process was placed by Waggoner in the context of an increasing accent on the work of the subjectively indwelling, mystical Christ.

When these emerging, "mystical" views of the atonement were put into the context of the subjective theme of the internal and immanent Christ who abides in the heart of any repentant soul, the stage was set for a version of "effective justification" that has the same, essential sense and scent of the Roman Catholic Council of Trent and the subjective justification views of the post-Reformation Lutheran scholar, Andreas Osiander.[15] While the views expressed in these similar teachings took some subtly different twists and turns, they all essentially ended up at the same place: the alleged, subjectively infused righteousness of Christ makes the believer righteous so that he is justified by the fruits of a transforming, internal work of grace. The *fruit* of sanctification forms the *root* basis for God's act of justification, not vice versa.

While there would be some seeming glimmers of forensic imputation from time to time in the thought of Waggoner during the 1892–1916 period, these expressions are best understood to be the results of the work of the immanent, indwelling Christ, via the ministration of His shed blood. This alleged mystical communication of Christ's blood effectively absorbs the guilt of sin and delivers from the power of sinful impulses. As a result of the working of the immanent, internally indwelling Christ, the believer is declared just and righteous for Christ's sake.

Using a literalistic method of biblical interpretation, which also often failed to take the varied literary contexts and genres into proper consideration, Waggoner would expound numerous passages (especially from the gospels and the epistles of the New Testament) to support his very subjective version of justification by faith. The following examples are quite representative of his hermeneutic which displays a virtually automatic or robotic effecting of Christ's justifying merits in the believer. This was a process that exhibited little evidence of Christ ministering the merits of His righteousness to the individual accounts of the believers in the heavenly sanctuary as an advocate before the Father. Everything was conceived as taking place in the heart or soul of the passively trusting, responsive, and yielding believer.

15  For helpful explanations of the Roman Catholic Council of Trent, the 16th-century Protestant Reformers and the thought of Andreas Osiander, see Alister E. McGrath, "The Doctrine of Justification by Faith," *Reformation Thought: An Introduction,* 3rd ed. (Oxford: Blackwell Publishers, 1999), 101–131, and Justo L. González, *A History of Christian Thought: From the Protestant Reformation to the Twentieth Century,* rev. ed., vol. 3 (Nashville, TN: Abingdon, 1975), 114–118, 150–151, 155, and 275.

Citing Romans 5:1, Waggoner asks: "What does this mean? What is it to be justified?" He points out that many think "it is a sort of halfway house to perfect favour with God," while others think "that it is a substitute for real righteousness. They think that the idea of justification by faith is that if one will only believe what the Bible says, he is to be counted as righteous when he is not. All this is a great mistake." Next he followed up with his usual definition of justification as "making just" or "to be righteous ... since the just man is the one who does the law, it follows that to justify a man, that is, to make him just, is to make him a doer of the law. Being justified by faith, then, is simply being made a doer of the law by faith."[16]

In order to leave no doubt as to his meaning, he then proceeds to claim that justification "does not mean that Christ's righteousness which He did eighteen hundred years ago is laid up for the sinner, to be simply credited to his account, but it means that His present, active righteousness is given to that man." And how is such righteousness given to the believer? "Christ comes to live in that man who believes, for he dwells in the heart by faith. So the man who was a sinner is transformed into a new man, having the very righteousness of God."[17]

In the very next paragraph, the claim is made "that there can be no higher state than that of justification. It does everything that God can do for a man short of making him immortal, which is done only at the resurrection."[18]

Thus in one fell swoop, Waggoner argued that justification completely encompasses sanctification and perfection of character, not just the settling of legal accounts. To really make the point unmistakably clear (that justification is the result of the working of the indwelling Christ), Waggoner concludes that the "one who obeys is the Lord Jesus Christ, and His obedience is done in the heart of everyone who believes. And as it is by His obedience alone that men are made doers of the law, so to Him shall be the glory forever and ever."[19]

This important article was the most comprehensive statement that Waggoner would ever offer on the subject of effective justification. But there were others, even ones that seemed tinged with his almost universalistic view which claims that Christ indwells even unconverted sinners.

> To believe that He [Christ] is the Son of God means to believe that He is come in the flesh, in human flesh, in our flesh, for His name is "God with us"; so to believe on His name means simply to believe that He dwells personally in every man – in all flesh. We do not make it so by believing it; it is so, whether we believe it or not; we simply accept the fact, which all nature reveals to us.[20]

16 E. J. Waggoner, "Being Justified," *Present Truth*, October 20, 1892, cited in Whidden, *E. J. Waggoner*, 294.
17 Ibid.
18 Ibid.
19 Ibid.
20 E. J. Waggoner, "The Epistle to the Galatians. 'Justified by the Faith of Christ'," *The Present Truth*, February 10, 1898, cited in Whidden, *E. J. Waggoner*, 295.

This came very close to suggesting that Christ even dwells in unbelievers and that His indwelling will be redemptively efficacious, even if unbelievers will not believe. But he then went on to claim that the indwelling Christ is the justifier:

> It follows then as a matter of course that, believing in Christ, we are justified by the faith of Christ, since we have Him personally dwelling in us, exercising His own faith. All power in heaven and earth is in His hands, and, recognizing this, we simply allow Him to exercise His own power in His own way ... The Gospel is no dead thing, no abstract doctrine, no "works done in righteousness."[21]

> "By the obedience of One shall many be made righteous." Rom. v. 19. Notice that it is not simply that by the obedience of One we are accounted righteous, but that it is by Christ's obedience that we are actually *made righteous*. His obedience is not a substitute for our disobedience, but it is actually our righteousness. Oneness with Christ is the Christian Standard ... He set the example when He was on earth, and now He comes to walk over the same road in us.[22]

Clearly, justification by faith was conceived by Waggoner as accomplished through the indwelling Christ. It is Christ who transforms the character of the believer so that it is made righteous enough to be declared as the means of justification via the subjectively produced righteousness of Christ. Furthermore, there is the constant downgrading of any elements of accounting or reckoning which were caricatured as "abstract" righteousness.

While there is a false and "abstract" notion of justification by faith alone, there is also a true, effective forensic version of it. Waggoner just never seemed to be able to grasp the powerful biblical notion of effective, forensic justification (received by faith) which truly and objectively declares the believer to be just for Christ's sake, based on the objective accounting of what He had done two thousand years ago.[23]

# Conclusion

It seems that when it comes to any truly *sola fide* convictions associated with 1888 and Minneapolis, we must rely upon the witness of Ellen G. White, not that of E. J. Waggoner and A. T. Jones. Led initially by Ellen White's and her husband's *sola Christus* and *sola scriptura* predilections, Seventh-day Adventism has been ultimately, yet gradually led to greater clarity on the primacy of both *sola gratia* and, ultimately *sola fide* in what has become an essentially Protestant soteriological pilgrimage.

---

21 Ibid.
22 E. J. Waggoner, "The Editor's Private Corner. 'As He walked'," *The Present Truth*, May 7, 1903, cited in Whidden, *E. J. Waggoner*, 296.
23 Whidden, *E. J. Waggoner*, 296.

*Johannes Hartlapp*

# Ludwig Richard Conradi's Understanding of Luther's Reformation

Abstract

Ludwig R. Conradi, with his numerous publications on the interpretation of biblical prophecy, has characterized the Adventist churches in Central and Eastern Europe for more than 40 years. He often mentions the Reformation of the sixteenth century. It is striking that his understanding of the Reformation differs significantly from the then dominant interpretations of the Reformation in Germany. Conradi viewed the message of Luther and the other Reformers exclusively from the perspective of biblical prophecies of Daniel and Revelation, as well as from the Sabbath-observing perspective. He does not mention other essential and fundamental elements of the Reformation message, such as the core concepts of *sola gratia, sola fide* or *solus Christus*. This points to a very one-sided understanding of the Reformation.

Introduction

On March 26, 1856, a boy was born in Karlsruhe, Baden, who, by human standards, was dealt a bad lot. His mother Elisabeth, the daughter of a Catholic barber from Constance named Anton Conradi, delivered him into the world 225 kilometers away in Karlsruhe, so that her relatives would not know of her indiscretion. Little Ludwig was raised by foster parents. He never met his father. We do not know if he even knew who his father was. Until the age of 10, he frequently moved from one small town to the next. According to his own autobiographical account, he went to school alongside being tutored by a priest.[1] Perhaps this priest recognized the boy's exceptional giftedness early on. Without being granted the opportunity of attending high school, he began an apprenticeship as a cooper. At the age of 16, he fled at the spur of the moment to America. He later wrote that the apprenticeship was so rough that he could not endure it any longer. In a document of the district court in Constance, this assertion is complemented by a further argument. In it, his mother confessed, "Until now, I have kept the existence of this son secret from my siblings,

---

1 Further biographical information can be found in Daniel Heinz, *Ludwig Richard Conradi – Missionar, Evangelist und Organisator der Siebenten-Tags-Adventisten in Europa*, Adventistica 2 (Frankfurt: Peter Lang, 1998); Ludwig Richard Conradi, *The Impelling Force of Prophetic Truth* (London: Thynne and Daily Prayer 1935), v–xiii; Corliss Fitz Randolph, "Rev. Louis Richard Conradi, D. D. – A Biographical Sketch," Supplement to the *Sabbath Recorder* (Plainfield, NJ, March 4, 1940).

with whom I live. I believe that my consideration for my relationship to my family was the main impetus behind his emigration."[2] An unwanted son, without a father, kept secret from the rest of the family. We can imagine the tension in the life of this freshly turned 16-year-old who sought to escape all this by attempting to flee to the New World. One thing, however, needs to be kept in mind: Conradi, baptized and raised a Catholic, would have up to this point only heard negative things about Protestants, the Reformation, and Martin Luther.

## Questions to Be Explored

The early Adventist churches in Central and Eastern Europe indisputably had their foundational theological outlook shaped by Ludwig Richard Conradi. For about 45 years, from 1886 to 1931, he contributed extensively to the establishment of churches in Europe and other mission fields. His exceptional rhetorical and organizational talent exerted an unmistakable influence. This influence was complemented and strengthened by a plethora of literature. The German National Library lists about 60 entries under his name (translations not being included in this count). For example, the tract *Gottes untrügliche prophetische Weltuhr (God's Infallible Prophetic World Clock)* was published to the number of 690,000 copies, the book *Christi glorreiche Erscheinung (Christ's Glorious Appearing)* to the number of 650,000 copies, and even such a comprehensive work as *Der Seher von Patmos (The Seer of Patmos)* to the number of 76,000 copies.[3] In addition, he was responsible for a series of periodicals, such as the church publication *Zions-Wächter (Zion's Watchman)* and the mission-minded *Herold der Wahrheit (Herald of Truth)*. Publication volumes of well over 100,000 – for example of the so-called "Missionsherold" ("Mission Herald"), which contained reports on mission stations in Africa and other fields in the world – were by no means uncommon. In other words, Conradi formed and shaped the Adventist churches, and his writings exerted a long-lasting influence well after his death in 1939.

It is not uncommon within Adventist circles in Germany and elsewhere, for the opinion to be held that Conradi's unmistakable influence contributed to the establishment of an independent, heavily Lutheran-influenced Adventism in Europe, in contrast to the Adventist world church, whose roots lie in Calvinism/Puritanism. As a son of the land of the sixteenth-century Reformation, he is said to have shifted the emphases in the Advent faith, because he oriented himself more by Martin Luther than other Adventist leaders did.

Against the backdrop of these views, the following questions will be explored: How did Conradi understand Martin Luther's Reformation in Central Europe? To what extent can the influence of Luther's Reformation theology be detected in his

2   Staatsarchiv Freiburg, B 715/1 Nr. 4219.
3   "Some of my smaller publications reached a circulation of one million" (Conradi, *The Impelling Force*, xi).

literature? Since he had a hold on the "Adventist market for books" in Central and Eastern Europe, the rich body of his literary legacy is a good source for this investigation. Still, I will restrict myself to two essential works: *Das goldene Zeitalter* (1923, *The Golden Age*) and *The Impelling Force of Prophetic Truth* (1935).[4]

The main focus of these books is the interpretation of Daniel and Revelation, in connection with the investigation of further relevant questions concerning the imminent second coming of Jesus. In this context, the volume *Das goldene Zeitalter* offers a comprehensive presentation of world history and church history as it relates to the aspect of hope in God's new earth, from the beginning of the world until the present. Many historical accounts are contained in them that Conradi had already partially dealt with in other works. Twelve years later, he once again published a similar presentation of prophetic interpretation in reference to the expectation of the second coming throughout the various centuries up to the present. The sharp difference between these works lies in two aspects: On the one hand, in *Impelling Force*, he worked numerous additional historical witnesses into his presentation (mostly from English sources). On the other hand, in 1931/1932, after sharp disputations, he parted ways with his church and founded the first Seventh Day Baptist Church in Germany. From this perspective, it is interesting to see in what way the presentation changed after this conversion.

Before pursuing the central messages of both books concerning the Reformation, it is necessary to note several biographical details. This information is indispensable for an accurate assessment of his view of the Reformation.

## Conradi's Conversion and Early Mission Success

Upon arriving in America, the adolescent Ludwig eked out a living for several years by doing odd jobs. Under the circumstances, school education was unthinkable. Fortunately for him, in 1878, he came across an Adventist farmer in the state of Iowa, who led him to experience conversion and to become a Seventh-day Adventist. Conradi describes the incident thus:

> Soon the Word of God took deep root in my heart, and the history of the world, so wonderfully outlined in the prophetic word, arrested my attention, and readily convinced me that God Himself had spoken here indeed. Out in the woods, for the first time the Spirit of God taught me to stammer: 'Abba, Father!', and Jesus became most precious to my soul. Gladly did I forsake all; my mother disinherited me as far as the law allowed her to, but leaving *all* for my Saviour, I found all in Him.[5]

From then on, he began to study. During the day he worked hard in the fields, and at night he studied the Bible and history. It was soon made possible for him to enroll in a program at Battle Creek College, which at the time was the training

---

4  Ludwig Richard Conradi, *Das goldene Zeitalter* (Hamburg: Advent-Verlag, 1923).
5  Conradi, *Impelling Force*, v.

center for the American Adventist Church. He completed the four-year program in 18 months, while simultaneously working as a typesetter and printer. The program appears to have been exceptionally easy for him. His longing for knowledge was insatiable. From this point on, for the rest of his life, he pursued a wide range of historical studies. But what did he learn in Battle Creek? Even though the curriculum he was exposed to there is not known, he doubtlessly did receive an American view of history, and certainly not an evangelical-Lutheran view!

## First Literary Work

Conradi thereafter successfully worked as pastor and missionary to the German-speaking Mennonites, and founded several churches. He referred to himself as more than mere "soul-winner." He continued to study further alongside his work. The results of this research were first published in brochures, and then in his first large work: a translation, revision, and comprehensive expansion of Andrews' history of the Sabbath.[6] "But," he writes,

> My real life's study became more and more the sure Word of Divine Prophecy. After writing, during 1897–98, editorials on Daniel and Revelation in German, I finally wrote a large Commentary on each of these books in German, of which fourteen editions appeared; over 200,000 of each were circulated, thus having the largest circulation of any commentary in German on Prophecy ... I became convinced that the only way to do justice to the impelling power of prophetic truth would be to thoroughly study all the old commentaries on Daniel and Revelation in the leading languages. Weeks were spent in the great continental libraries and twice three months in the British Museum ... My great aim now was to ascertain the gradual development of prophetic fulfilment, century after century, ever since these books have been written. To my great surprise I found that, quickly after the actual fulfilment, some interpreter would certify to it, and it gradually became an accepted fact, certified as such by many subsequent writers ... Another important fact became very evident – the wonderful effect the interpretation of the prophetic word had in causing mighty movements, such as that of the Donatists, the Waldensians, the Lollards, the great Reformation itself, and finally the wonderful 'Missionary Century,' when Bible and Mission societies fulfilled Matt. 24:14.[7]

Thus were his field of scholarship, his general view of history, and his central themes well-defined: Conradi's primary theme was the prophetic Word and its interpretation of history. His secondary theme was the Sabbath in the Bible and history. Both

---

6   The exact title reads: *Die Geschichte des Sabbats und des ersten Wochentages im Lichte der heiligen Schrift und der Geschichte von der Erschaffung der Welt bis auf die Gegenwart [The History of the Sabbath and the First Day of the Week in Light of the Holy Scriptures and History from the Creation of the World Until the Present]* (Hamburg: Internationale Traktatgesellschaft 1912.) As a basis, Conradi used John Nevins Andrews, *History of the Sabbath and First Day of the Week* (Battle Creek, MI: Steam Press of the Seventh-day Adventist Publishing Association, 1873).
7   Conradi, *Impelling Force*, v–vi.

formed the backdrop for the imminent second coming, The Golden Age. This knowledge in turn motivated him to mission, to which he dedicated all his strength. Conradi understood himself to be a treasure seeker, who rediscovers long-lost hidden treasure through a combination of textual exegesis and historical research.

## Conradi's Central Ideas on the Reformation

Conradi's historical research proceeded along the lines of a methodological approach that was widespread up until the nineteenth century. He understood the seven letters in Revelation 2 and 3 to be a brilliant outline of church history in compact form. He allotted each of the seven letters to a specific era and pursued all the details of the Bible text in history. It was within this context that he viewed the developments in church history, including the sixteenth-century Reformation. As was just mentioned, he found support from an enormous body of sources, through which he systematically searched. Such an achievement as this is worthy of admiration to this day, especially when kept in mind that alongside this research, he filled organizational positions of responsibility, such as Vice President of the General Conference from 1903 to 1922, and President of the European Division from 1913 to 1922. He was almost continuously on the road, participating in conferences and mission trips, about which he reported in *Zions-Wächter*. His talent for optimizing the limited time available was far superior to that of most of his colleagues.

Conradi's examination of the Reformation is markedly different from that of Ellen White. She presents Luther as *the* man of the sixteenth century, who restored the Bible to its rightful place. In order to describe this, she uses three chapters in her most famous book, *The Great Controversy Between Christ and Satan*, filling over 50 pages (60 in German). For Conradi, who discussed the Reformation in approximately 100 pages in *Das goldene Zeitalter (The Golden Age)*, this decisive episode in the history of Christianity does not have enough material to fill a single chapter. It only comprises the second part of the fourth section of the book under the heading, "Das vermeintliche goldene Millennium kirchlicher Vorherrschaft" ("The Supposedly Golden Millennium of Church Supremacy"). Thus he views the epoch of the Reformation (presented in the letter to Sardis) as merely a section of the era of church supremacy. His praise for the Reformation is very limited:

> Since the church ignored the ever louder call to reform, the men who were called by God to bring reform needed to – though they did not wish to at first – make a final break with the corrupt papacy and build something new. From the deepest inner faith experience, the Reformation began its utmost important work of renewal, based on the pure doctrine of Scripture, emphasizing righteousness by faith as well as Christ's role as High Priest, and rejecting the papal claims to power as characteristic of Antichrist.[8]

---

8   Conradi, *Das goldene Zeitalter*, 353f. Original: "Da sie [die Kirche] dem immer lauter erschallenden Ruf nach Reform nicht Gehör schenkte, mußten die von Gott zur Reform

After this generalized, rather restrained praise, the criticism immediately follows:

> On the other hand, they accepted the validity of the Romanist infant baptism, took this same outward ceremony of consecration and accepted everyone into their communion from the cradle on, viewed this as constituting the required new birth, likewise established state churches encompassing the entire population in territories under their control, and persecuted all those who insisted that baptism only applies to true believers and that only these should constitute the true church of God. Luther seeks to justify the resultant perpetuation of the carnal state church, in the same manner as the papacy created it through infant baptism, through his classic statement, 'Where baptism and gospel are, no one should doubt that saints are there, including the infant in the cradle.'[9]

berufenen Männer, ohne es anfänglich zu wollen, schließlich mit dem verderbten Papsttum brechen und etwas Neues schaffen. Aus innerster Glaubenserfahrung begannen die Reformatoren ihr hochwichtiges Werk der Erneuerung, beriefen sich auf die reine Schriftlehre, betonten die Glaubensgerechtigkeit sowie Christi Hohepriestertum und verwarfen die päpstlichen Machtansprüche als antichristlich." In Conradi's first published interpretation of Revelation, *Der Seher von Patmos – Eine Betrachtung über das letzte Buch der Bibel [The Seer of Patmos: A Consideration of the Last Book of the Bible]* (Hamburg: Internationale Traktatgesellschaft, 1907), regarding the meaning of the letter to Sardis, he describes the Reformation quite critically, even with respect to *sola scriptura*, *sola gratia*, and *solus Christus*: "The Reformation gave everyone an open Bible as the only standard of faith, a crucified Savior as the only justification for believers, and a resurrected, glorified Savior as the only Head of His church. But the true doctrine was not made alive in these confessors through God's Spirit, but solidified into the consciousness of so-called orthodoxy." [Original: "Die Reformation gab wohl jedem eine offene Bibel als die einzige Richtschnur des Glaubens, einen gekreuzigten Heiland als die einzige Rechtfertigung des Gläubigen und einen auferstandenen, verklärten Heiland als das einzige Haupt seiner Gemeinde, aber die richtige Lehre wurde nicht durch den Geist Gottes lebendig in dessen Bekennern, sondern erstarrte in dem Bewußtsein der sogenannten Rechtgläubigkeit," (72).] Eleven years later, the expanded commentary on Revelation, *Prophetischer Ausblick auf Zeit und Ewigkeit [Prophetic Outlook on Time and Eternity]* (Hamburg: Internationale Traktatgesellschaft, 1918) contained no more positive assessment of the Reformation at the same point in the discussion. Nevertheless, there were laudable exceptions: "Praise God that under the dead masses, Sardis had a tiny collection of holy seed, small in comparison to the large lot, and yet itself superb. Where holy conduct and true doctrine were found together, justification by faith and sanctification by faith were found together, and the name of the heavenly church shined, whether they went by the name Moravian Brethren, High Church-goers, Anabaptists, Pietists, Huguenots, or Puritans." [Original: "Gottlob hat auch Sardes unter der toten Masse doch ein Häuflein heiligen Samens, wenig im Verhältnis zum großen Haufen und doch an sich stattlich. Wo sich heiliger Wandel und rechte Lehre paarten, Glaubens- und Lebensgerechtigkeit sich zusammenfanden, da leuchteten auch Namen der himmlischen Gemeinde, ob sie nun mährische Brüder, Kirchliche, Taufgesinnte, Pietisten, Kamisarden oder Puritaner hießen." (74). In both instances, he did not name any of the big Reformers.

9   Conradi, *Das goldene Zeitalter*, 354. Original: "Dagegen erkannten sie die Gültigkeit der römischen Kindertaufe an, nahmen durch dieselbe äußerlich Weihehandlung jedermann von der Wiege an in ihre Gemeinschaft auf, sahen darin die geforderte Wiedergeburt, schufen in

In the introductory overview, the critical comment continues that the Reformation church was much too reliant upon right doctrine, outward confession, and predestination, thus soon manifesting a "shortage of real born again experiences, of true conversions to a new life and to the absolutely necessary obedience of faith to the divine commandments that belongs to sanctification."[10] The critical reader already senses a clear distancing from the Reformation.

After his introductory comments, the author begins the description of Reformation history with the controversy surrounding indulgences as the cause of the Reformation. Here begins the struggle with Rome. And now Conradi feels completely in his element. In the previous chapters, he had already written about the apostasy of the church and amassed a slew of references, and here the same line of evidence stands unmitigated. The headings of the following paragraphs read, "Luthers und Melanchthons keimende Erkenntnis vom Endchrist und dessen Abfall" ("Luther's and Melanchthon's Growing Recognition of Antichrist and His Apostasy"); "Luthers 'Kriegstrompete': 'Endlich muss man die Geheimnisse des Antichrists enthüllen!'" ("Luther's 'War Trumpet': 'Finally, We Must Reveal the Secrets of Antichrist!'"); "Luthers 'Offenbarung des Endchrists aus dem Propheten Daniel'" ("Luther's 'Revelation of Antichrist from the Prophet Daniel'").

Conradi describes the progression of the Reformation from two perspectives. On the one hand, he amasses a slew of references that describe the antichristian character of the Roman Church and the pope as Antichrist. On the other hand, he presents evidence how the prophetic Word was interpreted in the time of the Reformation. Suddenly he has much praise to lavish on Luther. This praise is primarily the praise of Luther's contemporaries. Luther's appearance before the Diet of Worms in 1521 impressed the Swabian Augustinian Michael Stifel so much, that he composed an ode to the Reformer, in which he compares him with the angel of Revelation 14:6:

> Johannes tut uns schreiben von einem Engel klar,
> Der Gottes Wort soll treiben ganz luter offenbar.
> Sein Herz zu Gott er neyget recht als ein Christen Mann.
> Die Gschrift er rein abseyget, kein Wust laßt er daran.
> Zu Worms er sich erzeyget, er trat keck auf den Plan;

---

ihrem Machtbereich gleichfalls Staatskirchen des Volksganzen und verfolgten alle, die darauf bestanden, daß nur an wirklich Gläubigen die Taufe vollzogen werde und nur solche die wahren Gottesgemeinde bilden sollen. Die sich daraus ergebende Fortdauer der fleischlichen Volkskirche, wie das Papsttums sie durch die Kindertaufe geschaffen hatte, sucht Luther als rechte Kirche der Heiligen im Glauben durch seinen klassischen Ausspruch zu rechtfertigen: 'Wo die Tauf und Evangelium ist, da soll niemand zweifeln, es sein Heiligen da und solltens gleich eitel Kind in den Wiegen sein.'"

10   Ibid. Original: "der Mangel an wahrer Wiedergeburt, an rechter Umkehr zu neuem Leben und an dem zur Heiligung unbedingt nötigen Glaubensgehorsam gegen die göttlichen Gebote."

Sein Feind her er geschweyget, keiner dorft ihn wenden an.[11]

Here, for the first and not the last time, we encounter a quotation by a contemporary of Luther comparing him to the angel of Revelation 14:6. This interpretation of the prophetic Word deeply impressed Conradi, and later seems to have contributed to his increasingly questioning the Millerite movement to be the starting point of the proclamation of the Three Angel's Messages of Revelation 14, rather than Luther's Reformation.

## Luther's Expectation of the Imminent Second Coming

On yet another point, Conradi had much praise for Luther. After the Reformer translated the New Testament into German in 1521/1522 at the Wartburg, and after his return to Wittenberg, he began – with assistance from friends – to translate the Old Testament. Interestingly, he did not systematically approach the task, but rather prioritized the book of Daniel above the other books. Luther defended this move with the following words:

> The world runs and rushes on so splendidly towards its end, that often strong impressions come to my mind, as if the Last Day were to dawn before we could possibly come to completely translate the Holy Scriptures into German. For it is certain, that in the Holy Scriptures there is nothing more pertaining to time to be waiting for. All has been revealed and fulfilled. The Roman Empire is at an end, the Turk has gained the ascendency, the glory of the papacy is fading, and the world is crumbling at the edges, almost if it would totally shatter and fall.[12]

---

11  Found in Conradi, *Das goldene Zeitalter*, 371. Unrhymed translation:
"John clearly wrote to us about an angel,
Who should drive us to God's Word, apparently Luther.
His heart was inclined toward God as a Christian man's should,
The Holy Scriptures he sieved to purity, leaving no rubbish behind.
In Worms he appeared, defiantly stepping into the arena.
He silenced his enemies, allowing no one to move him."
Reference is from Michael Styfel Augustiner von Esszlingen, Uon der Christfermigen / rechtgegründten leer Doctoris Martini Luthers / ein überauß schön kunstlich Lied / sampt seyner neben außlegung. Jn Bruder Veyten Thon. Augsburg 1522. (Index in the German language edition of the 16th century [VD16] S 9019).

12  Cited in Conradi, *Prophetischer Ausblick*, 264. Original: "Die Welt läuft und eilt so trefflich sehr zu ihrem Ende, daß mir oft starke Gedanken einfallen, als sollte der jüngste Tag eher einbrechen, denn wir die hl. Schrift gar aus verdeutschen könnten. Denn das ist gewiß, daß wir in der hl. Schrift nicht zeitlich Dinge zu gewarten haben, es ist alles aus und erfüllt. Das römische Reich ist am Ende, der Türke aufs höchsten kommen, die Pracht des Papsttums fällt dahin und knackt die Welt an allen Enden fast, als wollte sie schier brechen und fallen."

Thus Conradi addresses the two points that he was constantly keeping an eye out for: Foremost, the expectation of the imminent second coming; and related to it, the historical interpretation of Daniel chapter 2. He claims that Luther correctly interpreted the fourth world kingdom as Rome. But that is not all. Conradi noted further: "Concerning the fulfillment of the 490 days of Daniel 9, he [Luther] recognized that a prophetic day signifies a year, and that the prophecy of Daniel reaches until the end time. Thus the 1290 and 1335 days could also be prophetic days, that is, a day for a year, as was the case in chapter 9."[13] Thus, Conradi suggests, the Reformers grasped the correct accounting of prophetic time from Scripture, and in this way led many succeeding commentators to the correct interpretation of the books of Daniel and Revelation. This was, of course, merely the beginning, but since the time of the end – i.e., the point in time for the unsealing of the time prophecies – had not yet arrived, Luther for this reason was unable to explain the three and a half times along these lines.

## The Pope and the Turkish Threat as Sign of the Imminent End of the World

Yet another statement made Ludwig Richard Conradi enthusiastic concerning Luther: The prophetic interpretation of the Turks, who, during the Reformation era posed the greatest danger not only to the German nation of the Holy Roman Empire, but to the entire Christian world. Luther saw the threat of the Turks as fulfilling the biblical symbol of Gog in Revelation 20:8–9 (cf. Isa 38:2) as a harbinger of the soon second coming. In his "On War Against the Turks" ("Heerpredigt wider die Türken 1529"), he argued this using the prophecy of Daniel predicting two end-time tyrants, one spiritual – the pope – and one physical – Mohammed. He viewed the spiritual tyrant as the more dangerous, because he would kill not only the body, but the soul as well. But with the downfall of Gog, that is, with the imminent annihilation of the Turks, "we can predict with certainty, that the last day must be at the door."[14] It was therefore the threatening danger of the Turkish army that induced Luther to view the day of judgment as being at hand. This was the reason why he expedited the translation of the book of Daniel before the other books of the Old Testament. Luther's particular affinity for the book of Daniel, and Conradi's love of interpreting the prophecies of Daniel met above all at this point of the expectation of the soon coming of Christ.

---

13 Ibid. Original: "An der Erfüllung der 490 Tage in Dan. 9 erkannte er [Luther], daß ein prophetischer Tag ein Jahr bedeute, und da die Weissagung Daniels bis ans Ende herabreicht, so könnten auch die 1290 und 1335 Tage engelische Tage, das ist ein Tag, ein Jahr, wie droben Kap 9."
14 Conradi, *Das goldene Zeitalter*, 399. Original: "... können wir sicherlich weissagen, daß der Jüngste Tag vor der Tür sein müsse."

The high point in Conradi's view of Luther's Reformation is thus arrived at. With words of praise, he comments on the various statements of the Reformers concerning the calculations of the days of the second coming of Jesus, which Luther almost always calls the last day. Conradi notes how Luther characterized his age as the absolutely final age. He also perceives a consensus among Luther and many church fathers that world history would last approximately 6,000 years. Of the final 2,000 years, 1,500 had already passed. Since God often allowed the big events of world history to be fulfilled early (one must only think of the resurrection, where Christ was not a full three days in the grave), Luther therefore believed that Christ would come in his time. This leads Conradi to the conclusion: "This confidence of Luther and Melanchthon that the last day was imminently near, required them to prove the fulfillment of prophetic time. Since the 1260, 1290, and 1335 days did not mean days, but in fact years, both of them stood fast: but because the times were not yet up, finding the solution posed an insurmountable difficulty."[15]

Thus were explained the fundamental prophetic interpretations of Luther, except for those that did not harmonize with Conradi's model. The special importance of the Reformer Martin Luther lies therein that he marked the final era in the interpretation of prophecy, and with it, the beginning of the proclamation of Revelation 14. In this way, Luther was elevated to the status of one of the earliest fathers of the Advent movement.

## A Contemporary Explanation of the Three Angels' Messages of Revelation 14

In addition to Luther's interpretation of the prophet Daniel and Luther's expectation of the last day in the face of the Turkish threat, Conradi viewed Luther's constant struggle against the papacy in Rome as one of the most fundamental reasons for considering Luther as having initiated the fulfillment of Revelation 14. Conradi dedicated an entire chapter in his book *Das goldene Zeitalter* to this idea, under the title "Die Reformation und das Interim als Erfüllung von Offenbarung 14,6ff. gedeutet" ("The Reformation and the Interim Interpreted as the Fulfillment of Revelation 14:6ff."). Conradi writes with enthusiasm:

> Just as Stiefel in 1522 already saw in Luther the angel with the everlasting gospel, North German Reformer J. Bugenhagen, who saw in Luther the shining sun in the firmament of evangelical teaching (Dan 12:3), reinforced this at his graveside: "The powerful, holy, divine teaching of this dear man lives on to the uttermost. For without a doubt, he was the angel spoken of in Rev 14:6–8 ... This angel who says there, 'Fear God and give

---

15 Ibid., 425. Original: "Diese Gewissheit Luthers und Melanchthons, daß der Jüngste Tag unmittelbar bevorstehe, nötigte sie, die Erfüllung der prophetischen Zeit schon damals nachzuweisen. Daß diese nicht nur etwa 1260, 1290 und 1335 Tage bedeuteten sondern Jahre, stand beiden fest; da aber diese noch nicht abgelaufen waren, bereitete ihnen die Lösung unüberwindliche Schwierigkeiten."

glory to Him,' was Dr. M. Luther, and where it says 'Fear,' etc., these are the two parts of the teaching of Dr. Luther, the law and the gospel, through which all of Scripture is unlocked and Christ is recognized ... After the teaching of this angel, another follows who will preach comfort to the sorrowing and persecuted church; and upon their adversaries, the thunder and lightning of eternal judgment and condemnation, as the other angel says, 'She is fallen, Babylon, that great city.'"[16]

This statement by Luther's friend and confessor Johannes Bugenhagen not only revived the parallels between Martin Luther and the first angel of Revelation 14, but also introduced the second angel's message. In the struggle between the church of the Reformation and the papacy, the call of the second angel was consummated. Luther was considered to be the third Elijah by his followers and friends, whom God sent for the restoration of the true religion in the time of the Reformation. Conradi found apparent evidences of this in the commemorative medallions of 1630, the obverse side of which was inscribed with Luther's portrait and the Latin words for "The Third Elijah."[17] On the reverse side can be seen an angel flying in the midst of heaven with an open book, inscribed with "The Everlasting Gospel." He blows the words "She is fallen, fallen, that great Babylon" out of his trumpet. Underneath is the depiction of a collapsing city with the caption "Apoc. 14" (Rev 14).[18] For Conradi, this was proof that the second angel's message had the sixteenth-century Reformation as its starting point.

Conradi likewise found a fitting interpretation for the third angel's message as pertaining to the Reformation era. In the context of the so-called "Leipzig Interim," in which Protestants under the leadership of Melanchthon conceded in 1548 to some of the demands of the emperor constituting a return to Catholicism, a split arose among Luther's followers. One group, calling themselves Gnesio-Lutherans (literally, "authentic Lutherans"), fled from the laws to Magdeburg, among them being the Lutheran Bishop Amsdorf. From there, he railed against the "apostate" followers of Luther, using Revelation 13:15ff., and identified the following five steps of apostasy as signs of the immediate second coming of Christ:

16 Ibid., 444. Original: "Sah schon Stiefel 1522 in Luther den Engel mit dem ewigen Evangelium, so bekräftigte dies Norddeutschlands Reformator J. Bugenhagen, der in Luther die leuchtende Sonne im Sternenkreis evangelischer Lehrer sah (Dan 12,3), an dessen Sarge: ‚Die gewaltige, selige, göttliche Lehre dieses teueren Mannes lebt noch aufs allerstärkste. Denn er war ohne Zweifel der Engel, davon in Offb. 14,6–8 steht... Dieser Engel, der da sagt: Fürchtet Gott und gebet ihm die Ehre, war D. M. Luther und das hier steht: Fürchtet usw., das sind die zwei Stücke der Lehre D. L., das Gesetz und das Evangelium, durch welche die ganze Schrift geöffnet und Christus erkannt wird... Nach der Lehre dieses Engels wird folgen ein anderer, welcher Trost wird predigen der betrübten und angefochtenen Kirche und über die Widersacher Blitz und Donner ewiges Gerichts und Verdammnis, wie denn der andere Engel sprach: Sie ist gefallen, gefallen, Babylon, die große Stadt.'"
17 While *Das goldene Zeitalter* gives no source for the picture of the medallion, Conradi named the source in *The Impelling Force* as Christian Juncker, *Das Goldene und Silberne Ehrengedächtniß D. Martini Lvtheri* (Schleusingen: Georg Wilhelm Göbel 1706), 26–27.
18 Conradi, *Das goldene Zeitalter*, 457.

The apostasy of the pope; his being revealed as Antichrist; the disintegration of the German Holy Roman Empire; the cessation of the daily offering, (that is, evangelical preaching), along with the establishment abomination of desolation of human tradition; and lastly, laws making worship of the beast and acceptance of its mark compulsory. 'The beast is the Roman Empire, who supports, maintains, and operates the scarlet Babylonian whore, that is, the papacy, whose marks are the papal canons, decrees, and ceremonies.' 'That we should now worship this beast and should accept and keep his mark, especially the Mass, whether the old one or the new one with its amendments, the apathetic thus would urge and compel us with their advice and law. The last day can therefore not be long delayed.'[19]

Thus for Conradi, the third angel's message already found its first fulfillment in the Reformation.[20] The consequences of this interpretation were not long in coming.

## Conradi's Conversion to the Seventh Day Baptists

A further look into Ludwig Richard Conradi's biography is necessary at this point. He was a person with great zeal. His dedication to the furtherance of the Advent message can hardly be matched. We owe him great respect for this fact. At the same time, however, he was also a man of his time: a typical self-educated person with a

19 Ibid., 446. Original: "Abfall des Papstes, sein Offenbarwerden als Antichrist, Zerfall des Deutsch-Römischen Reiches, Aufhören des täglichen Opfers d. i. der evangelischen Predigt nebst Aufrichtung des Verwüstungsgreuels menschlicher Überlieferung und zuletzt Zwangsgesetze zur Anbetung des Tieres und Annahme seines Malzeichens. 'Das Tier ist da Römische Reich, so da trägt, erhält und handhabt die rote babylonische Buhlerin, nämlich das Papsttum, das Malzeichen sind dies Papstes Canones, Dekreta und Zeremonien.' 'Daß wir nun solches Tier anbeten und seine Malzeichen, sonderlich die Messe, es sei die alte oder neue mit ihrem Anhang annehmen und halten sollen, dazu zwingen und dringen uns die Gleichgültigen mit ihrem Ratschlagen und Gebot. Darum kann der Jüngste Tag nicht lange ausbleiben.'"
20 In his earlier published commentary on Revelation, concerning the interpretation of the three angels of Revelation 14, Conradi alludes to a fulfillment in the Reformation era and refers to citations from Heinrich Bullinger, Campegius Vitringa, and Johann Albrecht Bengel, who understood the angels to be those who proclaim biblical truth (*Der Seher von Patmos*, 423; *Prophetischer Ausblick*, 441). While in *Der Seher von Patmos*, he does not name any Reformers in this context, he becomes clearer in *Prophetischer Ausblick*, by quoting Pastor Robinson, who addressed the English Pilgrim Fathers at the beginning of their journey to America in 1620 with the following: "The Lord has yet more truth to break forth out of His holy Word. Luther and Calvin were great and bright lights in their time, but they did not perfectly perceive the council of God. Keep ever in mind that you must be ready to receive all truth that comes to your attention through the written Word of God." (466). Finally, he references Zinzendorf, who "brought more missions into being in two decades than the entirety of Protestantism in two centuries" and who, with his church in Bethlehem, Pennsylvania, decided to "observe the seventh day as a day of rest" (ibid.). Tennhardt is said to have acknowledged "the true Sabbath observance and the ungodly origin of Sunday," as early as 1709 in Nürnberg (ibid.).

wide range of scholarly interests. In addition, he was a child of the land of the Reformation, whose religious roots were first discovered through his own study of prophecy. In the same manner as he strove for great missionary success, for the largest numbers of souls won, and saw himself in a contest between the Old and New Worlds, so Conradi led a struggle for financial independence from the General Conference. He therefore established a European General Conference in 1901, seeking also a comparable theological independence from the brethren in the USA. Thus he emphasized European autonomy.[21]

The First World War brought this mid-European anomaly to an abrupt end. The unity of the church shattered the moment the front lines were drawn between enemy armies. Mission stations could no longer be cared for. Many missionaries ended up in internment camps for years. At home in Germany, tension in the church increased over the issue of military service and the end of the world. In short, Conradi's life work imploded. After the war, the General Conference held him responsible for the rise of the Reform Movement. He lost his positions as GC Vice President and as President of the European Division. He was elected as Secretary of the General Conference. As such, he could still provide representation, but could in no way continue to influence or independently make decisions. It all came together:

21 Cf. Heinz, *Ludwig Richard Conradi*, 101; Johannes Hartlapp, *Siebenten-Tags-Adventisten in der Zeit des Nationalsozialismus unter Berücksichtigung der geschichtlichen und theologischen Entwicklung in Deutschland von 1875 bis 1950*, Kirche – Konfession – Religion 53 (Göttingen: V&R unipress, 2008), 48–50. During the negotiations with the Reform Movement in 1920 in Friedensau, those opposing Conradi alleged that he forced an autonomous European Advent Movement upon them. As proof, they pointed to a quote from him given on the occasion of the opening of the 1920 school year in Friedensau: "It is all about knowing and showing that our message is not something English/American, but rather homegrown. This is evidenced by the preface of a book written in 1768." ("Eröffnungsfeier des neuen Schulkurses in Friedensau," *Zions-Wächter*, March 3, 1920, 35), (Original: Es komme auch darauf an, zu lernen und zu zeigen, daß unsere Botschaft nicht etwa eine englisch-amerikanische, sondern eine bodenständige sei. Die bestätige die Vorführung eines Buches aus dem Jahr 1768.) Conradi was referring to a brochure by Johann Philipp Petri from 1768 that he had found, in which the same prophetic outline was proposed that Miller later discovered, with the same starting point for the 70 weeks prophecy and the 2300 evening-mornings. Petri came to the conclusion, "4. The angel Gabriel here points us to AD 30, or the $483^{rd}$ year in the 70 weeks prophecy; and consequentially, to the $453^{rd}$ year before the birth of Christ, which would be the true and correct explanation of the dark face of the 2300 days: that 453 years would likewise be cut off from it until the birth of Christ; and that the rest or remainder of the number continues on until AD 1847, for 1847 and 453 add up to the number 2300." (Original: "4. Legte hiemit der Engel Gabriel vor Augen das 30te Jahr Christi oder das 483. Jahr in der 70. Wochen-Zahl; und einfolglich das 453. Jahr zum Geburts-Jahr Christ, so ware solches die richtige und rechte Erklärung von dem dunklen Gesicht der 2300., daß von denselben in der Geburt Christi eben zugleich auch 453. Jahr würden abgeflossen seyn. Und daß der Rest oder das übrige der Zahl von da fortgehet bis 1847. nach Christ Geburt. Wie dem denn 1847. und 453. die Zahl 2300. summiret.") Conradi published the little book in 1927 in the Advent-Verlag Hamburg as a reprint. The quote above is found on pages 9–10.

frustration, anger, disappointment, removal from his position, a great deal of senile stubbornness, and the inability to let go. In addition, he lost his wife, who died in 1928. She was possibly the only person who really understood and loved him.[22] All this, combined with the views on the history of the Reformation described above, led to a growing distance between him and the world church.

In 1930, Conradi wanted to publish a revised edition of his commentary on Revelation in the Advent-Verlag in Hamburg. However, as the church's literary committee sat in peer review of his interpretation of Revelation, conflict arose, and the manuscript was rejected. The committee explained the rejection in a long document, including, among other things, that,

> The bottom line is that the new interpretation of Revelation has almost entirely lost its character as an Adventist interpretation of Revelation ... Almost all of the symbols end with the age of the Reformation in this new interpretation of Revelation. Thus the Reformation has acquired the importance that, in our firmest convictions, belongs to the Advent message of the end times. Without belittling the merits of the Reformation or the Reformers in any way, we cannot share this viewpoint of the author that inflates the Reformation above its proper sphere, such that the Advent message appears to be a mere minor side note hardly worth mention. Upon reading it, one receives the impression that this manuscript is not an Adventist, but a mainline Protestant interpretation of Revelation ... It is especially regrettable that the author is so far removed from his earlier interpretation of Revelation 14:1-12, sidelining the Advent message entirely, and exalting the Reformation beyond all measure as if it were the Three Angels' Message, especially setting apart Luther as the angel or Elijah of God.[23]

22  A year earlier, she wrote him on their anniversary: "In thinking back, forty-five years ago, when you became all mine, what memories crowd into my mind. I've never been sorry, Richard, that I cast in my lot with you, you've been a good husband to me, and my love for you has grown instead of diminished. Now, Darling, God's blessing for the future on your work. With love, yours as ever, Lizzie." (Conradi, *The Impelling Force*, vii)

23  Letter of H. F. Schuberth to L. R. Conradi, June 10, 1931 (Historisches Archiv der Siebenten-Tags-Adventisten in Europa, Friedensau). Original: "Der wichtigste Punkt ist, daß die neue Offenbarungsauslegung den Charakter einer adventistischen Offenbarungsauslegung fast ganz verloren hat ... Fast alle Symbole schließen nach der neuen Offenbarungsauslegung mit dem Zeitalter der Reformation. Dadurch gewinnt die Reformation an Bedeutung, die nach unserer felsenfesten Überzeugung der Adventbotschaft der Endzeit zukommt. Ohne die Verdienste der Reformation oder der Reformatoren irgendwie schmälern zu wollen, kann unmöglich der Standpunkt des Autors geteilt werden, der die Reformation weit über ihren Rahmen heraushebt, wodurch dann die Adventbotschaft nur noch als nebensächliches Anhängsel erscheint und kaum der Erwähnung wert ist. So bekommt man beim Lesen schließlich den Eindruck, als ob es sich bei diesem MS. nicht um eine adventistische, sondern um eine von der protestantischen Kirche herausgegebene Offenbarungsauslegung handelt ... Es ist außerordentlich bedauerlich, daß der Schreiber in seiner Erklärung zu Offb. 14,1-12 völlig von seiner früheren eigenen Erklärung abweicht, die Adventbotschaft ganz beiseite schiebt und dafür die Reformation über alle Maßen verherrlicht und sie als die dreifache Engelsbotschaft hinstellt, unter besonderer Hervorhebung Luthers als dem Engel oder Elias Gottes."

The next step came very quickly. In the midst of a productive year, he separated from the church that he had substantially built up for the last 40 years, and became a Seventh Day Baptist. Once again, he founded new churches in Germany, mostly out of former Advent churches. From then on, he fought against his mother church in public presentations and through a series of publications.[24] What an irony!

## Conradi's Presentation of the Reformation in *The Impelling Force*

Once again, he published – as his *opus magnum*, so to speak – a comprehensive history of prophetic interpretation: *The Impelling Force of the Prophetic Truth*. Here he follows the same lines as in *Das goldene Zeitalter*. The single fundamental difference: now he grants the history of the Reformation its own chapter, and expands on the importance of the Reformation.

Already, in his concluding remarks on the Thyatira era, that is, the medieval papal church, Conradi comes to the conclusion,

> that in view of these facts the threefold message should be sounded world-wide as warning, the everlasting gospel should be evangelized or proclaimed in its purity against the perverted gospel of the papacy, the people were to be exhorted to come out of Babylon, and to beware of the worship of the beast, and of accepting its mark of subjection.[25]

Thus at the starting point of the discussion on the Reformation the interpretation is presupposed: the message of the three angels of Revelation 14:6–12 finds its fulfillment in Luther and the other Reformers. Accordingly, Conradi could save himself a general introduction to the Reformation similar to that of *Das goldene Zeitalter*. Consequently, after a reference to Luther's studies in Erfurt and his first teaching post in Wittenberg, he begins with a reference to Tetzel and indulgences. Immediately after describing the debate with the papal legate Cajetan in Augsburg, a short paragraph follows in which Luther's closest confidants, Karlstadt, Amsdorf, and Melanchthon are introduced. Then, out of the blue comes the sentence, "The doctrine of man's salvation by faith in Christ alone became the inspiring central

---

24  In addition to *The Impelling Force*, the following publications are worth mention here: *Die apostolischen und prophetischen Sondergaben (The Apostolic and Prophetic Gifts)*, 1932; *Ist Frau Ellen White die Prophetin der Endgemeinde (Is Mrs. Ellen White the Prophet of the Endtime Church?)*, 1933; *Fernblicke in die Zukunft – Ein Schlüssel zum Büchlein Daniel (Look into the Future – A Key to the Book of Daniel)*, 1934; *Der neue und lebendige Weg (The New and Living Way)*, n.d.; *Das ewige, lautere Evangelium Jesu Christi, (The Everlasting, Pure Gospel of Jesus Christ)*, n.d.; *Lebensbeschreibung von Prediger O. R. L. Crozier (Life Description of Pastor O. R. L. Crozier)*, 1937. All these publications and the periodical *Wahrheit – Licht – Leben (Truth – Light – Life)* were published privately.
25  Conradi, *The Impelling Force*, 242.

thought of all theological instruction at Wittenberg."[26] After words of praise for Melanchthon, whose precepts are always the original sources of the Holy Scriptures and of history, comes the text, as before, describing Reformation history measured by the standard of prophecy and ideas of Antichrist.

A bit later the author links his basic approach to the central concern of Luther, and interprets the Reformation as follows: "Luther and Melanchthon after having found Christ and the sufficiency of Holy Writ, enlightened by the sure word of prophecy they also discovered, in the corrupt papacy, and in the falsity of her traditions and decretals, the real Antichrist. Both were now ready to launch the Reformation."[27]

To a greater degree than he did in *Das goldene Zeitalter*, Conradi now relies upon testimony from the Anabaptists. Where he earlier mentioned the Nikolsburg Anabaptists, placing the spiritual interpretation of their Sabbath observance at the center of the discussion,[28] in *The Impelling Force*, he uses a variety of sources to describe a number of different Anabaptist groups, followed by the Sabbath observance of the Nikolsburg Anabaptists, as well as Karlstadt's thoughts on the Sabbath.[29] This ultimately led him to the conclusion that the Anabaptists held infant baptism and Sunday observance to be human inventions, introduced by the papacy as a sign of its authority. In contrast were the true baptism and the Sabbath as the Seal of God[30] as the literal fulfillments of Revelation 6:10. With this interpretation he goes beyond the argumentation he used in *Das goldene Zeitalter*, where he used the commemorative medallion for the Reformation jubilee as evidence.

An entire chapter is devoted to the passage in Revelation 14:6–12 as the "'Sum and Content' of the Evangelical Doctrine."[31] It mostly contains quotes from Luther's followers in the time after his death, most notably from Georg Nigrinus, theology professor in Giessen, who in his commentary on Revelation published in 1573 comes to the conclusion, "The three angels in Revelation 14 all signify evangelical preachers in this last time, beginning with the preaching of Luther until the end."[32]

Additional chapters in the section on the Reformation are devoted to the Jesuits, Cromwell's conception of the Fifth Monarchy, and other separatist movements in the seventeenth century. He closes the over 150-page presentation on the Reformation with the words,

> Though Lutherans, Reformed, Baptists, Brethren, Sabbatarians otherwise disagreed, yet one conclusion they all reached unanimously: Clear as the midday sun had shone the

26 Ibid., 244.
27 Ibid., 247.
28 Conradi, *Das goldene Zeitalter*, 416–417.
29 On the understanding of the Sabbath, see: Jürgen Kaiser, *Ruhe der Seele und Siegel der Hoffnung – Die Deutungen des Sabbats in der Reformation*, Forschungen zur Kirchen- und Dogmengeschichte 65 (Göttingen: Vandenhoeck & Ruprecht, 1996).
30 Conradi, *The Impelling Force*, 288.
31 Ibid., 337.
32 Ibid., 342.

light, that Rome, imperial and papal, was the predicted Antichrist, against whom the threefold message of Revelation 14:6–12 must be preached and through its proclamation a people must be gathered out, who in patience took the word of God as their only rule of faith, put their sole trust in Christ and walked in His footsteps, as He walked in His Father's commandments.[33]

Thus for Conradi, the significance of the Millerite Movement receded into the background. He mentions it on pages 533–542, but then turns attention to developments in England and the Ottoman Empire in the 1840s. The formation and development of Seventh-day Adventists through whom he first became acquainted with the prophetic word, is not ignored.[34] He describes it as a falsely led movement, in which he particularly analyzes the first vision of Ellen White and various prophetic interpretations in the early years, and presents their points of variation as being contradictory. Finally, he still has one positive remark left for Seventh-day Adventists: "When the great prophetic conferences were held in the old and new world, the S.D.A. were yet in their infancy, and when the great missionary century closed, they were about awakening to their duty to preach the Gospel to the heathen."[35]

## Conradi's Studies on the Reformation as Cause for His Separation from the Seventh-day Adventist Church?

Those who followed the argumentation of the author when *Das goldene Zeitalter* was published, recognized a broadened definition of Adventism. While in the United States, the term was understood as applying strictly to the followers of the former Millerite Movement, Ludwig R. Conradi used it in a much broader sense.[36] Several

33  Ibid., 400.
34  Ibid., 587–590.
35  Ibid., 590.
36  In *Das goldene Zeitalter,* after the presentation on the Reformation era, a discussion of church history continues with emphasis on Puritanism and Pietism, in which Conradi elevates alongside the Advent Movement in the USA a series of additional expositors whose prophetic calculations led them to the conclusion that Christ must return in the first half of the 19th century (e.g., the compilers of the Berleburg Bible, or Johann Albrecht Bengel). He especially underscores the work, *Aufschluß der Zahlen Daniels und der Offenbarung Johannis (Explanation of the Numbers in Daniel and the Revelation of John)* by Johann Philipp Petri in the year 1768, who described the coincident starting points of the 70 weeks of years and the 2300 evening-mornings, and even arrived at the year 1847. These publications possessed such a high value for Conradi, that in 1927 in the Advent-Verlag in Hamburg, he released them as reprint editions. Further, for Conradi, this is within the same timeframe as the "Father of the Advent Movement," Johann Albrecht Bengel. As evidence, he cites Stilling: "At the time of the Reformation and soon thereafter, one wished to suppose the end to be nearer than it really was, the expectation never being so high as 1730–1750. The many revivals everywhere and the many men who made calls to awaken, especially Franke, Zinzendorf, Rock, Haug, Tuchtfeld, Dippel, Petersen, Poiret, Hochmann, Gerhard,

of his colleagues adopted this understanding and published it in various articles in church publications.[37]

An open discussion on the historical location of the Adventist church could have proven useful to the world church and to its positioning within Protestantism. However, such a discussion was increasingly avoided in the early years of church practice after the death of Ellen White. The discussion during the Bible Conference of 1919 seems to be evidence for this. The General Conference repositioned itself, the end of the era of Daniells and Conradi as President and Vice President marking this development. Thus the opportunity for independent action became smaller. While in the United States, in the 1920s, fundamentalism clearly influenced public life, the effects were clearly noticed in the theological argumentation of the Adventist church. Thus, more and more of the common and unifying heritage was lost that was so decisive for Conradi. He felt quite alone. The time of the Advent pioneers came to an irrevocable end. Out of the competition that Conradi had earlier created between the American and European Adventists, developed a clear breakdown in the relationship with each other. This was foremost apparent in his relationship to his successor in leadership of the European Division, the American L. H. Christian.[38] On top of this was a series of additional factors that – as mentioned earlier – contributed to the differences that led to a complete separation.

It is not surprising therefore that Ludwig Richard Conradi gravitated towards the place where he had located quite early in his prophetic studies "the Three Angels' Message of the end time"[39] of Revelation 14: In a movement of church history that is not described as having the flaws of Sardis, but the praise of the church at Philadelphia (Rev 3:7ff.).[40] As a bridge between the starting point of

> Tersteegen and others, caused a general agitation ... Exactly at this time between 1740 and 1750, Bengel's writings came out. They kindled a new light that had not yet appeared, and with them, Revelation became clearer, more understandable, and more relevant" (Conradi, *Das goldene Zeitalter*, 447). (Original: "Zur Zeit der Reformation und bald nachher mochte man wohl auch das Ende näher vermuten als es wirklich war, allein niemals war die Erwartung so gespannt als 1730–1750. Die vielen Erweckungen allenthalben und die vielen Männer, welche zum Aufwachen aufriefen, vorzüglich Franke, Zinzendorf, Rock, Haug, Tuchtfeld, Dippel, Petersen, Poiret, Hochmann, Gerhard, Tersteegen and others verursachten ein allgemeine Aufregung ... Gerade in dieser Zeit 1740–1750 kamen nun die Schriften Bengels heraus; diese zündeten ein neues, noch nie erschienenes Licht an und bei diesem wird nun die Apokalypse klarer, verständlicher und anwendbarer.") Conradi commented with the words, "With him, the 'Church Father of Württemberg,' the Advent Movement began" (ibid.). (Original: "Mit ihm, dem 'Kirchenvater Württembergs,' setzte die Adventbewegung richtig ein ...")

37  Hartlapp, *Siebenten-Tags-Adventisten in der Zeit des Nationalsozialismus*, 224f.
38  Ibid., 156.
39  Conradi, *Prophetischer Ausblick*, 432.
40  In *Der Seher von Patmos* Conradi interprets the church of Philadelphia as the mission era of late 18th and early 19th centuries: "The precious Bible was published and distributed in hundreds of languages through the establishment of large missionary societies in England,

renewal in the Reformation and the missionary era of the nineteenth century, he finally discovered the Seventh Day Baptists, who stood for both the renewal as a free will church and the Sabbath.[41]

After his change of church affiliation, Conradi emphasized just how much his historical studies had contributed to his critical outlook. Writing on page 3 in the pamphlet *Höret meine Rechtfertigung! (Hear My Vindication!)* about the time after 1922, when he was no longer elected to serve as European Division President: "Now, for 6 months in London, I could finally secure historical evidence that in fulfillment of Revelation 14, the everlasting gospel was preached since Rome's fall,

America, and elsewhere; missionary societies multiplied quickly and sent their messengers to the darkest of heathen lands; tract societies made their contribution by bringing spiritual life to the dead masses through relevant writings; and great revivals proclaimed the power of the magnificent gospel of the kingdom. In the great Advent movement of the 30s and 40s, believers from different denominations were bound together by the blessed hope of the soon return of Christ, every barrier of separation was torn down, doctrinal differences disappeared, and pride and worldliness gave way to Christlikeness." (77) (Original: "Das köstliche Bibelbuch wurde durch die Gründung der großen Bibelgesellschaften in England, Amerika usw. in hunderten Sprachen veröffentlicht und verbreitet, Missionsgesellschaften mehrten sich rasch und sandten ihre Boten selbst in die dunkelsten Heidenländer, Traktatgesellschaften trugen das ihre bei, durch geeignete Schriften geistiges Leben unter die toten Massen zu bringen, und große Erweckungen bekundeten die Kraft des herrlichen Evangeliums vom Reich. In der großen Adventbewegung der 30er und 40er Jahre verband die selige Hoffnung von der nahen Wiederkunft Christi die Gläubigen der verschiedenen Gemeinschaften als eine Bruderschaft, jede trennende Schranke wurde niedergerissen, die Verschiedenheit der Glaubensbekenntnisse schwand und Hochmut und Weltsinn wichen dem Sinn Christ.") Conradi later shifted the era of Philadelphia back a hundred years earlier and included Pietism and Methodism: "What the Quaker Penn attempted to achieve outwardly with the founding of Philadelphia in 1683, the standard bearers of mission like Francke, Zinzendorf, Bengel, Wesley, Whitefield, and Carey achieved worldwide spiritually. Francke was God's instrument, 'to lead up to a new lively period of the evangelical church'; in the mission atmosphere of Halle, 'the first real mission hymn of Bogatzky, "Wach auf, du Geist der ersten Zeugen" ["Awake, O Spirit of the First Witnesses"] came into being, giving the mission and Reformation thought of Francke a poetic-classical expression' that in the process breathed a true Adventist spirit" (*Prophetischer Ausblick,* 77ff). (Original: "Was nun ein Quäker Penn durch die Gründung Philadelphias 1683 äußerlich fördern wollte, das schufen Bannerträger der Mission, wie Francke, Zinzendorf, Bengel, Wesley, Whitefield, Carey im geistlichen Sinne weltweit. Francke war Gottes Werkzeug, 'eine neue lebensvolle Periode der evangelischen Kirche heraufzuführen'; in der Halleschen Missionsatmosphäre entstand 'das erste wirkliche Missionslied Bogatzkys: "Wach auf, du Geist der ersten Zeugen," das den Missions- wie Reformationsgedanken Franckes einen poetisch-klassischen Ausdruck gab,' dabei auch den rechten Adventgeist atmete.")

41  On the establishment of Seventh Day Baptists in London in the 16th century, see: Bryan W. Ball, *The Seventh-Day Men – Sabbatarians and Sabbatarianism in England and Wales, 1600–1800* (Cambridge: James Clarke 2009); Mark R. Bell, *Apocalypse How? Baptist Movements During the English Revolution* (Macon, GA: Mercer, 2000).

and was the impetus for the Reformation."[42] In two lectures in Berlin-Neukölln presented on January 24 and 25, 1933, he presented to a group of Adventists his defense for his decision.[43] Although his position on Ellen White and her visions, as well as the whole issue of the sanctuary and 1844, occupied center stage here, he also refers quite specifically to his early sources on the fulfillment of Revelation 14:

> I believe in the Three Angels' Message wholeheartedly. And I will explain this to you. On the Three Angels' Message that is preached. From that time on, since the gospel was perverted in Rome, the pure gospel was preached. From that time on, all the children of God have known the message. From that time on, throughout the centuries the children of God have said: no mark and no image. Someone asks, 'Do you have evidence?' Absolutely. Here I have two little books – one printed in 1545 and the other in 1548 by Amsdorf, a colleague of Luther.[44]

Regarding the Millerite Movement, he explains:

> And what have I concluded in these years? That the Millerite Movement is not even the original movement. Someone asks, 'Br. Conradi, what then is before this?' Please. How many of you have a little book reproduced by the Advent-Verlag, an entire little book by Reverend Petri? (A few hands are raised). Very few. I beg you, write to the Advent-Verlag and request Reverend Petri's work. Why? Because in the reproduced little book – this is also in *Das goldene Zeitalter*, the pages are even exact photocopies, and you can receive it for almost nothing, I believe it was offered for 1.50 Reichsmark – there in this little book by Petri you will find nothing less than the numbers in Daniel. 1768. Is that before Miller? And what is in them? The entire pages are photocopied in *Das goldene Zeitalter*, page 548. That already in 1768, this man correctly calculated the 2300 years. Yes, before William Miller lived and Mrs. White as well, before SDAs existed. And where? In Seckbach near Frankfurt am Main in good ol' Germany. Some people think that everything has to come from America to be authentic. Thank God, that His Spirit is active in Germany as well. I think we too once had a Reformation in Germany. Martin Luther and quite a number of pious men were already there, when America was still in diapers.[45]

---

42  Ludwig Richard Conradi, "Höret meine Rechtfertigung," (Hamburg: Eigenverlag, [1934]), 3.
43  Since there are no historical audio recordings and, to my knowledge, no written transcripts of Conradi's sermons, these two sets of written notes are the only documents that allow us to experience the rhetoric of Ludwig Richard Conradi.
44  Ludwig R. Conradi, typewritten transcription of a lecture presented in Berlin-Neukölln, Bergstrasse 151, Tuesday, January 24, 1933, 10. Original: "Ich glaube an die dreifache Botschaft von ganzem Herzen. Und das werde ich euch erklären. An die dreifache Botschaft, die gepredigt wurde. Von der Zeit ab, da das Evangelium in Rom verkehrt wurde, wurde das reine Evangelium gepredigt. Von der Zeit ab haben alle Kinder Gottes die Botschaft gekannt. Von der Zeit ab schon die Jahrhunderte hindurch haben die Kinder Gottes sich gesagt: kein Malzeichen und kein Bild. Sagt jemand: Hast Du Beweise? Jawohl. Hier habe ich 2 Büchlein – ein gedruckt 1545 und das andre 1548 bei Amsdorf, dem Mitarbeiter von Luther."
45  Ibid, 5. Original: "Und was stellte ich fest in den Jahren? Dass die Miller-Bewegung gar nicht die ursprüngliche Bewegung ist. Ja sagt jemand, Br. Conradi, wer ist denn dann vorher?

In complete contrast to the enthusiasm surrounding his conversion, the reader can sense the deep bitterness of an old man who sees his life's work as slipping away from him. Nevertheless, he was as active as ever. Among other things, he continued to publish smaller brochures along with editions of *The Impelling Force*. This also included a condensed commentary on Revelation 14 with the title, *Das ewige, lautere Evangelium Jesu Christi (The Everlasting, Pure Gospel of Jesus Christ)*. His train of thought remained unchanged: "The Reformation put the everlasting, pure gospel in the spotlight."[46] In any case, for the first time he points to Luther's groundbreaking experience that led to the start of the Reformation:

> In his lectures, where he limited himself to the Holy Scriptures, he acquired from the Epistle to the Romans the assurance that whoever believes in Christ, has in Him 'the true, authentic righteousness,' and as He lives in the believers, He works out what the law demands by His grace. 'There I became happy; for the whole of Holy Scripture and heaven itself opened up to me.' Therefore, through constant reading of the gospel, we should make it our petition, that we who are born of God do not sin and sinfully enjoy good fortune.[47]

It appears that Conradi found it very difficult to understand that Luther's experience and understanding of justification by faith alone was so substantive and profound that the Reformer did not need to emphasize the law and the danger of sin in the same breath. Here he was miles away from the understanding of Ludwig Conradi.

---

Bitte. Wie viele von euch haben vom Advent-Verlag ein Büchlein wo photographiert ist, ein ganzes Büchlein von Pfarrer Petri? (Einige Hände werden gehoben). Sehr wenige. Ich bitte euch, schreibt an den Advent-Verlag und bittet um Pfarrer Petris Schrift. Ja, warum? Weil in dem photographierten Büchlein - das ist auch hier im *Goldenen Zeitalter*, die Seiten sind sogar photographiert, und das bekommt ihr ja fast geschenkt heute, war ja angeboten, ich glaube für RM 1,50 - da findet ihr in diesem Büchlein von Petri nicht weniger als die Zahlen Daniels. 1768. Ist das vor Miller gewesen? Und was steht in dem? Die ganze Seite photographiert im *Goldenen Zeitalter* 548. Dass der Mann schon 1768 die 2300 Jahre richtig ausgerechnet hatte. Ja, ehe W. Miller lebte und Frau White dazu, ehe die STA kamen. Und wo? In Seckbach bei Frankfurt a.M. Gutes Deutschland. Manche Leute glauben, es muss alles von Amerika kommen, dann ist es echt. Gott sei Dank, dass der Geist Gottes auch in Deutschland wirkt. Ich denke, wir hatten auch einmal eine Reformation in Deutschland. Haben Martin Luther und recht viele fromme Männer und da waren schon da, wo Amerika noch in den Windeln lag ..."

46 Conradi, *Das ewige, lautere Evangelium Jesu Christi*, 26.
47 Ibid., 27. Original: "Bei seinen Vorlesungen, die er auf die Hl. Schrift beschränkte, gewann er aus dem Römerbrief die Gewißheit, daß wer an Christus glaubt, der hat in ihm 'die rechte, grundgute Gerechtigkeit' und indem er in dem Gläubigen lebt, wirkt er aus Gnaden, was das Gesetz fordert. 'Da ward ich fröhlich; also tat sich mir die ganze Heilige Schrift und der Himmel selbst auf.' Darum sollen wir uns durch ständiges Lesen des Evangeliums anliegen sein lassen, daß wir als aus Gott Geborene nicht sündigen und sündigend des frohen Glücks genießen."

The question remains whether this path of Conradi led inevitably away from his Adventist church to the Seventh Day Baptists, or – at least in retrospect – if Conradi's enthusiasm for history could not have become more fruitful for the Adventist church. His broader horizon could have given the young church progress in its search for historical identity.

## Summary and Conclusion

Through his intensive studies, Conradi contributed an immense wealth of historical material on the topic of prophetic interpretation with emphases on both the second coming of Christ and the Antichrist, and compiled specifically in reference to the Reformation much more than Froom in his monumental work, *The Prophetic Faith of Our Fathers*.

Secondly, the presentation of Reformation history, even regarding specific issues, is to this day often influenced by a great deal of local patriotism. Conradi, by contrast, offered a broad overview of the many facets of the Reformation in various European countries, albeit within the narrow perspective of the aforementioned criteria.

Thirdly, Conradi's pointers to the interpretation of Revelation 14 in the Reformation era are accurate. Already then, the three angels' messages were interpreted as currently being fulfilled. In commemoration of this, until the first round of reforms were made under Prussian King Frederick William III in 1817, at every Reformation Day celebration, pastors preached on Revelation 14:1–6 in the worship services of the Lutheran state church.

Fourthly, Conradi's enthusiasm for the history of the Reformation contributed to the fact that several historical details in the 1911 revision of *The Great Controversy* were changed so as to be more in line with research. Not all his suggestions were accepted, however, probably because he viewed *The Great Controversy* more as a historical work than a devotional book. Thus he wrote to W. C. White: "Since writing my last about G/C, I have been very busy and especially on chapter 11, which I have nearly completed, in harmony with real facts in history." Regarding a quote from d'Aubigné Vol VII, chapter 7, he commented, "Now my dear brethren, this is not history. This is fancy, imagination. I dare any one now to find such a statement in any of Luther's writings."[48]

Fifthly, despite his immense knowledge of the Reformation, Conradi appears to have hardly, if at all, understood the essential statements of Luther, the basic framework of the Reformation so to speak. We find him offering no explanation of Luther's understanding of justification by faith alone, of the anthropology of the justification doctrine *(simul iustus et peccator)*, or of the difference between law and gospel. Nowhere does he seem to refer to Luther's central texts upon which he built the Reformation: Romans 1:17 and Romans 3:28. Herein lies a great tragedy. Obviously, Ludwig Conradi aimed to address the Reformation only from a specific

---

48 Letter to Brethren White and Town, July 25, 1915, GC Archive, Silver Spring, MD.

perspective in both works analyzed above. In doing so, he ignored essential statements without which a fundamental understanding of the Reformation is not possible. Even in his other writings, he constructs no broader view of Luther and the other Reformers. He views them exclusively from the perspective of historical prophetic interpretation.

With this, I return once more to the thesis proposed earlier: Did Conradi cause the Adventist church in Germany to be molded along Lutheran lines? The answer is simple: Since he did not have Luther's basic theological understanding, apparently he did not. Where he did influence the church was by possessing great missionary zeal along with a distinctive legalism, and in striving for an independent European identity.

Sixthly, when searching for the reasons for this misinterpretation of the Reformation, the method under which Conradi was operating must be noted. First came his comprehensive idea that had excited him since his conversion: the big idea of an Adventist-influenced interpretation of prophecy. To accomplish this, he diligently compiled every possible historical witness, though largely ignoring their historical context in the history of ideas. Anyone who proceeds so selectively can paint an apparently "accurate" overall picture. Such an overall presentation is bought at the price of inevitably ignoring all the other historical witnesses and contexts that contradict the broad vision.

Finally, Conradi's methodology led to misinterpretations that had negative consequences in the history of Seventh-day Adventism. For example, in connection with evangelistic meetings and publications in the years before World War I, the "Ottoman Question" was frequently put in the foreground as a relevant topic. Luther's statement was readily used for this: "Weil aber dennoch Christus hat Zeichen gegeben, dabei man kennen soll, wenn der jüngste Tag nahe sei, und dennoch, wenn der Türke ein Ende haben werde, so können wir sicherlich weissagen, daß der jüngste Tag müsse vor der Türe stehen." ("But because Christ still gave signs so that one should know when the last day is near, and when the Turk will come to an end, thus we can surely foretell that the last day must be at the door.") [49]

49 Ludwig R. Conradi, *Die Weissagung Daniels oder die Weltgeschichte im Lichte der Bibel* (Hamburg: Internationale Traktatgesellschaft, 1905), 316. Cf. pamphlet from Ludwig R. Conradi, *Das Ende der Türkei? Das Ende unserer Weltzeit? (The End of Turkey? The End of Our World History?)* (Hamburg: Internationale Traktatgesellschaft, 1912), and Otto Lüpke, *Die orientalische Frage (The Oriental Question)* (Hamburg: Internationale Traktatgesellschaft, 1913). The original quotation is taken from WA 30 II, 171. All citations are from *Weimarer Ausgabe: D. Martin Luthers Werke, Kritische Gesamtausgabe*, 127 vols. (Weimar: H. Böhlau, 1883–2009). It is grouped into Schriften/Werke [Writings] (WA), Tischreden [Table talks] (WA TR), Deutsche Bibel [German Bible] (WA DB) and Briefwechsel [Exchange of letters] (WA BR). On Luther's understanding, see Rudolf Mau, "Luthers Stellung zu den Türken" ("Luther's Position on the Turk") in *Leben und Werk Martin Luthers von 1525 bis 1546*, ed. Helmar Junghans (Göttingen: Vandenhoeck & Ruprecht 1983), 647–662.

This was supposed to prove the imminence of the second coming of Christ from the mouth of Luther. But as the world war broke out in the Balkans, many Adventists believed that the prelude to the second coming had begun, and it was therefore necessary to refuse any kind of military service. In contrast, Conradi and other responsible persons emphasized that the demands of the state must be obediently fulfilled. The differing views resulted in deep tensions, out of which came a church schism, and the beginning of various reform movements.

## Postscript

Conradi's great interest in church history bore positive fruits in Germany. In the mid-1930s, a young pastor and teacher at the Neanderthal Adventist Mission School near Mettmann, Walter Eberhardt (1902–1980), took up Conradi's view of history. Following the same model of viewing history from the perspective of the letters to the seven churches, he compiled ten volumes on the history of Christianity – an entire Adventist church history. In contrast to Conradi, he gave an overview of the whole of church history up to the present. Just before and after World War II, Eberhardt was the principal of Friedensau.

In retirement, Eberhardt published a four-volume church history that no longer explicitly follows the model of the seven letters, but is an excellent contribution to the understanding of history from an Adventist perspective. He especially details groups that were often oppressed by mainstream churches such as the Waldenses and the Anabaptists. The uniqueness of his church history lies in the fact that, alongside a concise but profound presentation, the footnotes offer a wealth of source materials that are seldom found in comparable works.[50] Here the reader finds the original soundtrack of church history and, from this, can paint his own picture of the events.

---

50 The four volumes appear under the title *Wege und Irrwege der Christenheit von der Urgemeinde bis zur Vorreformation* (Berlin: Union-Verlag, 1968); *Reformation und Gegenreformation* (Berlin: Union-Verlag, 1973); *Aufklärung und Pietismus 1648–1800* (Berlin: Union-Verlag, 1979); *Zwischen den Revolutionen* (Hamburg: Advent-Verlag, 1993).

*Gilbert M. Valentine*

## The Reformation and the Shaping of Conflict over the Meaning of "Righteousness by Faith" in Seventh-day Adventism 1960–1978

Abstract

During the almost two decades between 1960 and 1978, the Adventist church in the South Pacific and North America was roiled by fractious theological ferment over the doctrines of Christian perfection, Christian assurance and the meaning of righteousness by faith. The "Sanctuary Awakening Movement" led by Robert Brinsmead promoted an extreme version of sinless perfectionism within an Adventist eschatological framework claiming it to be "Historic Adventism." Both E. E. Heppenstall and Desmond Ford in formulating responses emphasized the implications of the doctrine of justification by faith. A later emphasis on forensic justification particularly in the context of the response to Tridentine doctrine framed by Martin Chemnitz, led to more sharply focused gospel teaching and significantly polarized the debate. The 1974 Palmdale Conference organized by the General Conference sought unsuccessfully to resolve the conflict. Perceptions of sixteenth-century reformers such as Chemnitz and the forensic emphasis on justification provoked and shaped the contours of this debate. Understandings of soteriology continue to divide opinion within the Adventist church.

Introduction

The theological turmoil that roiled the Seventh-day Adventist Church during the 1960s and 1970s in what was then the Australasian Division (now the South Pacific Division) was no inconsequential storm in the proverbial teacup. While the conflict began in the South Pacific, it soon spilled over into North America involving conferences and colleges and the General Conference and its agencies. It divided churches in both territories, led to the dis-fellowshipping of church members, cost numerous ministers and some college Bible teachers their jobs and pitted leading denominational periodicals against each other *(Ministry, Australasian Record* and *Adventist Review)*.[1] While anxious church administrators worried about the distraction from mission occasioned by the controversy, ironically significant developments towards the end of the conflict gave wide exposure of the

1    A brief overview of the outlines of the debate can be found in George Knight, *A Search for Identity* (Washington, DC: Review and Herald, 2000), 171–177. A broad analysis from a well-informed historical and sociology of religion perspective can be found in Malcom Bull and Keith Lockhart, *Seeking a Sanctuary: Seventh-day Adventism and the American Dream*, 2nd ed, (Indianapolis, IN: Indiana University Press, 2007) 83–98.

Adventist church to the larger Protestant world and stimulated the editors of *Ministry* magazine to embark on a wider mission to non-Adventist clergy.[2]

Beginning as a small lay-led cluster of agitators, "The Awakening Movement" soon morphed into a substantial faction, which stirred vigorous debate focused on soteriological issues involving particularly the doctrine of Christian perfection, assurance, original sin and the human nature of Christ. The "agitation" eventually generated a large body of polemical literature.[3] At its core, the debate swirled around questions about the meaning of the term "righteousness by faith" which were perceived by participants to have existential implications for the survival of authentic Adventism.

This paper will first address the background and context of the conflict, trace the contours of the debate as it developed during the two decades and show how those crucial developments were specifically shaped by particular understandings of the sixteenth-century Reformation's explication of the theme. The teaching of such figures as Martin Luther, John Calvin, Phillip Melanchthon but particularly Martin Chemnitz figured prominently in the debate and shaped both its development and its outcomes.[4]

---

2    The commencement of the ongoing expanded complimentary subscription program of *Ministry* magazine (PREACH) for non-Adventist clergy (currently 60,000) began in 1975 and provided 25,000 issues to non-Adventist clergy on an every-other-month basis. See *Seventh-day Adventist Encyclopedia* (Washington, DC: Review and Herald, 1976), 902. Brinsmead's *Present Truth* served as a model for the endeavor and prompted the initiative.

3    In a sampling of the literature, Tarling lists 22 books, pamphlets, reports, publications produced between 1959 and 1970. Prominent individual authors represented include E. E. Heppenstall, D. Ford, P. Jarnes, F. G. Clifford, L. C. Naden, H. K. LaRondelle, C. Mervyn Maxwell, H. E. Douglass, and K. H. Wood. The agitation engaged the attention and investment of substantial time for study groups such as the General Conference Biblical Research Committee (2), Defense Literature Committee of the General Conference (4), and endorsements of the Executive Committees of the General Conference and the Australasian Division; see Lowell Tarling, *The Edges of Seventh-day Adventism* (Barragga, NSW: Galilee Publications, 1981), 201. A graduate of Avondale and denominational school teacher during the 1970s, Tarling provides a sociological perspective on the movement with much helpful detail.

4    It is important to note that the debate was shaped in the pre-E. P. Sanders era of Pauline Studies. The insights of Krister Stendahl, "The Apostle Paul and the Introspective Conscience of the West" published first in the *Harvard Theological Review* 56 (1963), 199–215, were still being absorbed in the academic community. Sanders' *Paul and Palestinian Judaism*, published in 1977, gave rise to a number of new perspectives on Paul and Judaism. The importance of the "righteousness by faith" issue for the participants in the debate was conditioned by the fact that all subscribed to the primacy of the penal-substitution theory of the atonement as espoused by the sixteenth-century Reformers which was in its turn a variant of Anselm's satisfaction theory. The dominance in Adventism of the period of this framework for understanding the atonement related to the centrality of Adventist emphasis on law keeping and the sanctuary theme with its focus on the investigative judgement. Alternate theories such as Hugo Grotius' governmental theory of the atonement tended to be viewed as complementary to the penal-substitution view rather than in any way a negation of it.

## The Sanctuary Awakening Movement

Birthed in late 1959, the "Sanctuary Awakening Movement" began as a series of small unofficial camp meetings for a few interested families on Robert Brinsmead's farm near the Tweed River in northern New South Wales (Australia). Brinsmead at age 22 had enrolled at Avondale College in 1955 to undertake the ministerial course but in 1959 was not permitted to complete his program.[5] During his studies at Avondale however, the charismatic Robert, in his mid-twenties, had encountered the writings of A. T. Jones and E. J. Waggoner, studying them "quietly" in the college library. Shortly afterwards he read the iconoclastic ideas of Robert J. Wieland and Donald K. Short who challenged the standard interpretation of the 1888 Minneapolis Conference.[6] He was also disturbed by the new theology of the recently published *Questions on Doctrine* which attempted to distance the church from its previous positions on the human nature of Christ and reinterpret its understanding of a final atonement in 1844.[7] Enthused by the new insights about how to achieve perfection for the end times, he began to organize more regular meetings on his farm and elsewhere and developed extensive curriculum materials such as *The Sanctuary Institute Syllabi* articulating his ideas.

5  College administrators held reservations about his *bona fides* because of his family background (his parents had for a time been part of the Seventh Day Adventist Reform Movement) and his sister had come into conflict with church administration over doctrinal issues surrounding the book *Questions on Doctrine* and had been dis-fellowshipped. Prejudices and apprehensions nurtured misunderstandings and eventually resulted in doubts about Brinsmead's suitability for ministry. A further complication was occasioned by a verse-by-verse commentary which he had written on Daniel 11 in which he had challenged traditional interpretations arguing that the Roman Catholic Church was the King of the North of verse 40 and that it had succeeded in invading the Seventh-day Adventist Church through the subversive teaching of *Questions on Doctrine. The Vision by the Hiddekel* was first distributed in mimeographed form in 1958, and later published by International Health Institute, Denver, Colorado, 1970. For a perspective by church officials see *The Brinsmead Agitation: Its Background, Attitudes, and Some of Its Teachings* (Washington DC: Biblical Research Institute, 1969). An account that adopts a broader sociological perspective can be found in Tarling, 185–190.

6  The Wieland and Short manuscript, *1888 Re-examined*, prepared in 1950 was circulating widely in mimeographed form at this time. See Robert Brinsmead's *Sanctuary Institute Syllabus No 1* [1960], 214–216, for further details about the background of the emergence of the Awakening Movement in Australia. The Heritage Room, La Sierra University Library (LSUHR) has an extensive collection of Awakening Movement materials as does the Pacific Union College Heritage Collection (PUCHC).

7  Brinsmead's harsh criticism of church leadership over "the Barnhouse-Martin episode" particularly troubled church administrators. Brinsmead had written: "No informed person will question that worldliness has been the main sin down through our history. The episode of 1955, 1956, is a supreme demonstration of our desire to receive the approbation of the world." *Sanctuary Institute Syllabus I.* See *The Brinsmead Agitation*, 23–24.

Robert Brinsmead's generation of Adventists had been nurtured on a theology of end-time events that emphasized the challenges and perils of the time of trouble. The theology was built around Ellen White's graphic explanations that when probation closed (Rev 22:11) the saints would have to stand alone "in the sight of a holy God without a mediator."[8] The peril of the close of probation was the focal motivational point of much of Ellen White's own revivalist preaching and of the typical Adventist preacher.[9] In popular Adventist understanding this meant that believers would have to become perfectly sinless – not needing forgiveness anymore.

M. L. Andreasen's book *The Sanctuary Service*, a standard text used for college religion classes, had taken the idea a step further and with an extra twist taught that such sinless living was a necessary part of God's plan and that by this sinless living "in the last generation God gives the final demonstration that men can keep the law of God and that they can live without sinning." If the last generation of saints can do this "with all the odds stacked against them and the sanctuary closed, what excuse is there for men's ever sinning?" Thus, "through the last generation of saints God stands fully vindicated."[10] Other writers of the period taught a more vague Adventist view of the necessity of end-time perfection but without the "demonstration" feature.[11]

The burning issue for Brinsmead, as it had been for generations of Adventists, was how to stand in the judgement. Justification was understood to be "merely" for sins of the past. The real dilemma was how to live sinlessly when forgiveness and justification were no longer possible because the sanctuary was closed. Brinsmead recalled later, according to Geoffrey Paxton, an Anglican observer, "because of this doctrine ... very few people that I questioned had any real buoyant hope of being able to pass the scrutiny of the soon coming judgement of the living. It is no exag-

---

8   Ellen G. White, *Great Controversy* (Washington, DC: Review and Herald, 1911), 425. See also *Early Writings*, 280.
9   The close of probation functioned psychologically in a similar way to the concept of hellfire used by other evangelical revivalist preachers of the day. See for example Ellen White's first stenographically reported sermons, "Practical Remarks," *Review and Herald*, March 29, 1870, 113–114; and April 12, 1870, 130–131.
10  M. L. Andreasen, *The Sanctuary Service* (Washington, DC: Review and Herald, 1937, 1947), 299–321, 318.
11  For example see, W. H. Branson, *Our Firm Foundation* (Washington DC: Review and Herald, 1953), vol. 2, 573–618; also T. H. Jemison in the same volume, 412. The two volume publication contained the papers presented at a church-wide Bible Conference held in Washington, DC in September 1952 to affirm the doctrinal structure of historic Adventism. Samuele Bacchiocchi in assessing the difference between the writers observed that Brinsmead had "driven to a logical conclusion what others have left in suspense or expressed as an opinion or possibility." *An Analysis of Robert Brinsmead's Teachings Regarding the Cleansing of the Sanctuary*, Andrews University term paper, April 1963. Later circulated as a published booklet by Faith for Today, New York 1963, 4.

geration to say that most live in real fear and dread of the judgement."[12] It was the investigative judgement, courtroom setting of the problem that gave it its existential qualities and cast the subsequent debate exclusively in terms of the courtroom model of the atonement at the expense of other biblical models.

Paxton observes in his analysis of Brinsmead's teaching in this early period that Brinsmead drew from the sixteenth-century Reformers in his seeking of an answer to the anthropological problem of original sin. The problem loomed large in his thinking and was accentuated by the Adventist emphasis on the imminence of the tribulation. In what Paxton describes as a "monumental effort" to hold together the Reformation understanding of original sin and the mutually exclusive necessity of last day perfectionism, Brinsmead's theology became like "an ellipse with two focal points."[13] His peculiar solution to the sin problem was to develop a scheme of achieving perfection in the end time by the final atonement act of "blotting out of sin" from the subconscious mind of the believer – a physical eradicating of the sinful nature. Paralleling the sanctuary in heaven, each believer could also be understood on the basis of Pauline teaching as a temple of God in which the spirit dwells. Prior to the close of probation in a final cleansing of this "soul temple" as an act of God's gracious intervention, original sin and its effects would be finally "blotted out" of the temple of the soul by the "final atonement."[14]

Thus, Brinsmead was able to theoretically reject any claim to "here-and-now perfectionism" because he emphasized that perfection could only be achieved in the end time. Milton Hook observes, however, while this "brand" of perfection was only to be experienced in the last days, because "it was advocated simultaneously with a belief that the last days were already at hand, it made little difference whether perfection could be had then or in the future." [15] Edward Heppenstall of Loma Linda University also observed that the end result was the same. "The worst feature of this intensive search for sinless perfection, the most destructive impulse, is the anxiety, the despair, the self-condemnation and frustration which its victims feel."[16]

Brinsmead linked his sanctuary cleansing emphasis with a renewed interest in strict health reform, and "Awakeners" in local churches often adopted a vegan diet, which frequently was accompanied by a critical "holier than thou" attitude towards others and particularly the established church, as they quoted Ellen White endlessly. In common perception therefore at the local congregational level they were perceived simply as teaching the necessity of perfection and that the final events

---

12 Cited in Geoffrey J. Paxton, *The Shaking of Adventism* (Wilmington, DE: Zenith Publishers, 1977), 99–100.
13 Ibid.
14 Robert D. Brinsmead, *A Review of the Awakening Message*, part 1, 4.
15 Milton Hook, *Desmond Ford Reformist Theologian, Gospel Revivalist* (Riverside, CA: Adventist Today, 2008), 95.
16 *Evaluation of Brinsmead Doctrine* (Santa Ana, CA: P. H. Freeman, 1969), available at LSUHR.

would not come without it.[17] While Brinsmead never collected any tithe, other former Adventist ministers associated with him did and this for administrators was the litmus test of disloyalty for the movement. The Awakening Movement also tended to attract a range of "new lighters" and dissenters who brought to the movement their own axes of disaffection to grind.

In 1961 Brinsmead was disfellowshipped by his home congregation at Innisfail in Northern Australia for his divisive activities, and the movement soon spread more aggressively. Most conferences in the South Pacific were affected in some way as "Awakeners" agitated in local churches. And contrary to the view that the movement was largely a South Pacific phenomenon, Brinsmead attracted significant numbers of supporters in North America, some of whom had small, independent publishing outlets and substantial income from wealthy supporters that enabled him to circulate publications widely. In a 1970 sociological study of the movement, Robert W. Gardner reported that the group had a subscription list of 20,000 mostly USA addresses for their monthly newsletter. There were 225 fellowship groups and a donor list of 10,000, forty percent of whom had donated during 1969.[18]

A magazine entitled *Present Truth* was soon developed as a vehicle for promotion of the group's teaching. "Awakeners" took courage from the quiet endorsement of people such as H. E. Douglass, Bible teacher at Atlantic Union College who reported that he was teaching the same "basic thesis" as a significant part of his eschatology class.[19] The core perfectionist teaching of the movement also drew in teachers at other colleges, reaching perhaps its high point of appeal when in 1968 the Union College Theology Department Chair, Peter C. Jarnes, articulated awakening perfectionist teaching in his self-published book *The Sanctuary Restored*.[20] The effort cost him his job.

## The Church's Response

The first public theological response to Brinsmead's perfectionism in a church publication came from the pen of British-born Edward Heppenstall in 1963. He directly challenged the idea of the "eradication of the sinful nature" and denied on the basis of Scripture the possibility of sinless perfection in this life.[21] In a further

---

17  Hook, 95.
18  Fellowship group membership varied between 3 and 30. Hardy reports that an operating budget of $200,000 had resourced activities in 1970 and that a budget of $500,000 for 1971 anticipated expanded activities. Robert W. Gardner, "The Awakening: A Religious Movement in the Seventh-day Adventist Church," MA thesis, Loma Linda University (January 1971), 84, 90, 102. Tarling also provides detail of the kind of support Brinsmead was able to attract, 192.
19  H. E. Douglass to C. L. Conley, January 19, 1963 cited in Tarling, 200.
20  See https://goo.gl/auvkA9 (December 4, 2017).
21  Edward Heppenstall, "Is Perfection Possible?" *Signs of the Times*, December 1963, 10–11, 30. "Some Christians believe that it is possible in this life to reach a point in spiritual

hard-hitting response in 1969, Heppenstall argued that the teaching of Brinsmead on perfectionism (and by extension, also the teaching of Andreasen, W. H. Branson and T. H. Jemison) completely negated grace. "Sinless people do not need Grace." It was "egoism," the "product of self-seeking," and it exerted a "deadly influence upon oneself and one's relationship to others." Such perfectionism was "certainly" not "New Testament Christianity."[22] Heppenstall was widely respected in the church, and other voices in the church such as Harry W. Lowe, Norval Pease, E. W. Vick and Desmond Ford began to support his refutation of perfectionism.[23] The pushback from "Awakeners" was vigorous.

Spokesperson Jack Zwemer in a point-by-point reply to Heppenstall's evaluation alleged that Heppenstall's attack had "actually placed historic Adventism under assault." The teaching that "man must live in God's sight without a Mediator" was "distinctive Adventist belief" taught by the pioneers. Although it was "one appalling truth" Adventism had "stood on this truth with all its awful implications." In denying the possibility of sinless perfection Heppenstall had "essentially repudiated historic Adventism." From the Awakening perspective, he had rejected "the genius and destiny of Adventism" and returned to the "erroneous concepts of evangelical Protestantism."[24]

In the South Pacific region of the church Desmond Ford became the primary respondent to the 1960s Awakening Movement. Ford had studied with Heppenstall at the Adventist seminary in Michigan. The two had become friends and Heppenstall had persuaded Ford to undertake doctoral studies at the University of Michigan rather than confine himself to seminary studies at Berrien Springs. Ford had returned to Avondale in early 1961.[25] Ford had also been friends with Brinsmead since their college days together in the late 50s and Ford continued to maintain the friendship even as he challenged Brinsmead's teaching and divisive activities. Ford also worked

    development where the sinful nature is completely eradicated and, therefore, no longer operative" (ibid., 10). Heppenstall warned that "the pretension to sinless perfection at any time in this earthly life is the root of spiritual pride and self-righteousness." (ibid., 30).
22  *Evaluation of Brinsmead Doctrine*, 6.
23  Paxton documents these contributions during the late 1960s. From his perspective Heppenstall's refutation marked "a high point" in Adventist theology claiming that there was not an equal during this period (Paxton, 112). A 1985 questionnaire of North American Adventist lecturers revealed that Heppenstall was the Adventist writer who had most influenced them. See Bull, Malcolm and Lockhart, Keith, "The Intellectual World of Adventist Theologians," *Spectrum* 18:1 (1987), 33–34.
24  Jack D. Zwemer to E. Heppenstall, June 21, 1969, is published in *Evaluation of Brinsmead Doctrine*, 21, 24.
25  Heppenstall had tried to arrange a teaching appointment at the Seminary for Ford following the completion of his doctorate but contractual obligations to Australia prevailed. The two men continued a regular correspondence. See Hook, 76–82.

closely with Division President Laurence C. Naden in counteracting the influence. Both wrote pamphlets and books addressing the theological issues.[26]

Ford's distinctive response to the Awakening Movement's perfectionist teaching, as he explained to his biographer, Milton Hook, was not to engage in protracted dialogue and public debate with Brinsmead. Rather he focused on preaching and teaching the doctrine of Christian assurance and in many different ways highlighted the radical implications of justification by faith understood not just as forgiveness of the past but as a continuing status as one remained in a faith relationship with Christ. Ford's charismatic winsome style of preaching put him in much demand throughout Australia during this period and his emphasis on the positive dimensions of the gospel provided an effective corrective. In the occasional friendly dialogue with Brinsmead during walks through the bush or talks over a dinner table, Ford recalled that he would urge Brinsmead to read and study the sixteenth-century Reformers and that that exercise would correct his view of perfectionism.[27]

In his classes for undergraduate ministerial students at Avondale, Ford would be more specific in dealing with the perfectionist theology as students repeatedly raised direct questions about Brinsmead's teaching, often citing him, and sometimes if they came from families that were sympathetic to Brinsmead more directly challenged him. But Ford's distinctive response to students was largely the same as his response to Brinsmead himself. In his class on biblical theology a strong focus on Romans and Galatians anchored the class. In his systematics class students were assigned large swaths of Augustus Strong's *Systematic Theology* to read and some from Louis Berkhof. Ford required his students to read the sixteenth-century Reformers or those who articulated Reformation perspectives. Lengthy mimeographed selections from Luther and Calvin on justification and sanctification were provided and students were tested on them. Extracts from James Buchanan's recently published *The Doctrine of Justification by Faith* (1961) were required reading as was Charles Spurgeon's classic sermon on "Justification by Faith." Students were closely quizzed on their reading. Readings on the Reformationist understanding of original sin were also required as were critiques of predestination and the five points of Calvinism. Church History class required the reading of Roland Bainton's then still fairly new scholarly biography of Luther.[28] In distinctive ways, under Ford, Luther's unyielding stand for truth and "the gospel" became the iconic model for himself and for his ministerial students. It spoke to Adventism's call for loyalty and faithfulness in Sabbath keeping and in faithfulness to the gospel.

Extensive readings were also required from Wesley and the Arminian perspective on free will and the human dilemma. There were extensive discussions of Wesley's concept of entire sanctification not meaning sinless perfection but the

---

26 L. C. Naden, *The Perfecting of the Saints* (Warburton, AUS: Signs Publishing, 1964) and D. Ford, *Unlocking God's Treasury*, (Warburton, AUS: Signs Publishing, 1964). See Hook, 99, for a discussion of these.
27 Hook, 95, 100.
28 Roland Bainton, *Here I Stand: A Life of Martin Luther* (Nashville, TN: Abingdon, 1950).

experience of the divine "perfect love" and although he required his students to read and appreciate holiness authors such as Hannah Whitehall Smith, Thomas Gordon, and Judson Taylor, and even Thomas à Kempis's *Imago Dei*, for devotional nurture, his constant emphasis was on the primacy of justification by faith as the root and sanctification as the fruit of the Christian life.[29] As Milton Hook observes, Avondale was thus very effectively protected from the impact of the Awakening Movement. An analysis of Ford's writing and preaching during this period by Geoffrey Paxton notes that in his repudiation of perfectionism he was consistent in his affirmation of four cardinal reformation perspectives: *sola scriptura*, the doctrine of original sin, forensic justification and the sinlessness of Christ's human nature.[30] "During the 1960s Brinsmead's theories exerted no influence on the Avondale campus."[31]

## Brinsmead's Capitulation

According to Brinsmead's own recollection he had begun to doubt the validity of his convictions about perfectionism toward the end of 1969 and in the following year he completely jettisoned the idea.[32] A number of factors influenced the radical reversal. The artificial solution which required an eradication of the sinful nature prior to the Advent did not cohere easily with his other soteriological convictions. The effort of maintaining the tension between his eschatological perfectionism and the historic Reformation principle of *simul justus et peccator* eventually became intolerable.[33]

The crystalizing of the change in Brinsmead's theological understanding occurred in early 1971 when he found himself obliged to give much more time to the serious study of the writings of the sixteenth-century Reformers. The need for the study was occasioned by somewhat unusual circumstances. In April 1970 during the lead-up preparations for a papal visit to Australia in 1971 Brinsmead had publicly questioned the right of the Australian government to spend taxpayers' money for a religious dignitary. The challenge caught the attention of local press and TV and as a consequence a local Roman Catholic official challenged Brinsmead to a

---

29 Based on syllabi and class notes in the possession of the author who was a student in Ford's classes at Avondale 1965–1968.
30 Paxton, 116f. For examples, see Desmond Ford, *Unlocking God's Treasury*, 15–18; "What is Meant by Justification?" *Signs of the Times* (Australian edition), July 1959; "Grace or Works?" *Signs of the Times* (Australian edition), January 1960.
31 Hook, 95.
32 R. D. Brinsmead to "Brethren and Fellow Burden Bearers in the Awakening," September 10, 1969 cited in Tarling, 201.
33 Paxton, 102. Interaction with retired administrator Walter Scragg Sr. also helped in the theological reappraisal. See Hook, 125–126. Other readers of Brinsmead's articles at this time, such as Division President L. C. Naden also perceived a subtle change in tone and a sense of uncertainty. See Tarling, 193.

public debate which he brashly accepted. This necessitated a hurried, intense study of Roman Catholic theology to prepare himself for the debate. Brinsmead recounted that his preparation involved conversations with a theologian at the Catholic Seminary in Banyo, Brisbane, and with local Lutheran ministers about their respective understandings of their community's teaching on soteriology.

Brinsmead's preparation also involved him in wide reading in the literature of the Reformation. Martin Luther's *Lectures on Galatians* was particularly influential in persuading him that the Reformation meaning of righteousness by faith was to be understood as justification alone. Study of Calvin and Melanchthon reinforced this view. He reports that he came to see that his sinless perfection idea could not cohabit with a thoroughgoing Reformationist position on soteriology. He became convinced of the primacy of a forensic understanding of justification and that while justification and sanctification could never be separated they were nevertheless logically distinct. He was persuaded that justification as *imputed* righteousness and sanctification as *imparted* righteousness should not be fused together under the term "righteousness by faith."[34]

Brinsmead relates that an even more revolutionary insight occurred during the latter months of 1970 when he eventually read *Examination of the Council of Trent* by Martin Chemnitz (1522–1586) and works by Luther.[35] Whether he read the full four volumes of Chemnitz is not clear, but what Brinsmead took from his reading was a clearer perception of how the Reformation differentiated itself from Roman Catholicism as it was defined by the decretals of the Council of Trent. Brinsmead understood from these distinctive definitional and contrasting statements of Chemnitz that his own perfectionism, his historic Adventist insistence on merging both infused righteousness and imputed righteousness under the rubric of righteousness by faith made him no different theologically from Roman Catholic soteriology and that shocked and astounded him. He says that he saw with new clarity what Luther meant when he declared that the doctrine of justification by faith was the article of a standing or falling church. He found himself compelled to abandon his previous understanding.[36]

The picture clarified for Brinsmead over the year-end period and he thus excused himself from the debate, shared his changed perspective with his Awakening supporters and reportedly took "truckloads of perfectionist literature to the dump."[37] In a spirit of confession he and his brother John travelled to Washington, D.C., with a respected American colleague and supporter, Jack Zwemer, to apologize to General Conference officials for the divisiveness and distress they had brought to the

---

34 Brinsmead described these developments in interviews with Trevor Lloyd at Duranbah, NSW, March 18, April 16, 1996 cited in Hook, 124–127.
35 A student of Martin Luther, Martin Chemnitz became a major influence in the development of second generation orthodox Lutheranism and a primary author of its confessional expression in the *Formula of Concord*.
36 Paxton, 104.
37 Hook, 127.

church. The meetings developed into a week-long theological consultation between the parties and involved other invited scholars.

Although now ostensibly in harmony with the church, the former Awakening leaders were reluctant to discard their *Present Truth* publication because they saw it as a potential medium for sharing their new understanding about Adventism and the Reformation and the implications of justification by faith with a wider audience. Neal C. Wilson, observing that Brinsmead was not going to lose his interest in theology any time soon, suggested that the journal be utilized to communicate the now clarified justification by faith gospel message with the wider Protestant world. Within a short space of time Brinsmead and his associates changed the focus of the monthly publication, broadened its circulation base and published a range of articles exploring the doctrine of justification by faith in its many phases and discussing the wide range of implications of the doctrine for church life and belief. Discussion focused particularly on the meaning of the Reformation and frequently included extracts from the sixteenth-century Reformers.[38] During the years 1971–1974 the circulation, according to Lowell Tarling, reached 100,000 readers, only 10–20% of whom were Seventh-day Adventists. This was a larger penetration of the non-Adventist world than the establishment Adventist journals such as *Signs of the Times* and *These Times* had ever been able to achieve.[39] In 1974 the journal changed its name to *Verdict* to avoid confusion with other religious journals with similar initials but continued to engage with a wide range of clergy. The reader response pages regularly represented correspondence from a range of religious traditions.[40]

## The Influence of Martin Chemnitz and Polarization in the Righteousness by Faith Debate

Two far-reaching and rather paradoxical developments flowed from Brinsmead's surprise abandonment of perfectionism in 1971. Geoffrey Paxton observed them as "an almost unbelievable turn of events."[41] The first development was that while

---

38   Early issues focused on a critique of Pentecostalism and other holiness movements and were preoccupied with theological discussion of the danger of merging and confusing sanctification and justification together. Later issues broadened to discussions of the meaning of the atonement and other Reformation concerns such as predestination and the nature of sin including explorations of Arminianism and Wesleyanism. Files of the journals are available in LSUHR.
39   Tarling, 195.
40   The issue on predestination, for example, published letters from 26 respondents, 16 of whom identified themselves as pastors, one seminary dean and one professor emeritus. *Present Truth*, November 1976, 2–7.
41   Paxton, 124. Bull and Lockhart note that this was one of a number of ironies, among them the fact that Heppenstall's denial of perfectionism was "far more radical" than Brinsmead's assertion of it even if Brinsmead's form of it was "idiosyncratic." Bull and Lockhart, *Seeking a Sanctuary*, 87.

church leadership in the South Pacific interpreted Brinsmead's reorientation as a move in the right theological direction and saw it as a validation of the antiperfectionist stance of Heppenstall, Naden, and Ford, other powerful figures in church leadership in North America ironically saw the Heppenstall-Ford emphasis on justification by faith as distorted and "one-sided." *Review* editors, Kenneth Wood and Herbert Douglass in particular saw the new "gospel" emphasis as a serious threat to their final generation sinless demonstration theology and began to adopt an overt perfectionist emphasis through the pages of the *Review*. They soon claimed General Conference President Robert H. Pierson as an ally. The Washington, D.C. response to Brinsmead's strongly Reformationist and forensic perspective became even more specific and strident with the publication of a special "righteousness by faith" issue of the *Review* in mid-1974 which reaffirmed the traditional perspectives previously advocated by M. L. Andreasen, W. H. Branson and T. Housel Jemison.[42] Douglass's contribution to the special issue stressed the need for a here-and-now perfectionism and that God was waiting "for a people who will prove that what Jesus did ... could be done by his followers."[43] The special issue drew a provocative response from Brinsmead that directly challenged the assumption that sanctification could be legitimately embraced under the Pauline use of the term "righteousness by faith" and asserted that to do this was to side with the Council of Trent against the Protestant Reformation.[44]

The second development arising from Brinsmead's reversal was shaped particularly by the encounter with Martin Chemnitz. In Australia, significant numbers of church members were reading *Present Truth* and were finding it helpful in clarifying theological issues. Brinsmead's friends and followers were also reading Chemnitz and putting their sharpened perspectives into print. Cedrick Taylor's articles on the topic, for example, published in *Scope* magazine were widely read.[45] As Lowell Tarling noted, "by putting the issues in black and white it was the first time that Adventist laity in Australia could see the differences of thought within their church. It was, in fact, the first time," observed Tarling, "that there were such widespread and strong differences in Seventh-day Adventism on the plan of salvation."[46] Tarling's detailed narrative of the events of the 1970s describes how

---

42  The undated special issue was published on May 16, 1974 and emphasized that righteousness was an experience more than a doctrine. The special issue insisted that righteousness by faith embraced both justification and sanctification but it majored in its emphasis on sanctification with articles that spoke of victory over sin.

43  "Why God is Urgent and Yet Waits," *Review: Righteousness by Faith* (1974), 22.

44  Robert Brinsmead, *A Statement to My S. D. A. Friends*: [ca. July 1974]. The provocative lengthy subtitle of the pamphlet reads *Is Sanctification the Same as Righteousness by Faith? Rome says Yes; The Reformation says No; Where do Seventh-day Adventists Stand?*

45  C. Taylor, "Catholic or Protestant," *Scope,* July–September, 1973. Scope was a short-lived journal for Adventist young people attending public universities. The articles based on Chemnitz's response to the Council of Trent set out the issues in a stark black-and-white way for Australian Adventists.

46  Tarling, 196.

students at Avondale (he was a student there at the time) were quite taken by the harder-edged Chemnitzian approach in *Present Truth* whereby the issues were being sharpened by stating "what the Gospel *isn't* as well as what the Gospel *is*."[47] This approach was now viewed as an important strategy to help more clearly define the issues. The Chemnitzian approach brought a sharp new dimension to the debate and negated the assertion that the discussion was only a matter of semantics and it undercut the commonly held notion that "We're all saying the same thing [just] in a different way."[48]

Activist students excited by the Christian assurance that the gospel emphasis brought became involved in sharing their insights in local churches and also in evangelistic outreach through street preaching and coffee shop initiatives particularly in the Victorian Conference and to a lesser degree in other conferences. In Bible study groups students used discussion materials from *Present Truth* that, following Chemnitz, placed in parallel columns what the gospel was and what it was not. Other parallel columns, again in the fashion of Chemnitz contrasted the Protestant understanding and meaning of aspects of soteriology with Roman Catholic meaning and usage. These materials highlighted the contrast between such ideas as *declaring* righteous and *making* righteous, *infusing* and *imputing* and made it clear that traditional Adventist understanding and usage reflected the Roman Catholic understanding. (See App. 1) These activities created intense discussion and debate. Factions developed in churches and during 1974 a dissenting congregation united around a perceived need to defend so-called "historic Adventism" began to form in Melbourne which greatly alarmed church leaders.[49]

When Ford returned to Avondale from the United Kingdom at the end of 1972 following the completion of his second doctorate with F. F. Bruce at the University of Manchester he found a student body very much engaged with the issues. Milton Hook reports that some time shortly after his return, one of Ford's former students passed on to him a Brinsmead article or perhaps a copy of *Present Truth* with its extracts from Reformation sources and Ford turned to researching the sources for himself. In this way it seems Ford was introduced to the Chemnitz perspective. Given the pushback from the *Review* and its reassertion of final generation perfectionism Ford noted to his biographer that he too felt that the utilization of Chemnitz's contrasts and comparisons with Roman Catholic theology might now be helpful. As a result of his study of Chemnitz, he reports, he came to see righteousness by faith in sharper focus.[50] While still not willing to attack perfectionists head on and thus divide his audiences he nevertheless more clearly emphasized justification by faith as Hook notes, "with language that the laity could understand, often using vivid imagery, analogies, parables and Bible biography all

47  Ibid.
48  Ibid.
49  Ibid.
50  Desmond Ford, Interview with Trevor Lloyd, March 12, 1995, cited in Hook, 147.

laced with pithy one-liners."[51] Hook observes that Ford could not say that the perfectionism that his fellow church leaders advocated "was akin to Roman Catholicism's doctrine of sanctification as Brinsmead was doing," but his preaching and writing clearly emphasized the assurance of the gospel.[52] A typical sermon would assert,

> We stumble our way to the Kingdom of God in [a] progressive growth in holiness ... that is manifested in an increasing awareness of sinfulness ... The chimera of sinlessness in this life is not a New Testament hope. Romans 7.14–25 and Galatians 5.17 show that the flesh strives against the spirit continually through the Christian's experience ... The legalism in the New Testament was not the belief that we are saved by works, but that we are saved by faiths *[sic]* and works. Adventists are in danger of this error ... We are not saved by faith and works but by faith that works.[53]

While Ford understood and appreciated the clarity that Chemnitz gave to the discussion and as a helpful corrective to perfectionism, he had other reasons to avoid such a polarizing debate and unnecessarily offending those who held to traditional views. Opposition to his teaching at Avondale from several retired pastors had coalesced into a "Get Rid of Ford" (GROF) movement. The group who identified themselves as the Concerned Brethren (CBs) was motivated by a mix of personal jealousies and theological concerns.[54] Charges circulated around the Division office that Ford's preaching fostered antinomianism and more disturbing still for many church members who were not aware of Brinsmead's change of heart, Ford's name and Avondale also by association were being linked with Brinsmead. Damaging rumors of a "Ford-Brinsmead mateship" spread widely.[55] South Pacific Division leadership in late 1974 together with Heppenstall in California and his colleagues at Andrews became increasingly alarmed at the damage to Ford's reputation.[56]

51 Hook, 148. See, e.g., Desmond Ford, *The Cross and Other Sermons* (Sydney: Steam Press, 1977).
52 Hook, 148.
53 Desmond Ford, "The Two Faces of Redemption," *The Australasian Record*, February 10, 1975, 13. Douglass dissented strongly from such ideas. H. E. Douglass to Paul von Wielt, March 11, 1975, cited in Hook, 150.
54 Theological criticism focused on Ford's willingness to allow flexibility on the 6,000 year date for the age of the earth, his interpretations of Daniel 9 and 11 which differed from traditional Adventist interpretations, his questioning the geographic literalness of two apartments in the heavenly sanctuary and an unwillingness to see Ellen White as a determinant authority on doctrinal definition. Hook, 154f.
55 "Mate" in Australian culture is an iconic term conveying the idea of a close, confidential and mutually protective friendship in the sense of "close buddy." While Brinsmead and Ford were former classmates and maintained a cordial friendship and engaged in theological exchange they were not "close buddies" and the term "mateship" was misleading and derogatory in this context.
56 A twelve-part series of articles on Daniel published in the *Australasian Record* and *Ministry* in which Ford suggested the idea of recurring fulfilment as a way of augmenting historicist interpretation brought criticism (Hook, 136). Both Heppenstall and William Murdoch, then Dean of the Seminary, wrote supportively to Ford over the issues.

Division officers found themselves involved in defensive efforts to protect Ford's name and in the process falling increasingly out of step with General Conference President Robert Pierson who had allied himself with Kenneth Wood and Douglass. The latter misleadingly labeled the evangelical renewal perspective as "liberal" and actively promoted Douglass's version of Andreasen's end-time demonstration generation of sinless commandment keepers.[57] Douglass's view was that the church was "reaping the results of years of rudderless theology." He was reassured however that church administration had become aware "of the magnitude of this present diversion" from "solid historic Adventist thought." He assured a young correspondent in Australia that "Elders Pierson, Hackett and Wilson are reversing all that, believe me ..." and he asked to be kept informed about the "mateship."[58]

## Intensified Conflict and the Palmdale Conference

In mid-1975 the two sides in the debate over Christian perfection were highlighted in the publication of a volume by the church's Southern Publishing Association in its Anvil series entitled *Perfection: The Impossible Possibility*. The book contained two careful and civilly reasoned positions on each side of the question – one side by Heppenstall and Hans LaRondelle, and the other by C. Mervyn Maxwell and Herbert Douglass. The book added clarity but whether it changed people's minds is uncertain.

About this same time the debate was further inflamed in Australia by the publication of *The Soteriological Implications of the Human Nature of Christ* by Gillian Ford (Desmond Ford's wife). Published by Avondale Press, the 50-page manuscript had been originally prepared as a collation of materials for a Sabbath School class that Gillian was teaching at her local church in Cooranbong. It drew from class notes she had taken as a student in Norman Young's New Testament classes at Avondale and it affirmed the sinless nature of Christ position advanced by L. E. Froom and R. A. Anderson in *Questions on Doctrine*. Gillian supported her argument with extensive quotations from Ellen White – different quotations from those adduced by Douglass. The paper was reviewed by the six theology lecturers at Avondale and subsequently used as supplementary readings for class assignments.[59] The manuscript is a further illustration of the significant influence Martin Chemnitz had on the contours of the theological debate over the meaning of righteousness by faith in Adventism in the mid-1970s. As Lowell Tarling observes, the publication antagonized those who supported the perspective of Douglass and the *Review*

---

57 Hook, 142–145. See also Raymond Cottrell, "Architects of Crisis: A Decade of Obscurantism," (1984), Andrews University Center for Adventist Research (AUCAR).
58 H. E. Douglass to Paul von Wielt, March 11, 1975, cited in Hook, 140.
59 The manuscript was reviewed and endorsed by Raoul Dederen and others such as Division Ministerial Secretary Ray Stanley. Raoul Dederen to Desmond Ford, September 15, 1975; Ray Stanley to Desmond Ford, December 1, 1975, cited in Hook, 152.

because it utilized Chemnitz's comparison and contrast method and classified their perfectionism as "That Other Gospel" in contrast with "The True Gospel."[60]

Gillian Ford's book prompted a flurry of protests and petitions from perfectionists and members of the retired CB group. Division officers came under pressure to "restrain" Avondale if not clean out its apostate teachers. Fierce debates were held in Melbourne and Sydney about what specifically should be embraced in the term "righteousness by faith." Was it essentially a forensic legal term or not? Anti-perfectionist participants in the debate viewed this issue as crucial. They felt that on this matter it was vitally important to maintain the same distinctions as the sixteenth-century Reformers. Increasingly on the other hand, CBs interpreted the justification by faith emphasis as antinomianism and became convinced that they were locked in a battle for the soul of historic Adventism.

As Milton Hook documents, the new Division president Robert Frame became "increasingly alarmed by the promotion of perfectionism in American SDA literature," and former president Laurence Naden echoed his concern.[61] The fact that the Division journal *The Australasian Record* was being pitted against the *Review* alarmed Division leaders who decided to appeal to the General Conference for a consultation to resolve the issue of whether the biblical term righteousness by faith referred to justification or a fusion of both justification and sanctification. The question seemed pedantic but throughout the Division it had become the decisive issue for determining the orthodoxy of sinless perfectionism and last generation demonstration theology. Church administration felt that the ferment in Australia had reached boiling point and the situation could not continue without serious damage to the church. Frame finally persuaded Pierson of the necessity of a meeting where both parties could sort out the problem face to face.[62]

The two groups met in the high desert town of Palmdale in California for seven days, April 23–30, 1976. Nine representatives from Australia (Avondale, *Australasian Record* and Union and Division administrators) met with ten American representatives (Andrews University, *Review*, White Estate and General Conference administrators).[63] Prepared papers were considered on the key issues concerning the sinful nature of Christ, the possibility of sinless perfection and

60 Tarling notes the contrast method but does not source it to Chemnitz, see Tarling, 196.
61 Naden complained to Frame, "It has been distressing to me to note that at least two men in the States have been preaching and publishing the old Brinsmead view on the nature of Christ and sinless perfection." He named Herbert Douglass and Mervyn Maxwell. L. C. Naden to R. R. Frame, November 13, 1975, cited in Hook, 158, 159.
62 Hook, 159, references several letters from General Conference leaders who indicated that part of the reluctance to call such a meeting was because they felt the difference in perspective was merely semantic.
63 The study group, appointed jointly by the General Conference and the Australasian Division, was composed of Raoul Dederen, N. R. Dower, W. Duncan Eva, Desmond Ford, R. R. Frame, W. J. Hackett, Gordon M. Hyde, A. S. Jorgensen, C. D. Judd, Hans K. LaRondelle, L. C. Naden, Don F. Neufeld, Robert W. Olson, Robert H. Parr, Robert H. Pierson, A. P. Salom, C. R. Stanley, S. M. Uttley, and Kenneth H. Wood.

whether sanctification was to be understood as part of the Pauline expression "righteousness by faith." This latter was considered crucial from the anti-perfection perspective because it was important to avoid the sense that sanctification contributed to an individual's salvation combining "the accepting of what Christ has done with the Christian's doing" which then led to the widespread Adventist understanding that the more one had of imparted righteousness the less one needed imputed righteousness.[64]

The Chemnitz paradigm of providing a contrast with Tridentine theology continued to serve as a filter for at least the Australian group at Palmdale. According to Ford, after a presentation by one of the American delegates he was so exasperated he blurted out undiplomatically, "Well, that was Roman Catholic theology, lock stock and barrel."[65] Australian colleagues, Robert Frame and Alwyn Salom, Ford recalled, later remonstrated with him that at least in public such candid comments were not helpful. From Ford's perspective, the doctrine of sinless perfection was not a truly Protestant doctrine. The issues were not just semantic or fine issues of systematic theology. They had serious pastoral implications. The tone of the meeting was apparently amicable and participants came to appreciate the honesty of each other's motives and sincerity of convictions and Christian experience even though the conference did not change anyone's mind.[66]

The agreed consensus statement published after the conference was noted for its ambiguity. It affirmed two points and thus allowed each of the parties to claim that it represented their perspective. The statement began with a clear agreed affirmation "that when the words 'righteousness' and 'faith' are connected (by 'of', 'by' etcetera) in Scripture, reference is to the experience of Justification by Faith." This meant, the statement explained, that God "declared righteous" the person who believes in Jesus, and several paragraphs expanded this understanding of the distinction between justification and sanctification and the "aloneness" of this declaration as the basis of salvation "without any works of law" although the word "alone" is actually avoided in the text. The statement also allowed, however, that Seventh-day Adventists "have often used the phrase 'righteousness by faith' theologically to include both justification and sanctification." This had been done as a way of underlining the importance and necessity of obedience and regeneration.[67]

Ford returned to Avondale affirming that a decisive acknowledgement had been made at Palmdale concerning the meaning of the Pauline expression and that this protected the church from a soteriology that was essentially Roman Catholic. He was widely sought out as a speaker on the topic post-Palmdale. In the weeks that

64   This was argued to Frame in correspondence. Desmond Ford to Robert Frame, November 10, 1975, cited in Hook, 160.
65   Desmond Ford interview with Trevor Lloyd, March 12, 1965, March 10, 1996, cited in Hook, 161.
66   Hook, 163.
67   "Christ Our Righteousness Palmdale Statement," *Review*, May 27, 1976, 2; *Australasian Record*, May 31, 1972, 1.

followed Palmdale in America, however, the *Review* also ran a series of editorial commentaries on the Palmdale statement using it as a basis for justifying Wood's continued emphasis on last generation perfection and demonstration theology and defending the sinful nature of Christ.[68] R. H. Parr, editor of the *Australasian Record*, objected strongly to Wood about the misuse of his editorial position and the slant he gave to the statement.[69] The Palmdale statement failed to settle the dispute.[70]

Shortly after the conference two Australian medical doctors, John Clifford and Russell Standish who, according to Tarling, considered themselves as spokesmen for the traditionalists and who had been offended that they had not been invited to participate in the Palmdale Conference, prepared a 160-page document that in harsh and vituperative tones excoriated Ford and Avondale for teaching antinomianism and for their denial of historic Adventism. *Conflicting Concepts of Righteousness by Faith in the Seventh-day Adventist Church in the Australasian Division* alleged that "the Ford-Brinsmead apostasy" was "the most threatening and most serious ever to confront the Seventh-day Adventist Church. Never before have such views been suggested by Seventh-day Adventists."[71] The book concluded its six chapters with a Chemnitz style summary of forty-one topical headings under which parallel statements were listed. "Ford-Brinsmead say," contrasted with "God says."[72] The paper misleadingly claimed on its cover to be a Biblical Research Institute paper which greatly distressed the Division administration who lodged protests to the authors over the "audacity" of this breach of protocol.[73] Standish and Clifford refused to withdraw the manuscript – it had already been circulated extensively in Australia and North America and it thus prompted vigorous rebuttals from the Division Field Secretary, Ford, Brinsmead and several others.[74]

68  K. H. Wood, "FYI," *Review*, October 21, 1976, 3; November 18, 1976, 3.
69  R. H. Parr to D. Ford, Jan. 25, 1979, cited in Hook, 172.
70  Further follow-up consultations involving smaller groups of the participants chaired by General Conference Vice President Duncan Eva failed to resolve the differences.
71  A. J. Clifford and R. R. Standish, *Conflicting Concepts of Righteousness by Faith in the Seventh-day Adventist Church – Australasian Division*. (Wahroonga, NSW: Burnside Press, 1976), 156.
72  Ibid., 142–154.
73  Tarling, 211; A. S. Jorgenson to Russell Standish, June 28, 1976; A. S. Jorgenson to John Clifford and Russell Standish, July 21, 1976 cited in Hook, 178. See also A. S. Jorgenson, "Independent Publications," *The Australasian Record*, August 30, 1976, 12.
74  A. S. Jorgensen, "Circular Letter to Division Officers, Union and Local Conference Presidents, Departmental Directors and Division and Union Institutional Directors, R. H. Parr and D. Ford," July 19, 1976. Jorgensen explained that the document was unacceptable even for consideration by BRI because:
   • It has already been widely circulated prior to vetting
   • The claim that the manuscript spoke for a wide group of laymen and workers (the BRI felt such could speak for themselves)
   • It was an attack on Dr. Ford and Avondale College
   • It alleged that Ford imported heresy into Avondale from Brinsmead
   • It misrepresented Ford's positon

In the following year Brinsmead's continued emphasis on Reformationist teaching in Chemnitzian fashion of comparing the true gospel with its Roman Catholic opposite helped keep the conflagration alight. But two additional major publications soon added fuel to the fire. In early 1977 the General Conference Sabbath School Department-approved quarterly pamphlet for the second quarter was circulated worldwide. Prepared by Herbert Douglass and entitled *Jesus, The Model Man* the pamphlet boldly taught the sinful nature of Christ and last generation perfectionism which the Australasian church leaders had so strongly opposed. South Pacific administrators regarded the publication as incendiary and attempted to disallow its distribution in their region. They were unsuccessful but given the general theological context in the South Pacific it seems that most pastors distanced themselves from the pamphlet or actively countered its teaching in their Sabbath Schools. It was this flagrant promotion of the perfectionist point of view and its endorsement from the General Conference that, Hook observes, contributed to a sense of disillusionment and cynicism among many church members and pastors.[75]

The second major development that exacerbated the theological tensions both in Australia and the United States and brought them to a peak in late 1977 was the publishing of *The Shaking of Adventism* by Anglican clergyman observer of the Adventist scene, Geoffrey Paxton. Principal of the Queensland Bible Institute and a part-time tutor in the history of Christian thought at the University of Queensland, Paxton had become acquainted with Brinsmead and undertook a study of the recent soteriological developments in Adventism as a thesis for a graduate degree at Queensland University. His thesis analyzed the struggle within the Adventist church over soteriological issues and attempted to evaluate the Adventist claim to be "the true heirs" of the Protestant Reformation. As the basis for his evaluation he took the refined reformed positions of the later Luther as they had been expressed in the Formula of Concord and as articulated by Martin Chemnitz. Utilizing Chemnitz's expression of Reformation distinctives as framed in response to the Tridentine expression of Roman Catholicism, Paxton came to the conclusion that with its recent unprecedented intensity of stress on perfectionism, Adventism had unwittingly

- It claimed "Justification" came as a result of a person being regenerated and sanctified rather than these being the result of "Justification"
- It called into question the motives and credibility of the Division and Avondale leaders
- There was misrepresentation in the manuscript by misquoting authors

See also D. Ford, "Observations on Conflicting Concepts on Righteousness by Faith," (Australasian Division), 1976. This pamphlet was an official response requested by the Australasian Division BRI. R. D. Brinsmead, *An Answer to "Conflicting Concepts of Righteousness by Faith in the Seventh-day Adventist Church,"* (Sydney, NSW: Wittenberg Steam Press, 1976), 143ff. This latter volume is an edited transcript of talks Brinsmead gave in Melbourne in September 24–25, 1976.

75 Hook, 184.

aligned itself with the Roman Catholic articulation of its doctrine of salvation without of course adopting its sacramentalism or its idea of merit.[76]

Paxton's analysis disturbed Adventist leaders and evoked numerous critical reviews from Adventist scholars. LaRondelle faulted him on his definition of the Reformation gospel and argued that more modern interpreters of Luther saw his emphasis more broadly and that the emphasis on justification by faith alone was "purely theoretical" and "merely verbal" and "abstract."[77] William Johnsson suggested that Adventism's real link with the Reformation was with respect to *sola scriptura* rather than an acceptance of its precise expression of justification by faith.[78] Other reviews such as those by Ford and Richard Rice, while acknowledging things they disagreed with, were nevertheless more positive.[79] Rice affirmed the book's review of past and then-present views of salvation in Adventism as well-informed and generally accurate. He felt that it was "valuable as an analysis of SDA soteriology." He suggested, however, that Paxton read more into their claim to be heirs of the Reformation than most Adventists themselves did and artificially imposed "a certain construction" on the Adventist claim that Adventists "may not have in mind."[80]

In a response to his critics, Paxton pointed out that LaRondelle's stance was to fuse justification and sanctification and that was in fact the same position as the Council of Trent. Quoting Cardinal Bellarmine he noted that the central dividing issue was "an inherent righteousness or not." He observed that "nowhere in LaRondelle have I seen a clear upholding of justification unmixed with sanctification and statements about the union of the two." He will not "distinguish justification." Although he also observed that LaRondelle was perhaps trying to be vague and that "the ambiguity of LaRondelle's writing makes it quite unlikely that the average *Spectrum* reader would really know what he is saying."[81] In response to the issue of whether the link between Adventists and the Reformers was *sola scriptura* and not its soteriology, Paxton responded that Johnsson and LaRondelle "clearly do not understand the Reformation principle of *sola Scriptura*," for it was that principle that had underscored the "restoration of the gospel." He had not in his book tried to "define the distinction between justification and sanctification more minutely than 'inspiration'," as Johnsson had alleged, but had simply tried "to make clear the basic relation of the two for the health of the soul. The distinction between the *for us* work of Christ and the *in us* work of the Spirit is vital to understanding the

---

76 He noted that Erwin Gane among a number of Adventist authors with a similar approach seemed to give the "clearest expression" of Roman Catholicism. Paxton, 140.
77 H. K. LaRondelle, "Paxton and the Reformers," *Spectrum* 9:3 (July 1978), 45–57.
78 William Johnsson, "An Evaluation of *The Shaking of Adventism,*" *Focus* (Spring 1979), 31.
79 D. Ford, "The Truth of Paxton's Thesis," *Spectrum* 9:3 (July 1978) 38, 42.
80 R. Rice, "Questions for Paxton," unpub. MS, 1979.
81 Geoffrey J. Paxton, *The Shaking of Adventism Paxton responds to the reviews of his book by Drs Gane, Johnsson and LaRondelle* (Fallbrook, CA: Verdict Publications, 1980), 17. *Spectrum* is the journal of the Association of Adventist Forums which has a focus on Adventist studies.

gospel."[82] The Adventist responses to Paxton's *The Shaking of Adventism* confirmed for its author that "Seventh-day Adventist thinking is anything but united on the heart of its mission and message," and that this demonstrated for him that there was a "nest of crypto-Catholic sentiment in the heart of Adventism's theologcal endeavors."[83]

## Conclusion

If the publication by Paxton brought the righteousness by faith conflict in Adventism to a peak, the issue nevertheless remained unresolved. In an effort to lessen the theological temperature in Australia, Desmond Ford accepted an exchange teaching appointment to Pacific Union College in California. After 1979 attention turned to other issues as the interpretation of righteousness by faith understood in its Pauline context and in its evangelical formulation was considered to pose a challenge to other traditional eschatological teachings of the church. These developments led to the landmark Glacier View meetings in 1980, developments which lie outside the scope of this paper.

This paper has demonstrated that differing Adventist perceptions of the Reformation theologians not only gave rise to vigorous debate over the meaning of righteousness by faith in Adventism during the 1960s and 70s, but they also shaped the contours and development of the debate and contributed to polarization within the community over core doctrines and the very nature of its mission. The portrayal of one position as "the true gospel" and truly Protestant and the other as "that other gospel," which reflected the soteriology of Roman Catholicism, gave a sharp edge to the discussion in Adventism during this period. If the sharp edge to the debate has dulled in recent decades, the two perspectives still nevertheless stand in tension with each other and continue to polarize the church.

The polemical approach drawn from Chemnitz may have been helpful as an educational strategy in clarifying the distinction between justification and sanctification and thus facilitating an exposure of the error of sinless perfectionism. This was clearly apparent for a generation of believers for whom the incipient legalism and works orientation of their Adventism had robbed their Christian experience of assurance and joy. The approach, however, also had inherent limitations. The inadequacy of the approach as a comprehensive corrective to perfectionism becomes apparent in its assumption that all talk of perfection necessarily is focused on behavior in a legalistic way. The approach fails to account for the mature Wesleyan understanding of Christian perfection as relationship to God in the sense of "perfect love." If participants in the debate of the 1960s and 70s had been able to draw on the theology of complimentary biblical models of the atonement such as adoption,

---

82 Ibid., 4, 15.
83 Ibid., 18.

redemption or the *Christus Victor*[84] emphasis perhaps the debate would not have been so polarizing and divisive. The parallel metaphors of the atonement need to be considered in nuancing soteriological formulations. This may have broadened categories of understanding and lessened the tensions arising from the use of just the courtroom model of the atonement. It may be of no value to speculate as to whether, if available earlier, the insights of Krister Stendahl and E. P. Sanders, whose broadened understanding of the first-century context emphasizes the social implications of Pauline teaching on righteousness by faith, would have dissipated tensions. Such perspectives, however, certainly need to be allowed to influence the discussion today. Pauline soteriology is ultimately about bringing communities of faith together rather than polarizing them.

The two distinct and competing theological strands in Adventist teaching, that which emphasizes grace and the forgiveness of God as the heart and focus of Adventist mission, and that which sees the achieving of perfection in a last generation of Adventists as its distinctive focus continue to vie with each other as the expression of authentic Adventism. Broadening understanding beyond the comparative categories of Chemnitz may point out ways to help resolve such tensions.

---

84  Gustaf Aulén, *Christus Victor* (New York, NY: Macmillan, 1958).

## Appendix 1

### Are you Catholic or Protestant?

Please record your answers to the 10 questions. Then read the following study entitled "The Basic Catholic Doctrine of Justification by Faith." After that check your answers again, comparing them with the key on page 8.
In each of the following 10 choices, mark either (a) or (b), whichever is correct:

1  (a) God gives a man right standing with Himself by mercifully accounting him innocent and virtuous.
   (b) God gives a man right standing with Himself by actually making him into an innocent and virtuous person.

2  (a) God gives a man right standing with Himself by placing Christ's goodness and virtue to his credit.
   (b) God gives a man right standing with Himself by putting Christ's goodness and virtue into his heart.

3  (a) God accepts the believer because of the moral excellence found in Jesus Christ.
   (b) God makes the believer acceptable by infusing Christ's moral excellence into his life.

4  (a) If a Christian becomes "born again" (regenerate, transformed in character), he will achieve right standing with God.
   (b) If the sinner accepts right standing with God by faith, he will then experience transformation in character.

5  (a) We receive right standing with God by faith alone.
   (b) We receive right standing with God by faith which has become active by love.

6  (a) We achieve right standing with God by having Christ live out His life of obedience in us.
   (b) We achieve right standing with God by accepting the fact that He obeyed the law perfectly for us.

7  (a) We achieve right standing with God by following Christ's example by the help of his enabling grace.
   (b) We follow Christ's example because His life has given us right standing with God.

8  (a) God first pronounces that we are good in His sight, then gives us His Spirit to make us good.
   (b) God sends His Spirit to make us good, and then He will pronounce that we are good.

9  (a) Christ's intercession at God's right hand gives us favor in the sight of God.
   (b) It is the indwelling Christ that gives us favor in God's sight.

10 (a) Only by faith in the doing and dying of Christ can we fully satisfy the claims of the Ten Commandments.
   (b) By the power of the Holy Spirit living in us, we can fully satisfy the claims of the Ten Commandments.

*Present Truth*, May 1972, p. 5.

*Rolf J. Pöhler*

## Are Seventh-day Adventists "Heirs of the Reformation"? Between Aspiration and Reality

**Abstract**

Seventh-day Adventists have – both humbly and proudly – claimed to be "(the) heirs of the Reformation." What did they mean by it and in what respect did, and do, they live up to this aspiration? To begin with, the essay defines the terms and shows the difficulties and intricacies in answering the question with a simple Yes or No. In the second part, the claim is analyzed on the basis of the chapters in this book and evaluated in regard to its accord with Reformation and Adventist history and theology. As long as the spirit of the Reformers is alive among Adventists, they may rightly claim to be heirs of the Reformation.

### Introduction

The Friendship Issue of *Adventist World* dated May 2016 contains "A Brief History of Seventh-day Adventists." On page 30, it lists eleven dates, among them – as would be expected – the years 1844, 1863, and 1888. Surprisingly, however, the list begins with the year 1517, to which the following explanation is attached: "Martin Luther posts his 95 theses, questions, or propositions about the gospel in faith and practice." An editorial mistake? Certainly not. The usurpation of the founding date of the sixteenth-century Reformation by a denomination that arose 300 years later on a far-away continent? Some may view it like that. Or just another indication that Adventists see themselves as standing in more or less direct lineage to the Protestant Reformers?

The linkage between 1517 and 1844/1888 is a startling reminder of a claim often raised by Adventists, namely, to be the true heirs of the Reformation.[1] Frequently, in evangelistic preaching, church history was, and is, presented as a long chain of decline and deterioration of the pure, primitive Christian faith, on the one hand, and of continuous phases of reformation and restoration, on the other. According to this scenario, the sixteenth-century Reformation remained unfinished, to be carried forward by the so-called "free churches" like Baptists and Methodists and, finally, Adventists – the unspoken implication being that Seventh-day Adventists will finally complete the Reformation that had begun centuries ago.

---

1 For details and documentation, see Stefan Höschele, "Reform, Reformation – Protest, Protestant: Adventist Terminology and Rhetoric," 25–28 above. The international Adventist television network "Hope Channel" has produced a film series covering the history of the Reformation leading up to today's Adventism, entitled "Heirs of the Reformation."

## Redefining the Question

In perusing this claim, this concluding essay will consider two related questions. Firstly, what do Adventists actually mean by the phrase "heirs of the Reformation"? And, secondly, how does this self-designation match with reality – both of the sixteenth-century Reformation and of the modern Seventh-day Adventist Church?

By "the Reformation" Adventists mean the events unfolding in the late Middle Ages and early modern times, set in motion by some laypeople and clergy who wanted to reform the church of their days. Following Peter Waldo (1140–1205), John Wycliffe (1330–1384), John Hus (1369–1415) and others, reform movements like the Waldenses, Lollards, and Hussites challenged a worldly and corrupt church, calling it back to biblical faithfulness and the pure gospel. One hundred years after the Czech Reformer was burnt at the stake, another theology professor, this time in the university town of Wittenberg, also challenged the entrenched religious-political system by appealing directly to the Bible and by claiming the right to follow the dictates of his own conscience. He was followed by others – like Calvin, Zwingli, and the Radical Reformers – who shared many of Luther's views and developed them further, leading to the successive establishment of Lutheran and Reformed churches and their different branches, predominantly in Europe and North America.

According to Collins English Dictionary (Digital Edition 2012), the term "heir," if used in a general (rather than a legal) sense, denotes "any person or thing that carries on some tradition, circumstance, etc., from a forerunner." In a broad sense, then, the question raised in the title of this paper is simply this: are Seventh-day Adventists carrying on the tradition of the above-named Reformers? The answer is straightforward: yes, indeed. Without question, Adventists are much indebted to the Reformers for many of their beliefs and practices and strive to emulate them with regard to their focus on the Bible and their faithfulness and determination.

However, upon closer examination, additional questions arise that cannot be answered as easily by a simple Yes or No. For example, Adventists have by no means adopted everything the Reformers believed, taught, and practiced – like the teaching on divine predestination, eternal hell fire, sacramental communion, infant baptism, and episcopal church structure, to name but a few.[2] Thus, for the question to be meaningful (and for the answer to be informative), it needs to be expressed more pointedly: Are Seventh-day Adventists in agreement with the key biblical insights and fundamental theological concerns of the Protestant Reformation?

Again, it is difficult to answer this question straightforwardly. Inasmuch as the Reformers and the churches growing out of the Reformation disagree(d) on quite a

---

2   See above, Thomas Domanyi, "John Calvin's Legacy in Seventh-day Adventist Belief," 155–163, and Reinder Bruinsma, "The Sixteenth-Century Reformation and Adventist Ecclesiology," 165–178.

number of doctrinal and ethical points – for example, on the meaning of the Lord's Supper and Christ's real presence at Communion,[3] the relationship of divine grace and human free will, the condition and mode of baptism, state vs. free church, religious liberty, and the use of violence – what is to be regarded as the true hallmark of the Protestant faith?[4] Is it the least common denominator or rather a specific conception of Protestantism – like the Lutheran, Reformed, or Radical, or even a subgroup of one of these? In any case, all denominations in the Protestant tradition can rightly claim to be in substantial agreement and obvious continuity with the Reformers, while still disagreeing on quite a number of important points of belief and practice.[5]

As there are as many views on the Reformation as there are branches on the Protestant tree, all churches claiming to be "heirs of the Reformation" will, for all practical purposes, define for themselves what they consider the true legacy of their spiritual progenitors. Thus, the answer to our question will inevitably reflect a church's particular set of beliefs and values. In other words, what a denomination regards as true Reformation heritage may actually tell more about this church than about the sixteenth-century Reformers. Obviously, then, the Adventists' claim to be heirs of the Reformation mirrors their own belief system and thus serves to reinforce the latter for church members. We must be aware of the unavoidable circular reasoning involved in any claim to be the heirs of the Reformation.

By raising this claim, Seventh-day Adventists are expressing, not only their self-understanding as a true Protestant church, but also their unique calling and mission. This can be illustrated by a quotation from the book *Heirs of the Reformation,* which presents the history of Seventh-day Adventism in Europe:

> Seventh-day Adventists seriously endeavor to contribute to an ongoing Reformation in three ways:
> 1. *Keepers of the Flame.* Seventh-day Adventists keep alive the biblical truths which the Reformation rediscovered: the Bible as the only foundation of faith, and the conviction that we owe all and everything regarding our salvation to God.
> 2. *Restorers of early Church tenets.* Seventh-day Adventists have an obligation to restore the understanding of some aspects of the early Christian faith which the Reformation Churches neglected and even ignored ... [like the Sabbath].

---

3   See above, Michael Campbell, "Martin Luther, Seventh-day Adventism and the Lord's Supper," 139–154.
4   Compare, e.g., the soteriological views of Philip Melanchthon as set forth by Timothy J. Arena (see above, 179–203) with those of Martin Chemnitz as described by Gilbert M. Valentine (see above, 287–309). Adventists are closer to Melanchthon than to Chemnitz.
5   Trevor O'Reggio argues that Adventists are particularly indebted to the Radical Reformers; see above, 219–238 ("The Radical Reformers [Anabaptists] and Seventh-day Adventism"). For more information on the Radical Reformation and Adventism's similarity and affinity to it, see above, Martin Rothkegel, "The Anabaptist Reformation Experience," 205–217, and Charles Scriven, "The Radical Reformation and the Transformation of Adventism," 239–249.

3. *Revivers of neglected truths.* Seventh-day Adventists call for a revival of Reformation truth through a renewed emphasis on biblical eschatology. Luther's ardent longing for the return of Christ was nourished by Bible prophecies. ...
By preserving, restoring and reviving biblical teachings the Seventh-day Adventist Church strives to continue the agenda of the Reformation.[6]

In view of the particular Adventist self-understanding as the "remnant church" of Bible prophecy, our lead question needs to be phrased even more pointedly: "Are Seventh-day Adventists *the last and only true* heirs of the Reformation?" Following the historicist interpretation of apocalyptic prophecy, "the remnant" are the final restorers of biblical truth and will not, by definition, bequeath a legacy to later generations of believers. As the final generation of faithful Christians, they will, by God's grace, complete the work of restoration before the second coming of Christ. As the counterpart of fallen spiritual Babylon, they constitute the true church of Christ and "the pillar and bulwark of the truth" (1 Tim 3:15 RSV). The following quotation may serve to illustrate this ambitious Adventist self-image.

> The Seventh-day Adventist Church, it may be humbly claimed, is nothing less than God's ecumenical movement of truth, providentially bringing together truths of the ongoing Reformation, neglected or even rejected by many Protestant churches, but vitally relevant to our time. In fact, in its modern manifestation it is the "final remnant" of His true church spanning the centuries. The fascinating story of the full recovery of "the faith which was once delivered unto the saints" and is now being proclaimed as "the everlasting gospel," God's last message of mercy to a doomed world, is the theme of this volume.[7]

Can Adventists deliver what they claim? Do they actually live up to the principles and insights of the Reformation? The presentations given at the Symposium of the Institute of Adventist Studies in Friedensau in 2016, published in this volume, can serve as a reference point in assessing this pretension. How did Adventists perceive the Reformation and how does this perception compare to what the Protestant Reformers actually stood for? What can be said about the Adventists' assertion to be the (last and only true) heirs of the Reformation?

## Reconsidering the Answer

Looking at the Reformation through the lens of the distinctive Adventist teachings reveals some converging ideas. For example, the moral government of God view of Hugo Grotius, based on Arminian free will theology, resembles the great controversy motif of Ellen White. Both want to protect God's reputation by denying any

---

6   Daniel Heinz, Introduction to *Heirs of the Reformation*, ed. by H. Dunton, D. Heinz, D. Porter and R. Strasdowsky (Grantham, England: The Stanborough Press, 1997), 15f.
7   W. L. Emmerson, *The Reformation and the Advent Movement* (Hagerstown, MD: Review and Herald, 1983), 7.

arbitrariness in his dealings with humanity. A few sixteenth-century Anabaptists (e.g., Oswald Glait) propagated the Sabbath. Both motives were brought together by seventeenth-century Seventh Day Baptist Thomas Tillam. However, while there are certain parallels in language and conceptions, no direct influence on Sabbath-keeping Adventists can be substantiated. Still, the moral government view of God reached America and provided the soil on which the distinctive Adventist view on the great controversy could grow. It seems that Ellen White, in particular, was receptive to this concept through her Methodist upbringing and her familiarity with Albert Barnes's *Notes on the New Testament*.[8]

(Re)interpreting the past in the light of the present is not limited to those beliefs that set Adventists apart from other Christian traditions. Rather, it is a common way of relating historic events to contemporary concerns. For example, early Adventists, regarding themselves as a reform movement, were inclined to see in Martin Luther a zealous moral reformer rather than the theologian-preacher of grace and justification by faith. To them, the Reformation appeared more like a protest movement against a sinful and worldly church, echoing the Adventists' own negative perception of the Christian world of their time.[9] This suggests that the perception of the sixteenth-century Reformation was (and always is) colored by the experience and concern of the present, making room for different and shifting interpretations.

Claiming to be the heirs of the Reformation entails the necessity of defining the characteristic features of the revered past. For example, Luther's intense longing for the coming of Christ and his strong interest in the "signs" preceding this glorious event strike a chord in the Adventist heart and mind. Today, and paradoxically, Adventists are closer to the Reformer in this regard than the Protestant church bearing his name. However, while Luther was looking for this day in joyful anticipation, for many Adventists it is beset by apprehension and fear *(Heilsangst)*.[10]

This striking difference appears to be due, in part, to the regrettable effects which the traditional doctrine of the pre-Advent (Investigative) Judgment had on Adventists. Luther's faith and hope, on the other hand, was closely tied to the assurance of salvation *(Heilsgewissheit)*, which overcame his fear of the judgment. What, then, does it mean today to be Luther's heirs regarding the blessed Advent hope? Is setting up prophetic time tables, engaging in arbitrary interpretations, and raising conjectures about the pope or Islam an adequate expression of Reformation faith? Or rather living the Christian life with calm assurance, without fear of the heavenly judgment, based on an experiential understanding of justification by faith?

---

8   See above, 31–46 (Nicholas Miller, "The Reformation and the Remnant: The Reformers, the Great Controversy and the Sabbath").
9   See above, 13–29 (Stefan Höschele, "Reform, Reformation – Protest, Protestant: Adventist Terminology and Rhetoric").
10  See above, 67–78 (Daniel Heinz, "'Komm, lieber Jüngster Tag!' An Appraisal of Luther's Eschatological Worldview").

As Jón H. Stefánsson points out in his essay, "Luther's apocalyptic was the future prolongation of his contemporary realities mingled with the hope God would intervene at last."[11] Something similar can be said about Ellen White's description of final events in the concluding chapters of the *Great Controversy*. This raises the question to what degree both end-time views are subject to the contingencies of history, allowing for no definitive predictions about future events apart from the certain outcome of human history? But there are also differences. "Luther had discovered what the Antichrist *was* doing [in his own lifetime] – Adventists discovered what he *would* do [in a projected future]."[12] "Luther used *theology* to expose the Antichrist, but Adventists did so with *history*."[13] What, then, is the Reformer's lasting eschatological legacy, which Adventists should build upon? This question deserves further attention in view of the radical changes in world and religious history.

Next to Ellen G. White, among the seminal Adventist pioneers and authors that paid special attention to the Reformation, the European church leader Ludwig R. Conradi stands out. In his numerous books, he focused predominantly on Luther's interpretation of the book of Daniel and other apocalyptic Bible prophecies, unmasking the pope as the Antichrist ("little horn"). He even saw Luther's battle with Rome as fulfillment of the three angels' messages of Revelation 14. However, when it came to the core Reformation teaching on justification by faith *(sola gratia, sola fide)*, Conradi virtually fell silent. While he focused on the Reformation, he missed its central concerns. According to Johannes Hartlapp, "this points to a very one-sided understanding of the Reformation."[14]

In light of this, Adventists need to self-critically reflect on their claim to be in line with the Reformation. While it is widely recognized that early Adventism had some legalistic threads woven into its fabric, the 1888 General Conference is usually regarded as the decisive turning point from law to grace, from a focus on works to one on faith. However, the 1890s and 1900s saw pronounced perfectionistic trends among Adventist leaders like E. J. Waggoner and A. T. Jones. While Woodrow W. Whidden draws a sharp line of demarcation between Ellen White and her one-time protégées,[15] still their writings on salvation issues contains numerous overlaps, which reflects a lack of precision on the part of the prophet's soteriological terminology.

This was confirmed by twentieth-century developments generating overtly perfectionistic views and movements (Andreasen, Brinsmead) that shook the church to the

11 See above, 86 (Jón Hjörleifur Stefánsson, "Luther's Antichrist and His Reception by Seventh-day Adventists," 79–97).
12 Ibid., 89.
13 Ibid., 92 (emphasis added).
14 See above, 263 ("Ludwig Richard Conradi's Understanding of Luther's Reformation," 263–286). For Ellen White's view on Luther, see Denis Kaiser, "'God Is Our Refuge and Strength' – Martin Luther in the Perception of Ellen G. White," 49–65 above.
15 See above, 253–262 ("The Ground-Breaking General Conference of 1888: What Kind of Reformation Experience Was It About?").

very foundations and found support even among top leaders. Unsurprisingly, these movements invoked Ellen White, whose writings provided apparent justification for their extreme views. As Gilbert M. Valentine concludes, soteriological issues still divide opinion in the Adventist church.[16] It seems that Seventh-day Adventism is still struggling with its diverse soteriological legacy, making the claim to be the true heirs of the Reformation debatable to some degree. While official statements of belief clearly support the Protestant solae *(sola gratia, sola fide, solus Christus)*, there also exist views in the church that notably deviate from the Reformers' position.

To honor the legacy of the Reformation and to continuously reflect on the proper ways to understand and interpret it is a formidable hermeneutical challenge. While Adventists fully resonate with Luther's *sola scriptura* emphasis, it is less clear whether they understand it in the way he did. As Christian Lutsch demonstrates, Martin Luther's Bible hermeneutic was decidedly Christocentric ("Take Christ out of the Scripture, and what will you find left in them?") with a strong existential-experiential flavor, while Adventists tend to read the Bible in a fundamentalist and biblicist manner with a predominantly doctrinal focus.[17]

Would the great Reformer recognize our handling of the Bible as "his" Scripture principle, faithfully applied to the living Word of God? Do Seventh-day Adventists read it with the same radical openness and unconditional commitment *(devotio)* needed in order to hear and understand what God is saying to us? Is the Bible today less bound by the shackles of ecclesiastical authority than it was in Reformation times – or does it need to be set free again in today's church? In his thoughtful essay, Sully Sanon challenges us to face these disquieting questions squarely.[18]

## Reclaiming the Heritage

After two hundred years of modern Adventist history – reckoning from William Miller's meticulous study of the Bible culminating in 1818 –, an impressive amount of biblical, historical, doctrinal, ethical, prophetic, and hermeneutical insights has been accumulated and placed into the hands of the Seventh-day Adventist Church. This tradition is a great asset, benefitting the church as it continues to spread around the world and move further into the twenty-first century. At the same time, it may become a serious liability if this rich heritage ever encroaches upon the final authority of the Scriptures and the gospel of salvation by grace through faith in Jesus Christ alone. The church needs to continually (re)focus its attention on the center of divinely revealed truth.

---

16  See above, 287–309 ("The Reformation and the Shaping of Conflict Over the Meaning of 'Righteousness by Faith' in Seventh-day Adventism 1960–1978").
17  See above, 99–116 ("Martin Luther's View of the Scripture Principle").
18  See above, 117–135 ("*Sola Scriptura* as *Devotio:* An Appeal to Theological Dialogue").

The torch of truth is to be passed on to those coming after us. Either we keep the flame burning or we become mere preservers of the ashes. One of the participants of the symposium said during the plenary discussion: "Truth cannot be inherited, it has to be discovered." Perhaps it is this insight that lay at the very heart of the Protestant Reformation and made Martin Luther such a towering witness to the Truth. Instead of regarding the views and actions of the sixteenth-century Reformers as final and prescriptive, we should follow them in their radical openness to (present) truth, their unswerving dedication to the Bible, and their firm determination to follow sound reason and conscience whatever the outcome may be. In this sense, the sixteenth-century Reformation was, not a normative set of new beliefs and practices, but a genuine movement – a movement that must never come to a halt but continue for as long as time will last. *Ecclesia semper reformanda.*

As long as Seventh-day Adventists – both individually and collectively – embody the spirit of the Reformers and continue to move onward, they too will remain a divinely-inspired movement. Then, and only then, can they rightly claim to be true "heirs of the Reformation."

# Contributors

**Timothy J. Arena,** MDiv
PhD student, Seventh-day Adventist Theological Seminary, Andrews University, Mich., USA
timothy.arena@gmail.com

**Reinder Bruinsma,** PhD
Retired church administrator, scholar and author
reinder@bruinsmas.com

**Michael W. Campbell,** PhD
Associate Professor of Religion, Southwestern Adventist University, Keene, Texas, USA
mcampbell@swau.edu

**Thomas Domanyi,** Prof. Dr. em.
Retired scholar, lecturer and author
tdomanyi@bluewin.ch

**Johannes Hartlapp,** Dr. theol.
Lecturer of Church History, Faculty of Theology, Friedensau Adventist University, Germany
johannes.hartlapp@thh-friedensau.de

**Daniel Heinz,** PhD
Director of the European Archives of Seventh-day Adventist History, Friedensau, Germany
daniel.heinz@thh-friedensau.de

**Stefan Höschele,** PhD
Lecturer of Systematic Theology and Mission Studies, Friedensau Adventist University, Germany
stefan.hoeschele@thh-friedensau.de

**Denis Kaiser,** PhD
Assistant Professor of Church History, Seventh-day Adventist Theological Seminary, Andrews University, Michigan, USA
denis@andrews.edu

**Christian Lutsch,** M.A.
Pastor (Youth Ministry), Bad Aibling, Germany
christian.lutsch@adventisten.de

**Nicholas P. Miller,** JD, PhD
Professor of Church History, Seventh-day Adventist Theological Seminary,
Andrews University, Michigan, USA
nicholas@andrews.edu

**Trevor O'Reggio,** PhD, DMin
Professor of Church History, Discipleship and Religious Education,
Seventh-day Adventist Theological Seminary, Andrews University, Michigan, USA
toreggio@andrews.edu

**Rolf J. Pöhler,** ThD
Professor of Systematic Theology, Friedensau Adventist University, Germany
rolf.poehler@thh-friedensau.de

**Martin Rothkegel,** ThD, Dr. phil.
Professor of Church History, Theologische Hochschule Elstal, Germany
martin.rothkegel@th-elstal.de

**Sully Sanon,** MTS, MPTh
Student of International Social Sciences, Friedensau Adventist University, Germany
sanon.sully@gmail.com

**Charles Scriven,** PhD
Board Chair of Adventist Forum, publisher of *Spectrum*
c.scriven@live.com

**Jón Hjörleifur Stefánsson**
PhD candidate, Vrije Universiteit Amsterdam
j.hjorleifur.stefansson@gmail.com

**Gilbert M. Valentine,** PhD
Retired Professor of Leadership and Administration, School of Education,
La Sierra University, California, USA
gvalenti@lasierra.edu

**Woodrow W. Whidden II,** PhD
Em. Professor of Religion, College of Arts and Sciences, Andrews University, Michigan, USA
woodrow.whidden@gmail.com

www.ingramcontent.com/pod-product-compliance
Lightning Source LLC
Chambersburg PA
CBHW020121240426
43673CB00038B/552